INUBAKA

CRAZY FOR DOGS

9

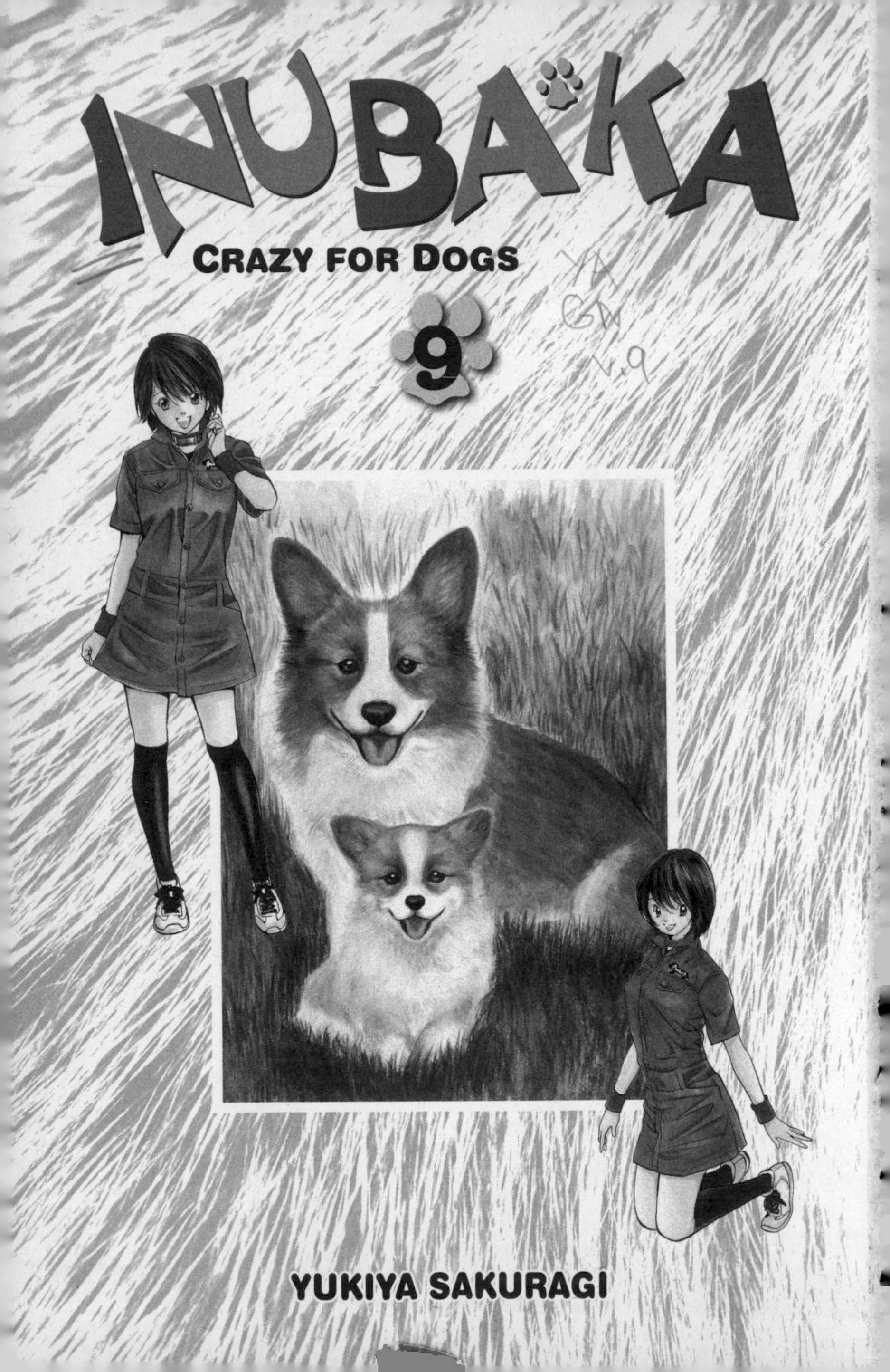

YUKIYA SAKURAGI

Contents

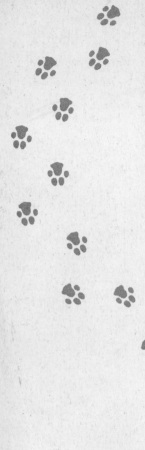

Story thus far

Teppei is the manager of the recently opened pet shop Woofles. He intended to breed his black Labrador Noa with a champion dog, but instead Noa was "taken advantage of" by an unknown and unfixed male dog!

The unknown dog's owner was Suguri Miyauchi and her dog was a mutt named Lupin. Suguri is now working at Woofles to make up for her dog's actions.

Suguri's enthusiasm is more than a little unique. She has eaten dog food (and said it was tasty), caught dog poop with her bare hands, and caused dogs to have "happy pee" in her presence. Teppei is starting to realize that Suguri is indeed a very special girl.

Woofles has been open for six months now and has welcomed some new staff members to their team, bringing a refreshed energy to the store. Everyone's been busy, but the days continue to be very fulfilling. On holidays Teppei travels to various places in search of the perfect puppies for Woofles. Suguri becomes curious about where the puppies at Woofles actually come from, so Teppei suggests that Suguri visit the breeding ranch run by the owner of Woofles.

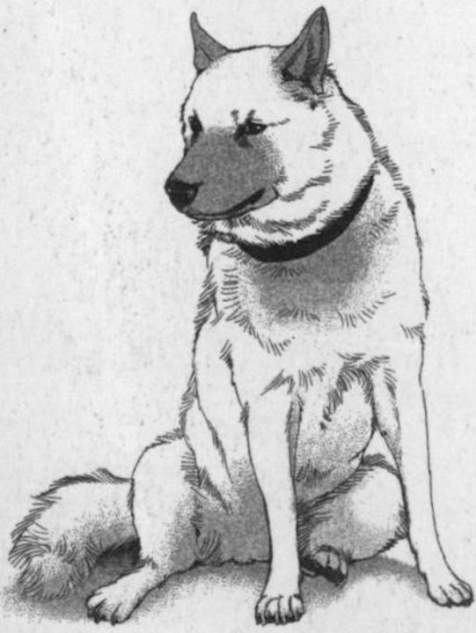

CHARACTERS

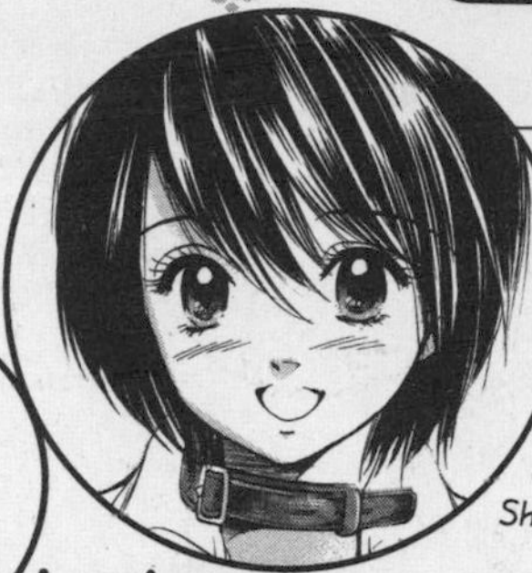

Suguri Miyauchi

She seems to possess an almost supernatural connection with dogs. When she approaches them they often urinate with great excitement! She is crazy for dogs and can catch their droppings with her bare hands. She is currently a trainee at the Woofles Pet Shop.

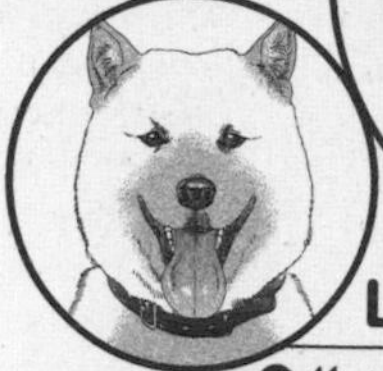

Lupin

♂ *Mutt (mongrel)*

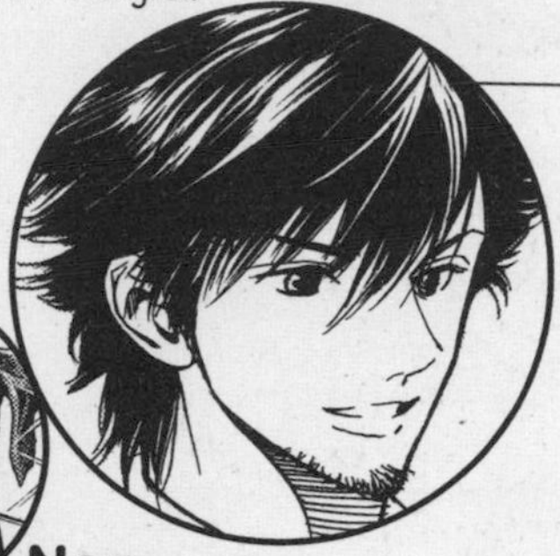

Teppei Iida

He is the manager of the recently opened pet shop Woofles. He is aware of Suguri's special ability and has hired her to work in his shop. He also lets Suguri and Kentaro crash with him.

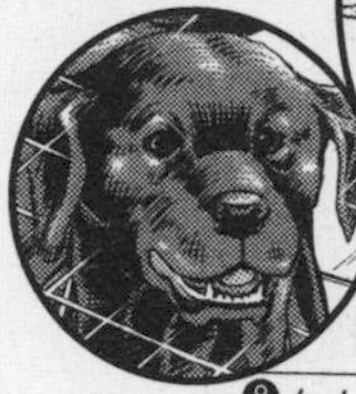

Noa

♀ *Labrador retriever*

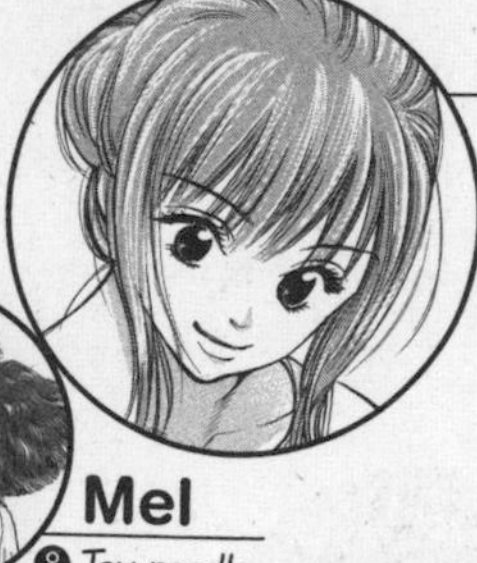

Momoko Takeuchi

Woofles Pet Shop (second location) pet groomer. At first she was a girl with many problems and she rarely smiled. But after meeting Suguri, she's changed, and the two are now best friends.

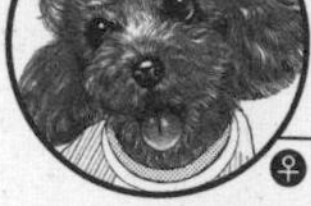

Mel

♀ *Toy poodle*

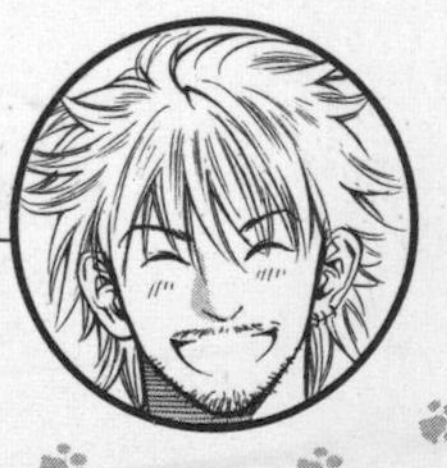

Kentaro Osada

A wannabe musician and buddy of Teppei's from high school. Teppei saved Kentaro when he was a down-and-out beggar. He has a crush on the piano instructor Kanako, but not her dog...

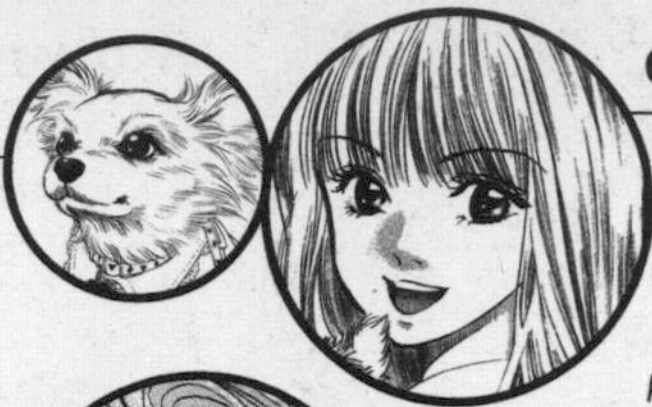

Chizuru Sawamura

She adopted a Chihuahua, Melon, after her long-time pet golden retriever Ricky alerted her that Melon was ill. She works at a hostess bar to repay Melon's medical fees.

Melon

♂ *Chihuahua*

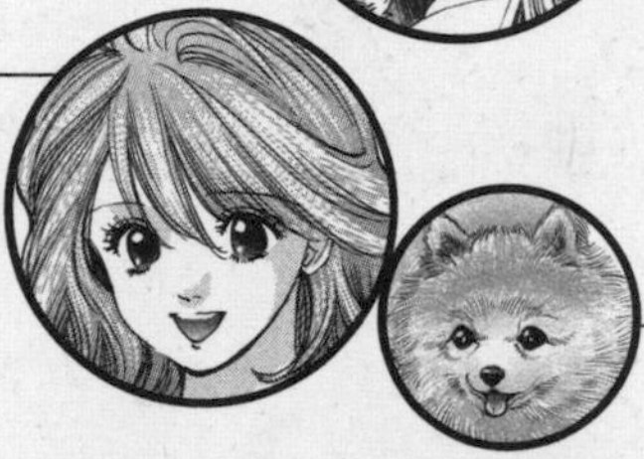

Kanako Mori

She teaches piano on the second floor of the same building as Woofles. Her love for her dog, Czerny, is so great that it surprises even Suguri!

Czerny

♀ *Pomeranian*

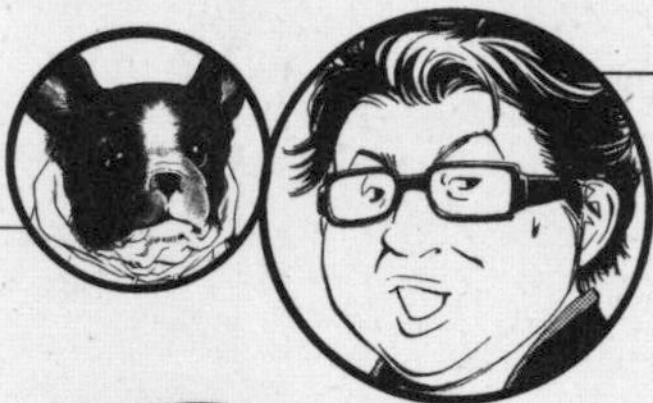

Hiroshi Akiba

Pop-idol otaku turned dog otaku. His dream is to publish a photo collection of his dog, Zidane. He is a government employee.

Zidane

♂ *French bulldog*

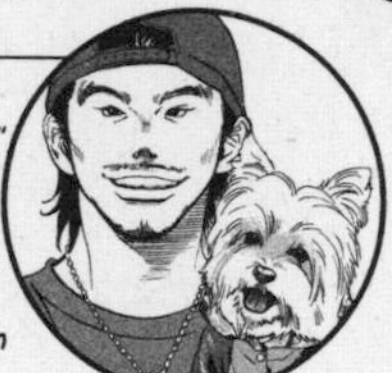

JIN

A mysterious self-employed "entrepreneur." His speech is unpolished and sometimes blunt, but kindness and compassion show through when he's with dogs. Being a student of Kanako-sensei's piano class shows that there are unexpected sides of him.

Mosh

♂ *West Highland white terrier*

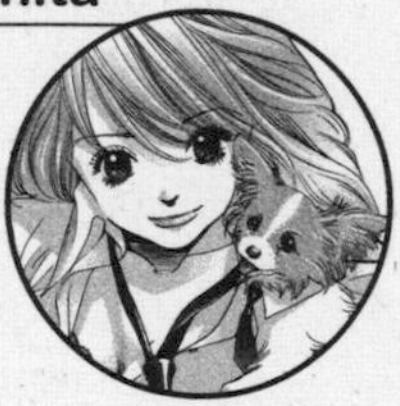

Mari Yamashita

She is a model whose nickname is Yamarin. She decided to keep an unsold papillon, Lucky, which was her costar in a bread commercial.

Lucky

♂ *Papillon*

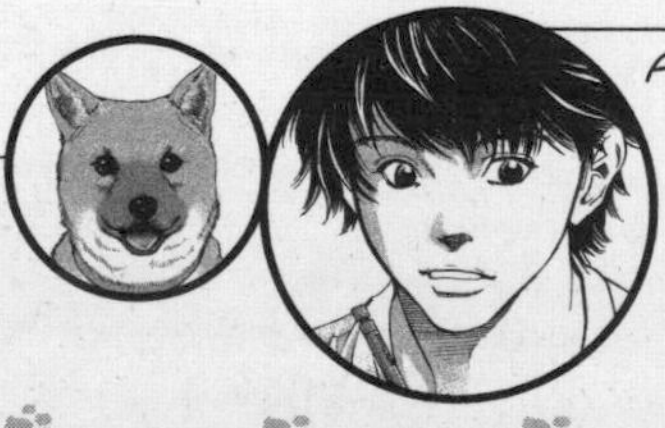

Kim

A Korean friend of Kentaro. He had a phobia of dogs, but he has been working hard to get over it in order to get close to Suguri, whom he has a crush on. He bought a Shiba dog!

Chanta

♀ *Shiba*

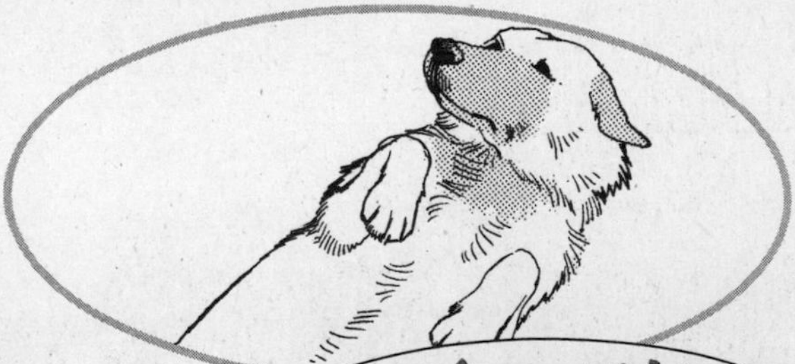

INUBAKA

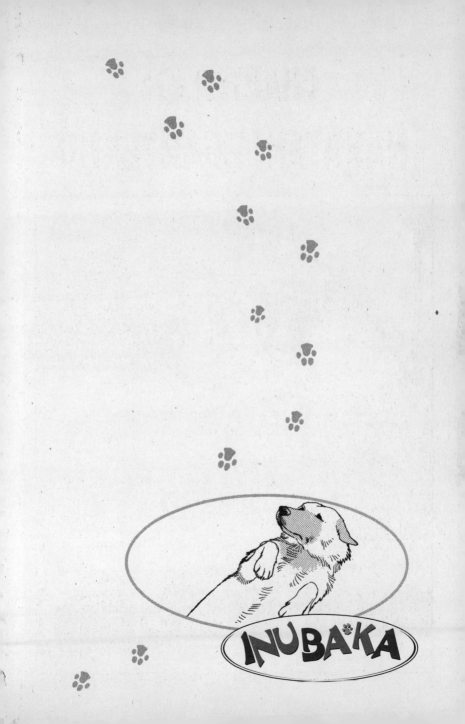

CHAPTER 87: NAKATANI HEARTLAND

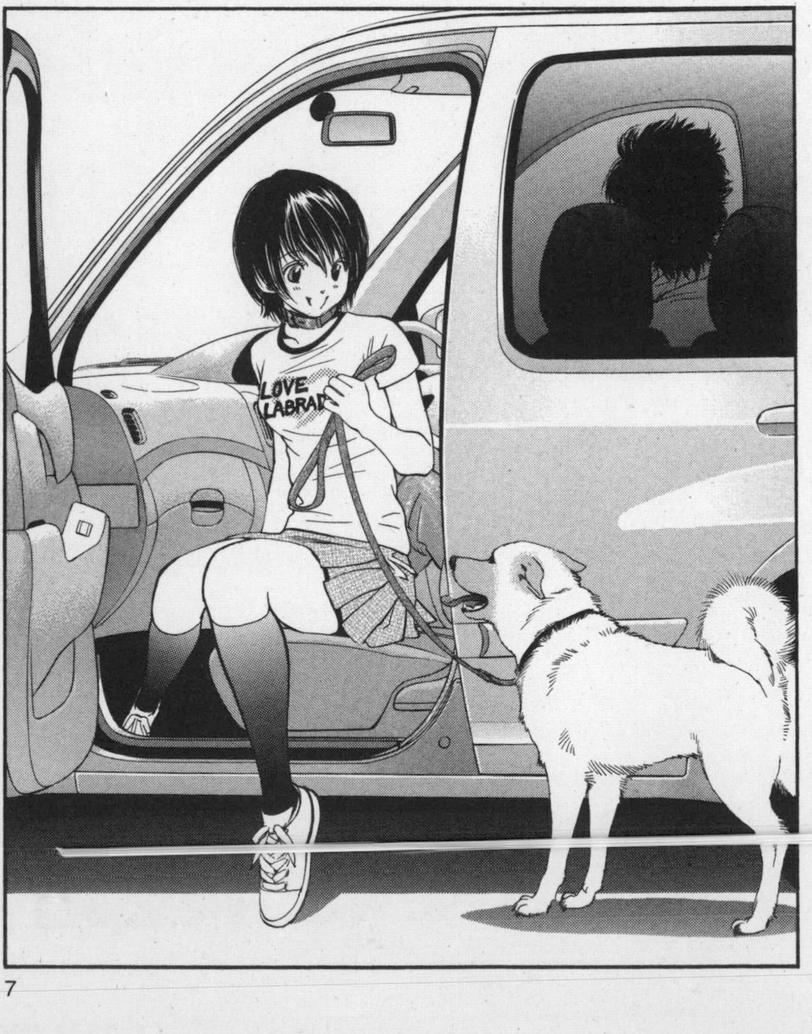
LOVE
LABRAD

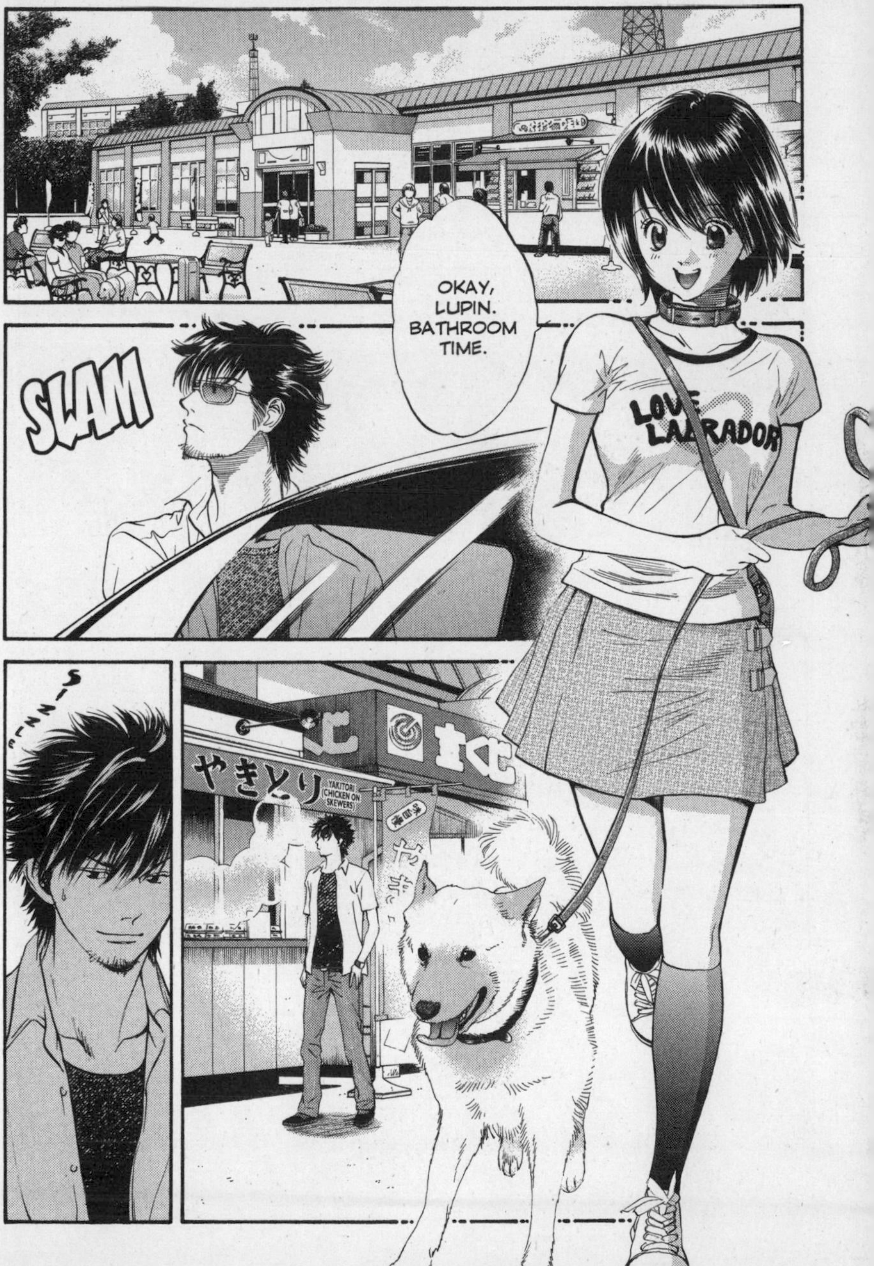
OKAY, LUPIN. BATHROOM TIME.
LOVE LABRADOR
SLAM
やきとり
YAKITORI (CHICKEN ON SKEWERS)
SIZZLE

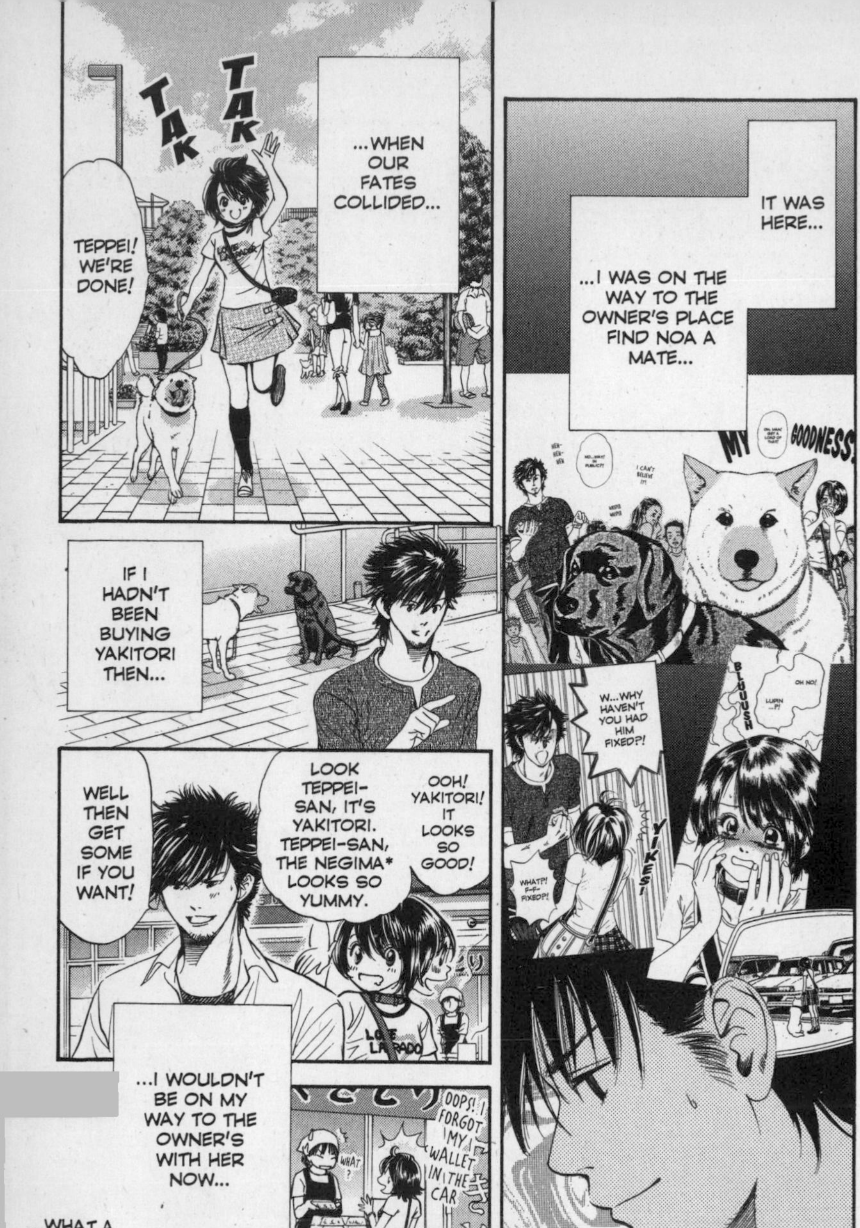
IT WAS HERE...
...I WAS ON THE WAY TO THE OWNER'S PLACE FIND NOA A MATE...
MY GOODNESS!
I CAN'T BELIEVE IT!
HEH-HEH-HEH
OH NO!
LUPIN ...?!
BLUUUSH
W...WHY HAVEN'T YOU HAD HIM FIXED?!
YIKES!
WHAT?! F-F-FIXED?!
...WHEN OUR FATES COLLIDED...
TAK TAK
TEPPEI! WE'RE DONE!
IF I HADN'T BEEN BUYING YAKITORI THEN...
OOH! YAKITORI! IT LOOKS SO GOOD!
LOOK TEPPEI-SAN, IT'S YAKITORI. TEPPEI-SAN, THE NEGIMA* LOOKS SO YUMMY.
WELL THEN GET SOME IF YOU WANT!
...I WOULDN'T BE ON MY WAY TO THE OWNER'S WITH HER NOW...
OOPS! I FORGOT MY WALLET IN THE CAR
WHAT ?
...WHAT A WEIRD FEELING.

*NEGIMA IS YAKITORI WITH GREEN ONIONS

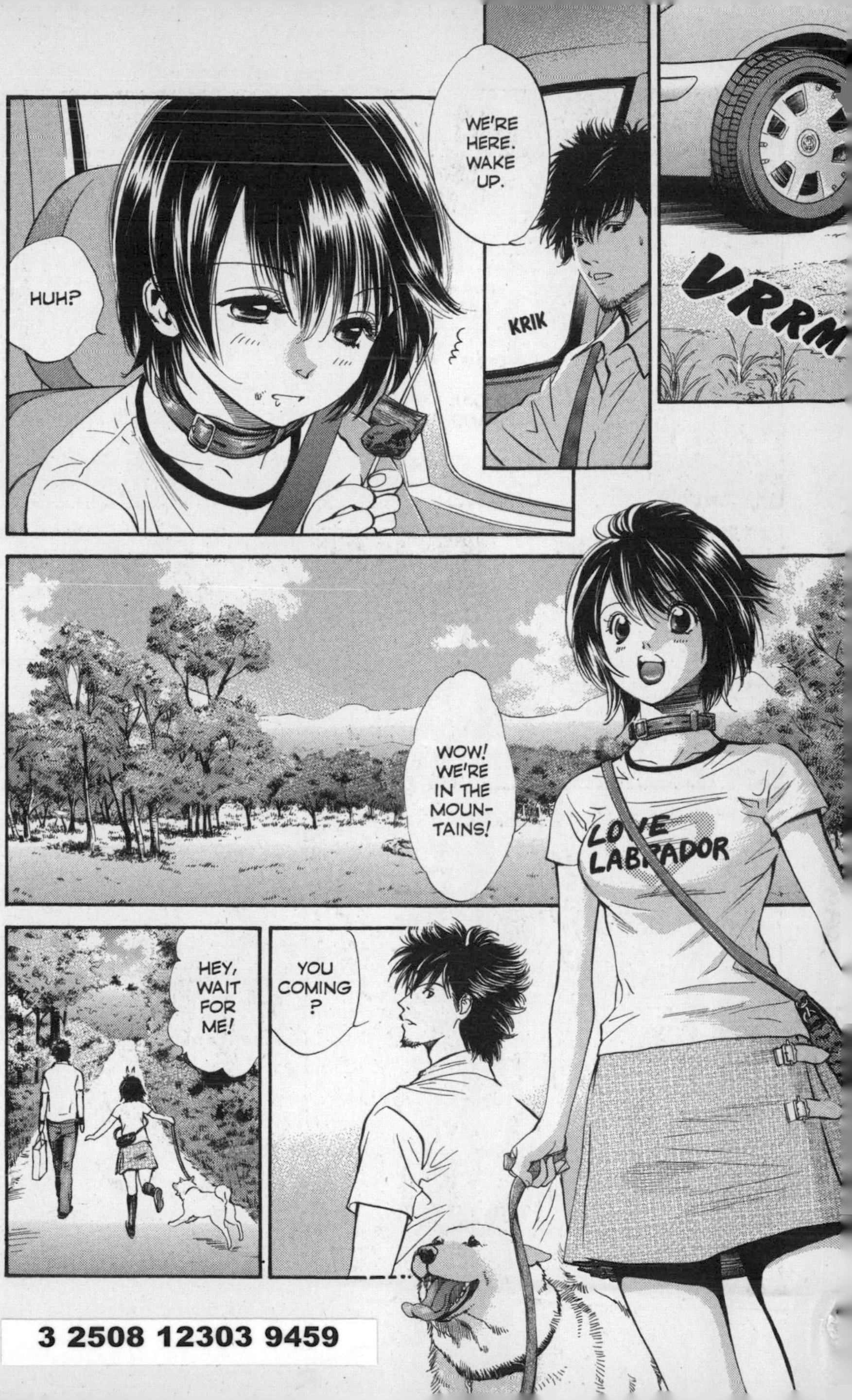
VRRM
WE'RE HERE. WAKE UP.
KRIK
HUH?
WOW! WE'RE IN THE MOUN-TAINS!
LOVE LABRADOR
YOU COMING?
HEY, WAIT FOR ME!

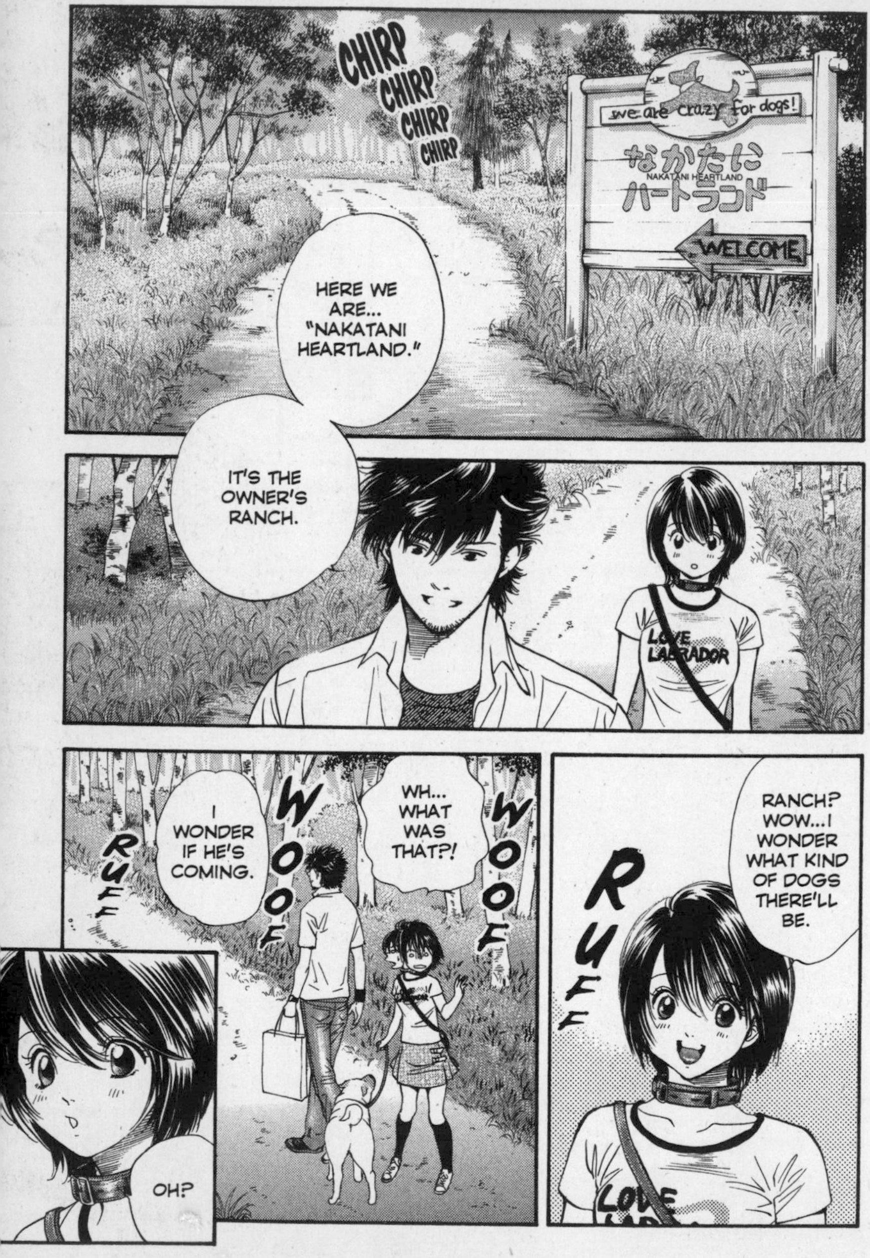
CHIRP CHIRP CHIRP CHIRP
we are crazy for dogs!
なかたに
NAKATANI HEARTLAND
ハートランド
WELCOME
HERE WE ARE... "NAKATANI HEARTLAND."
IT'S THE OWNER'S RANCH.
LOVE LABRADOR
RANCH? WOW...I WONDER WHAT KIND OF DOGS THERE'LL BE.
RUFF
WOOF
WH... WHAT WAS THAT?!
WOOF
I WONDER IF HE'S COMING.
RUFF
OH?

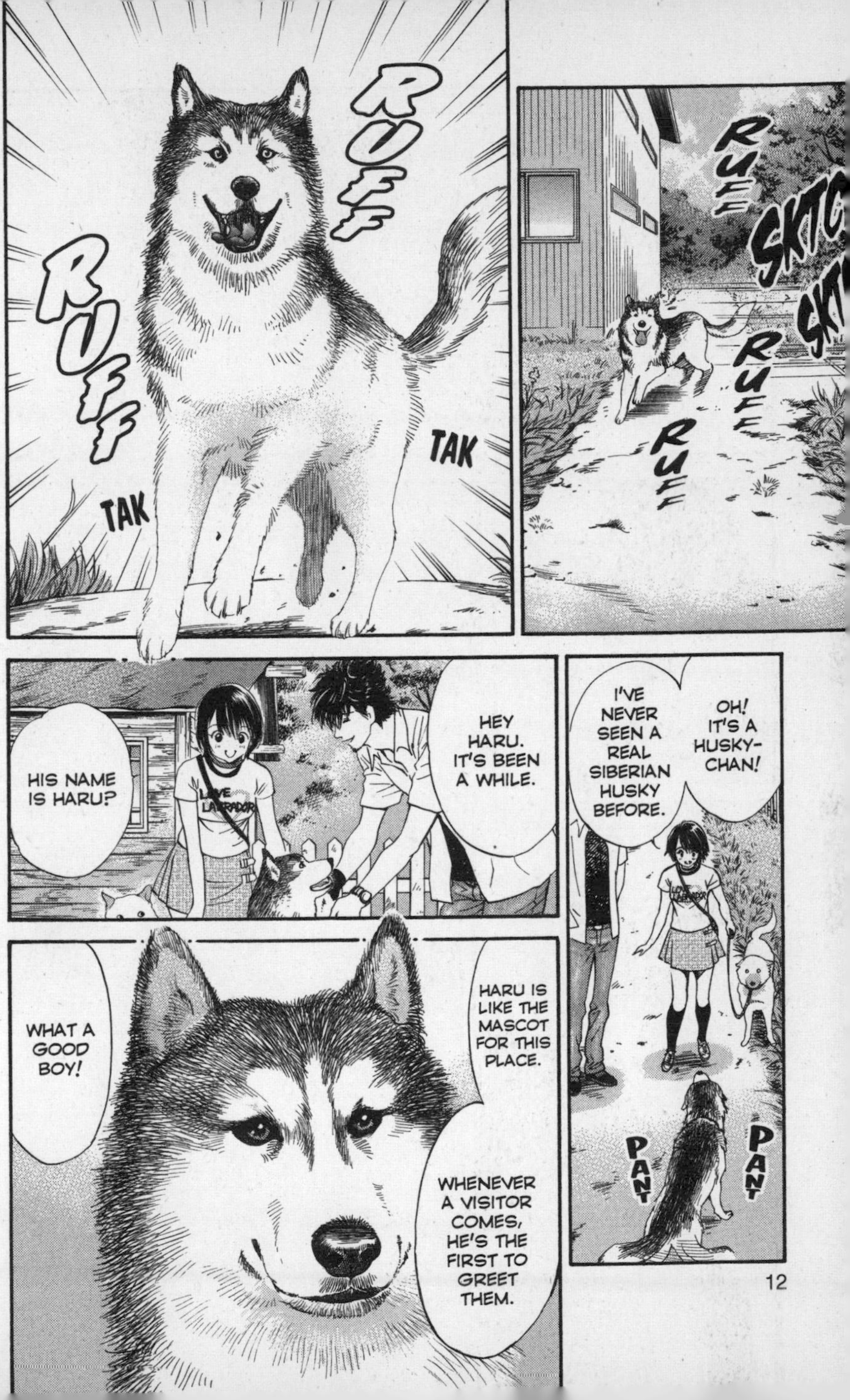
RUFF
RUFF
RUFF
RUFF
RUFF
TAK
TAK
OH! IT'S A HUSKY-CHAN!
I'VE NEVER SEEN A REAL SIBERIAN HUSKY BEFORE.
PANT
PANT
HEY HARU. IT'S BEEN A WHILE.
HIS NAME IS HARU?
HARU IS LIKE THE MASCOT FOR THIS PLACE.
WHENEVER A VISITOR COMES, HE'S THE FIRST TO GREET THEM.
WHAT A GOOD BOY!

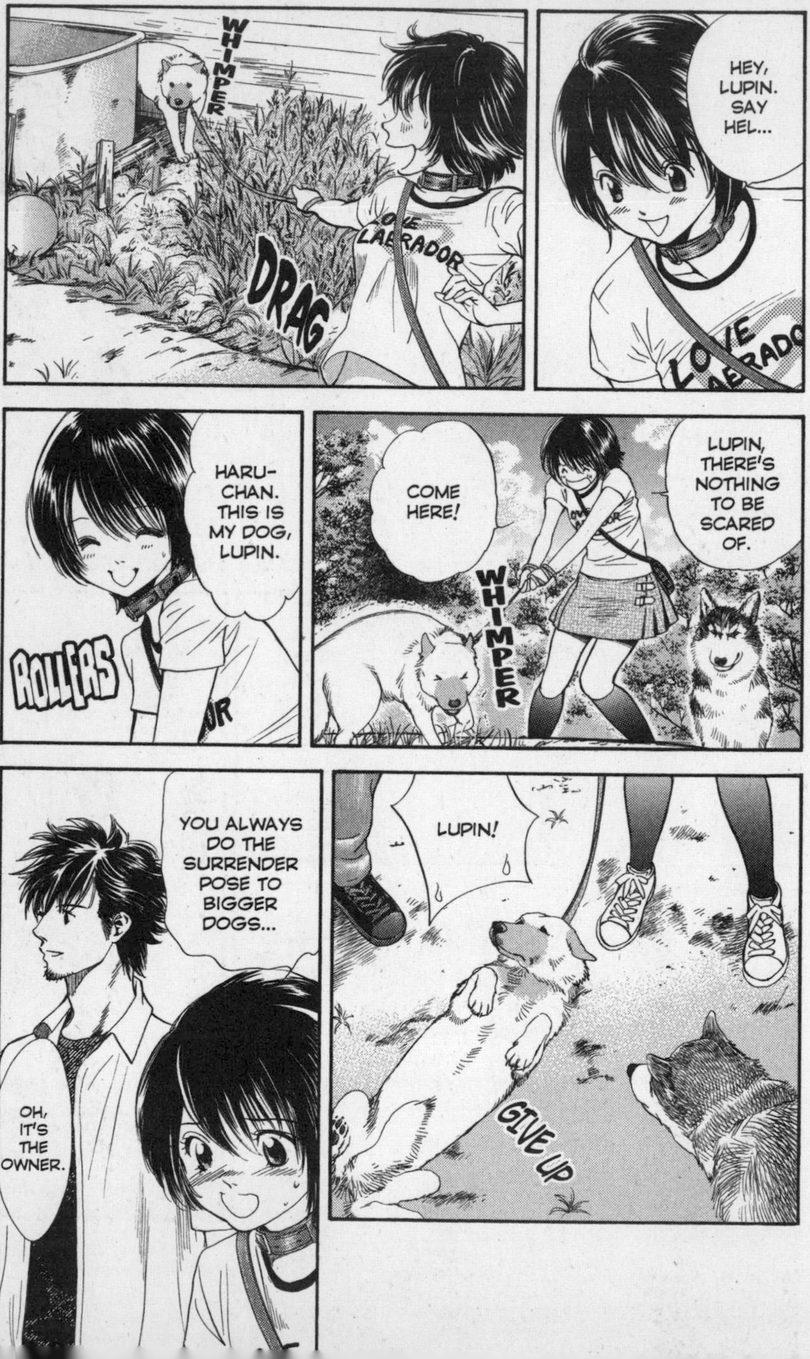
HEY, LUPIN. SAY HEL...
WHIMPER
DRAG
LUPIN, THERE'S NOTHING TO BE SCARED OF.
COME HERE!
WHIMPER
HARU-CHAN. THIS IS MY DOG, LUPIN.
ROLLERS
LUPIN!
GIVE UP
YOU ALWAYS DO THE SURRENDER POSE TO BIGGER DOGS...
OH, IT'S THE OWNER.

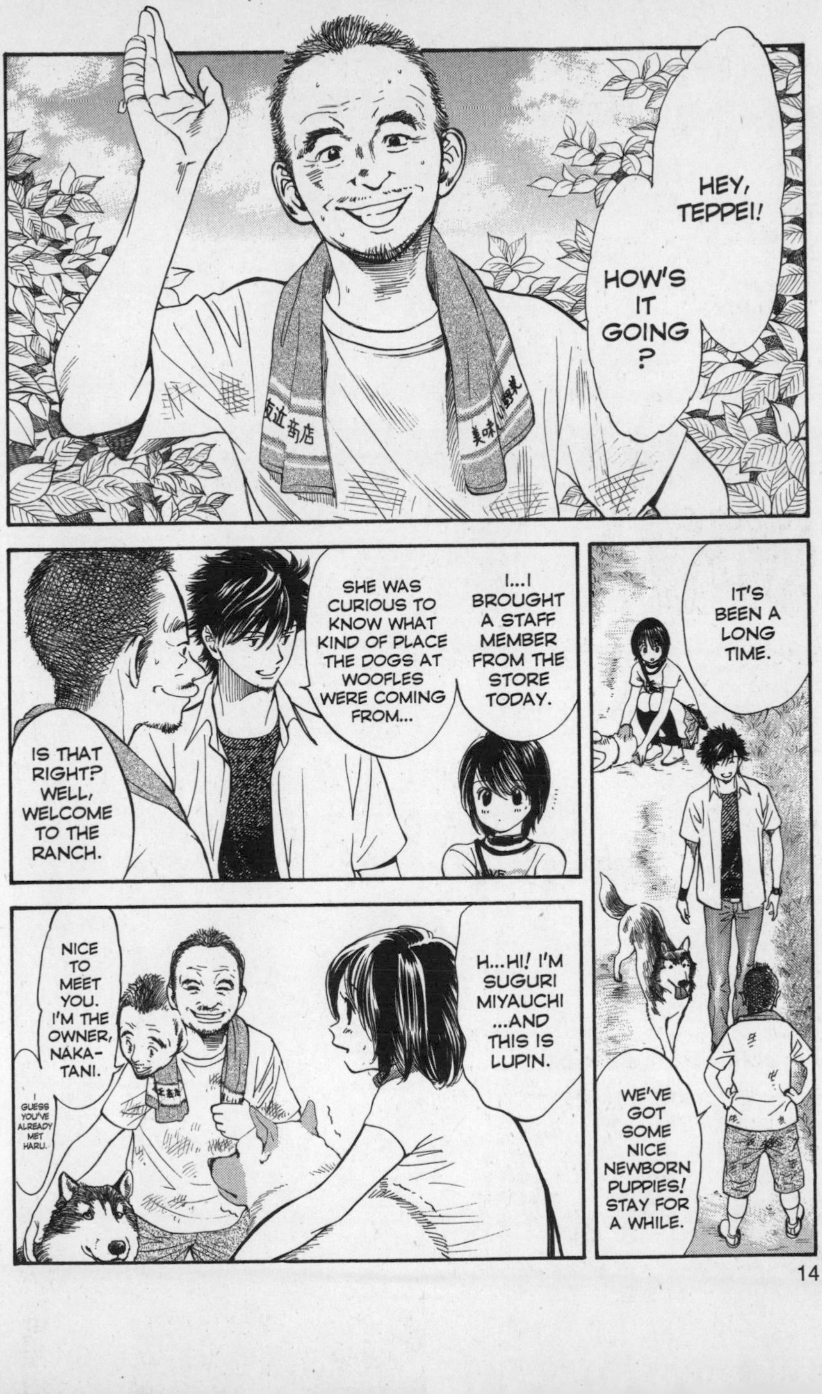
HEY, TEPPEI!
HOW'S IT GOING?
IT'S BEEN A LONG TIME.
WE'VE GOT SOME NICE NEWBORN PUPPIES! STAY FOR A WHILE.
I...I BROUGHT A STAFF MEMBER FROM THE STORE TODAY.
SHE WAS CURIOUS TO KNOW WHAT KIND OF PLACE THE DOGS AT WOOFLES WERE COMING FROM...
IS THAT RIGHT? WELL, WELCOME TO THE RANCH.
H...HI! I'M SUGURI MIYAUCHI ...AND THIS IS LUPIN.
NICE TO MEET YOU. I'M THE OWNER, NAKATANI.
I GUESS YOU'VE ALREADY MET HARU.

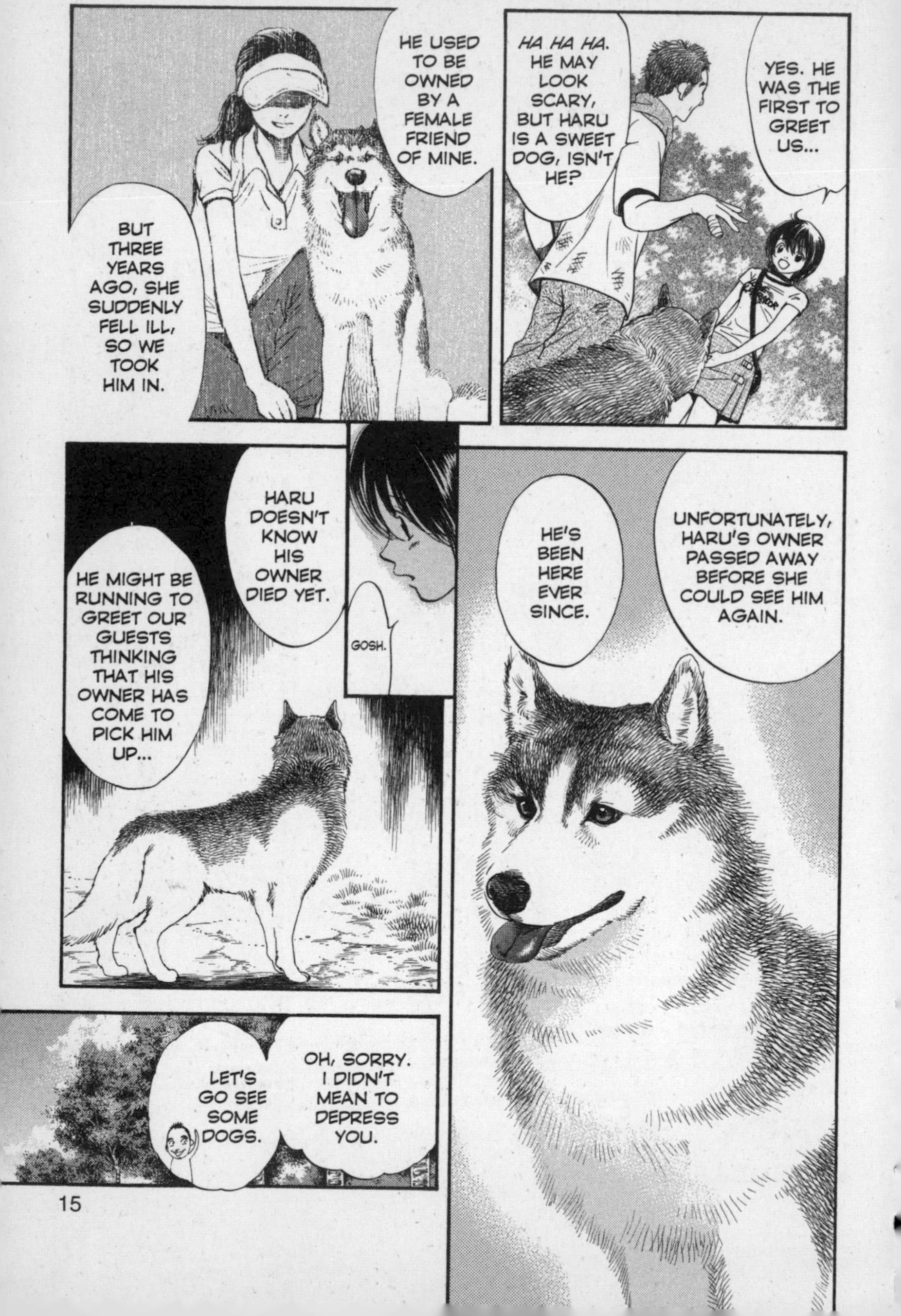
YES. HE WAS THE FIRST TO GREET US...
HA HA HA. HE MAY LOOK SCARY, BUT HARU IS A SWEET DOG, ISN'T HE?
HE USED TO BE OWNED BY A FEMALE FRIEND OF MINE.
BUT THREE YEARS AGO, SHE SUDDENLY FELL ILL, SO WE TOOK HIM IN.
UNFORTUNATELY, HARU'S OWNER PASSED AWAY BEFORE SHE COULD SEE HIM AGAIN.
HE'S BEEN HERE EVER SINCE.
GOSH.
HARU DOESN'T KNOW HIS OWNER DIED YET.
HE MIGHT BE RUNNING TO GREET OUR GUESTS THINKING THAT HIS OWNER HAS COME TO PICK HIM UP...
OH, SORRY. I DIDN'T MEAN TO DEPRESS YOU.
LET'S GO SEE SOME DOGS.

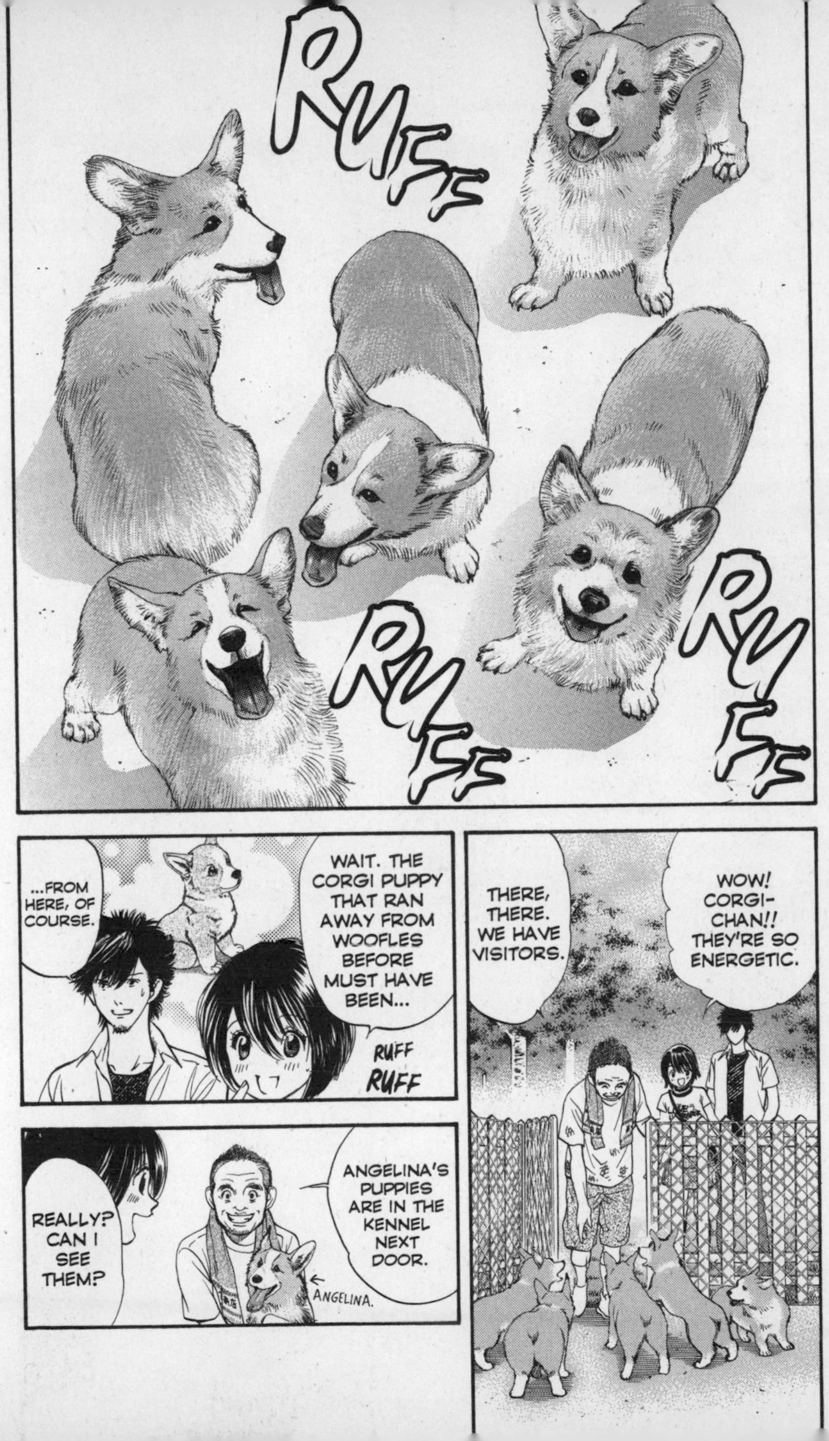
RUFF
RUFF
RUFF
WOW! CORGI-CHAN!! THEY'RE SO ENERGETIC.
THERE, THERE. WE HAVE VISITORS.
WAIT. THE CORGI PUPPY THAT RAN AWAY FROM WOOFLES BEFORE MUST HAVE BEEN...
...FROM HERE, OF COURSE.
RUFF RUFF
ANGELINA'S PUPPIES ARE IN THE KENNEL NEXT DOOR.
ANGELINA.
REALLY? CAN I SEE THEM?

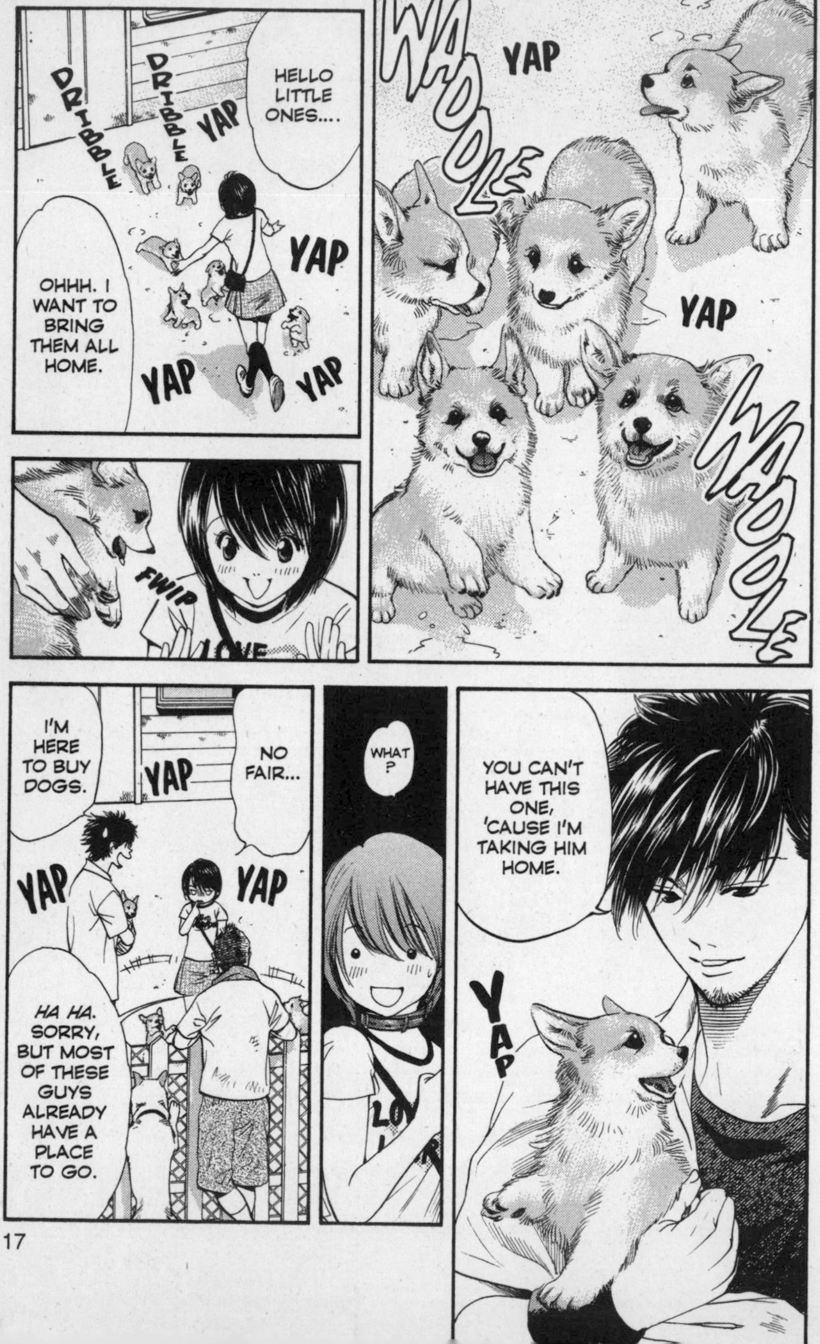
YAP
WADDLE
YAP
WADDLE
HELLO LITTLE ONES....
DRIBBLE
DRIBBLE
YAP
YAP
OHHH. I WANT TO BRING THEM ALL HOME.
YAP
YAP
FWIP
LOVE
YOU CAN'T HAVE THIS ONE, 'CAUSE I'M TAKING HIM HOME.
YAP
YAP
WHAT?
NO FAIR...
I'M HERE TO BUY DOGS.
YAP
YAP
YAP
HA HA. SORRY, BUT MOST OF THESE GUYS ALREADY HAVE A PLACE TO GO.

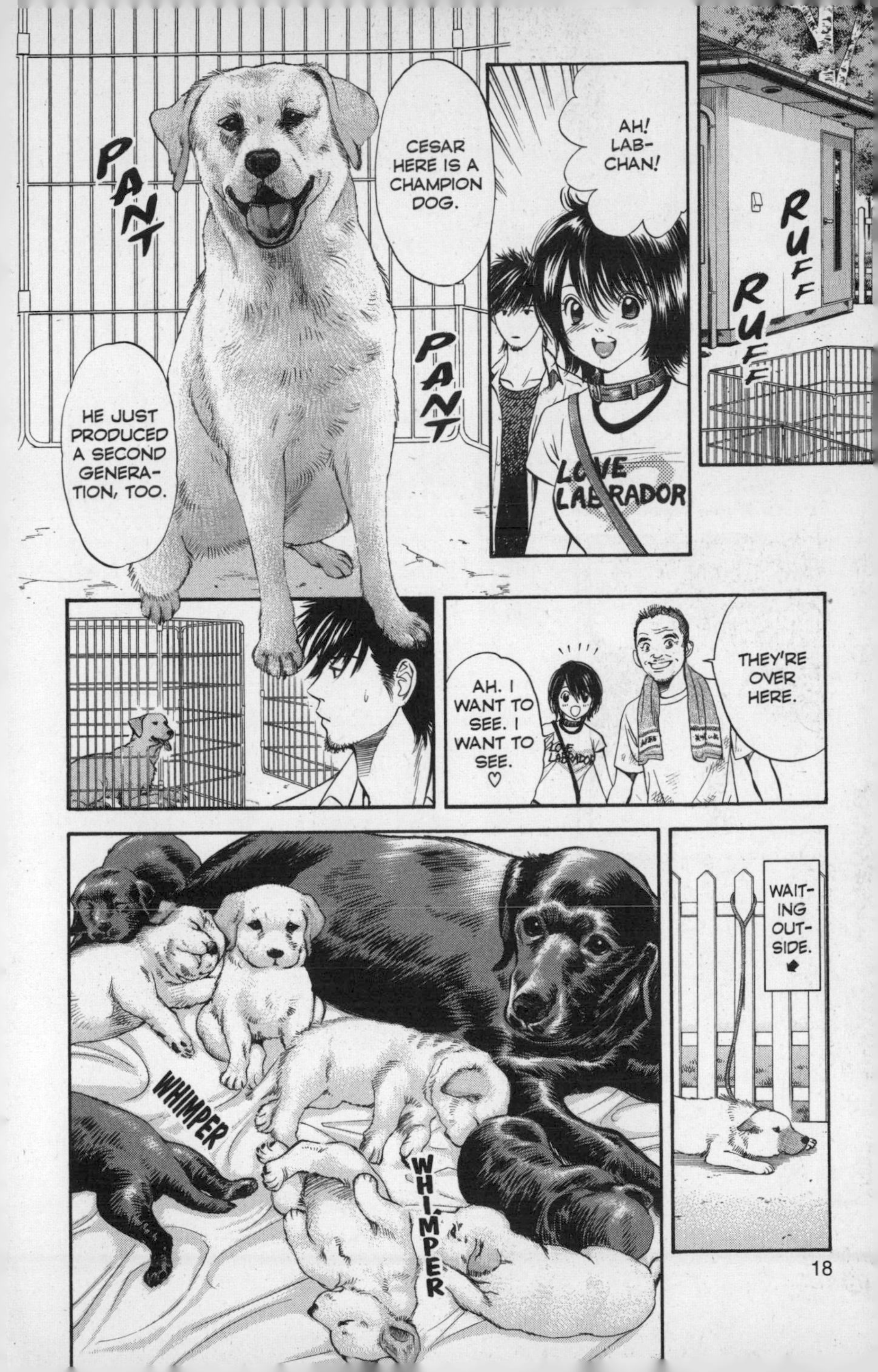

RUFF
RUFF
AH! LAB-CHAN!
LOVE LABRADOR
CESAR HERE IS A CHAMPION DOG.
PANT
PANT
HE JUST PRODUCED A SECOND GENERATION, TOO.
THEY'RE OVER HERE.
AH. I WANT TO SEE. I WANT TO SEE. ♡
LOVE LABRADOR
WAITING OUTSIDE.
WHIMPER
WHIMPER

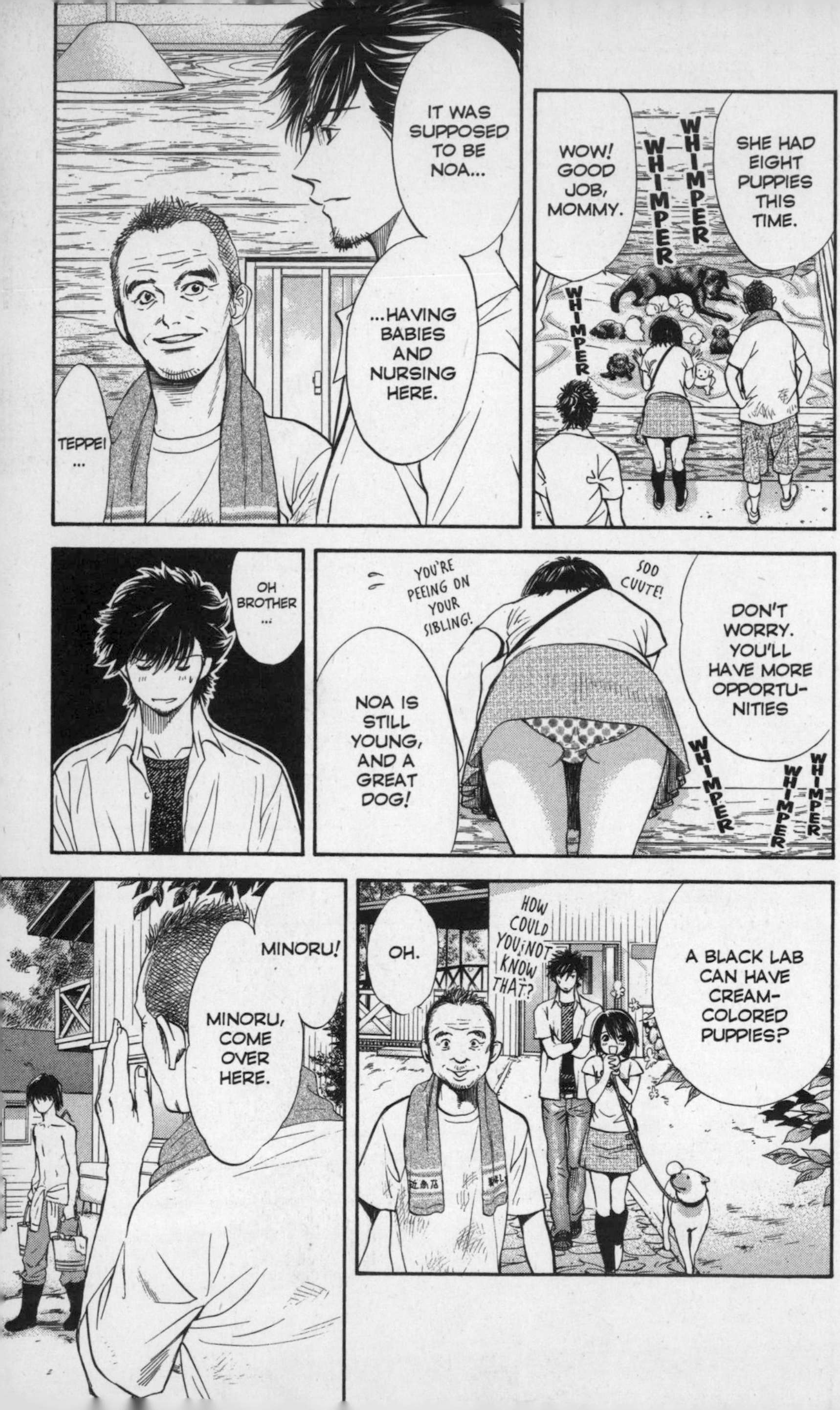
SHE HAD EIGHT PUPPIES THIS TIME.
WHIMPER WHIMPER
WOW! GOOD JOB, MOMMY.
WHIMPER
IT WAS SUPPOSED TO BE NOA...
...HAVING BABIES AND NURSING HERE.
TEPPEI ...
DON'T WORRY. YOU'LL HAVE MORE OPPORTU-NITIES
WHIMPER WHIMPER WHIMPER
SOO CUUTE!
YOU'RE PEEING ON YOUR SIBLING!
NOA IS STILL YOUNG, AND A GREAT DOG!
OH BROTHER ...
A BLACK LAB CAN HAVE CREAM-COLORED PUPPIES?
HOW COULD YOU NOT KNOW THAT?!
OH.
MINORU!
MINORU, COME OVER HERE.

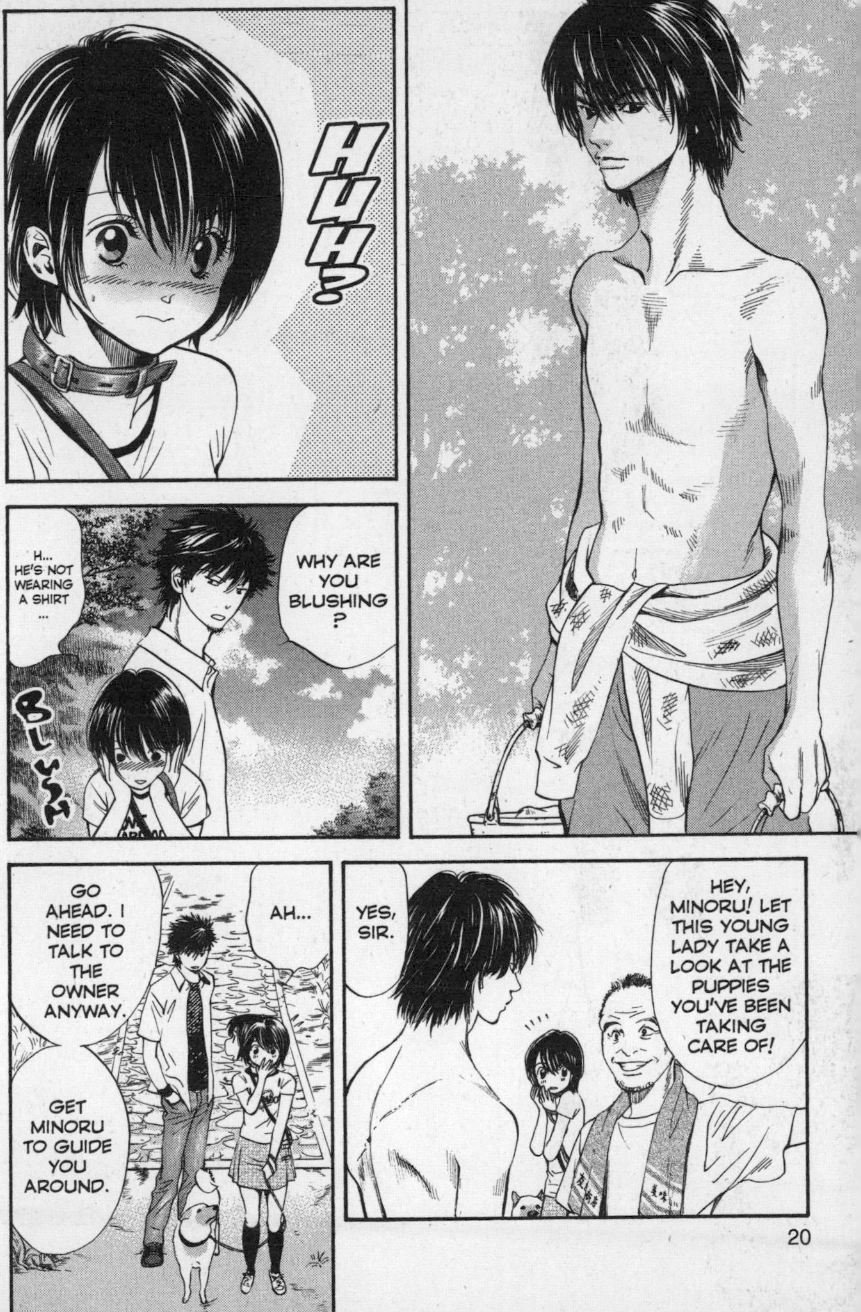
HUH?!
WHY ARE YOU BLUSHING?
H... HE'S NOT WEARING A SHIRT...
BLUSH
HEY, MINORU! LET THIS YOUNG LADY TAKE A LOOK AT THE PUPPIES YOU'VE BEEN TAKING CARE OF!
YES, SIR.
AH...
GO AHEAD. I NEED TO TALK TO THE OWNER ANYWAY.
GET MINORU TO GUIDE YOU AROUND.

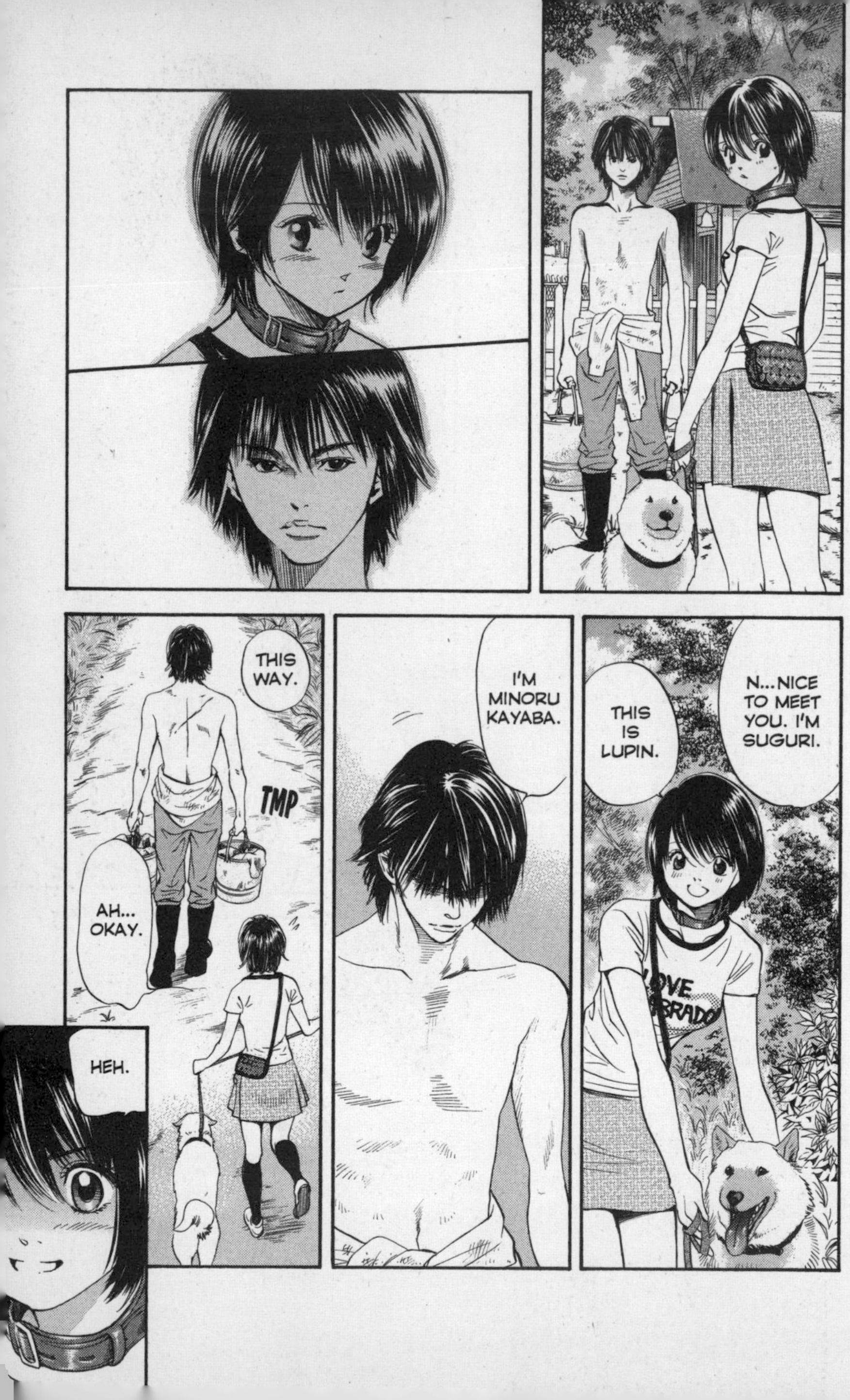
N...NICE TO MEET YOU. I'M SUGURI.
THIS IS LUPIN.
I'M MINORU KAYABA.
THIS WAY.
TMP
AH... OKAY.
HEH.

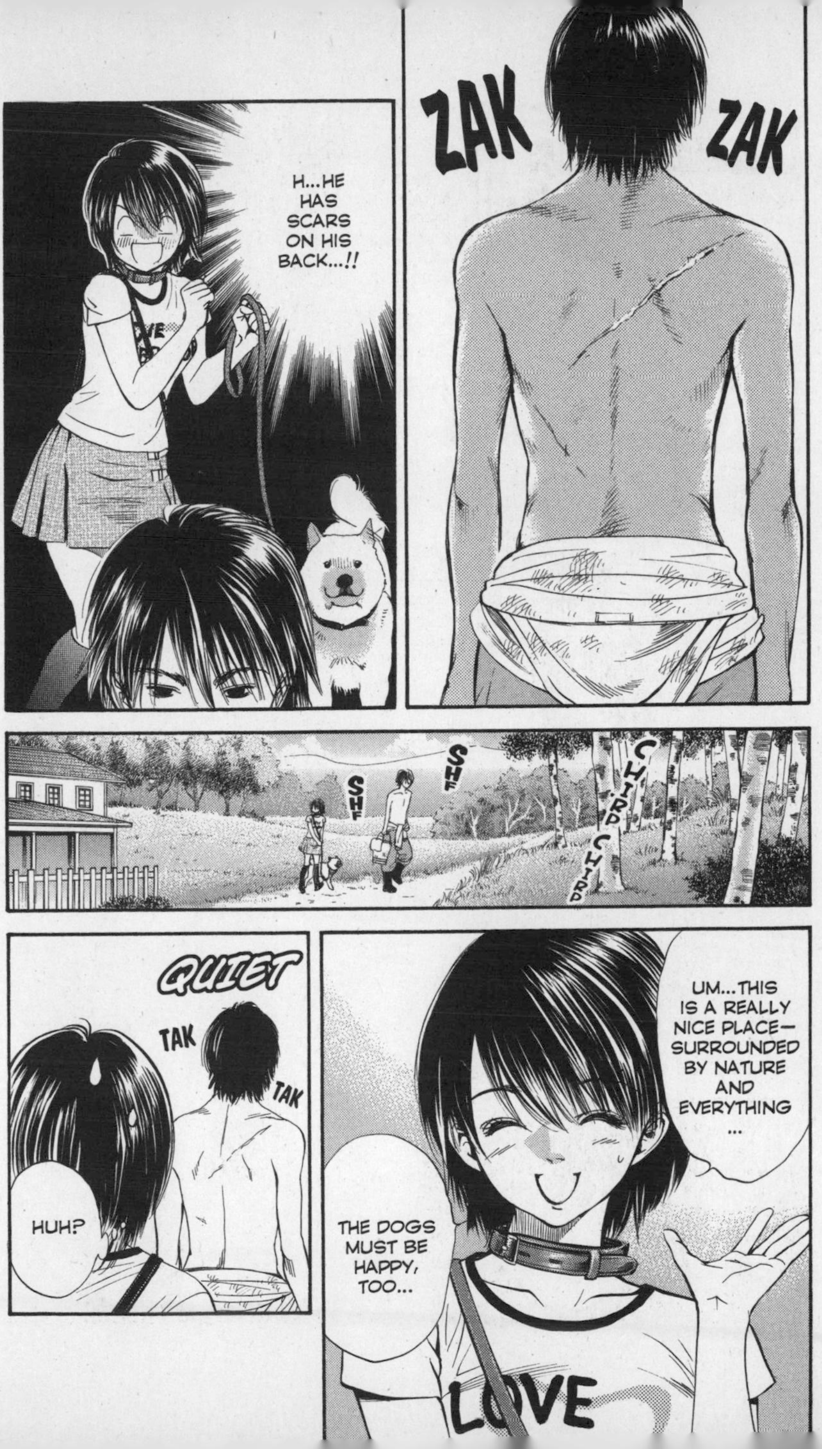
ZAK
ZAK
H...HE HAS SCARS ON HIS BACK...!!
CHIRP CHIRP
SHF
SHF
UM...THIS IS A REALLY NICE PLACE—SURROUNDED BY NATURE AND EVERYTHING...
THE DOGS MUST BE HAPPY, TOO...
LOVE
QUIET
TAK
TAK
HUH?

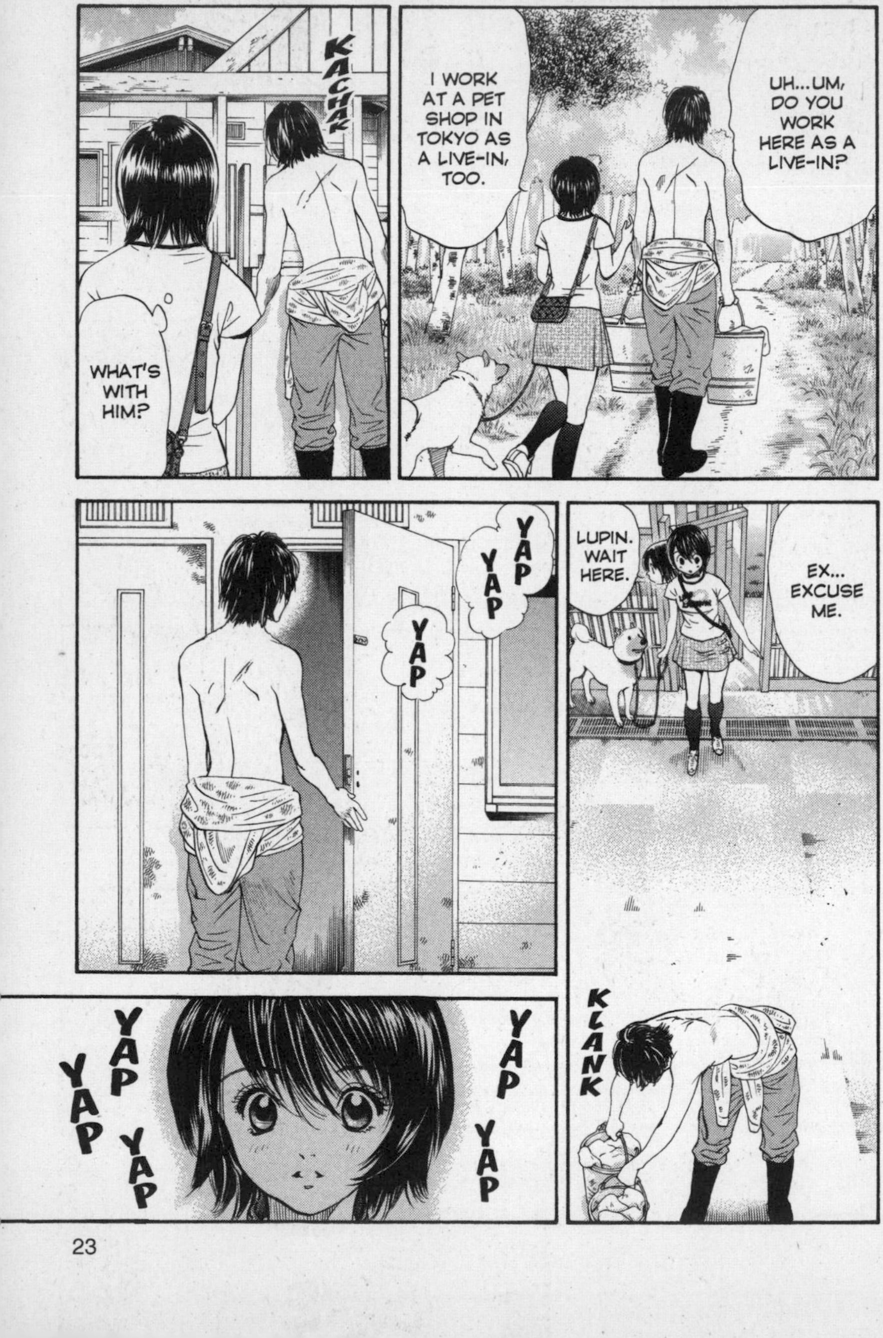
UH...UM, DO YOU WORK HERE AS A LIVE-IN?
I WORK AT A PET SHOP IN TOKYO AS A LIVE-IN, TOO.
KACHAK
WHAT'S WITH HIM?
EX... EXCUSE ME.
LUPIN. WAIT HERE.
KLANK
YAP YAP
YAP YAP
YAP
YAP YAP
YAP YAP
YAP YAP
YAP YAP

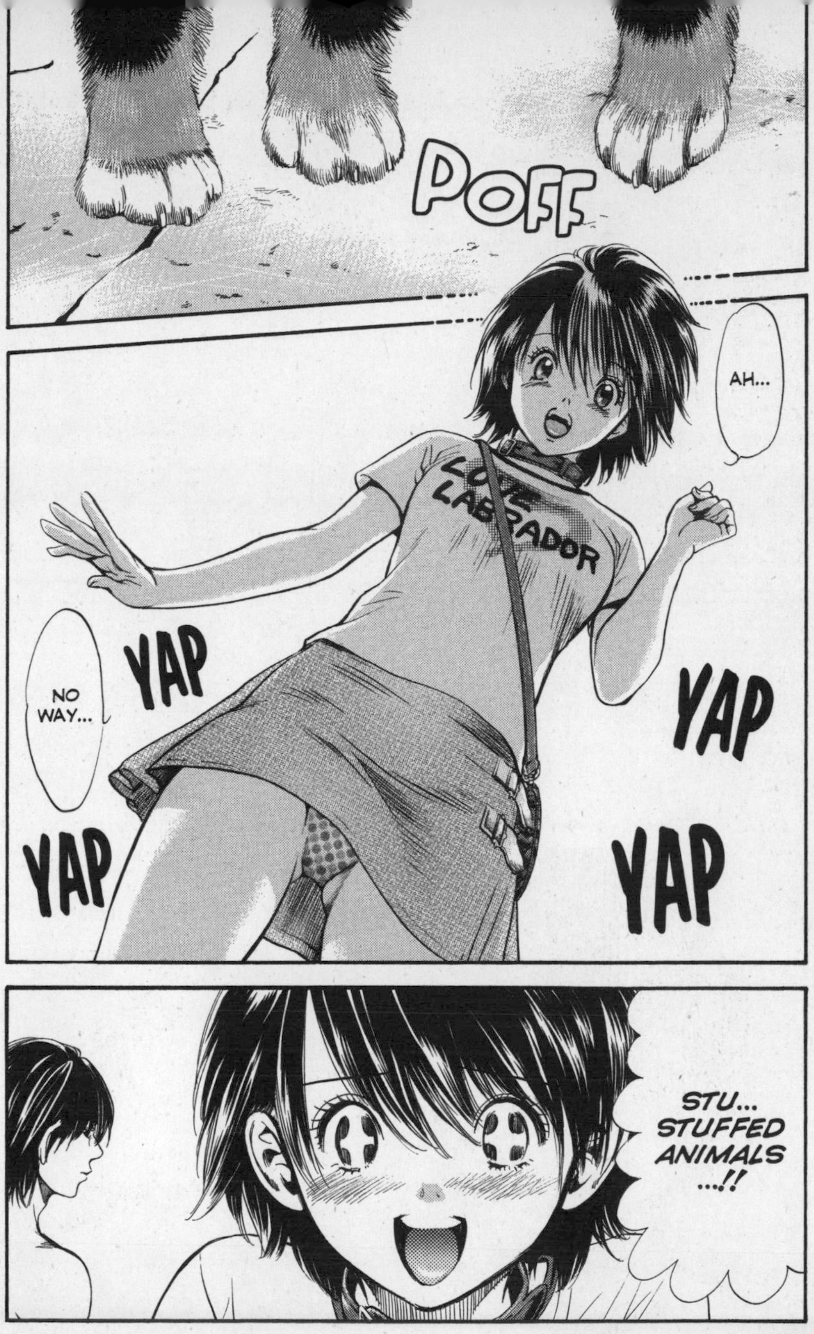
POFF
AH...
YAP
YAP
LOVE LABRADOR
YAP
NO WAY...
YAP
STU... STUFFED ANIMALS ...!!

CHAPTER 88: WALKING "STUFFED ANIMALS" AND MEN'S DREAMS

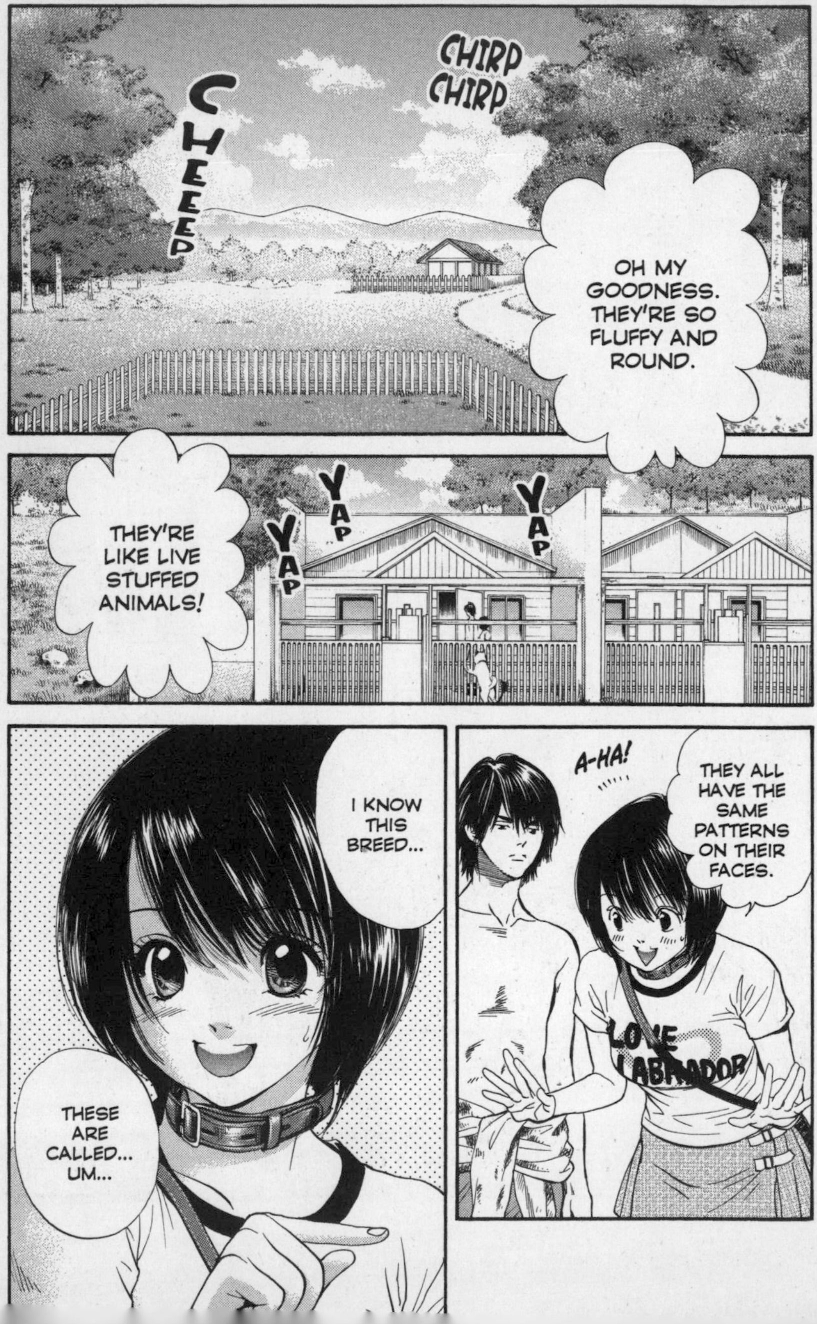
CHIRP CHIRP
CHEEEP
OH MY GOODNESS. THEY'RE SO FLUFFY AND ROUND.
YAP
YAP
YAP
THEY'RE LIKE LIVE STUFFED ANIMALS!
A-HA!
THEY ALL HAVE THE SAME PATTERNS ON THEIR FACES.
I KNOW THIS BREED...
THESE ARE CALLED... UM...

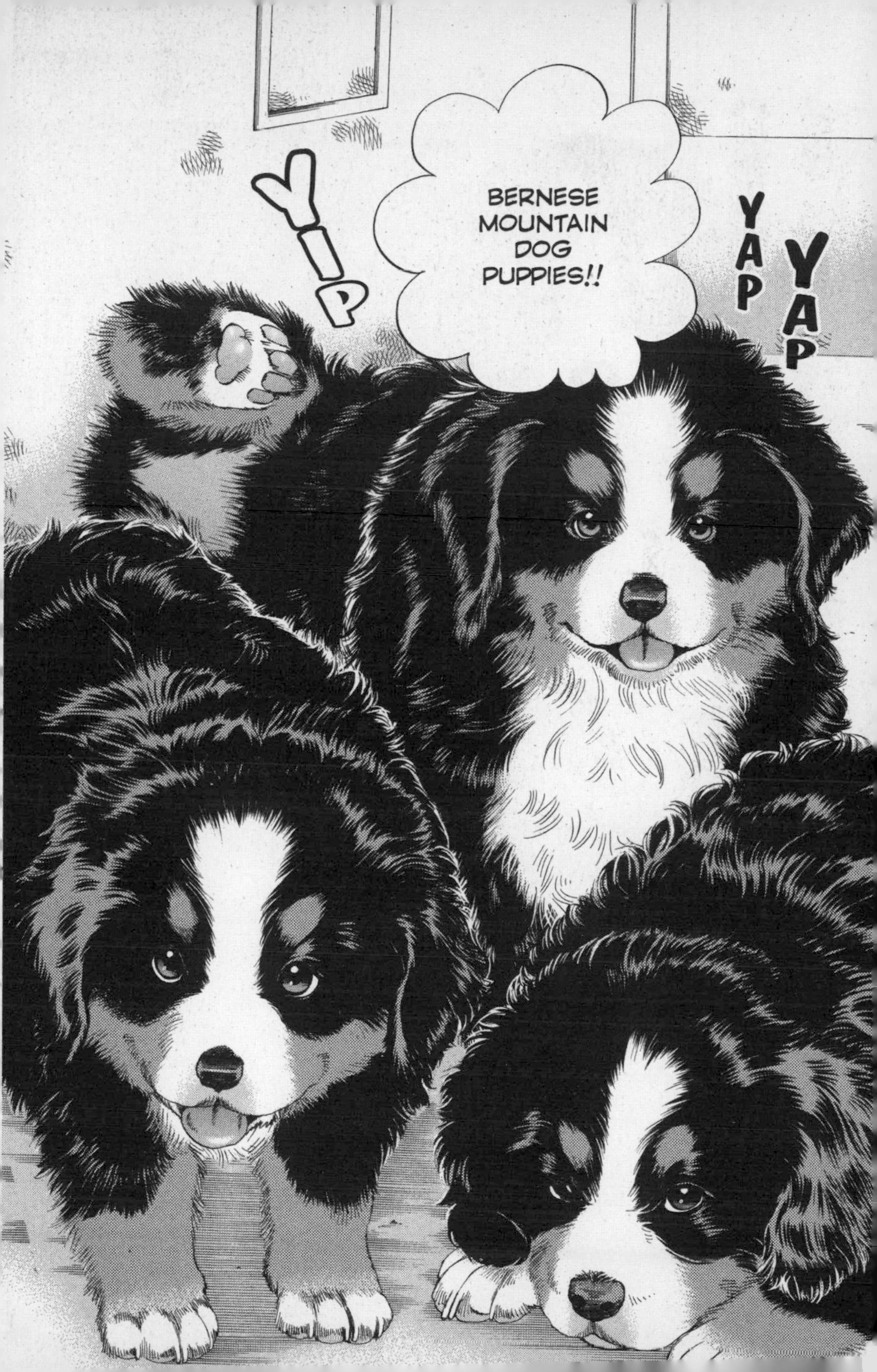
YAP YAP YAP
BERNESE MOUNTAIN DOG PUPPIES!!
YIP

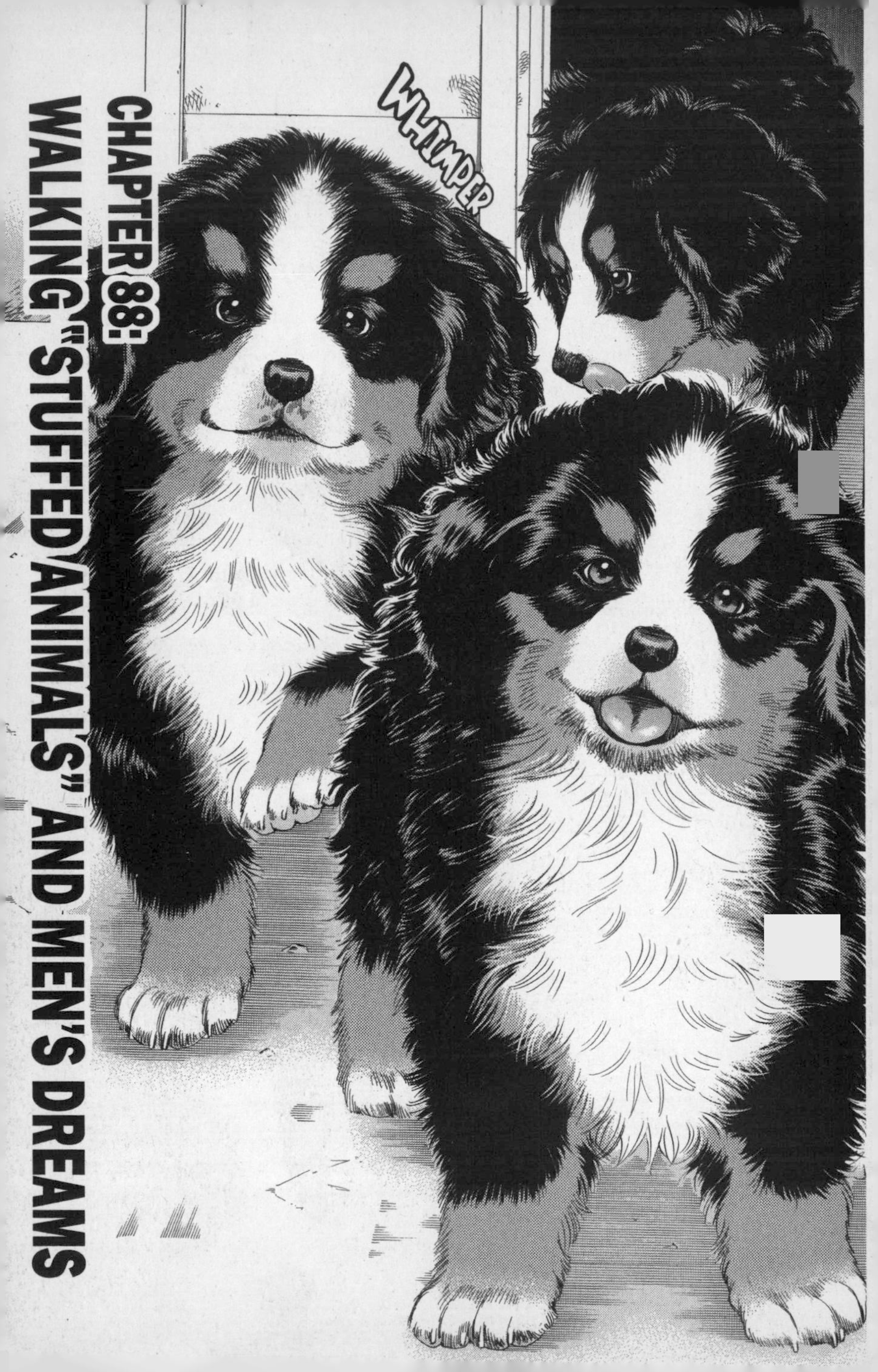
WHIMPER
CHAPTER 88:
WALKING "STUFFED ANIMALS" AND MEN'S DREAMS

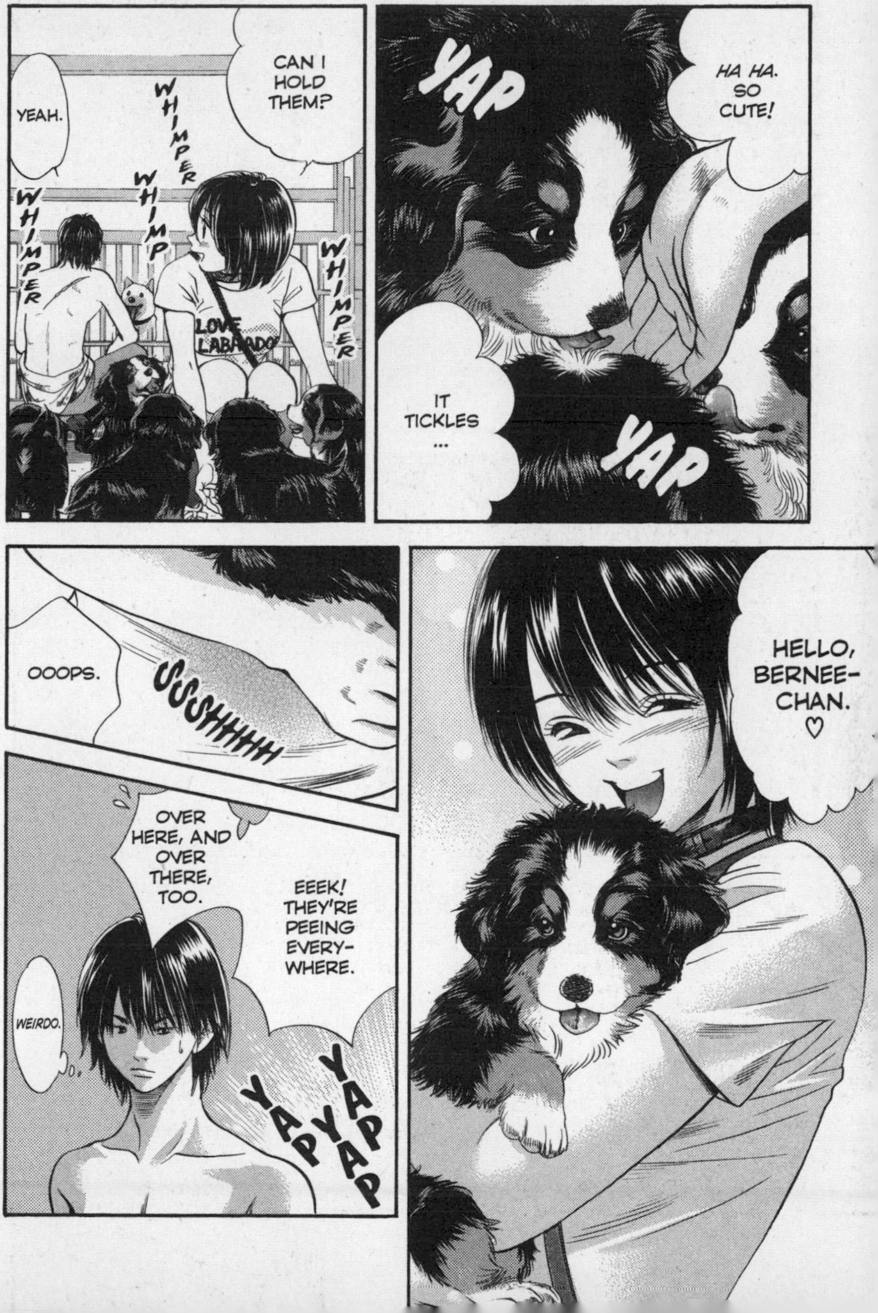
HA HA. SO CUTE!
YAP
IT TICKLES ...
YAP
CAN I HOLD THEM?
WHIMPER
YEAH.
WHIMPER
WHIMP
WHIMPER
LOVE LABRADO
HELLO, BERNEE-CHAN. ♡
SSSHHHHH
OOOPS.
EEEK! THEY'RE PEEING EVERY-WHERE.
OVER HERE, AND OVER THERE, TOO.
YAP YAP YAP
WEIRDO.

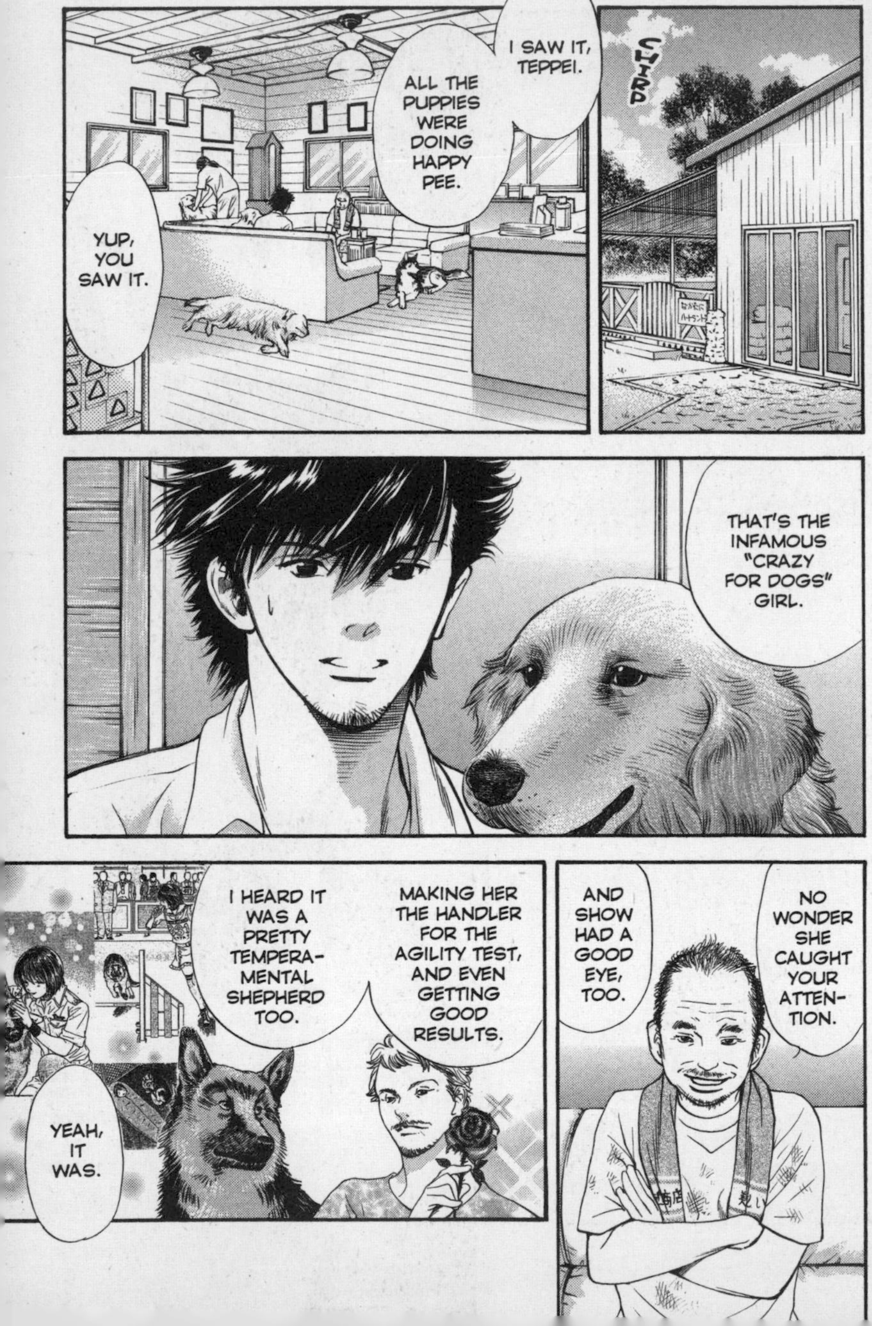
CHIRP
I SAW IT, TEPPEI.
ALL THE PUPPIES WERE DOING HAPPY PEE.
YUP, YOU SAW IT.
THAT'S THE INFAMOUS "CRAZY FOR DOGS" GIRL.
NO WONDER SHE CAUGHT YOUR ATTENTION.
AND SHOW HAD A GOOD EYE, TOO.
MAKING HER THE HANDLER FOR THE AGILITY TEST, AND EVEN GETTING GOOD RESULTS.
I HEARD IT WAS A PRETTY TEMPERAMENTAL SHEPHERD TOO.
YEAH, IT WAS.

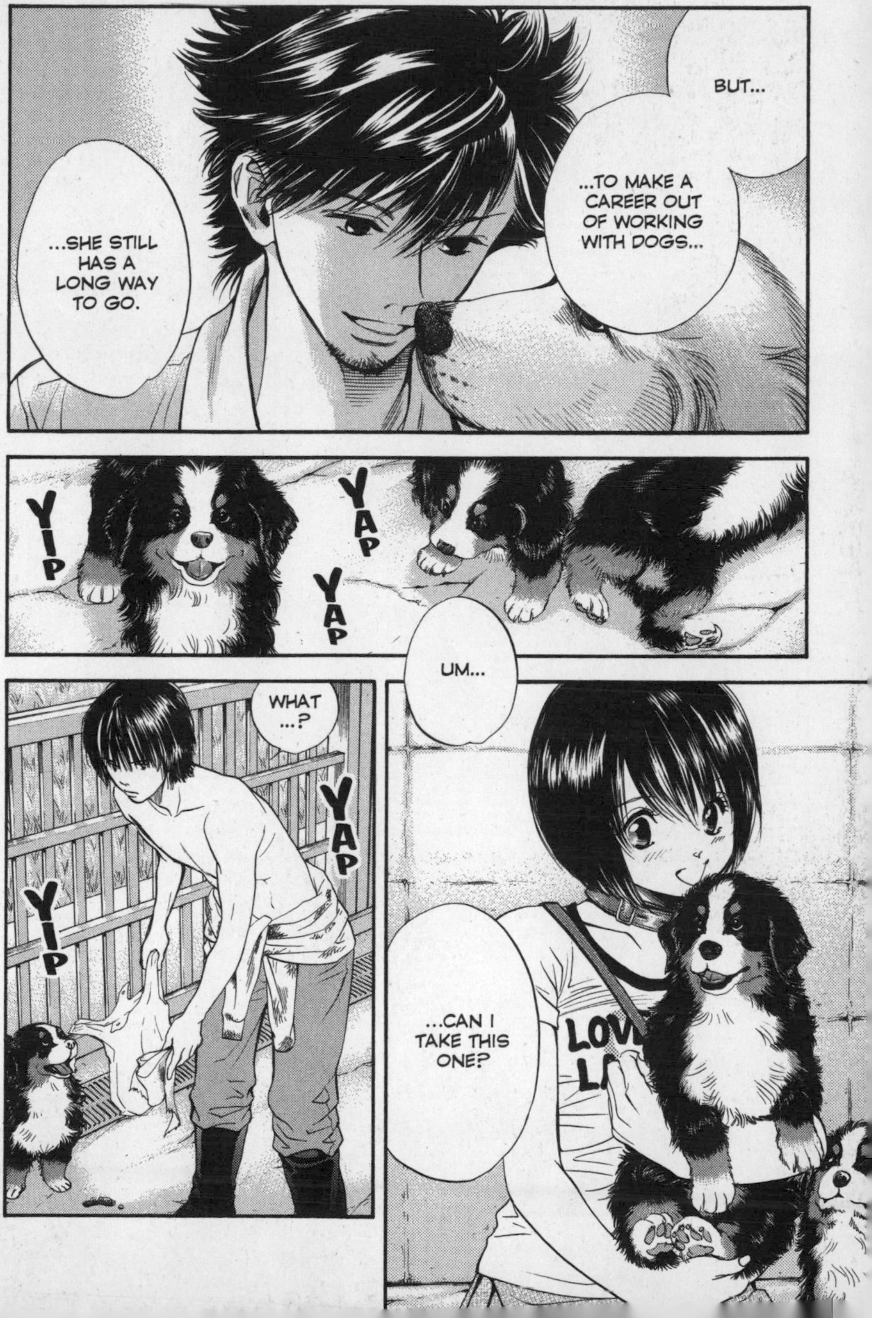
BUT...
...TO MAKE A CAREER OUT OF WORKING WITH DOGS...
...SHE STILL HAS A LONG WAY TO GO.
YAP
YAP
YIP
UM...
...CAN I TAKE THIS ONE?
WHAT ...?
YAP
YIP

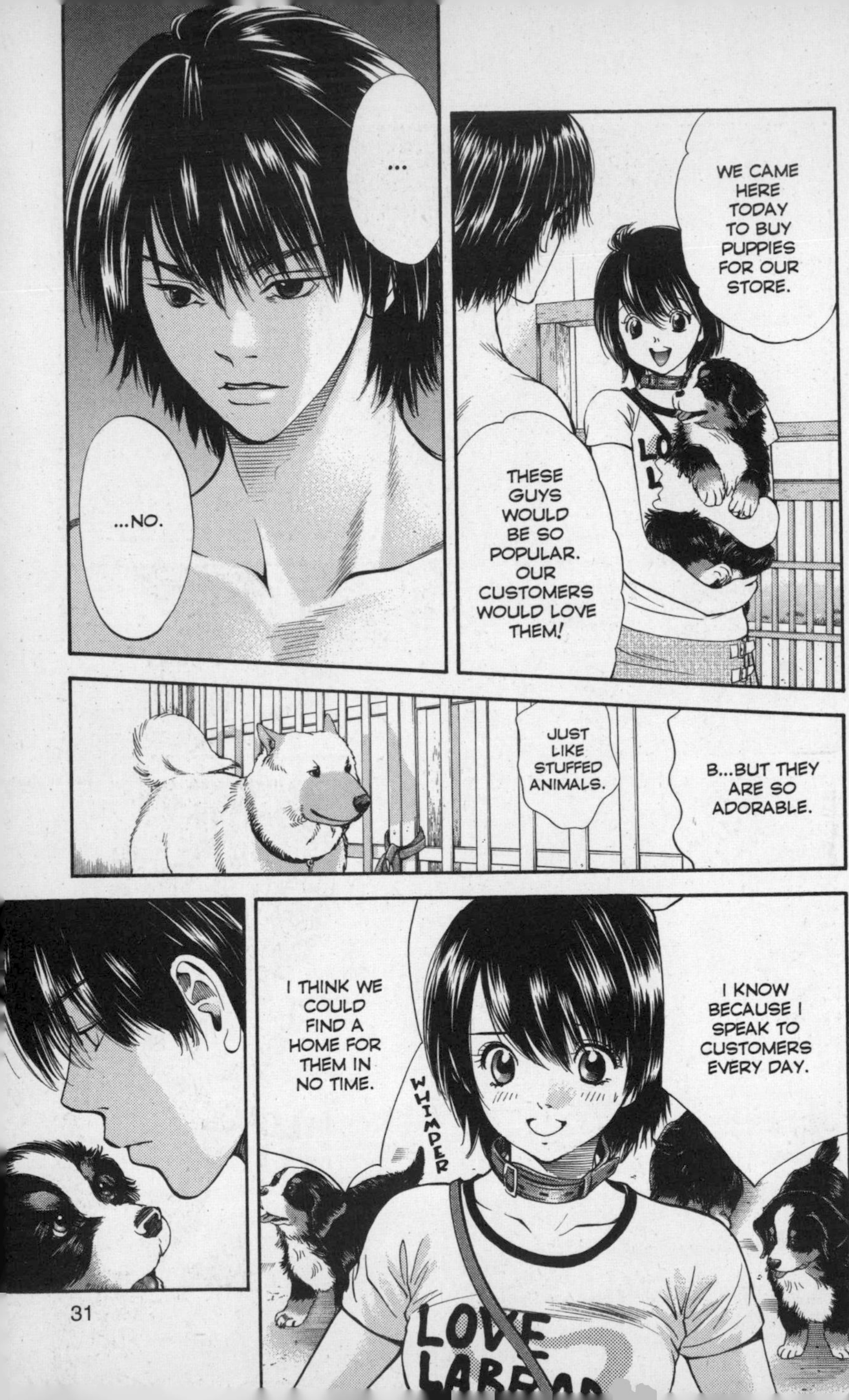
WE CAME HERE TODAY TO BUY PUPPIES FOR OUR STORE.
THESE GUYS WOULD BE SO POPULAR. OUR CUSTOMERS WOULD LOVE THEM!
...
...NO.
B...BUT THEY ARE SO ADORABLE.
JUST LIKE STUFFED ANIMALS.
I KNOW BECAUSE I SPEAK TO CUSTOMERS EVERY DAY.
I THINK WE COULD FIND A HOME FOR THEM IN NO TIME.
WHIMPER

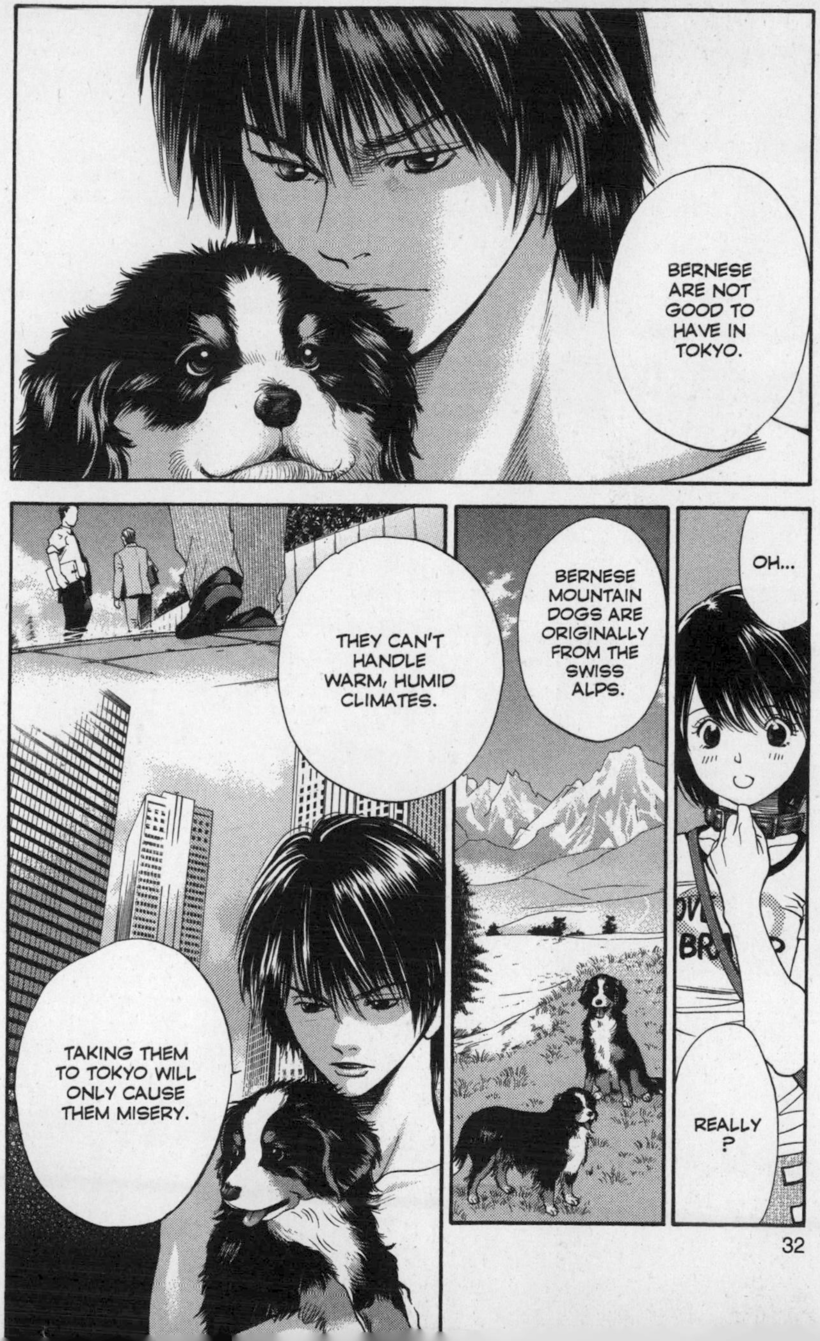
BERNESE ARE NOT GOOD TO HAVE IN TOKYO.
OH...
REALLY?
BERNESE MOUNTAIN DOGS ARE ORIGINALLY FROM THE SWISS ALPS.
THEY CAN'T HANDLE WARM, HUMID CLIMATES.
TAKING THEM TO TOKYO WILL ONLY CAUSE THEM MISERY.

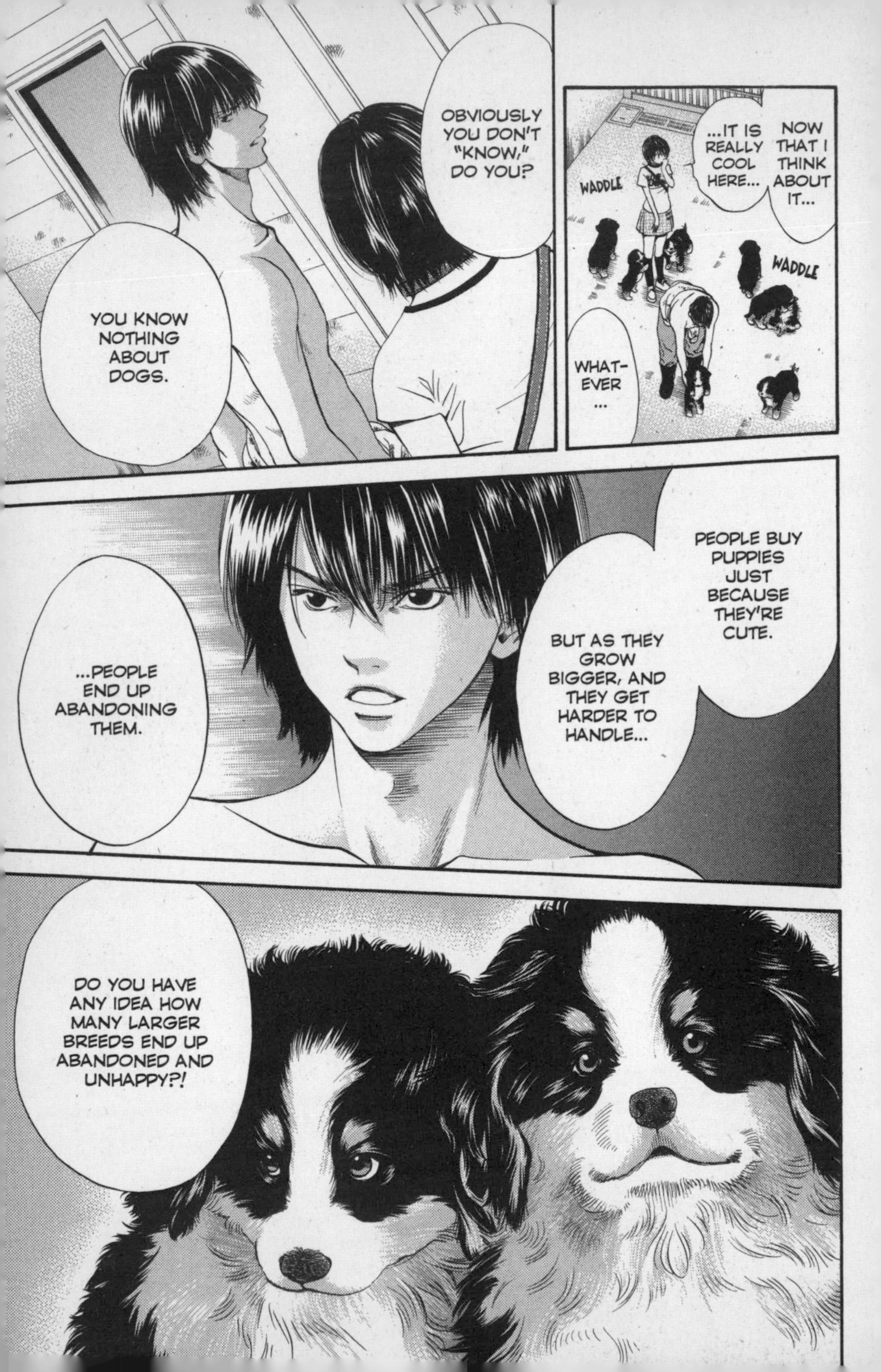
NOW THAT I THINK ABOUT IT...
...IT IS REALLY COOL HERE...
WADDLE
WADDLE
WHAT-EVER...
OBVIOUSLY YOU DON'T "KNOW," DO YOU?
YOU KNOW NOTHING ABOUT DOGS.
PEOPLE BUY PUPPIES JUST BECAUSE THEY'RE CUTE.
BUT AS THEY GROW BIGGER, AND THEY GET HARDER TO HANDLE...
...PEOPLE END UP ABANDONING THEM.
DO YOU HAVE ANY IDEA HOW MANY LARGER BREEDS END UP ABANDONED AND UNHAPPY?!

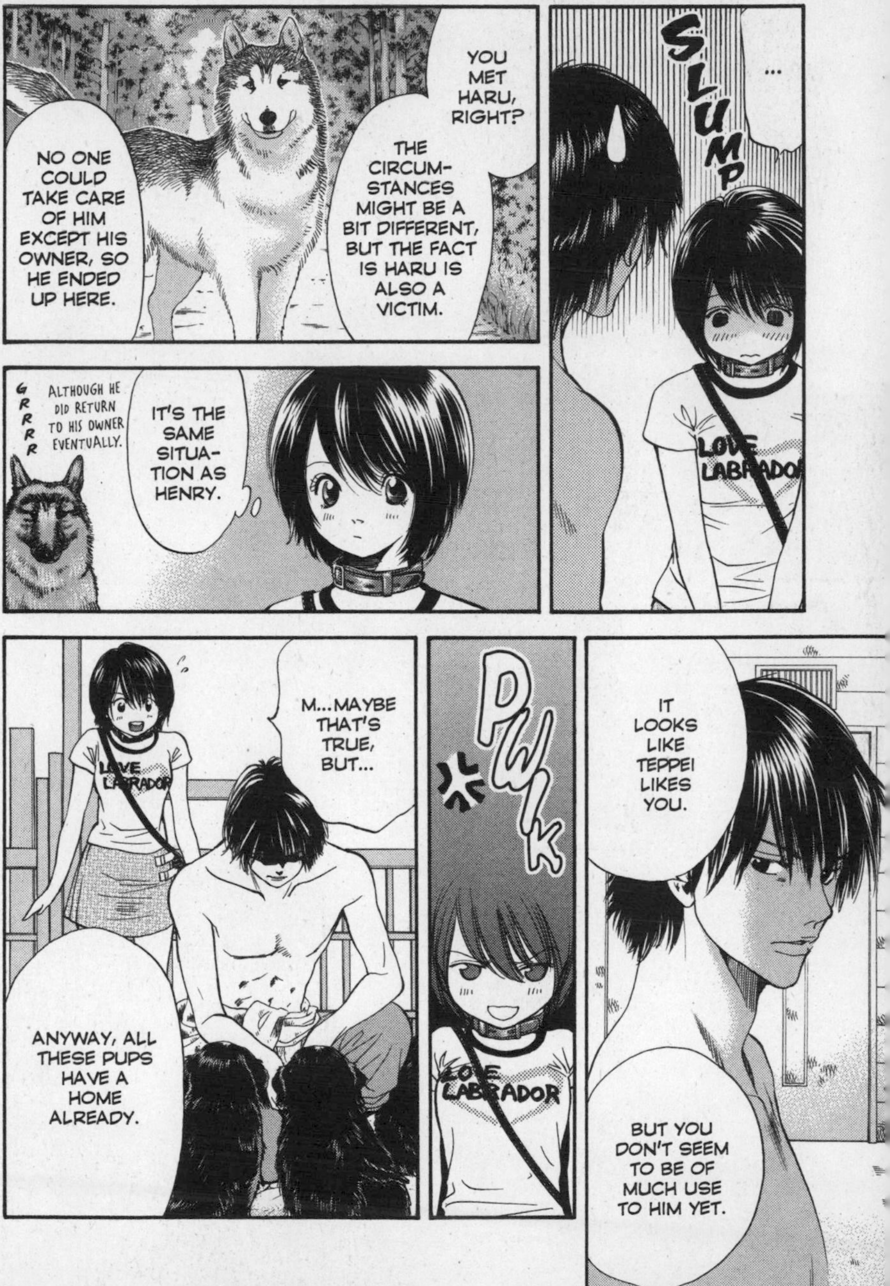
SLUMP
...
YOU MET HARU, RIGHT?
THE CIRCUM-STANCES MIGHT BE A BIT DIFFERENT, BUT THE FACT IS HARU IS ALSO A VICTIM.
NO ONE COULD TAKE CARE OF HIM EXCEPT HIS OWNER, SO HE ENDED UP HERE.
IT'S THE SAME SITUA-TION AS HENRY.
ALTHOUGH HE DID RETURN TO HIS OWNER EVENTUALLY.
GRRRR
LOVE LABRADOR
IT LOOKS LIKE TEPPEI LIKES YOU.
BUT YOU DON'T SEEM TO BE OF MUCH USE TO HIM YET.
PWIK
LOVE LABRADOR
M...MAYBE THAT'S TRUE, BUT...
ANYWAY, ALL THESE PUPS HAVE A HOME ALREADY.
LOVE LABRADOR

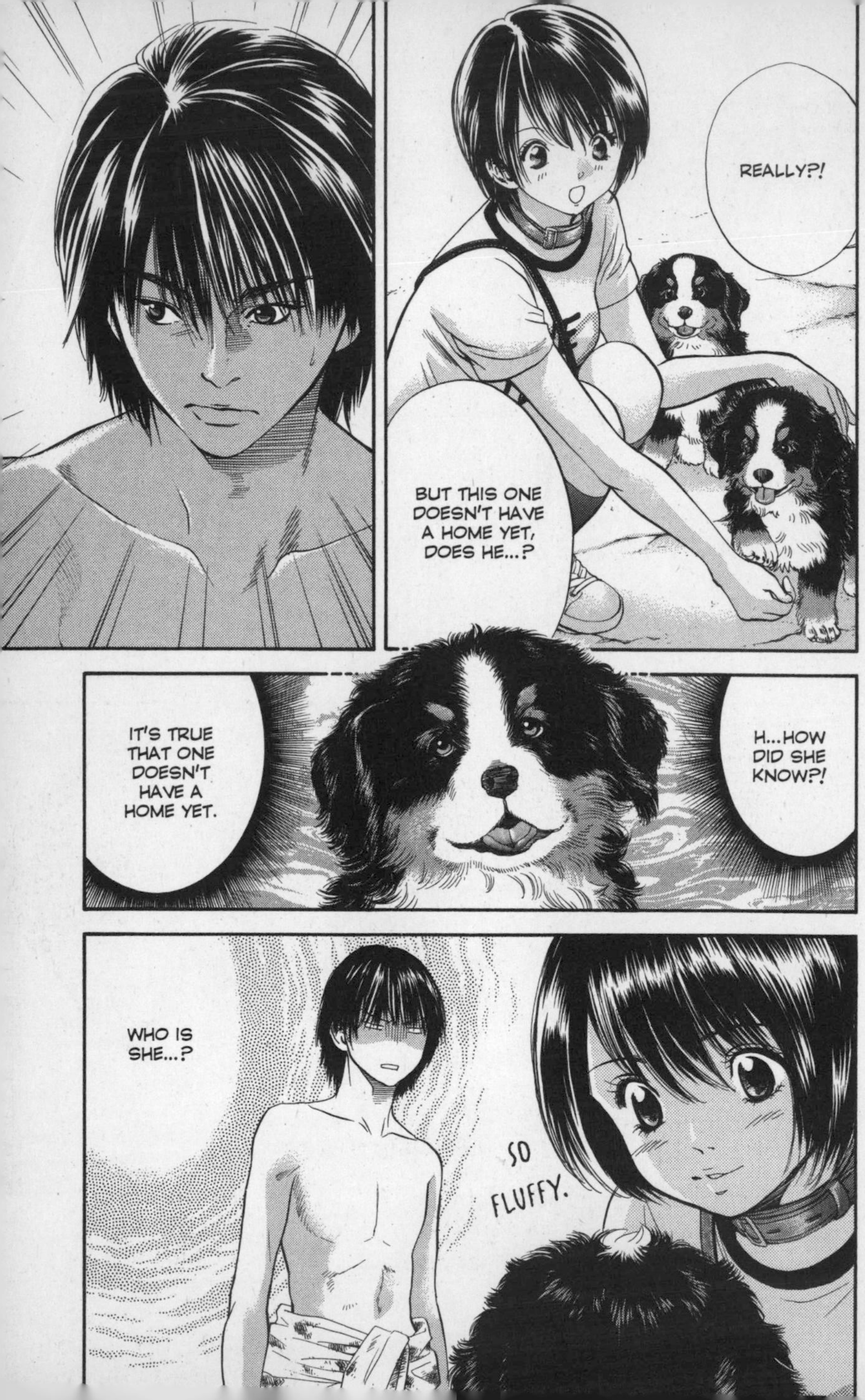
REALLY?!
BUT THIS ONE DOESN'T HAVE A HOME YET, DOES HE...?
H...HOW DID SHE KNOW?!
IT'S TRUE THAT ONE DOESN'T HAVE A HOME YET.
SO FLUFFY.
WHO IS SHE...?

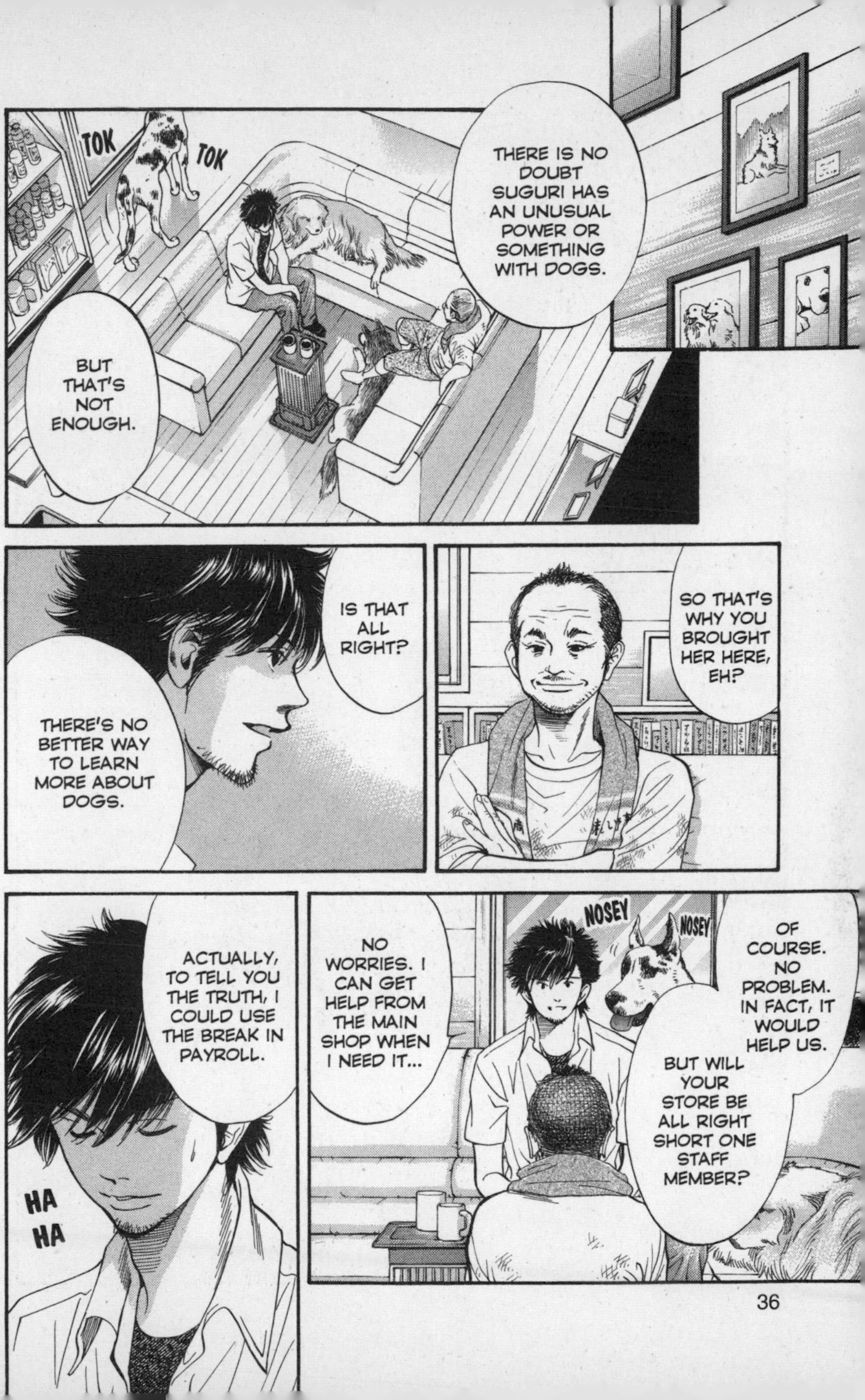
TOK
TOK
THERE IS NO DOUBT SUGURI HAS AN UNUSUAL POWER OR SOMETHING WITH DOGS.
BUT THAT'S NOT ENOUGH.
SO THAT'S WHY YOU BROUGHT HER HERE, EH?
IS THAT ALL RIGHT?
THERE'S NO BETTER WAY TO LEARN MORE ABOUT DOGS.
NOSEY
NOSEY
OF COURSE. NO PROBLEM. IN FACT, IT WOULD HELP US.
BUT WILL YOUR STORE BE ALL RIGHT SHORT ONE STAFF MEMBER?
NO WORRIES. I CAN GET HELP FROM THE MAIN SHOP WHEN I NEED IT...
ACTUALLY, TO TELL YOU THE TRUTH, I COULD USE THE BREAK IN PAYROLL.
HA
HA

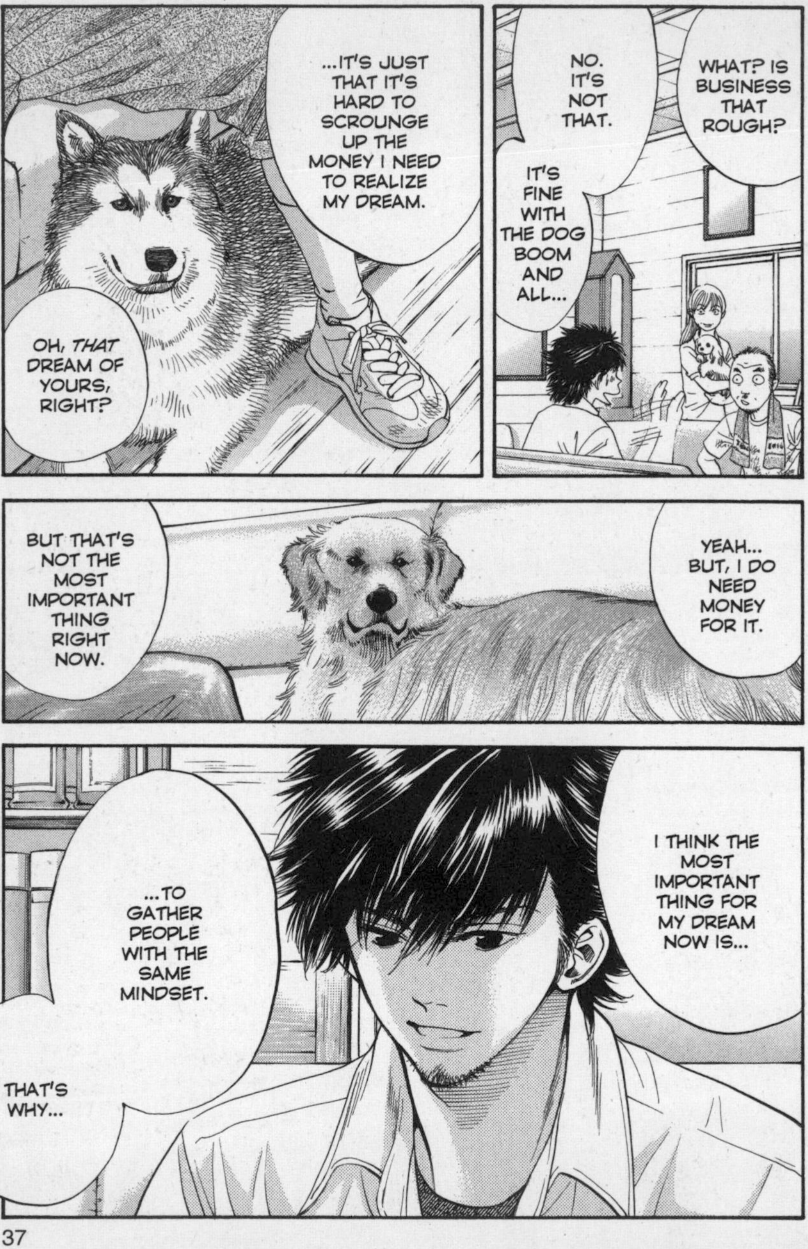
WHAT? IS BUSINESS THAT ROUGH?
NO. IT'S NOT THAT.
IT'S FINE WITH THE DOG BOOM AND ALL...
...IT'S JUST THAT IT'S HARD TO SCROUNGE UP THE MONEY I NEED TO REALIZE MY DREAM.
OH, *THAT* DREAM OF YOURS, RIGHT?
YEAH... BUT, I DO NEED MONEY FOR IT.
BUT THAT'S NOT THE MOST IMPORTANT THING RIGHT NOW.
I THINK THE MOST IMPORTANT THING FOR MY DREAM NOW IS...
...TO GATHER PEOPLE WITH THE SAME MINDSET.
THAT'S WHY...

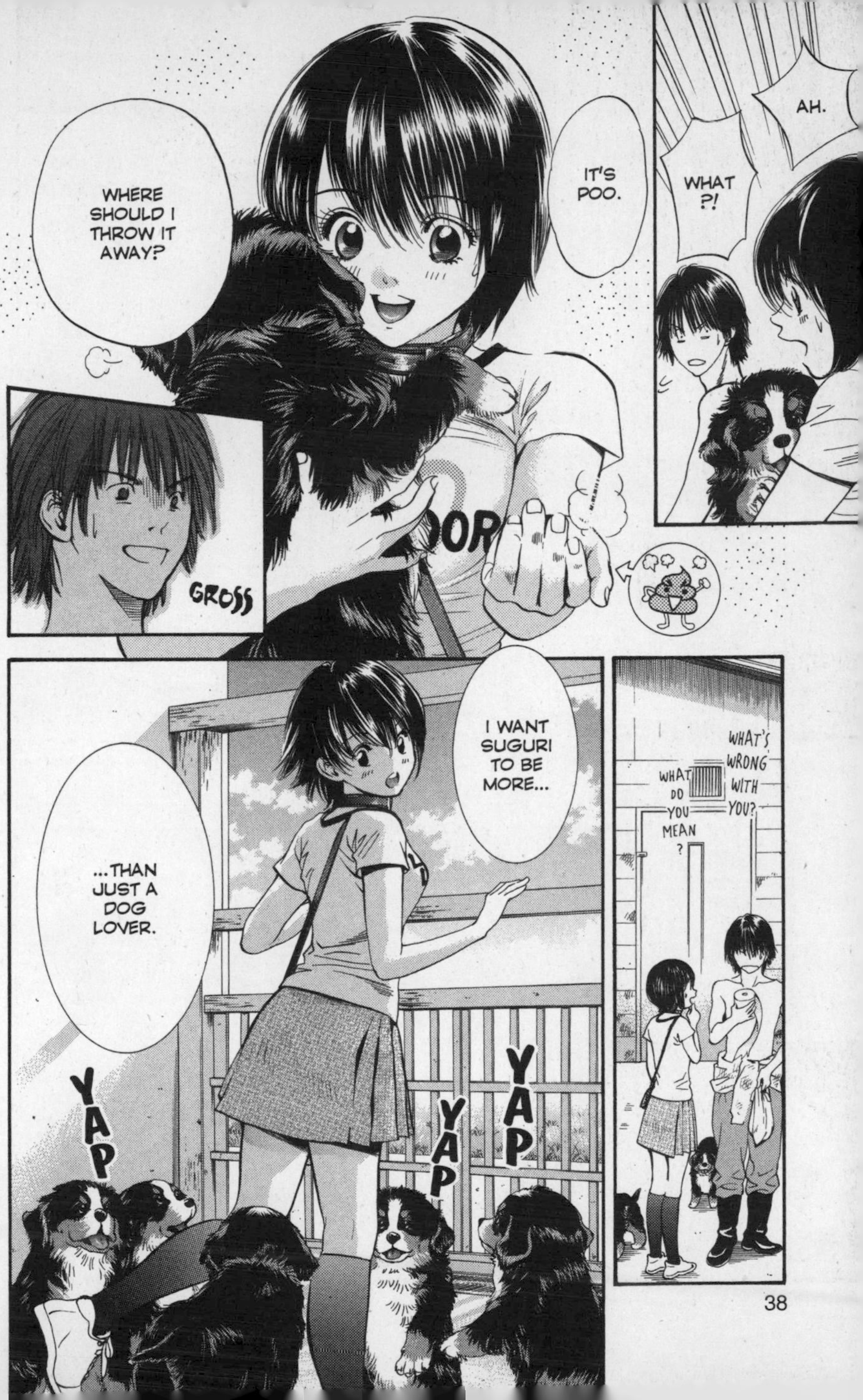
AH.
WHAT ?!
IT'S POO.
WHERE SHOULD I THROW IT AWAY?
GROSS
WHAT'S WRONG WITH YOU?
WHAT DO YOU MEAN ?
I WANT SUGURI TO BE MORE...
...THAN JUST A DOG LOVER.
YAP
YAP
YAP

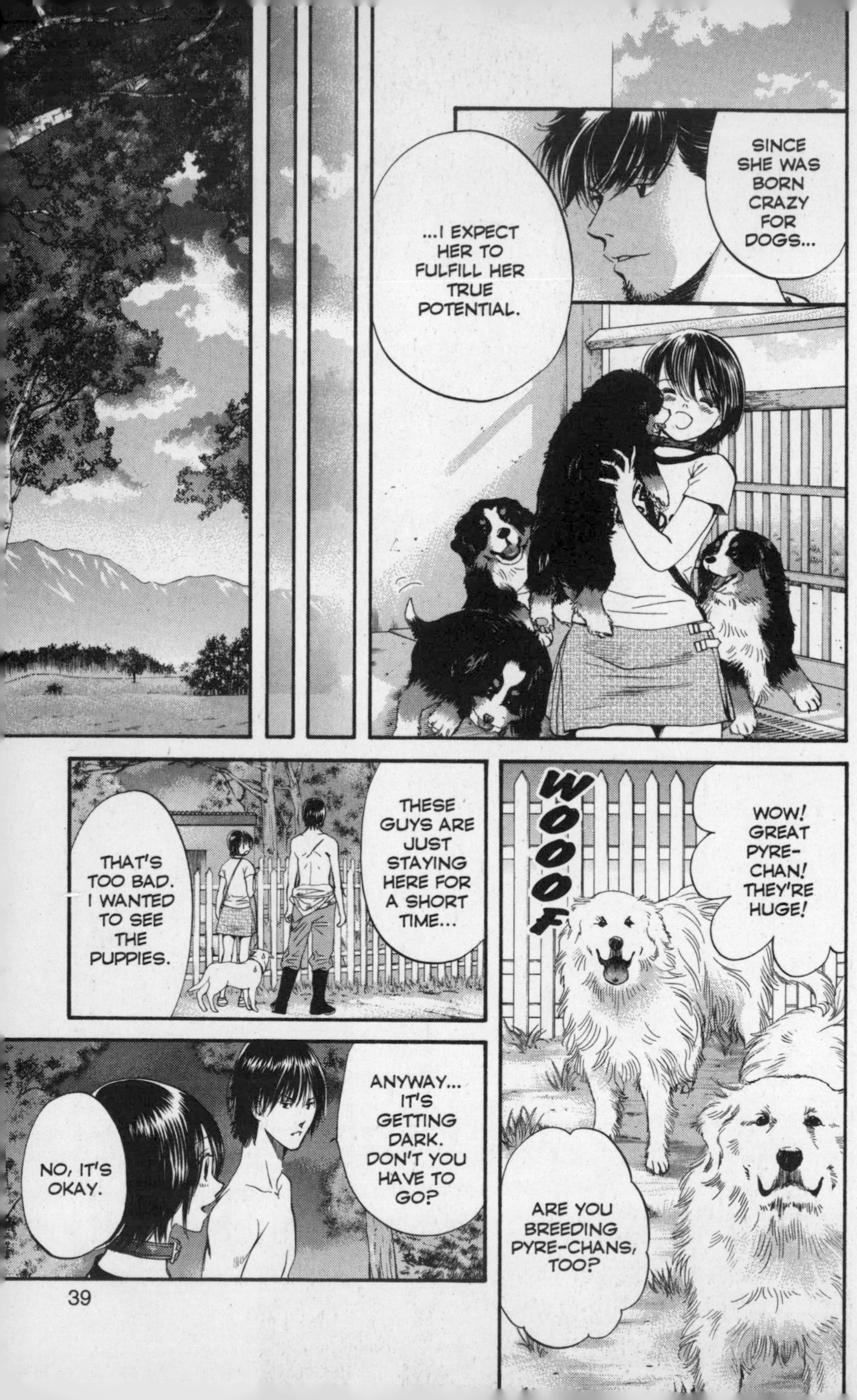
SINCE SHE WAS BORN CRAZY FOR DOGS...
...I EXPECT HER TO FULFILL HER TRUE POTENTIAL.
WOOOF
WOW! GREAT PYRE-CHAN! THEY'RE HUGE!
ARE YOU BREEDING PYRE-CHANS, TOO?
THESE GUYS ARE JUST STAYING HERE FOR A SHORT TIME...
THAT'S TOO BAD. I WANTED TO SEE THE PUPPIES.
ANYWAY... IT'S GETTING DARK. DON'T YOU HAVE TO GO?
NO, IT'S OKAY.

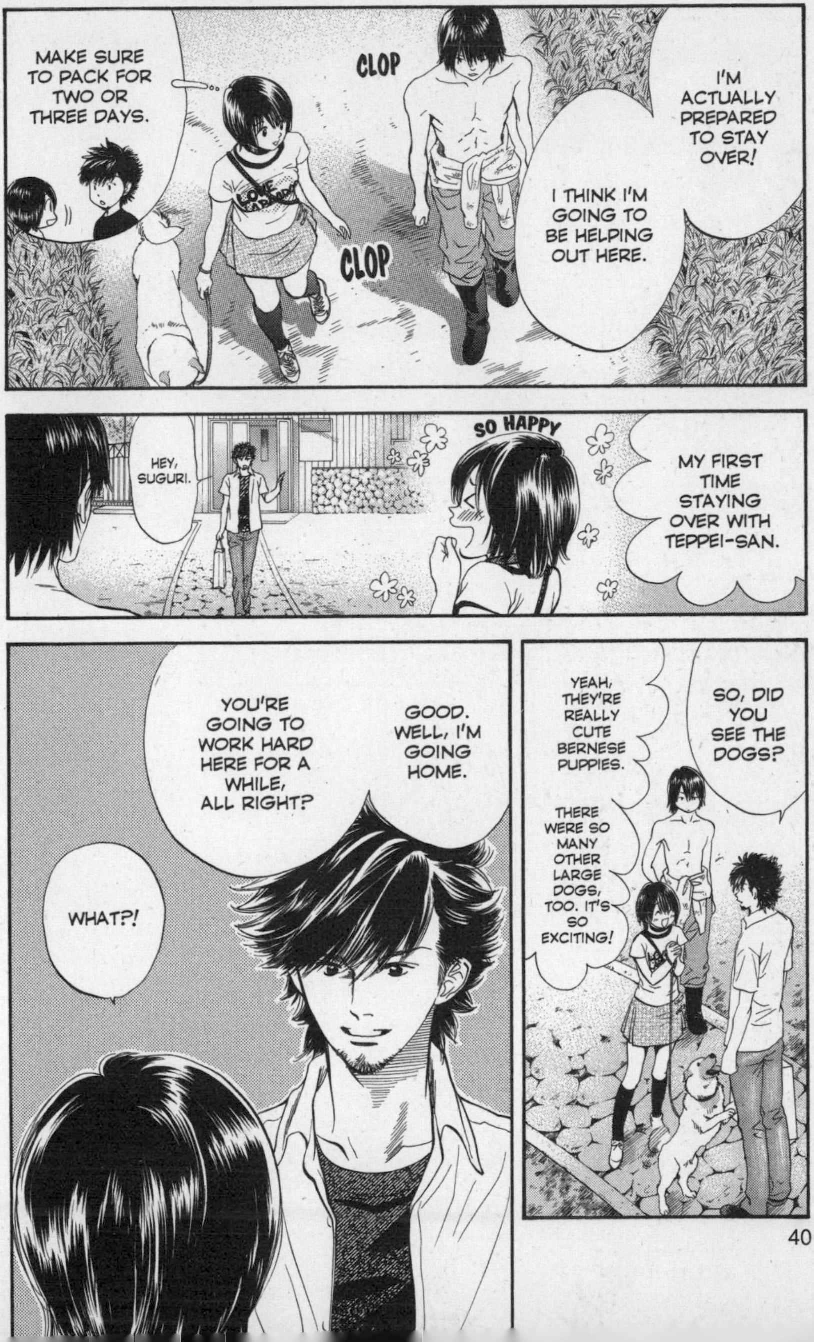
I'M ACTUALLY PREPARED TO STAY OVER!
I THINK I'M GOING TO BE HELPING OUT HERE.
CLOP
CLOP
MAKE SURE TO PACK FOR TWO OR THREE DAYS.
MY FIRST TIME STAYING OVER WITH TEPPEI-SAN.
SO HAPPY
HEY, SUGURI.
SO, DID YOU SEE THE DOGS?
YEAH, THEY'RE REALLY CUTE BERNESE PUPPIES.
THERE WERE SO MANY OTHER LARGE DOGS, TOO. IT'S SO EXCITING!
GOOD. WELL, I'M GOING HOME.
YOU'RE GOING TO WORK HARD HERE FOR A WHILE, ALL RIGHT?
WHAT?!

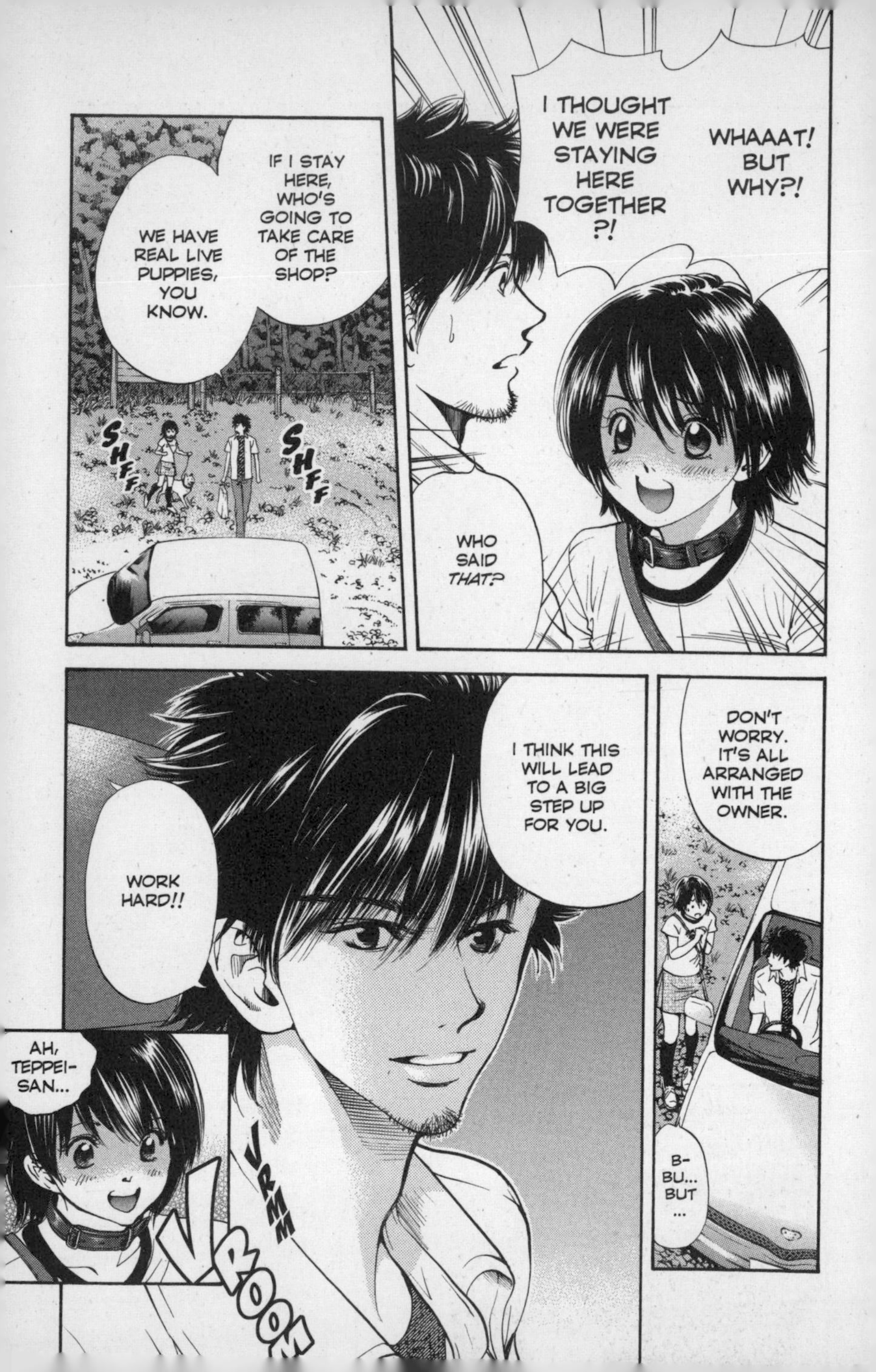
WHAAAT! BUT WHY?!
I THOUGHT WE WERE STAYING HERE TOGETHER?!
WHO SAID THAT?
IF I STAY HERE, WHO'S GOING TO TAKE CARE OF THE SHOP?
WE HAVE REAL LIVE PUPPIES, YOU KNOW.
SHFF
SHFF
DON'T WORRY. IT'S ALL ARRANGED WITH THE OWNER.
B-BU... BUT ...
I THINK THIS WILL LEAD TO A BIG STEP UP FOR YOU.
WORK HARD!!
VRMM
VROOM
AH, TEPPEI-SAN...

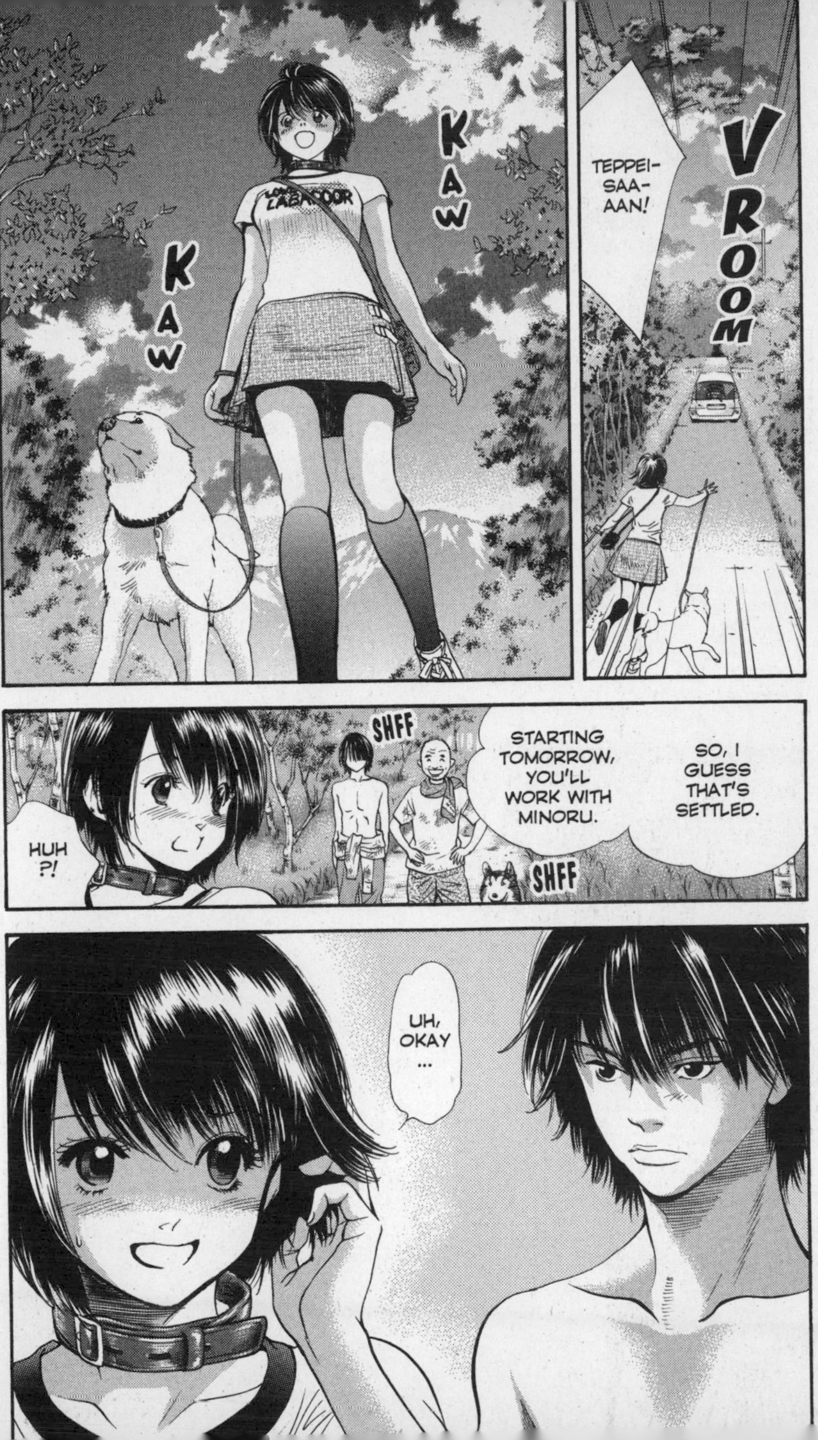
VROOM
TEPPEI-SAAA-AAN!
KAW KAW
KAW KAW
SO, I GUESS THAT'S SETTLED.
STARTING TOMORROW, YOU'LL WORK WITH MINORU.
SHFF
SHFF
HUH?!
UH, OKAY ...

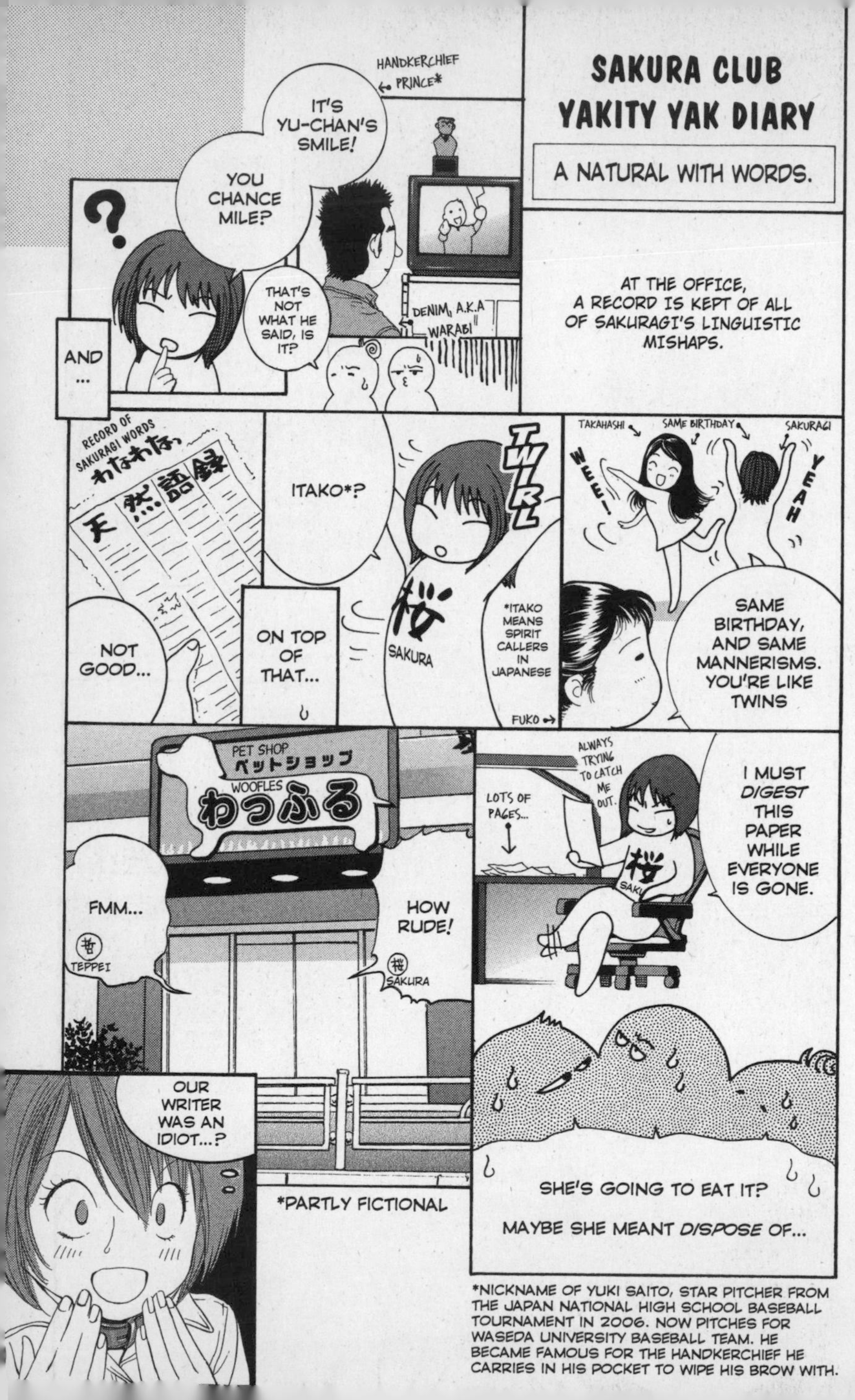
SAKURA CLUB
YAKITY YAK DIARY
A NATURAL WITH WORDS.
AT THE OFFICE, A RECORD IS KEPT OF ALL OF SAKURAGI'S LINGUISTIC MISHAPS.
HANDKERCHIEF PRINCE*
IT'S YU-CHAN'S SMILE!
YOU CHANCE MILE?
THAT'S NOT WHAT HE SAID, IS IT?
DENIM, A.K.A WARABI
AND ...
TAKAHASHI
SAME BIRTHDAY
SAKURAGI
WEE!
YEAH
SAME BIRTHDAY, AND SAME MANNERISMS. YOU'RE LIKE TWINS
FUKO
TWIRL
ITAKO*?
桜
SAKURA
*ITAKO MEANS SPIRIT CALLERS IN JAPANESE
ON TOP OF THAT...
RECORD OF SAKURAGI WORDS
わなわな
天然語録
NOT GOOD...
ALWAYS TRYING TO CATCH ME OUT.
LOTS OF PAGES...
I MUST *DIGEST* THIS PAPER WHILE EVERYONE IS GONE.
SHE'S GOING TO EAT IT?
MAYBE SHE MEANT *DISPOSE* OF...
PET SHOP
ペットショップ
WOOFLES
わつふる
HOW RUDE!
SAKURA
FMM...
TEPPEI
OUR WRITER WAS AN IDIOT...?
*PARTLY FICTIONAL

*NICKNAME OF YUKI SAITO, STAR PITCHER FROM THE JAPAN NATIONAL HIGH SCHOOL BASEBALL TOURNAMENT IN 2006. NOW PITCHES FOR WASEDA UNIVERSITY BASEBALL TEAM. HE BECAME FAMOUS FOR THE HANDKERCHIEF HE CARRIES IN HIS POCKET TO WIPE HIS BROW WITH.

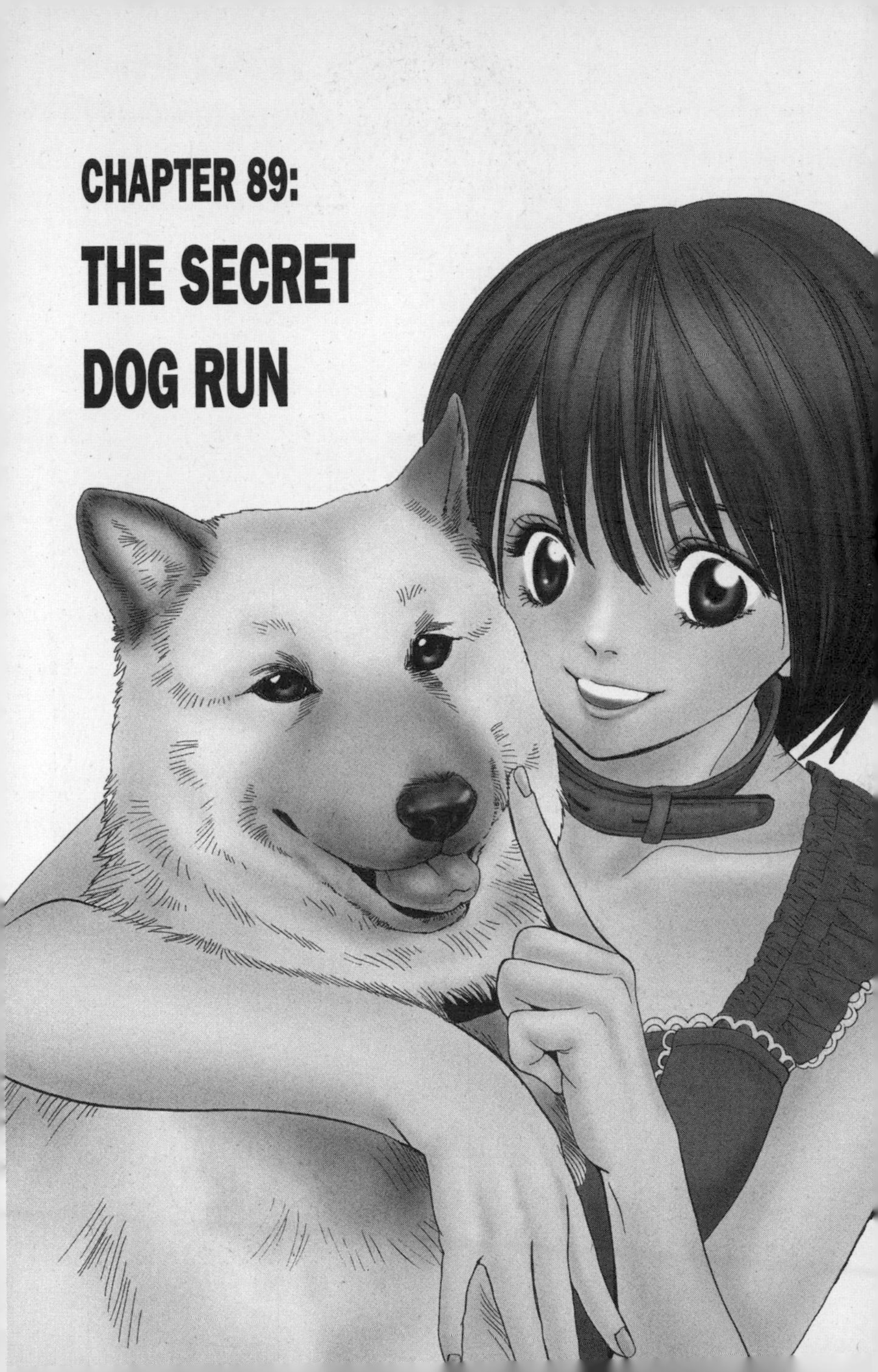
CHAPTER 89:
THE SECRET
DOG RUN

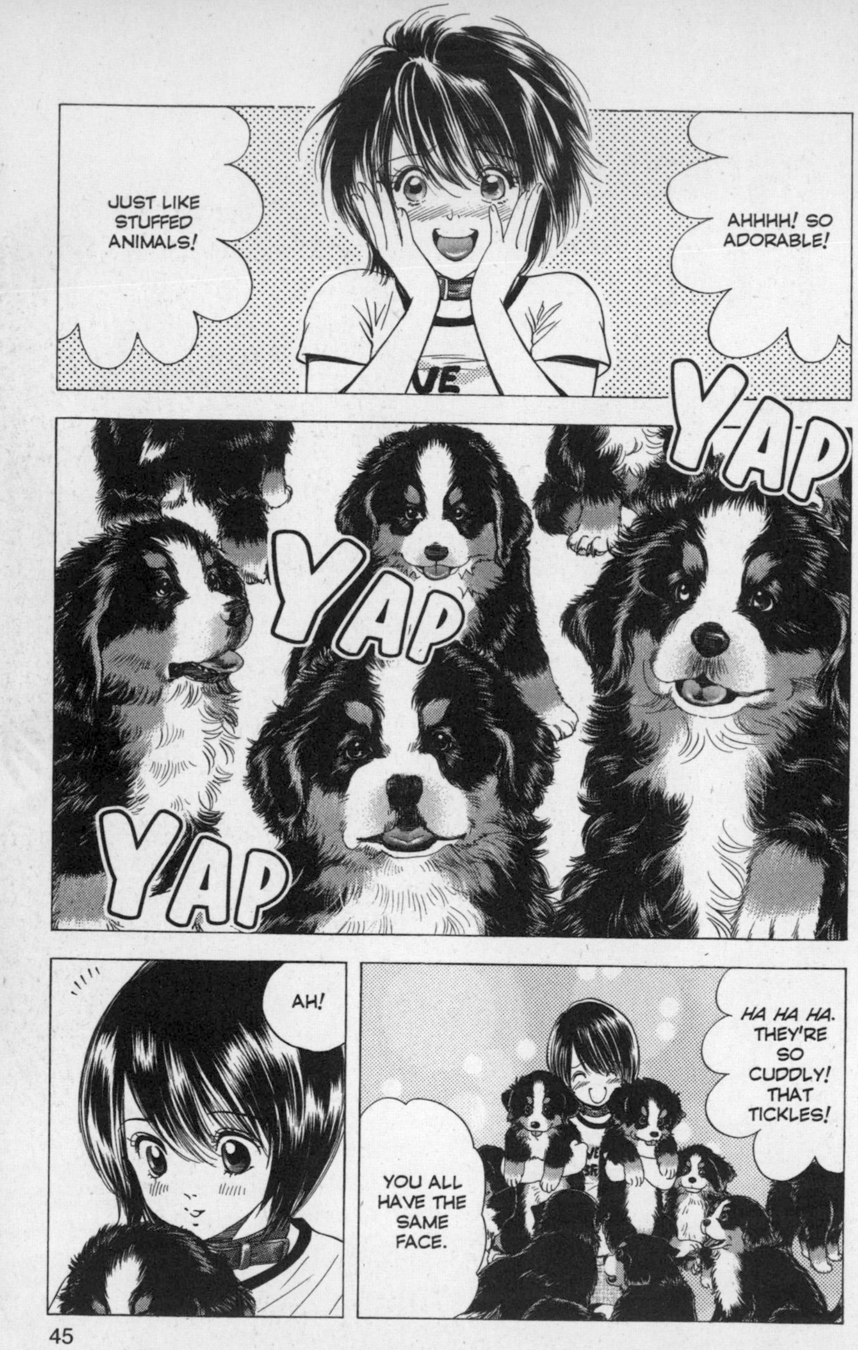
AHHHH! SO ADORABLE!
JUST LIKE STUFFED ANIMALS!
YAP
YAP
YAP
HA HA HA. THEY'RE SO CUDDLY! THAT TICKLES!
YOU ALL HAVE THE SAME FACE.
AH!

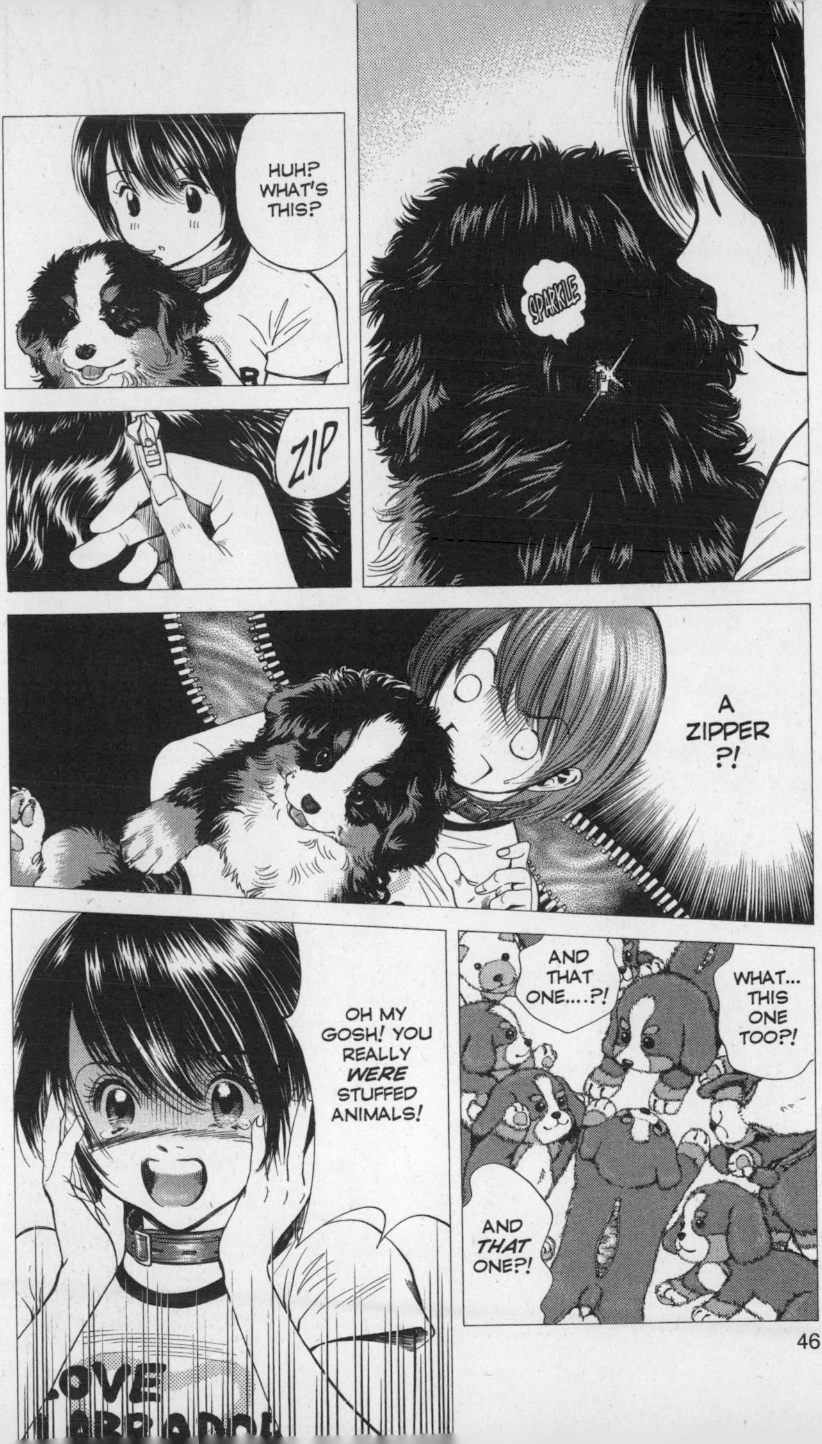
SPARKLE
HUH? WHAT'S THIS?
ZIP
A ZIPPER ?!
WHAT... THIS ONE TOO?!
AND THAT ONE....?!
AND *THAT* ONE?!
OH MY GOSH! YOU REALLY *WERE* STUFFED ANIMALS!
LOVE

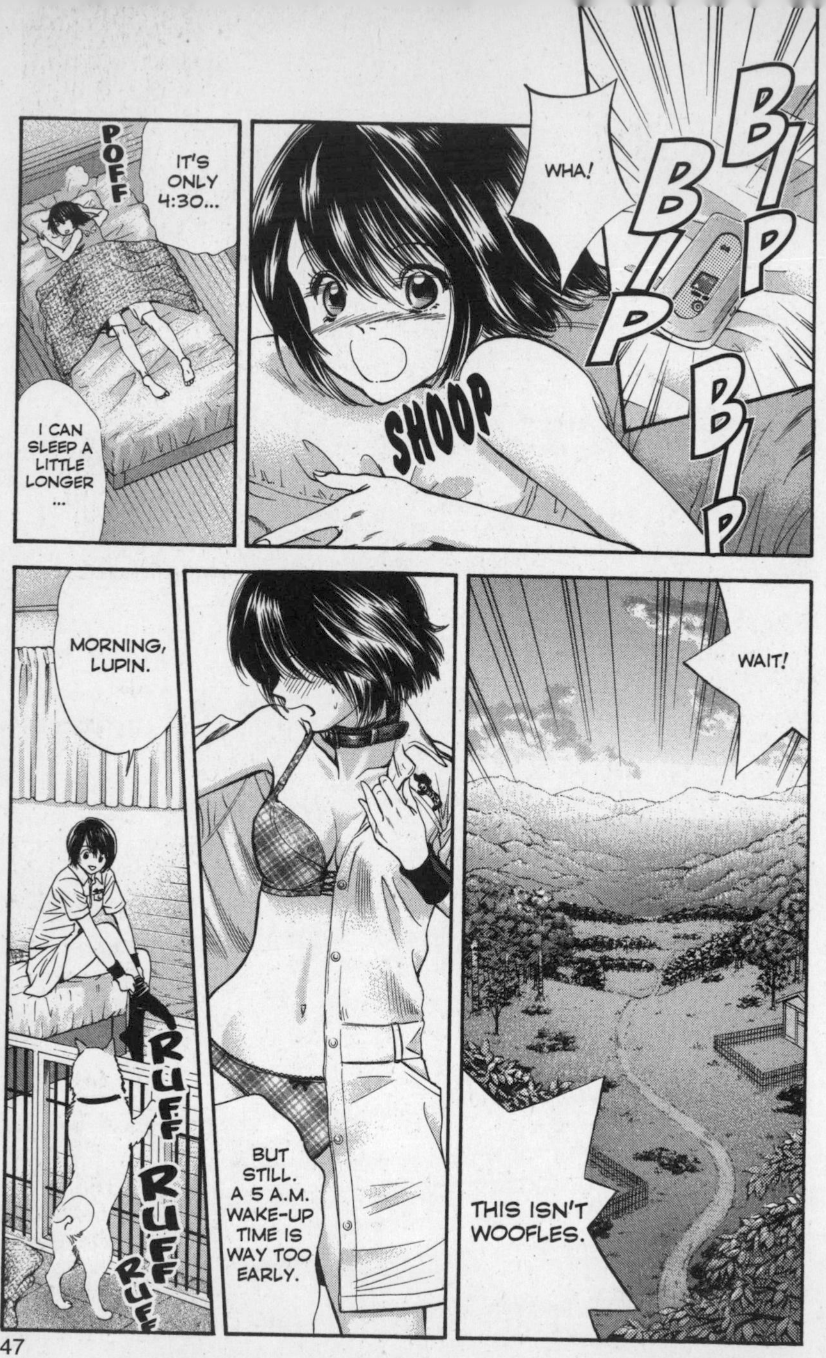
BIP BIP
BIP BIP
BIP BIP
WHA!
SHOOP
POFF
IT'S ONLY 4:30...
I CAN SLEEP A LITTLE LONGER ...
WAIT!
THIS ISN'T WOOFLES.
BUT STILL. A 5 A.M. WAKE-UP TIME IS WAY TOO EARLY.
MORNING, LUPIN.
RUFF
RUFF
RUFF

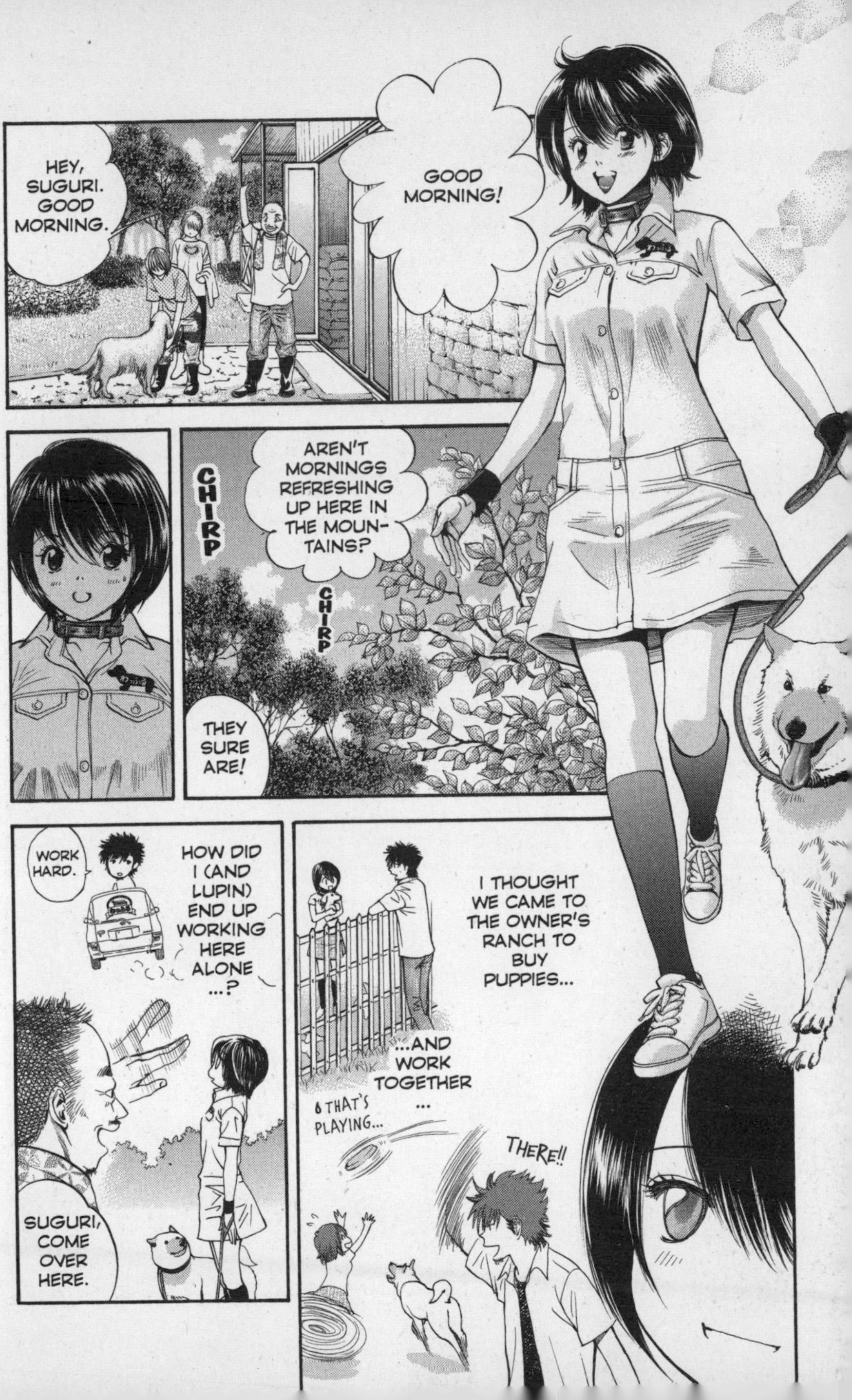
GOOD MORNING!
HEY, SUGURI. GOOD MORNING.
AREN'T MORNINGS REFRESHING UP HERE IN THE MOUN-TAINS?
CHIRP
CHIRP
THEY SURE ARE!
I THOUGHT WE CAME TO THE OWNER'S RANCH TO BUY PUPPIES...
...AND WORK TOGETHER...
♪ THAT'S PLAYING...
THERE!!
HOW DID I (AND LUPIN) END UP WORKING HERE ALONE...?
WORK HARD.
SUGURI, COME OVER HERE.

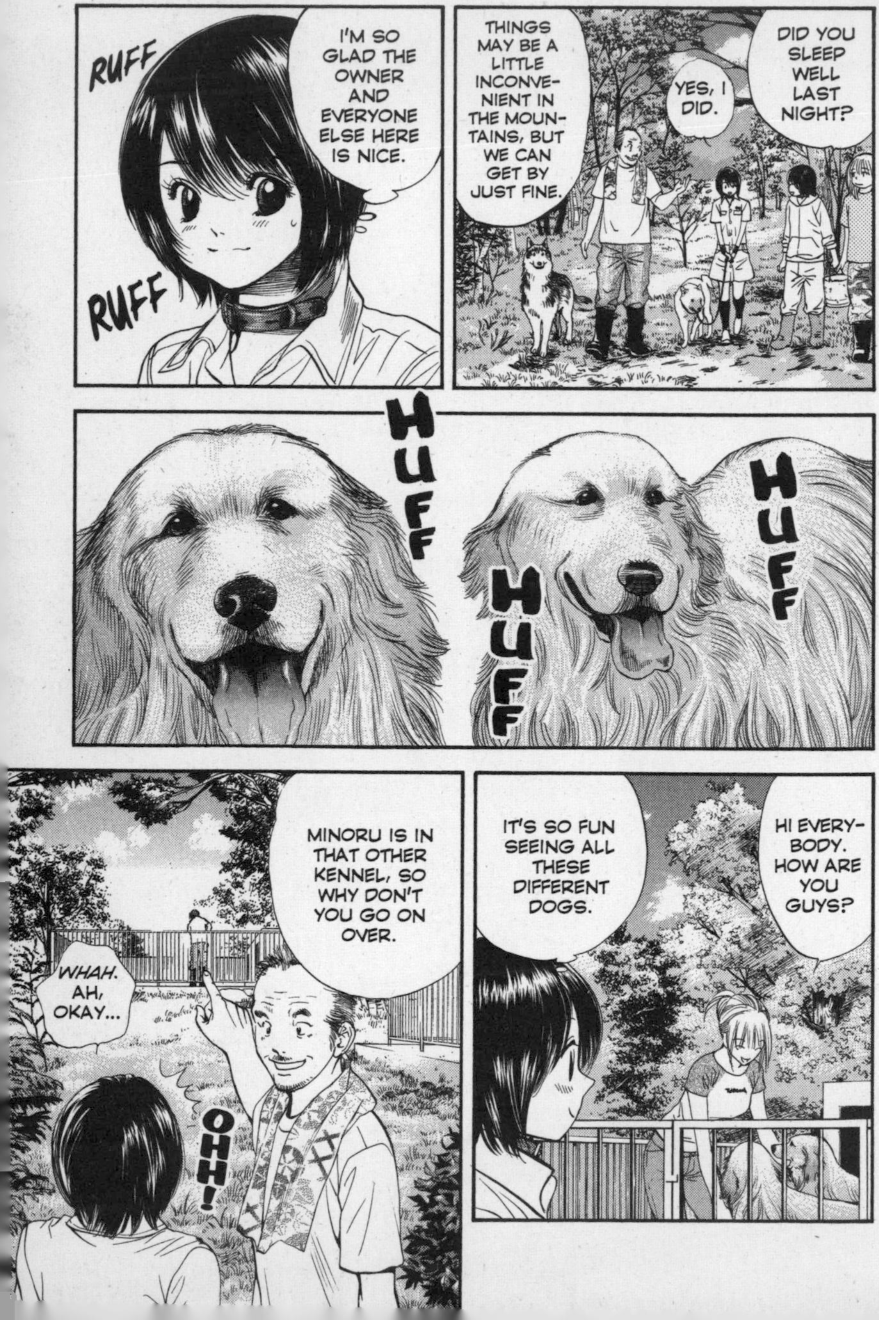
DID YOU SLEEP WELL LAST NIGHT?
YES, I DID.
THINGS MAY BE A LITTLE INCONVENIENT IN THE MOUNTAINS, BUT WE CAN GET BY JUST FINE.
RUFF
I'M SO GLAD THE OWNER AND EVERYONE ELSE HERE IS NICE.
RUFF
HUFF
HUFF
HUFF
HI EVERYBODY. HOW ARE YOU GUYS?
IT'S SO FUN SEEING ALL THESE DIFFERENT DOGS.
MINORU IS IN THAT OTHER KENNEL, SO WHY DON'T YOU GO ON OVER.
WHAH. AH, OKAY...
OHH!

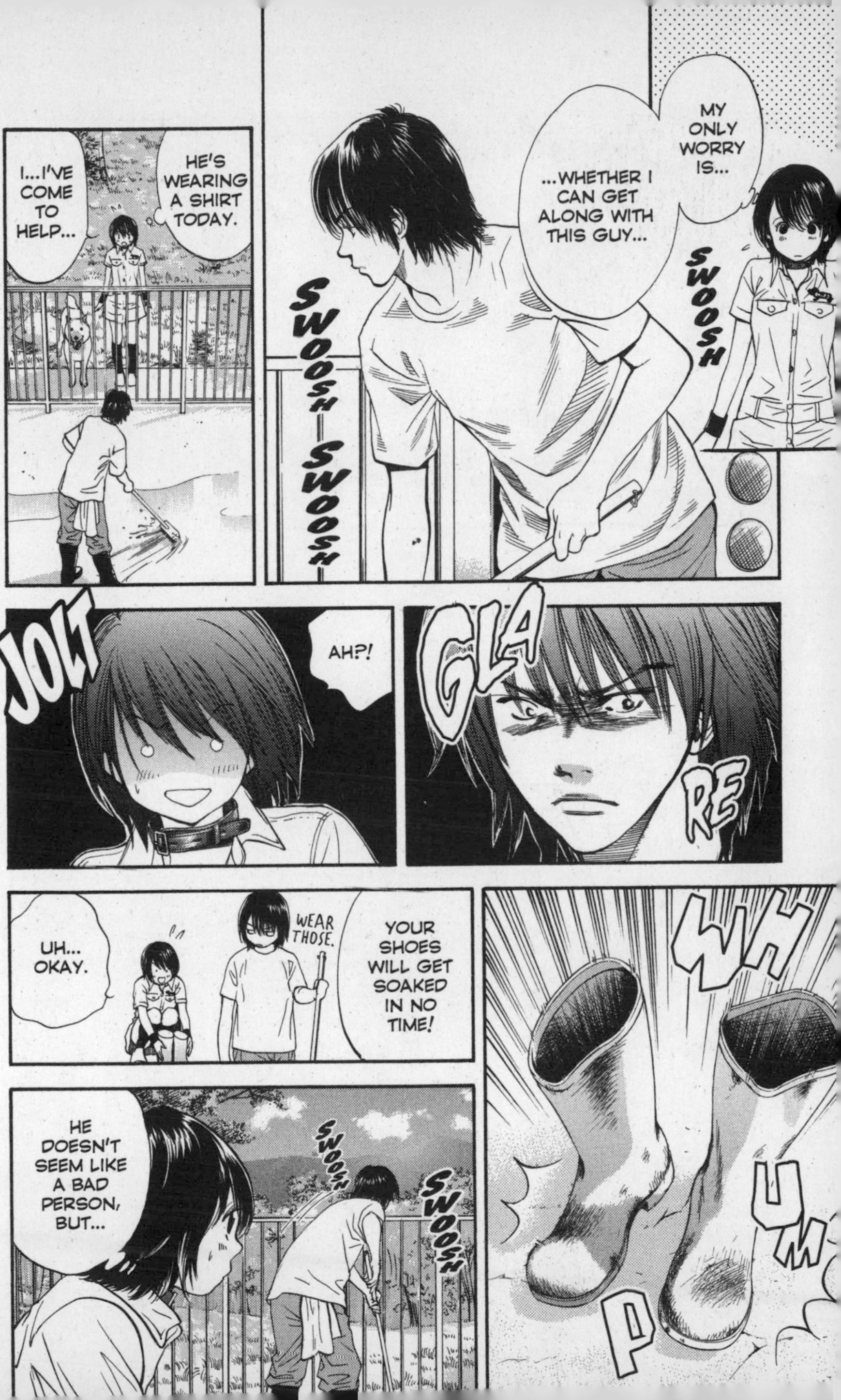
MY ONLY WORRY IS...
SWOOSH
...WHETHER I CAN GET ALONG WITH THIS GUY...
SWOOSH SWOOSH
HE'S WEARING A SHIRT TODAY.
I...I'VE COME TO HELP...
GLARE
AH?!
JOLT
WHUMP
YOUR SHOES WILL GET SOAKED IN NO TIME!
WEAR THOSE.
UH... OKAY.
SWOOSH
SWOOSH
HE DOESN'T SEEM LIKE A BAD PERSON, BUT...

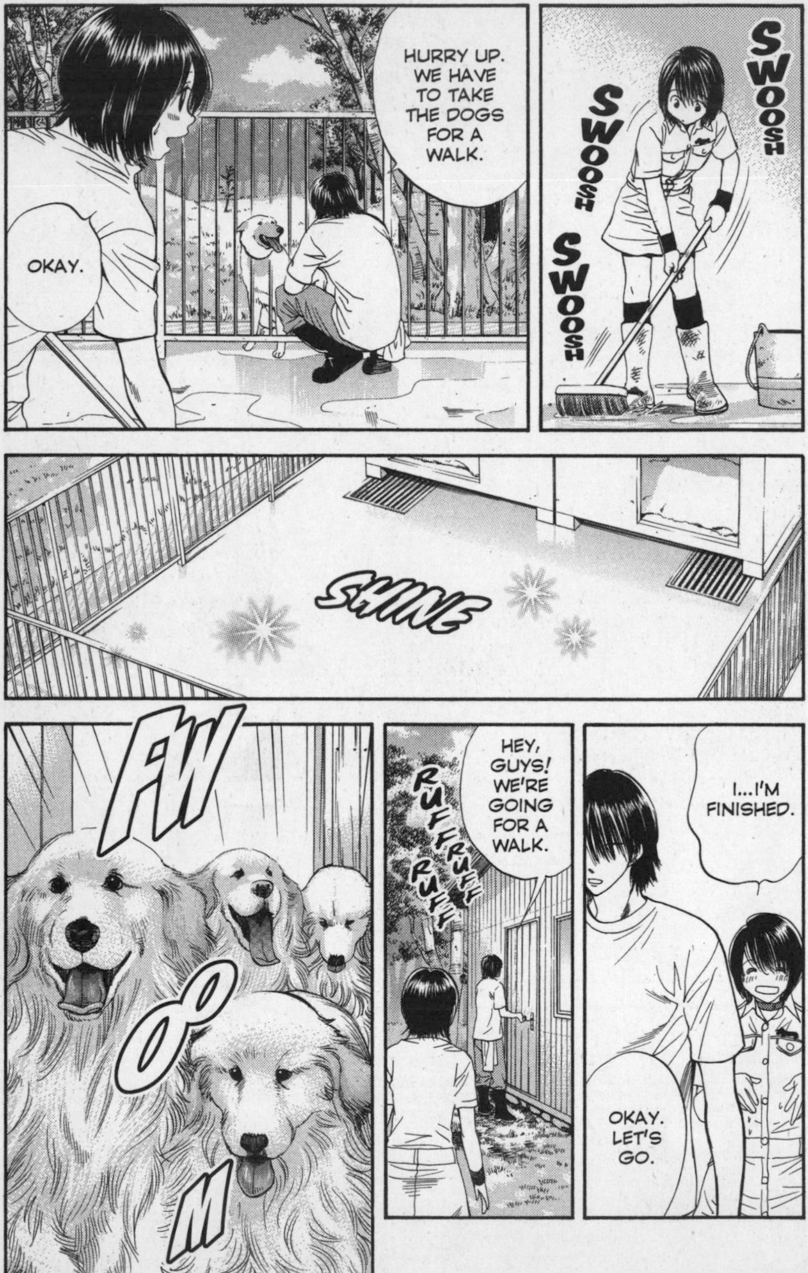
SWOOSH
SWOOSH
SWOOSH
HURRY UP. WE HAVE TO TAKE THE DOGS FOR A WALK.
OKAY.
SHINE
I...I'M FINISHED.
OKAY. LET'S GO.
HEY, GUYS! WE'RE GOING FOR A WALK.
RUFF RUFF RUFF
FWOOM

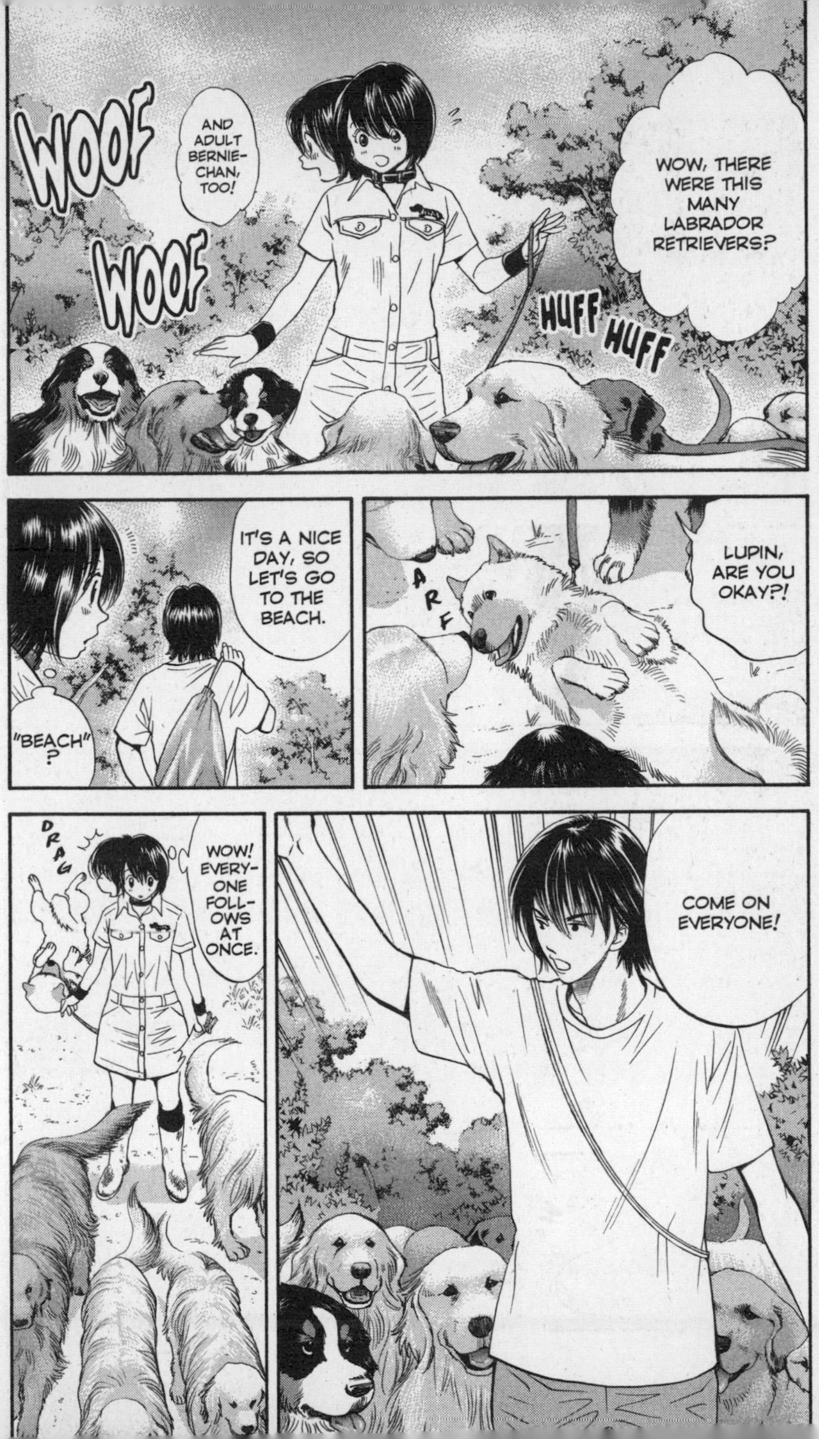
WOW, THERE WERE THIS MANY LABRADOR RETRIEVERS?
AND ADULT BERNIE-CHAN, TOO!
HUFF HUFF
WOOF
WOOF
LUPIN, ARE YOU OKAY?!
ARF
IT'S A NICE DAY, SO LET'S GO TO THE BEACH.
"BEACH"?
COME ON EVERYONE!
WOW! EVERY-ONE FOLL-OWS AT ONCE.
DRAG

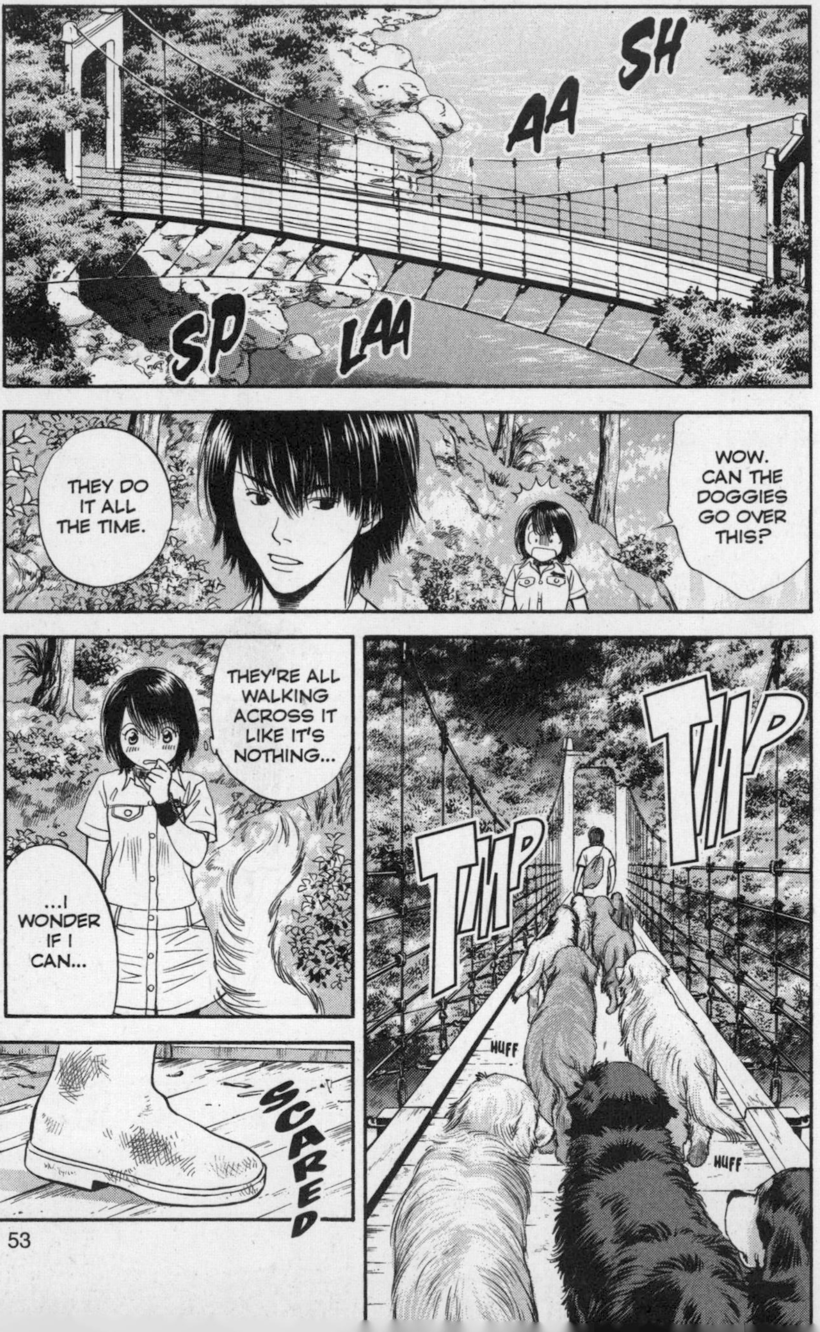
SP
LAA
AA
SH
WOW. CAN THE DOGGIES GO OVER THIS?
THEY DO IT ALL THE TIME.
TMP
TMP
HUFF
HUFF
THEY'RE ALL WALKING ACROSS IT LIKE IT'S NOTHING...
...I WONDER IF I CAN...
SCARED

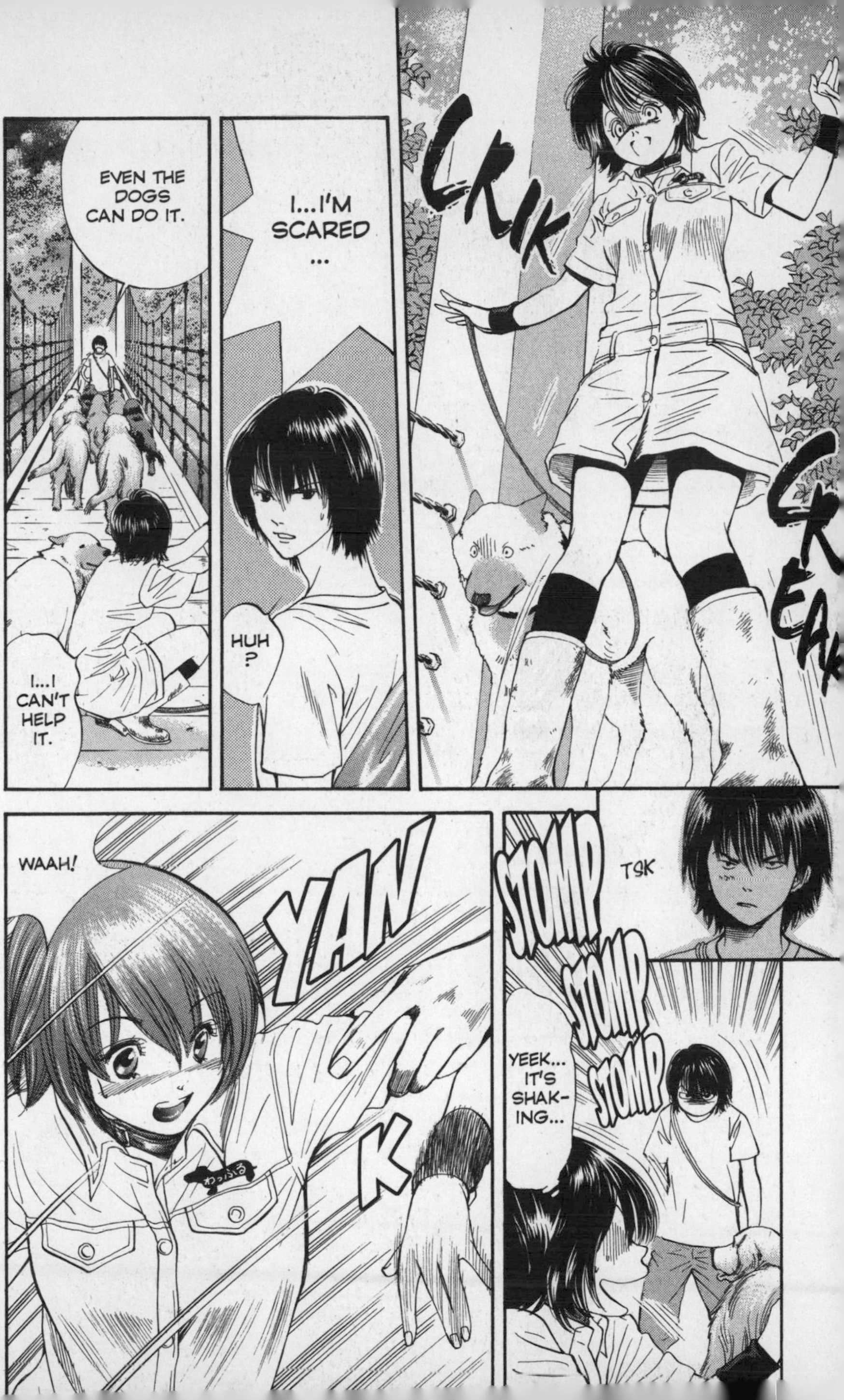
CRIK
CREAK
I...I'M SCARED ...
HUH ?
EVEN THE DOGS CAN DO IT.
I...I CAN'T HELP IT.
TSK
STOMP
STOMP
STOMP
YEEK... IT'S SHAK-ING...
WAAH!
YANK

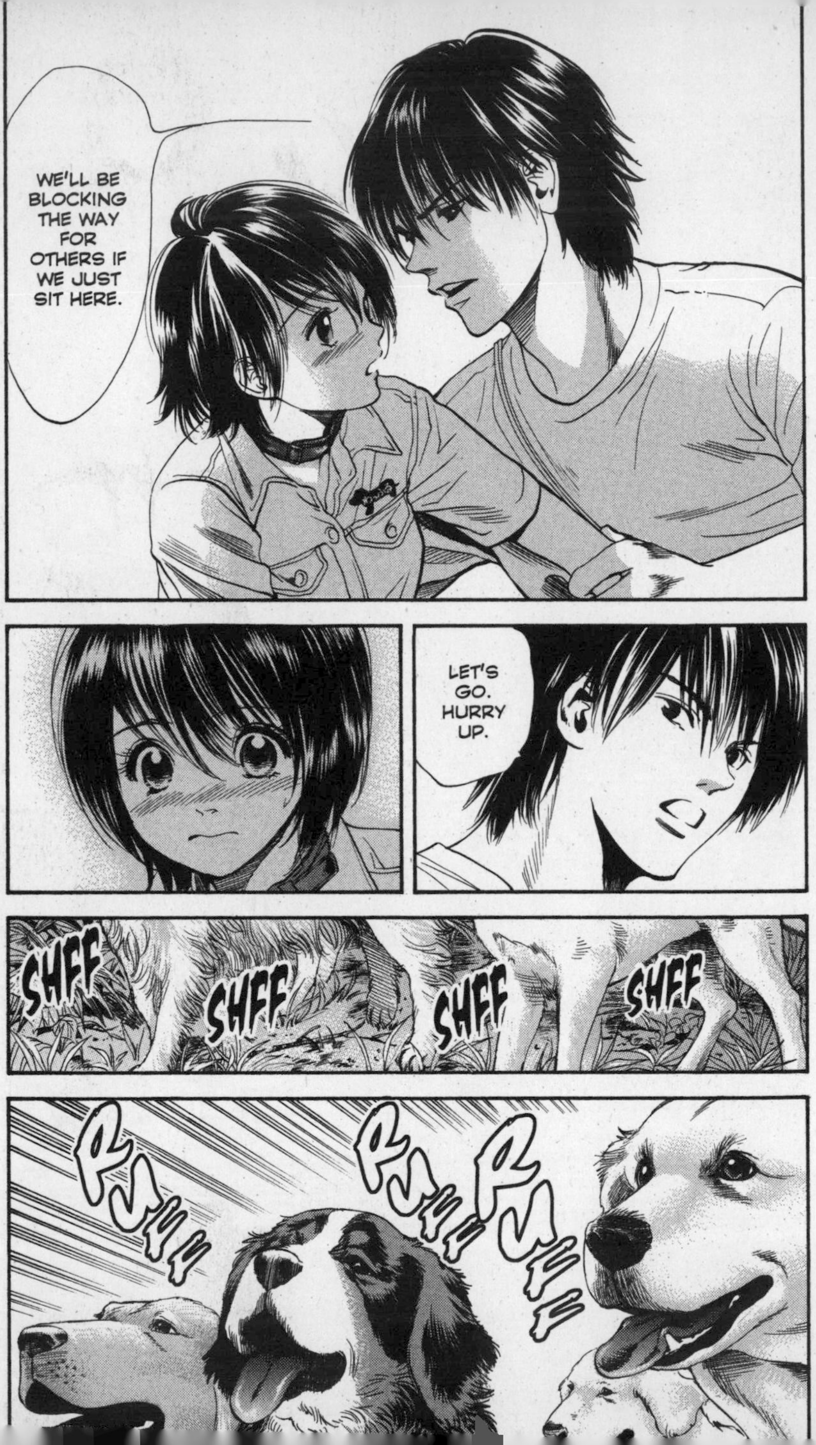
WE'LL BE BLOCKING THE WAY FOR OTHERS IF WE JUST SIT HERE.
LET'S GO. HURRY UP.
SHFF
SHFF
SHFF
SHFF

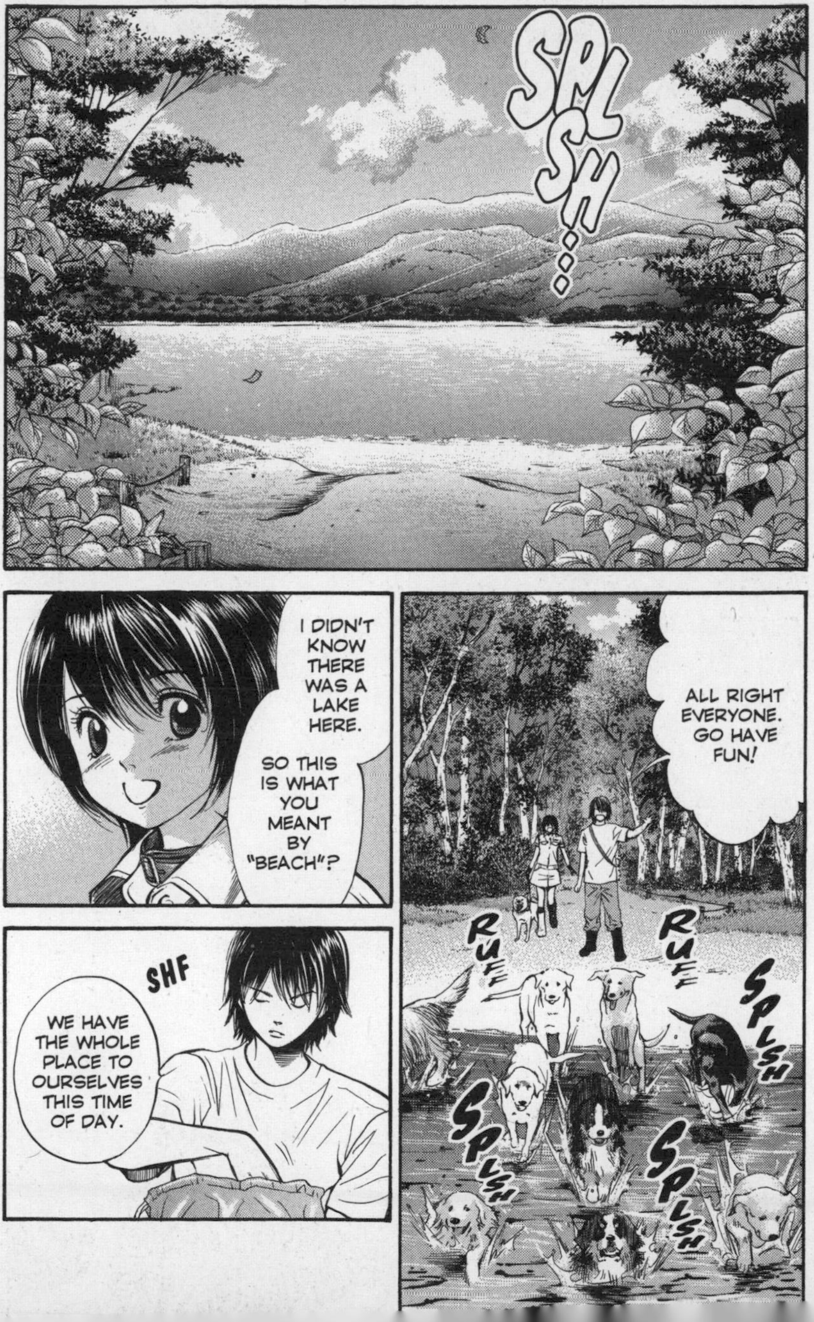
SPLSH...
ALL RIGHT EVERYONE. GO HAVE FUN!
RUFF
RUFF
SPLSH
SPLSH
SPLSH
I DIDN'T KNOW THERE WAS A LAKE HERE.
SO THIS IS WHAT YOU MEANT BY "BEACH"?
SHF
WE HAVE THE WHOLE PLACE TO OURSELVES THIS TIME OF DAY.

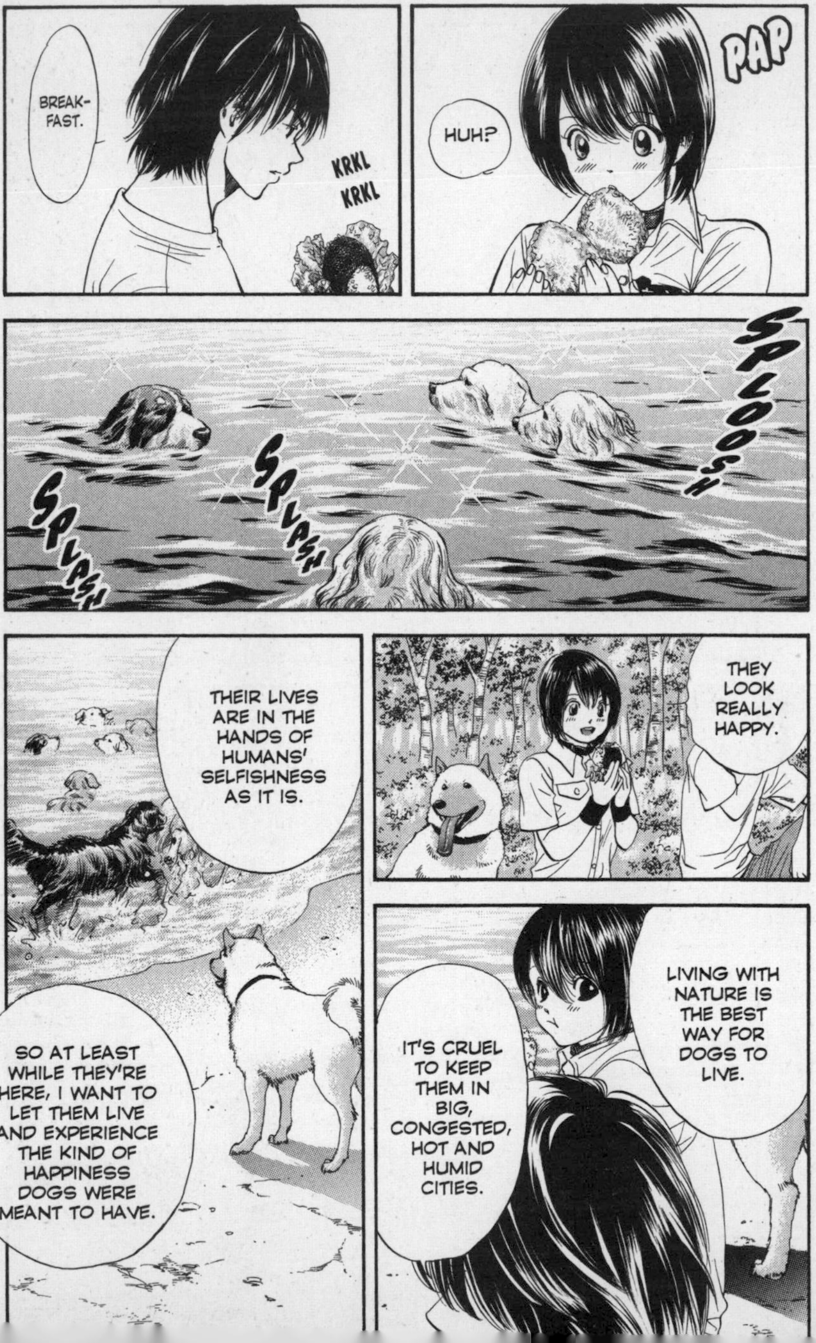
PAP
HUH?
KRKL KRKL
BREAK-FAST.
SPLOOSH
SPLASH
SPLASH
THEY LOOK REALLY HAPPY.
LIVING WITH NATURE IS THE BEST WAY FOR DOGS TO LIVE.
IT'S CRUEL TO KEEP THEM IN BIG, CONGESTED, HOT AND HUMID CITIES.
THEIR LIVES ARE IN THE HANDS OF HUMANS' SELFISHNESS AS IT IS.
SO AT LEAST WHILE THEY'RE HERE, I WANT TO LET THEM LIVE AND EXPERIENCE THE KIND OF HAPPINESS DOGS WERE MEANT TO HAVE.

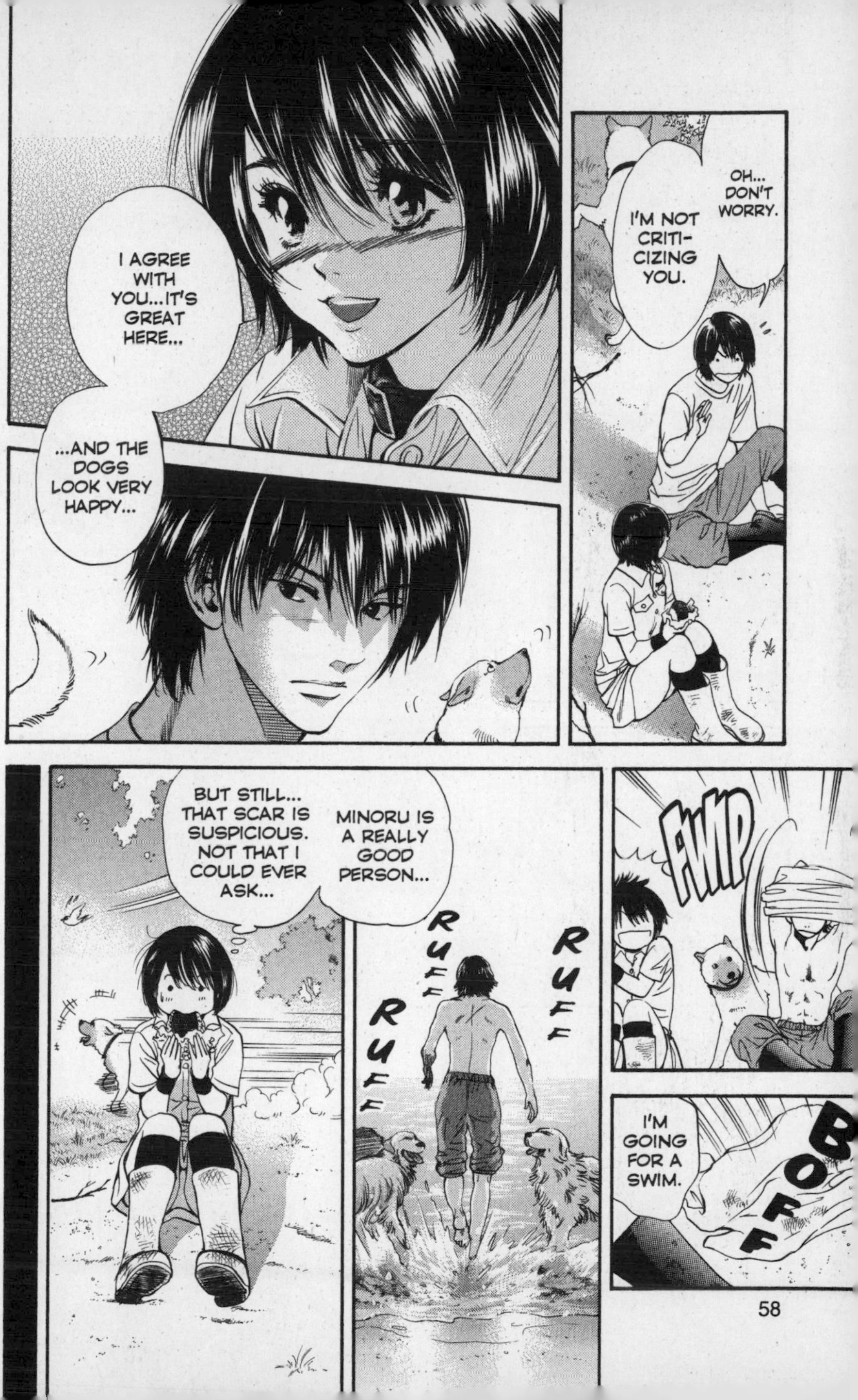
OH... DON'T WORRY.
I'M NOT CRITI-CIZING YOU.
I AGREE WITH YOU...IT'S GREAT HERE...
...AND THE DOGS LOOK VERY HAPPY...
FWIP
I'M GOING FOR A SWIM.
BOFF
RUFF
RUFF
RUFF
MINORU IS A REALLY GOOD PERSON...
BUT STILL... THAT SCAR IS SUSPICIOUS. NOT THAT I COULD EVER ASK...

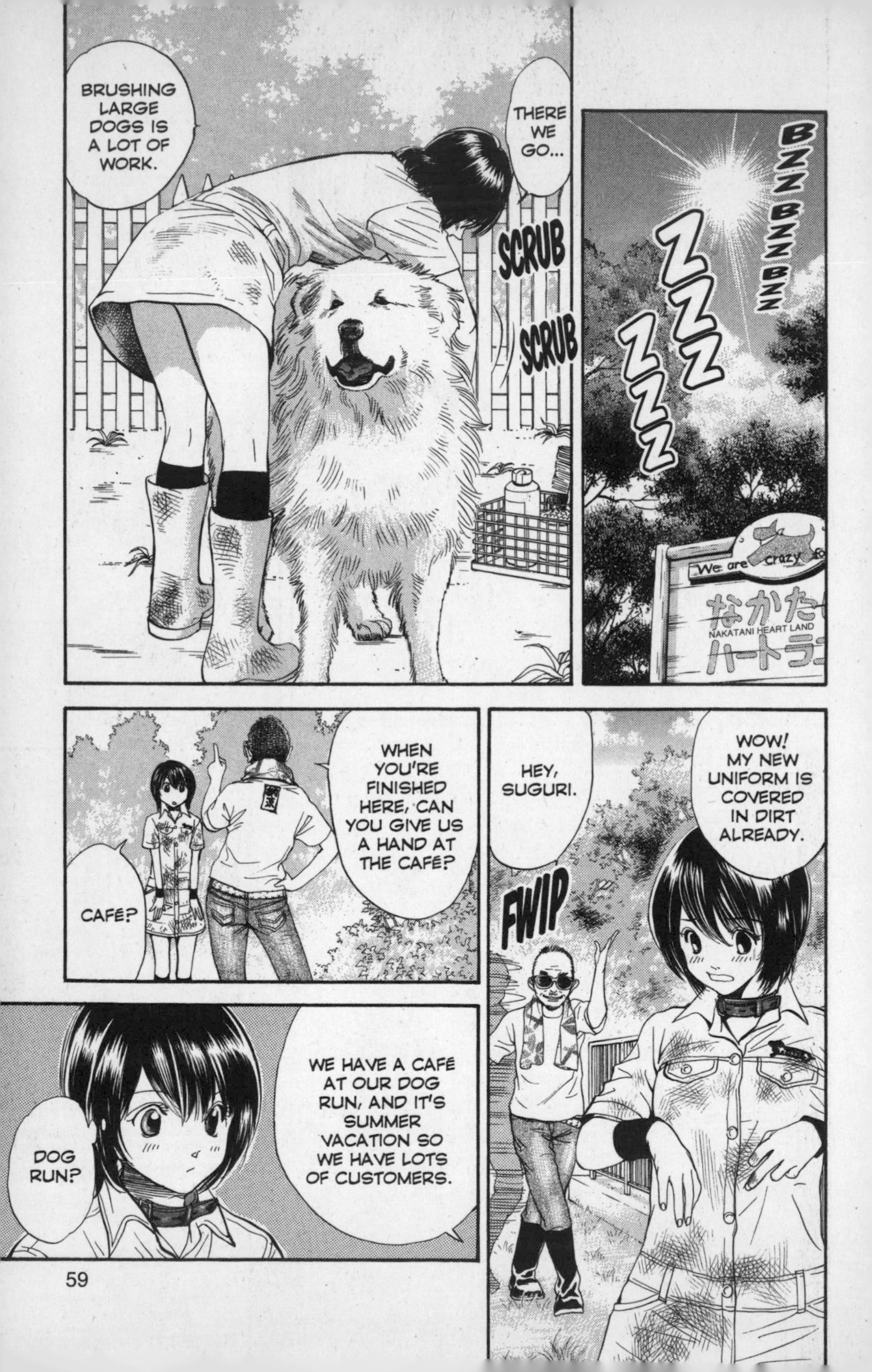
BZZ BZZ BZZ
ZZZ
ZZZ
We are crazy
NAKATANI HEART LAND
THERE WE GO...
SCRUB
SCRUB
BRUSHING LARGE DOGS IS A LOT OF WORK.
WOW! MY NEW UNIFORM IS COVERED IN DIRT ALREADY.
HEY, SUGURI.
FWIP
WHEN YOU'RE FINISHED HERE, CAN YOU GIVE US A HAND AT THE CAFÉ?
CAFÉ?
WE HAVE A CAFÉ AT OUR DOG RUN, AND IT'S SUMMER VACATION SO WE HAVE LOTS OF CUSTOMERS.
DOG RUN?

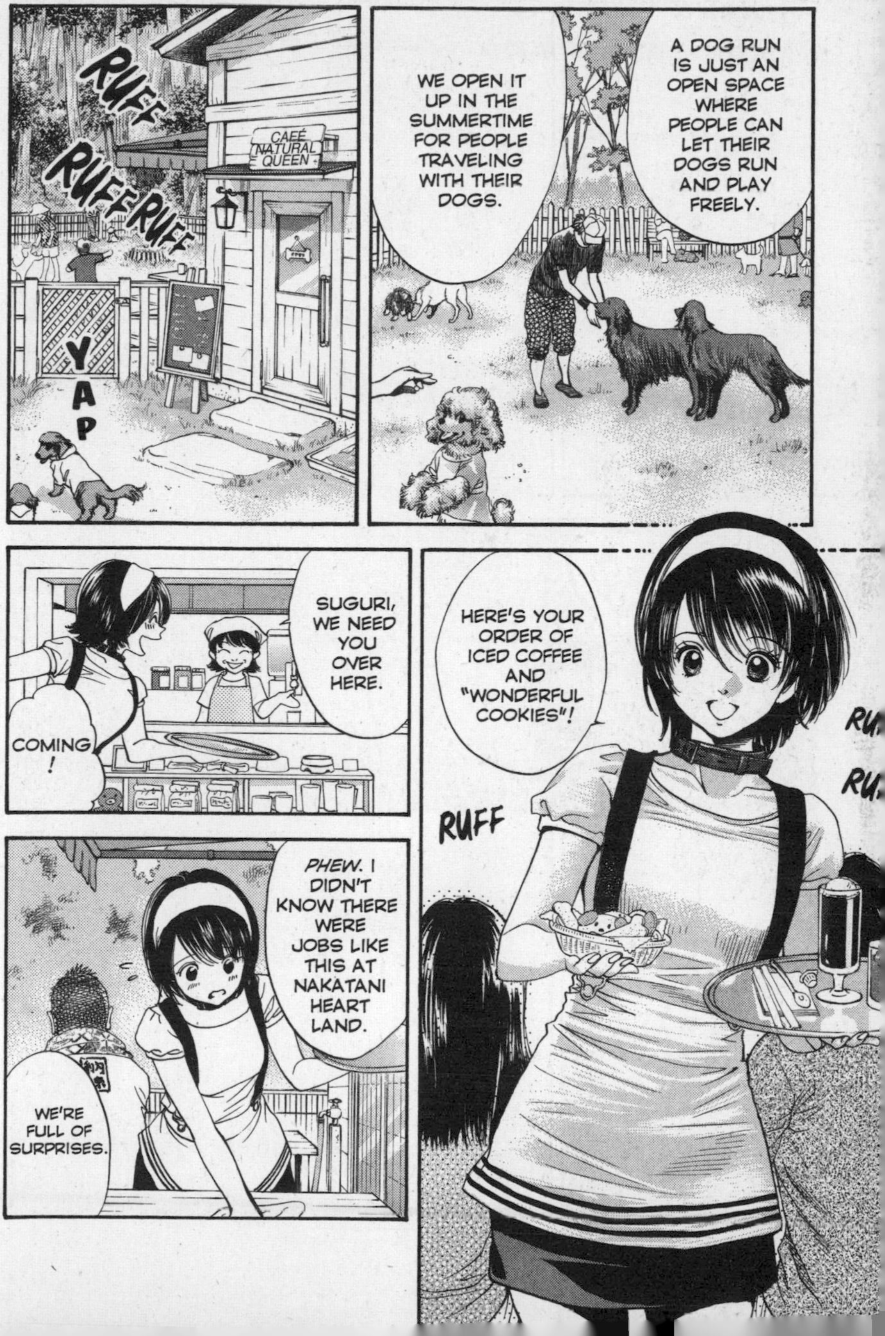
A DOG RUN IS JUST AN OPEN SPACE WHERE PEOPLE CAN LET THEIR DOGS RUN AND PLAY FREELY.
WE OPEN IT UP IN THE SUMMERTIME FOR PEOPLE TRAVELING WITH THEIR DOGS.
RUFF
RUFF RUFF RUFF
CAFÉ NATURAL QUEEN
YAP
HERE'S YOUR ORDER OF ICED COFFEE AND "WONDERFUL COOKIES"!
RUFF
SUGURI, WE NEED YOU OVER HERE.
COMING!
PHEW. I DIDN'T KNOW THERE WERE JOBS LIKE THIS AT NAKATANI HEART LAND.
WE'RE FULL OF SURPRISES.

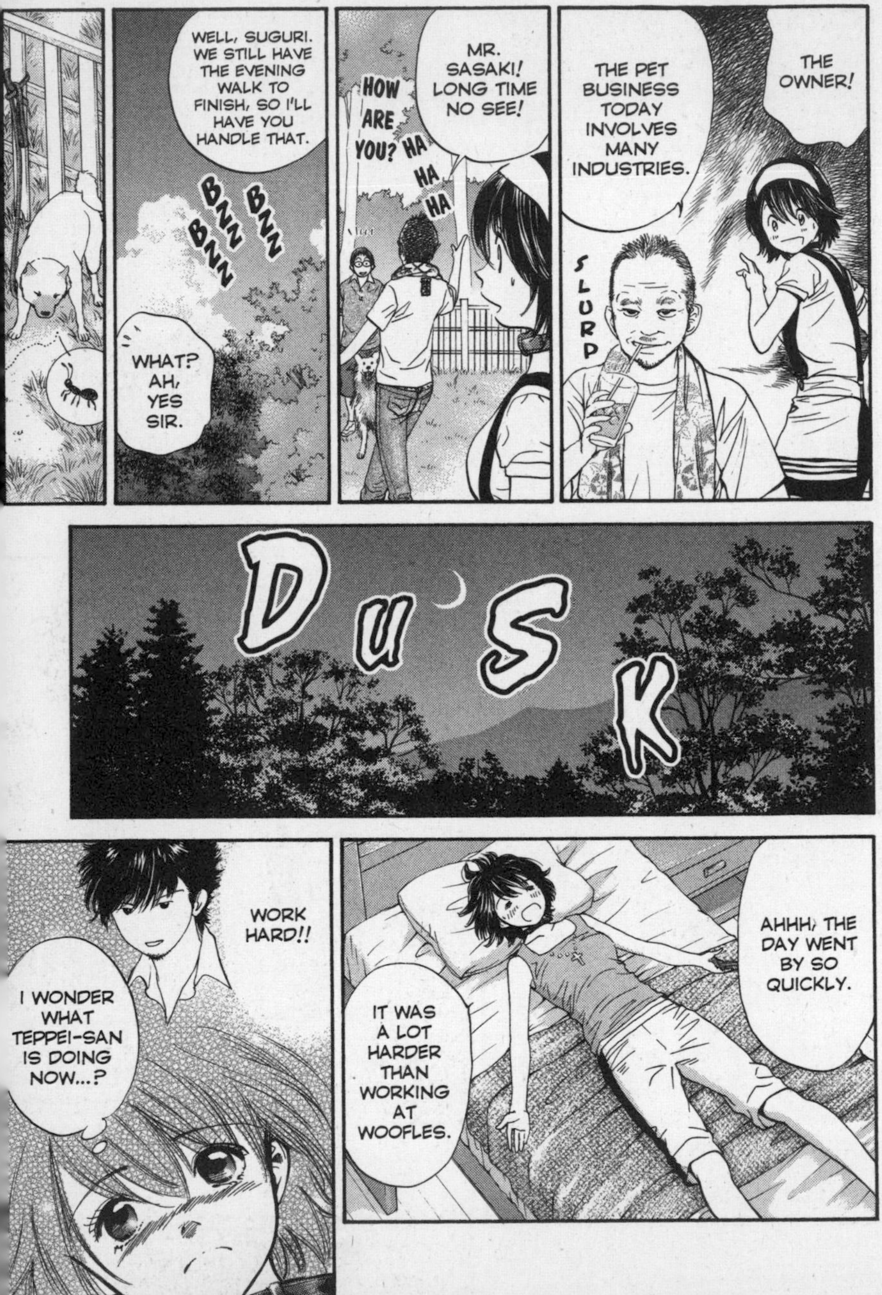
THE OWNER!
THE PET BUSINESS TODAY INVOLVES MANY INDUSTRIES.
SLURP
MR. SASAKI! LONG TIME NO SEE!
HOW ARE YOU? HA HA HA
WELL, SUGURI. WE STILL HAVE THE EVENING WALK TO FINISH, SO I'LL HAVE YOU HANDLE THAT.
BZZ BZZ
BZZ
WHAT? AH, YES SIR.
DUSK
AHHH, THE DAY WENT BY SO QUICKLY.
IT WAS A LOT HARDER THAN WORKING AT WOOFLES.
WORK HARD!!
I WONDER WHAT TEPPEI-SAN IS DOING NOW...?

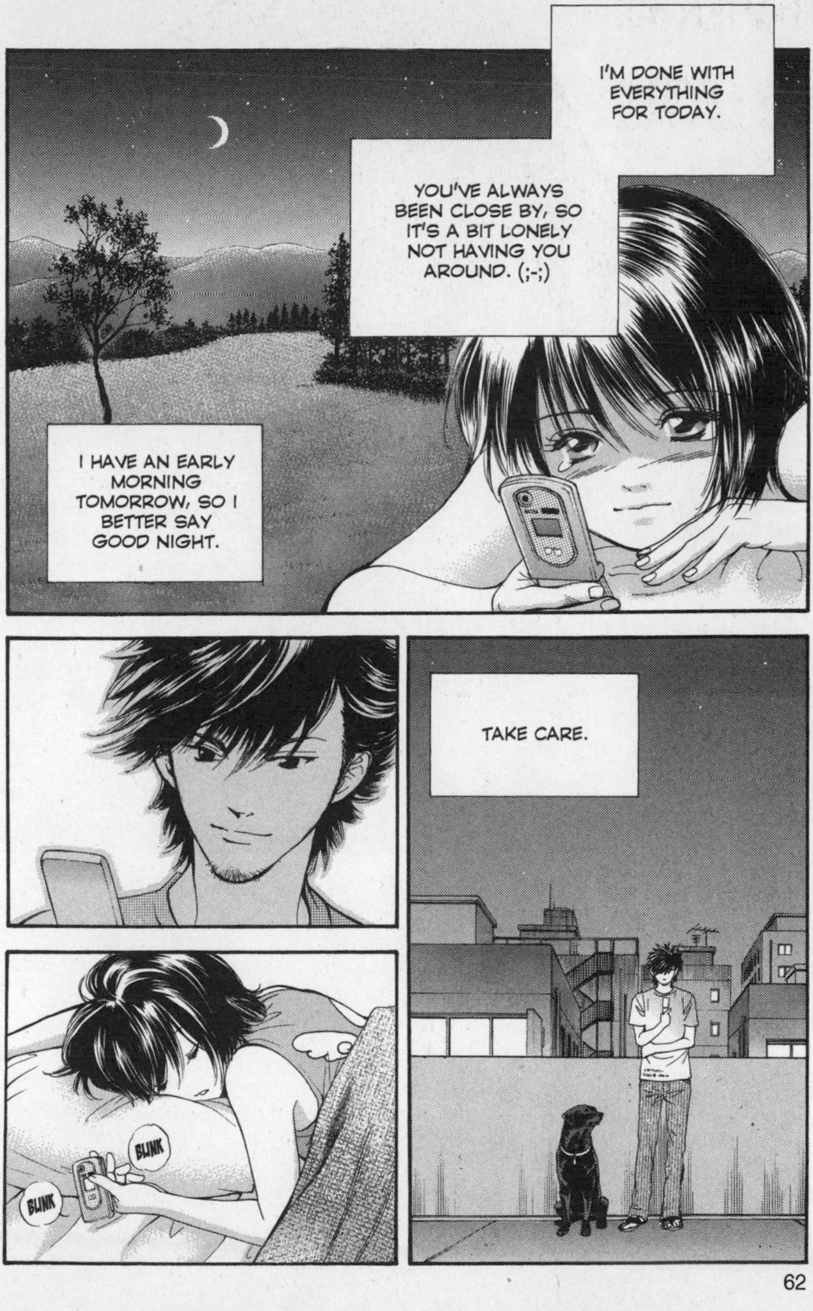
I'M DONE WITH EVERYTHING FOR TODAY.
YOU'VE ALWAYS BEEN CLOSE BY, SO IT'S A BIT LONELY NOT HAVING YOU AROUND. (;-;)
I HAVE AN EARLY MORNING TOMORROW, SO I BETTER SAY GOOD NIGHT.
TAKE CARE.
BLINK
BLINK

CHAPTER 90: THE LITTLE ANGEL

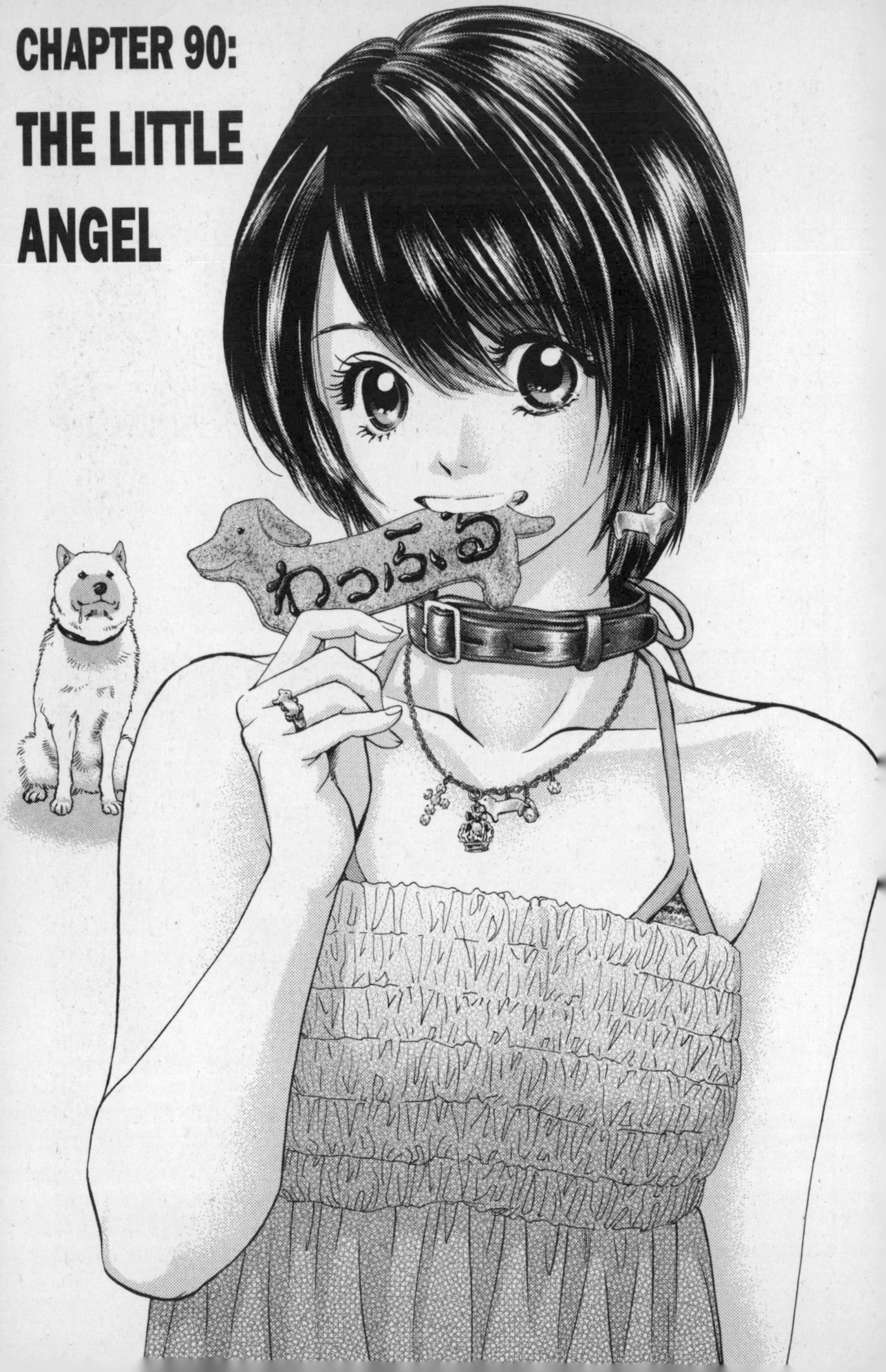

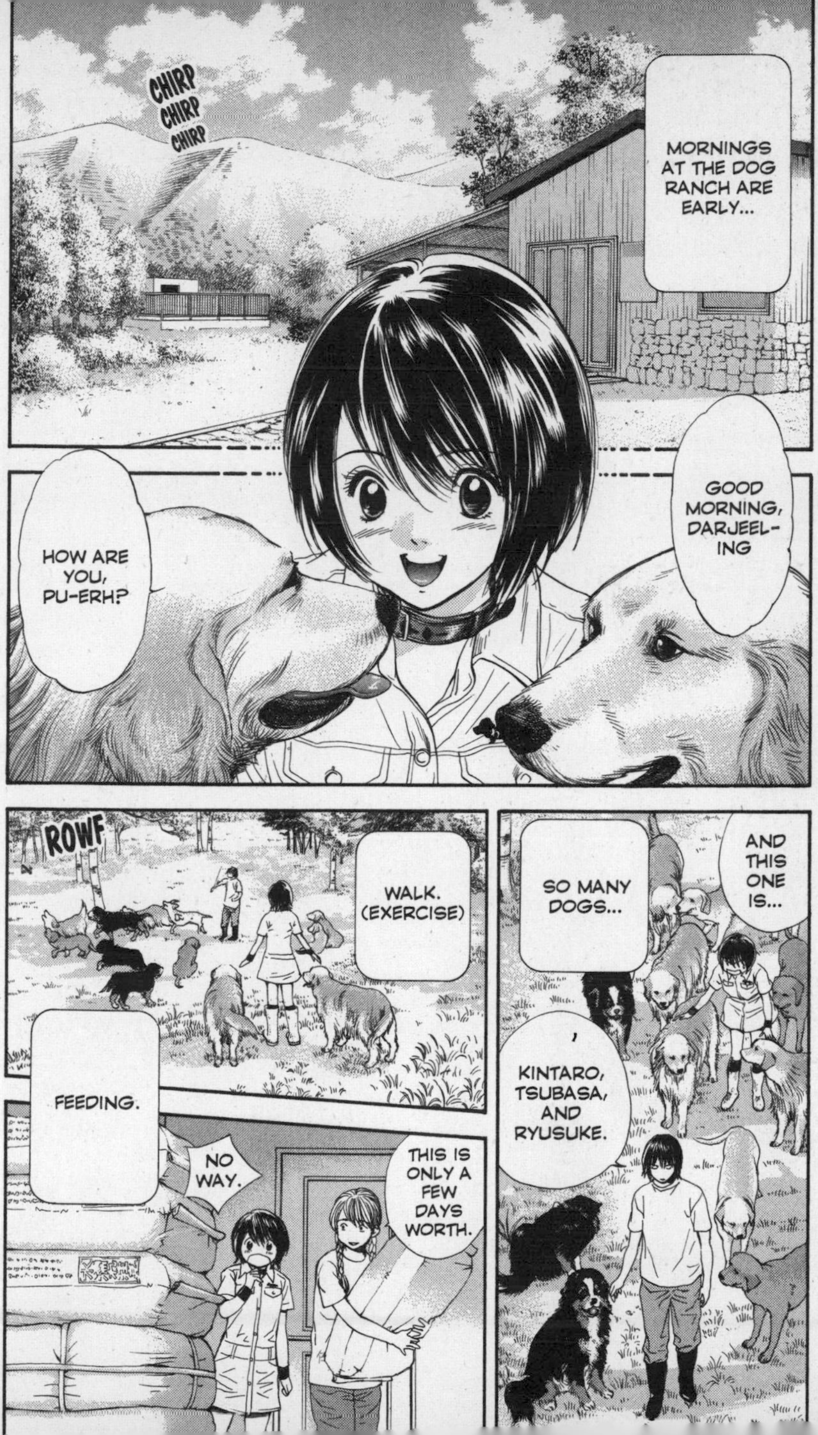
CHIRP
CHIRP
CHIRP
MORNINGS AT THE DOG RANCH ARE EARLY...
GOOD MORNING, DARJEEL-ING
HOW ARE YOU, PU-ERH?
AND THIS ONE IS...
SO MANY DOGS...
KINTARO, TSUBASA, AND RYUSUKE.
ROWF
WALK. (EXERCISE)
FEEDING.
THIS IS ONLY A FEW DAYS WORTH.
NO WAY.

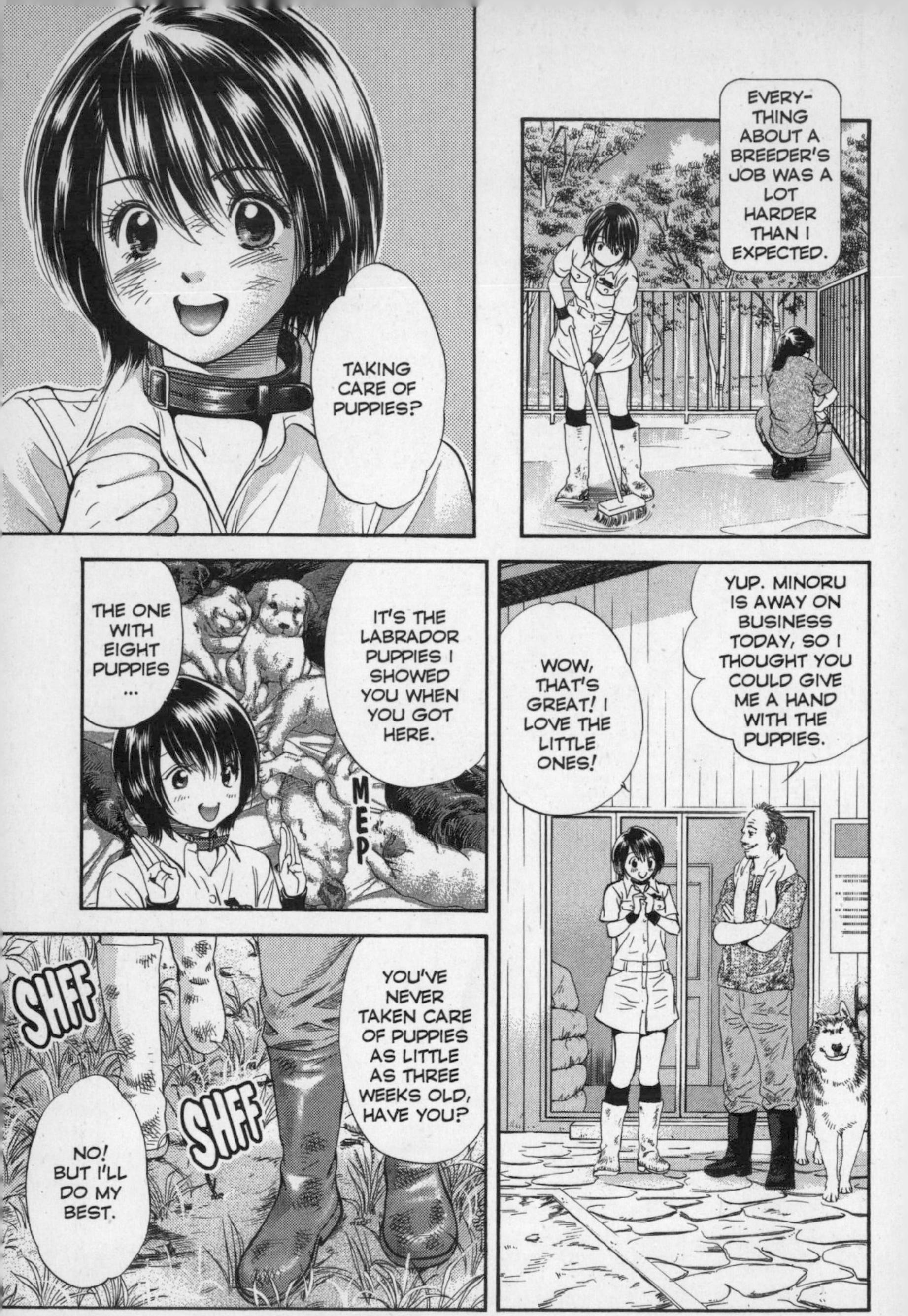
EVERY-THING ABOUT A BREEDER'S JOB WAS A LOT HARDER THAN I EXPECTED.
TAKING CARE OF PUPPIES?
YUP. MINORU IS AWAY ON BUSINESS TODAY, SO I THOUGHT YOU COULD GIVE ME A HAND WITH THE PUPPIES.
WOW, THAT'S GREAT! I LOVE THE LITTLE ONES!
IT'S THE LABRADOR PUPPIES I SHOWED YOU WHEN YOU GOT HERE.
THE ONE WITH EIGHT PUPPIES ...
MEP
YOU'VE NEVER TAKEN CARE OF PUPPIES AS LITTLE AS THREE WEEKS OLD, HAVE YOU?
SHFF
SHFF
NO! BUT I'LL DO MY BEST.

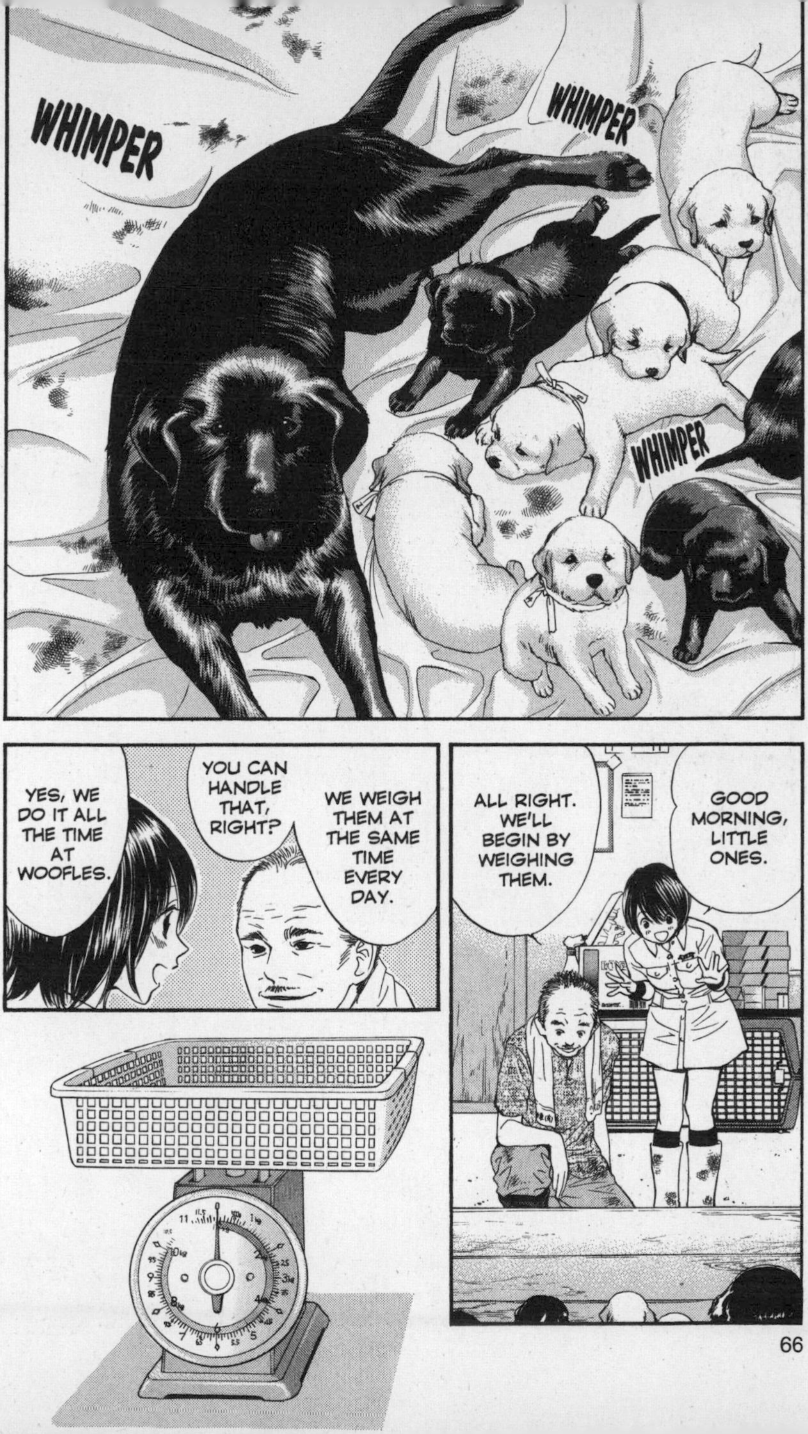
WHIMPER
WHIMPER
WHIMPER
GOOD MORNING, LITTLE ONES.
ALL RIGHT. WE'LL BEGIN BY WEIGHING THEM.
WE WEIGH THEM AT THE SAME TIME EVERY DAY.
YOU CAN HANDLE THAT, RIGHT?
YES, WE DO IT ALL THE TIME AT WOOFLES.

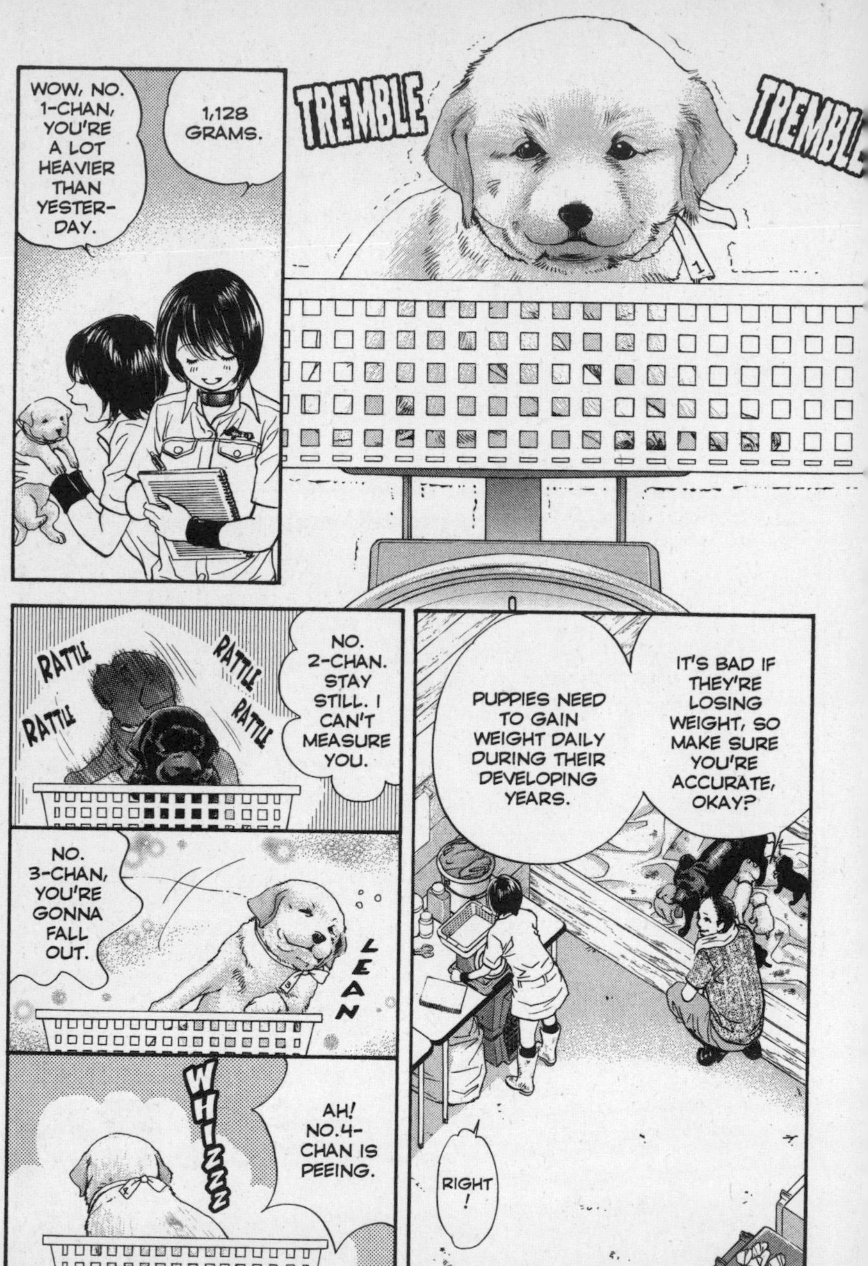
TREMBLE
TREMBLE
1,128 GRAMS.
WOW, NO. 1-CHAN, YOU'RE A LOT HEAVIER THAN YESTER-DAY.
IT'S BAD IF THEY'RE LOSING WEIGHT, SO MAKE SURE YOU'RE ACCURATE, OKAY?
PUPPIES NEED TO GAIN WEIGHT DAILY DURING THEIR DEVELOPING YEARS.
RIGHT!
NO. 2-CHAN. STAY STILL. I CAN'T MEASURE YOU.
RATTLE
RATTLE
RATTLE
RATTLE
NO. 3-CHAN, YOU'RE GONNA FALL OUT.
LEAN
AH! NO.4-CHAN IS PEEING.
WHIZZZ

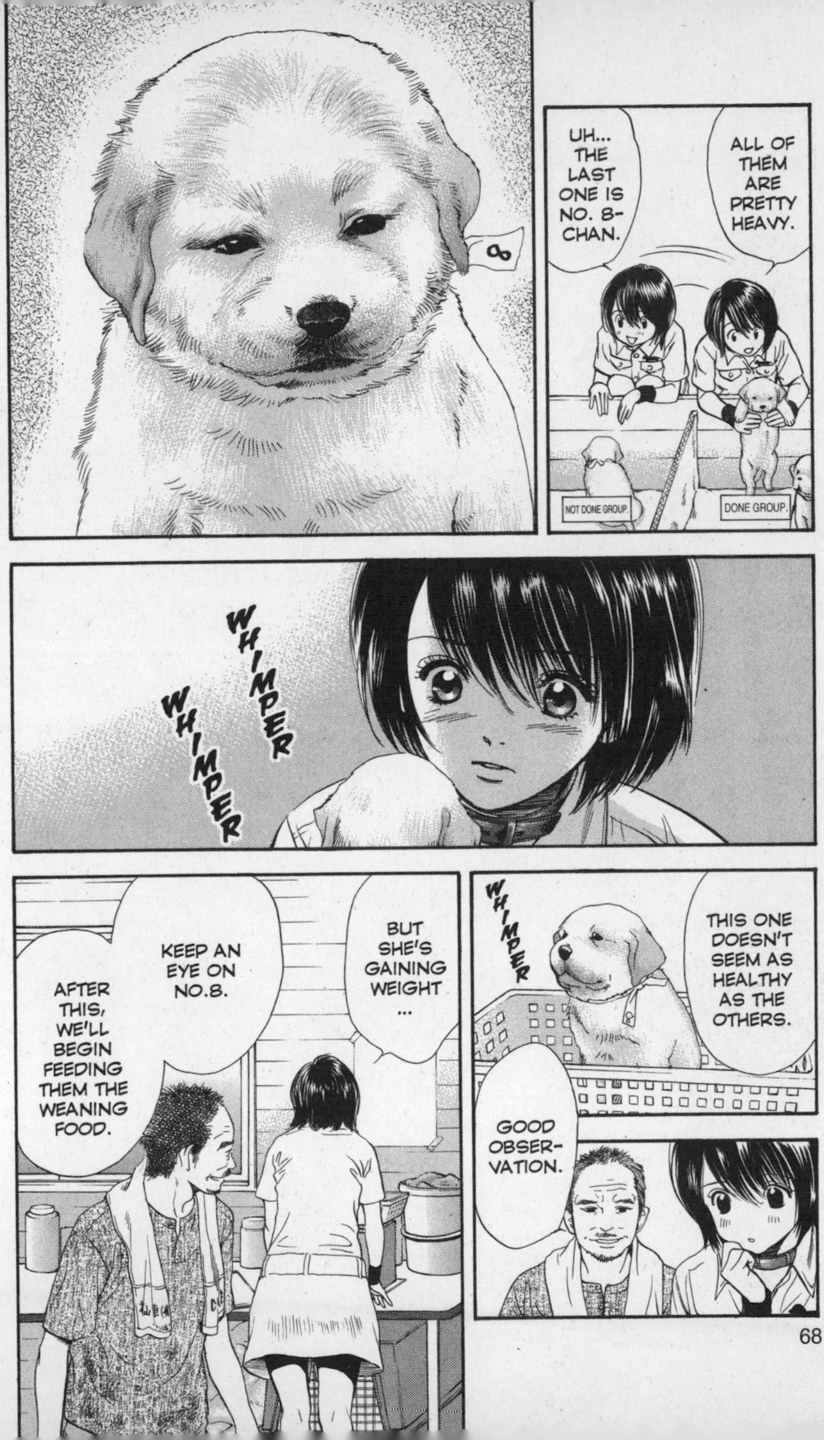
ALL OF THEM ARE PRETTY HEAVY.
UH... THE LAST ONE IS NO. 8-CHAN.
DONE GROUP.
NOT DONE GROUP.
WHIMPER
WHIMPER
WHIMPER
THIS ONE DOESN'T SEEM AS HEALTHY AS THE OTHERS.
GOOD OBSERVATION.
BUT SHE'S GAINING WEIGHT ...
KEEP AN EYE ON NO.8.
AFTER THIS, WE'LL BEGIN FEEDING THEM THE WEANING FOOD.

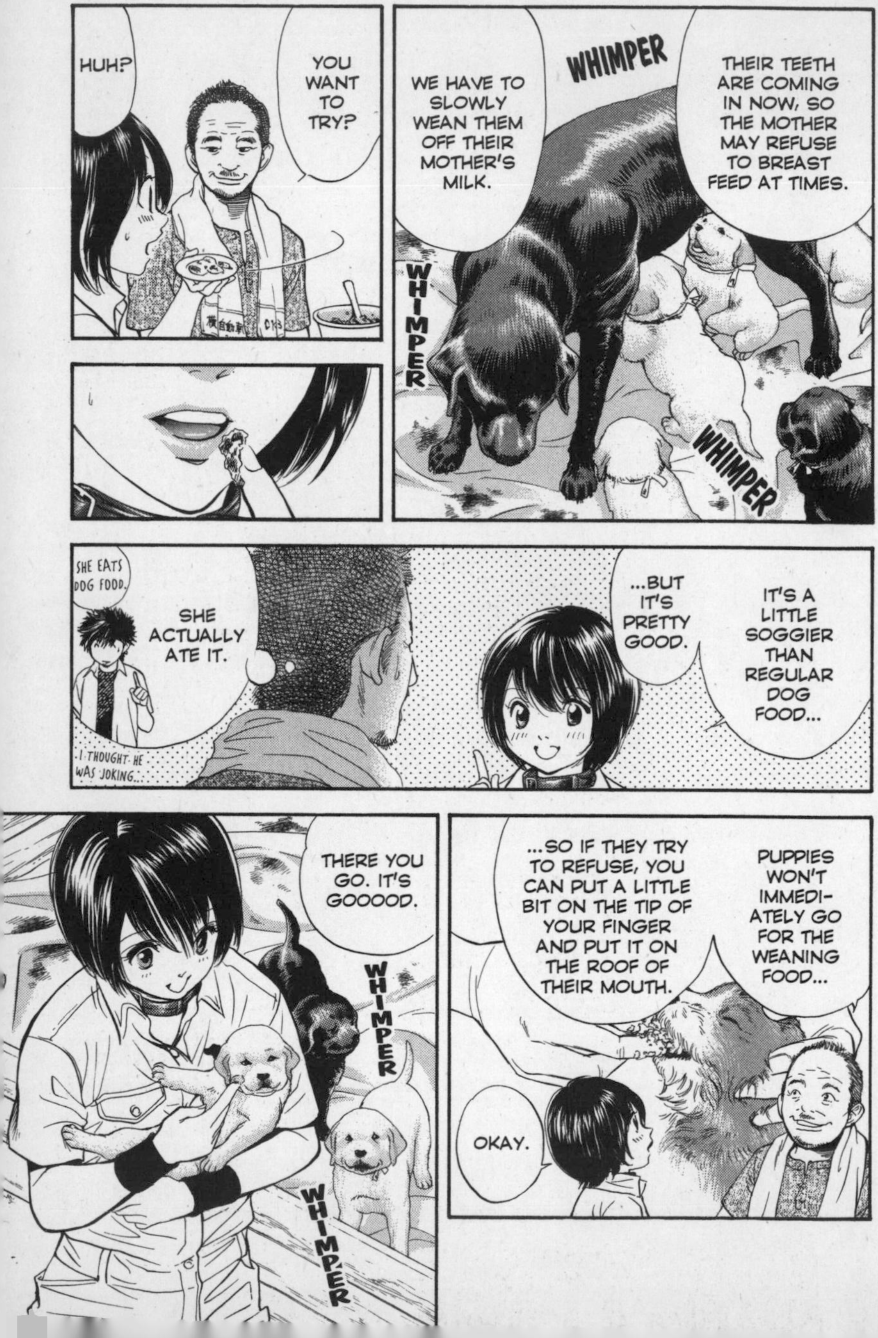
THEIR TEETH ARE COMING IN NOW, SO THE MOTHER MAY REFUSE TO BREAST FEED AT TIMES.
WHIMPER
WE HAVE TO SLOWLY WEAN THEM OFF THEIR MOTHER'S MILK.
WHIMPER
WHIMPER
YOU WANT TO TRY?
HUH?
IT'S A LITTLE SOGGIER THAN REGULAR DOG FOOD...
...BUT IT'S PRETTY GOOD.
SHE ACTUALLY ATE IT.
SHE EATS DOG FOOD.
I THOUGHT HE WAS JOKING...
PUPPIES WON'T IMMEDIATELY GO FOR THE WEANING FOOD...
...SO IF THEY TRY TO REFUSE, YOU CAN PUT A LITTLE BIT ON THE TIP OF YOUR FINGER AND PUT IT ON THE ROOF OF THEIR MOUTH.
OKAY.
THERE YOU GO. IT'S GOOOOD.
WHIMPER
WHIMPER

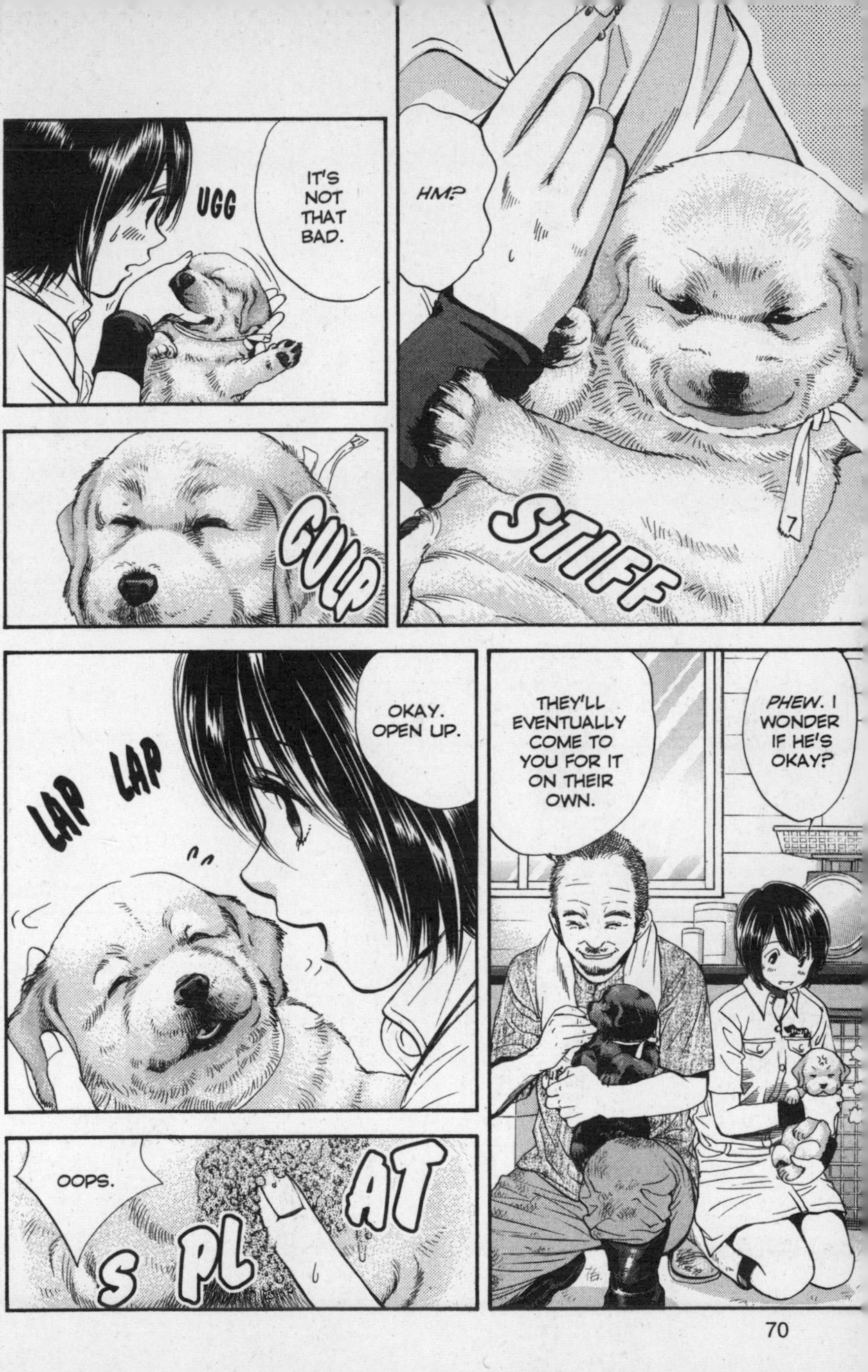
HM?
STIFF
IT'S NOT THAT BAD.
UGG
GULP
PHEW. I WONDER IF HE'S OKAY?
THEY'LL EVENTUALLY COME TO YOU FOR IT ON THEIR OWN.
OKAY. OPEN UP.
LAP LAP
OOPS.
S PL AT

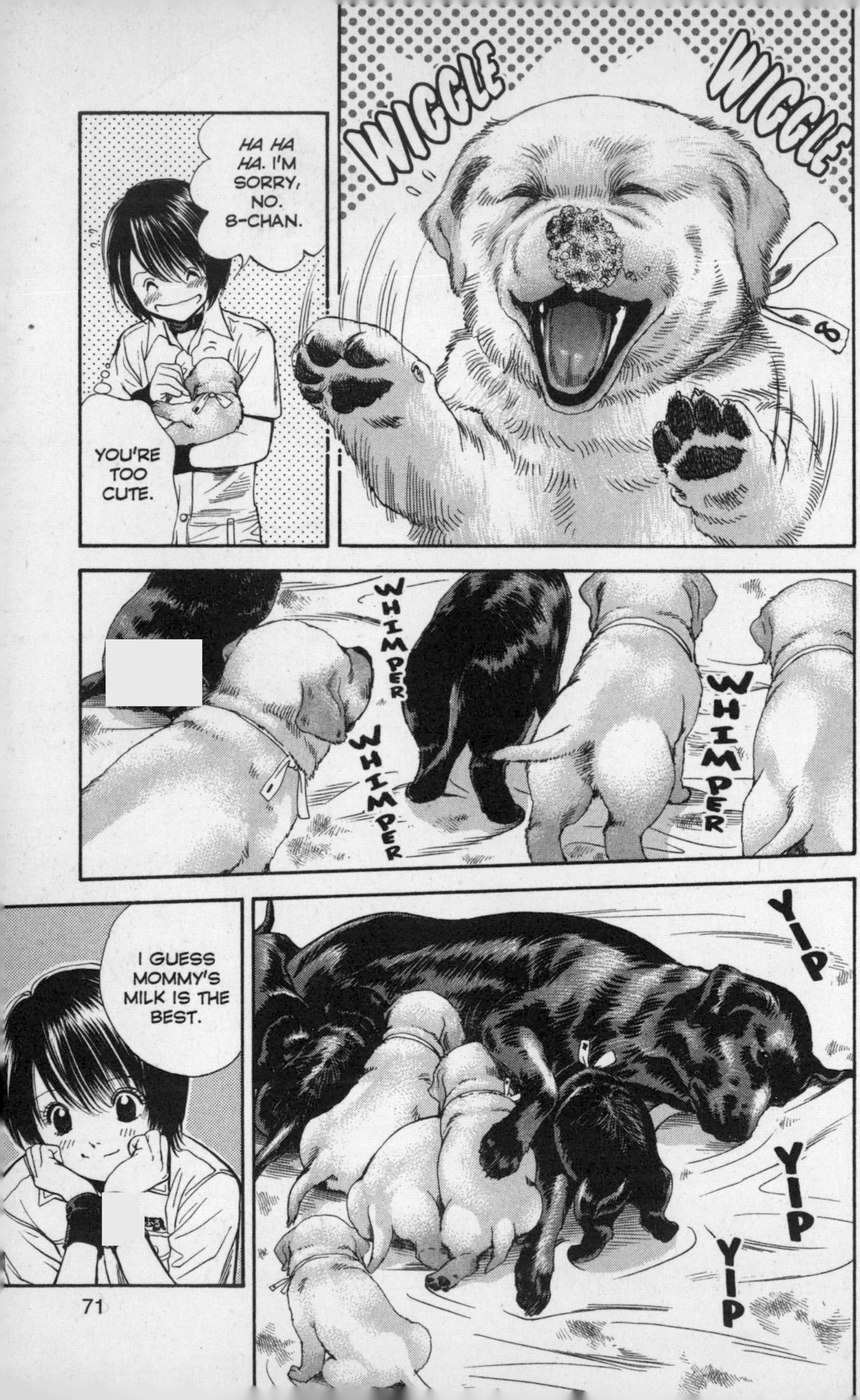
WIGGLE
WIGGLE
HA HA HA. I'M SORRY, NO. 8-CHAN.
YOU'RE TOO CUTE.
WHIMPER
WHIMPER
WHIMPER
YIP
YIP
YIP
YIP
I GUESS MOMMY'S MILK IS THE BEST.

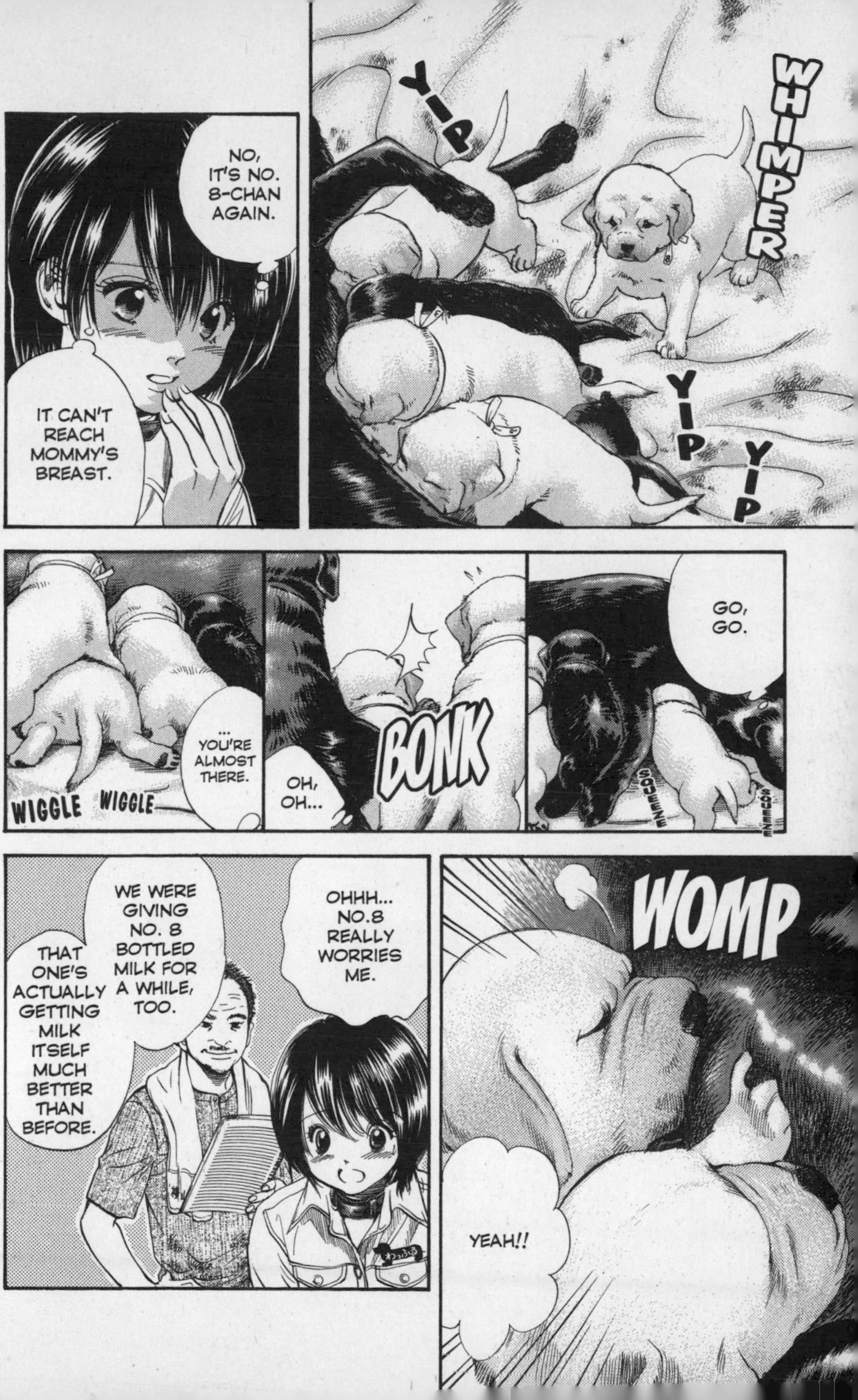
WHIMPER
YIP
YIP
YIP
NO, IT'S NO. 8-CHAN AGAIN.
IT CAN'T REACH MOMMY'S BREAST.
GO, GO.
SQUEEZE
SQUEEZE
BONK
OH, OH...
... YOU'RE ALMOST THERE.
WIGGLE WIGGLE
WOMP
YEAH!!
OHHH... NO.8 REALLY WORRIES ME.
WE WERE GIVING NO. 8 BOTTLED MILK FOR A WHILE, TOO.
THAT ONE'S ACTUALLY GETTING MILK ITSELF MUCH BETTER THAN BEFORE.

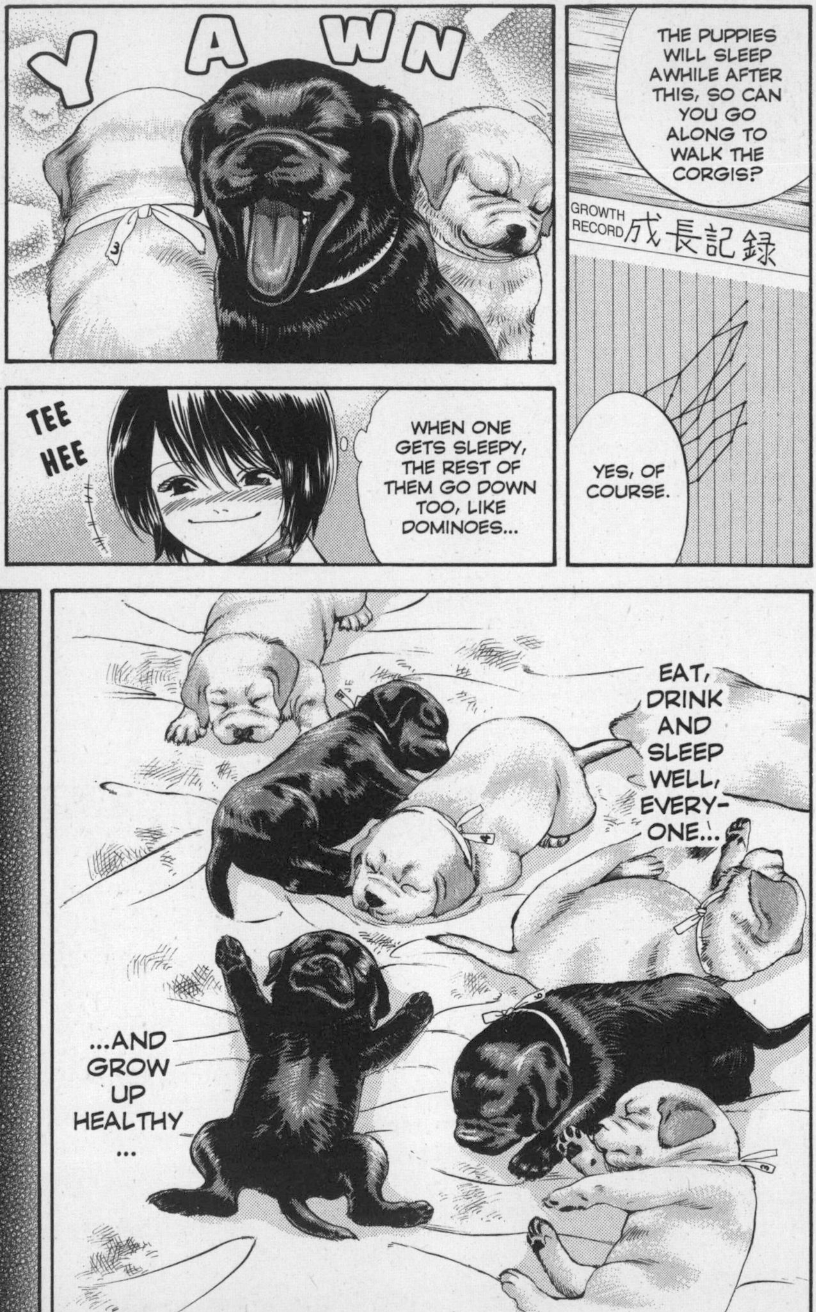
THE PUPPIES WILL SLEEP AWHILE AFTER THIS, SO CAN YOU GO ALONG TO WALK THE CORGIS?
GROWTH RECORD 成長記録
YES, OF COURSE.
YAWN
TEE HEE
WHEN ONE GETS SLEEPY, THE REST OF THEM GO DOWN TOO, LIKE DOMINOES...
EAT, DRINK AND SLEEP WELL, EVERY-ONE...
...AND GROW UP HEALTHY ...

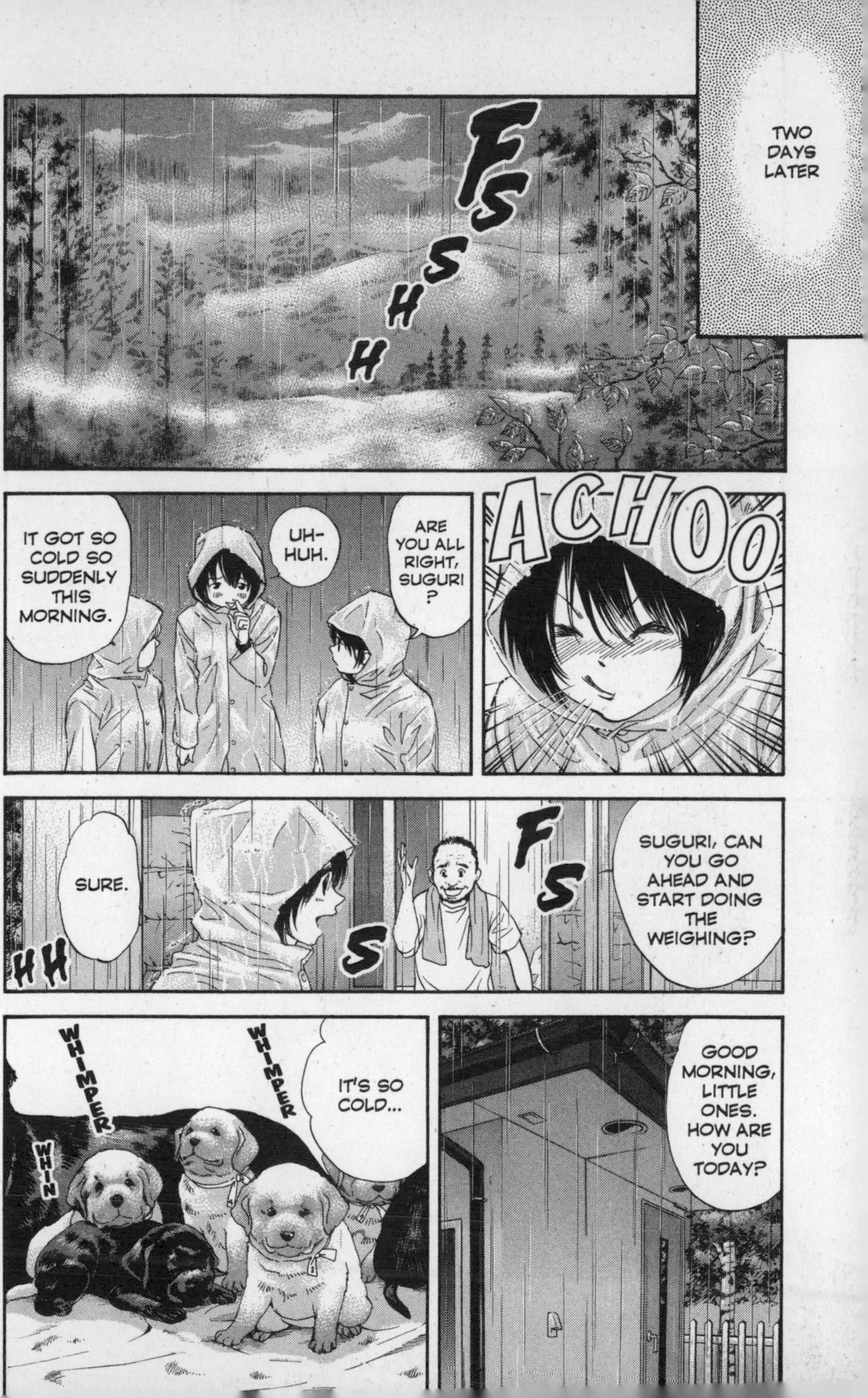
TWO DAYS LATER
FSSHH
ACHOO
ARE YOU ALL RIGHT, SUGURI?
UH-HUH.
IT GOT SO COLD SO SUDDENLY THIS MORNING.
SUGURI, CAN YOU GO AHEAD AND START DOING THE WEIGHING?
FSSHH
SURE.
GOOD MORNING, LITTLE ONES. HOW ARE YOU TODAY?
WHIMPER
IT'S SO COLD...
WHIMPER
WHIN

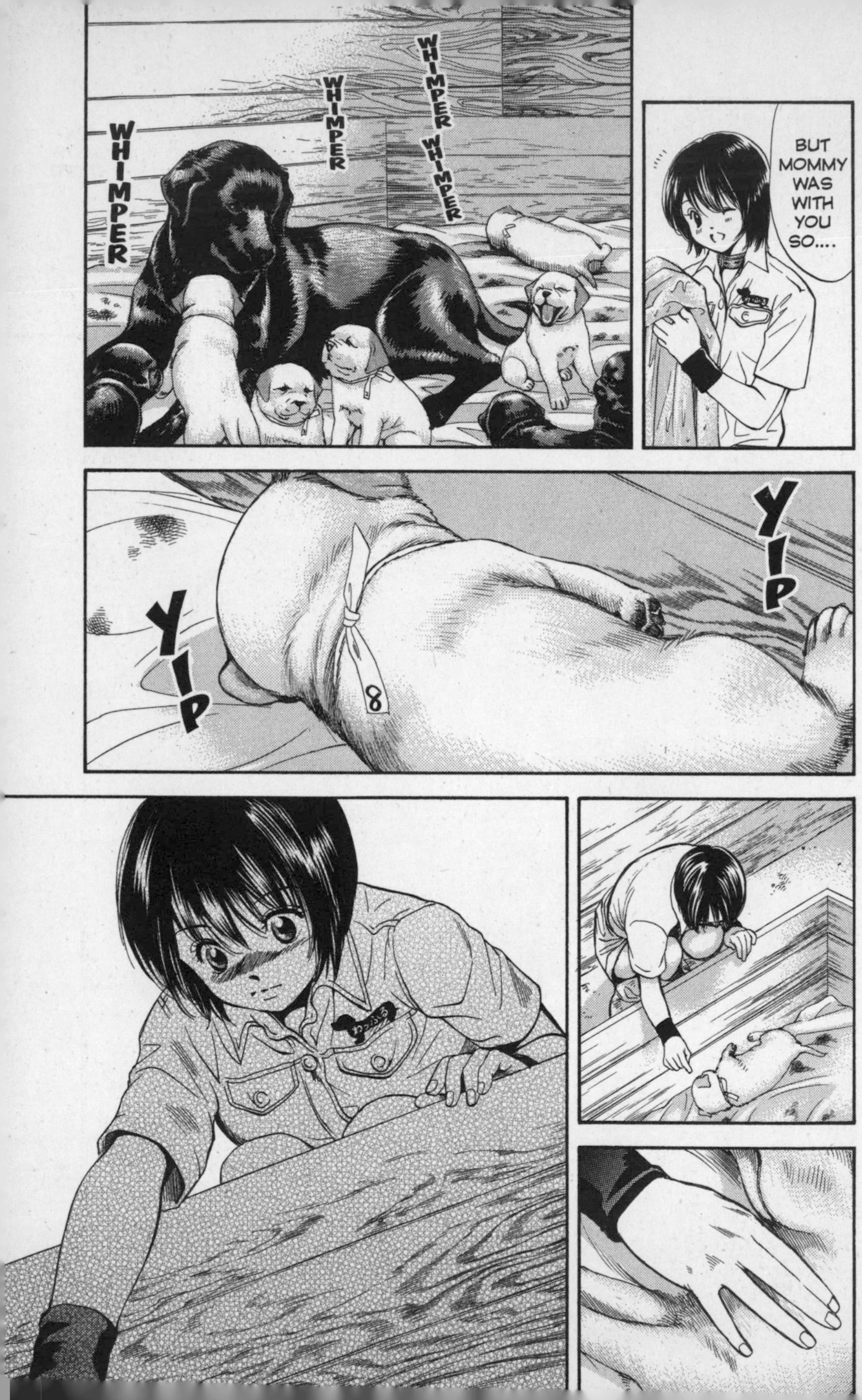
BUT MOMMY WAS WITH YOU SO....
WHIMPER WHIMPER
WHIMPER
WHIMPER
YIP
YIP

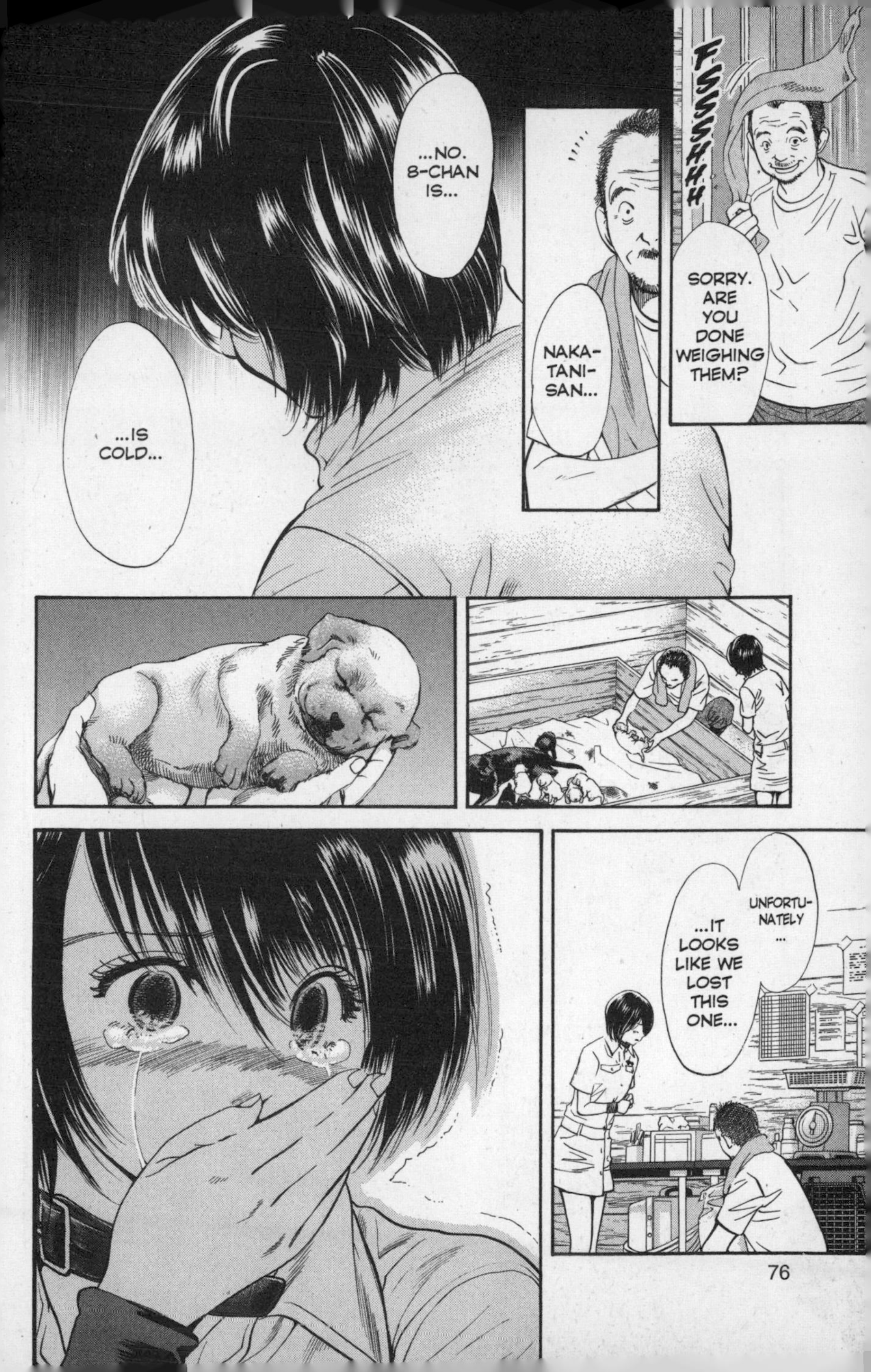
FSSSHHH
SORRY. ARE YOU DONE WEIGHING THEM?
NAKA-TANI-SAN...
...NO. 8-CHAN IS...
...IS COLD...
UNFORTU-NATELY...
...IT LOOKS LIKE WE LOST THIS ONE...

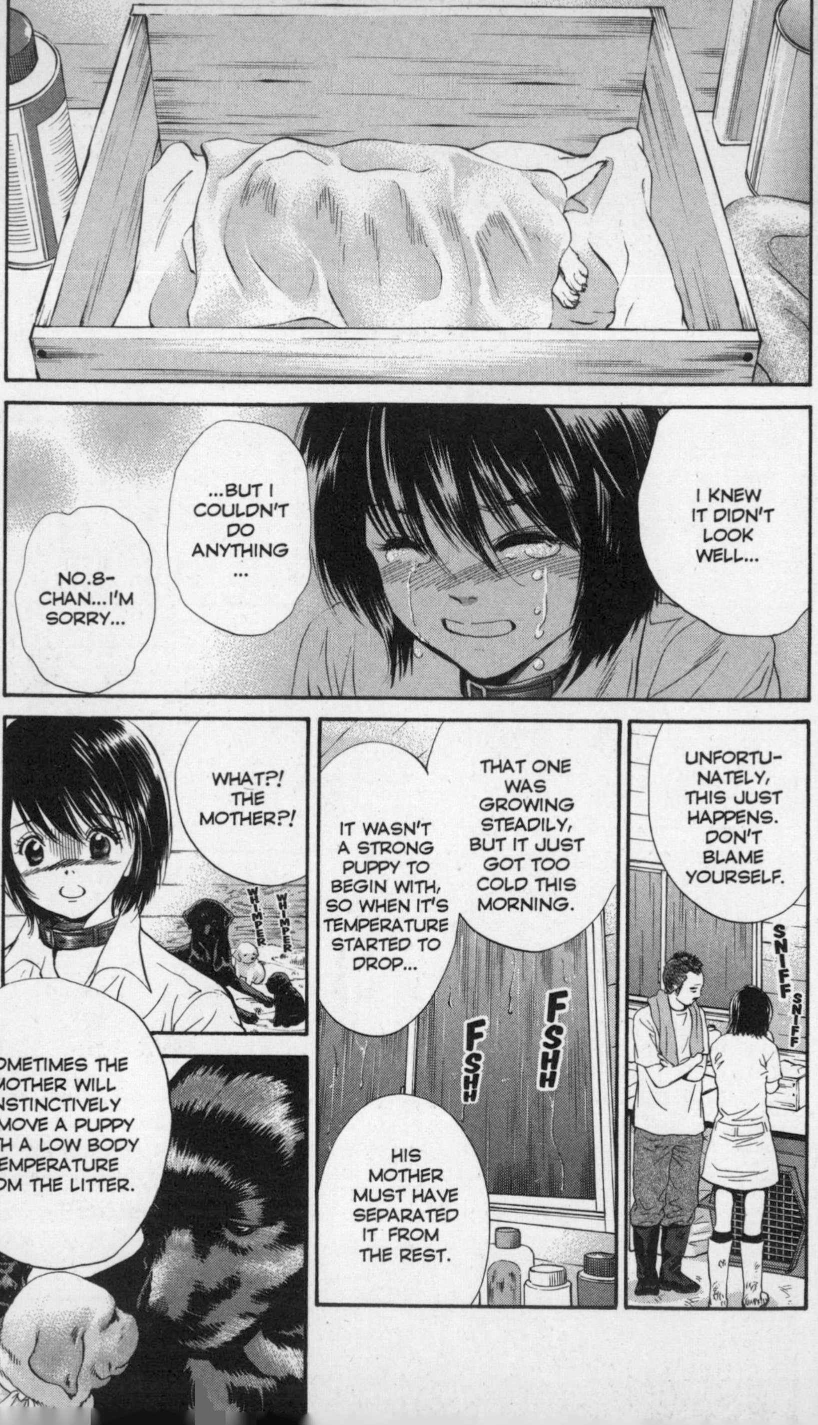
I KNEW IT DIDN'T LOOK WELL...
...BUT I COULDN'T DO ANYTHING ...
NO.8-CHAN...I'M SORRY...
UNFORTUNATELY, THIS JUST HAPPENS. DON'T BLAME YOURSELF.
SNIFF
SNIFF
THAT ONE WAS GROWING STEADILY, BUT IT JUST GOT TOO COLD THIS MORNING.
IT WASN'T A STRONG PUPPY TO BEGIN WITH, SO WHEN IT'S TEMPERATURE STARTED TO DROP...
FSHH
FSHH
HIS MOTHER MUST HAVE SEPARATED IT FROM THE REST.
WHAT?! THE MOTHER?!
WHIMPER
WHIMPER
SOMETIMES THE MOTHER WILL INSTINCTIVELY REMOVE A PUPPY WITH A LOW BODY TEMPERATURE FROM THE LITTER.

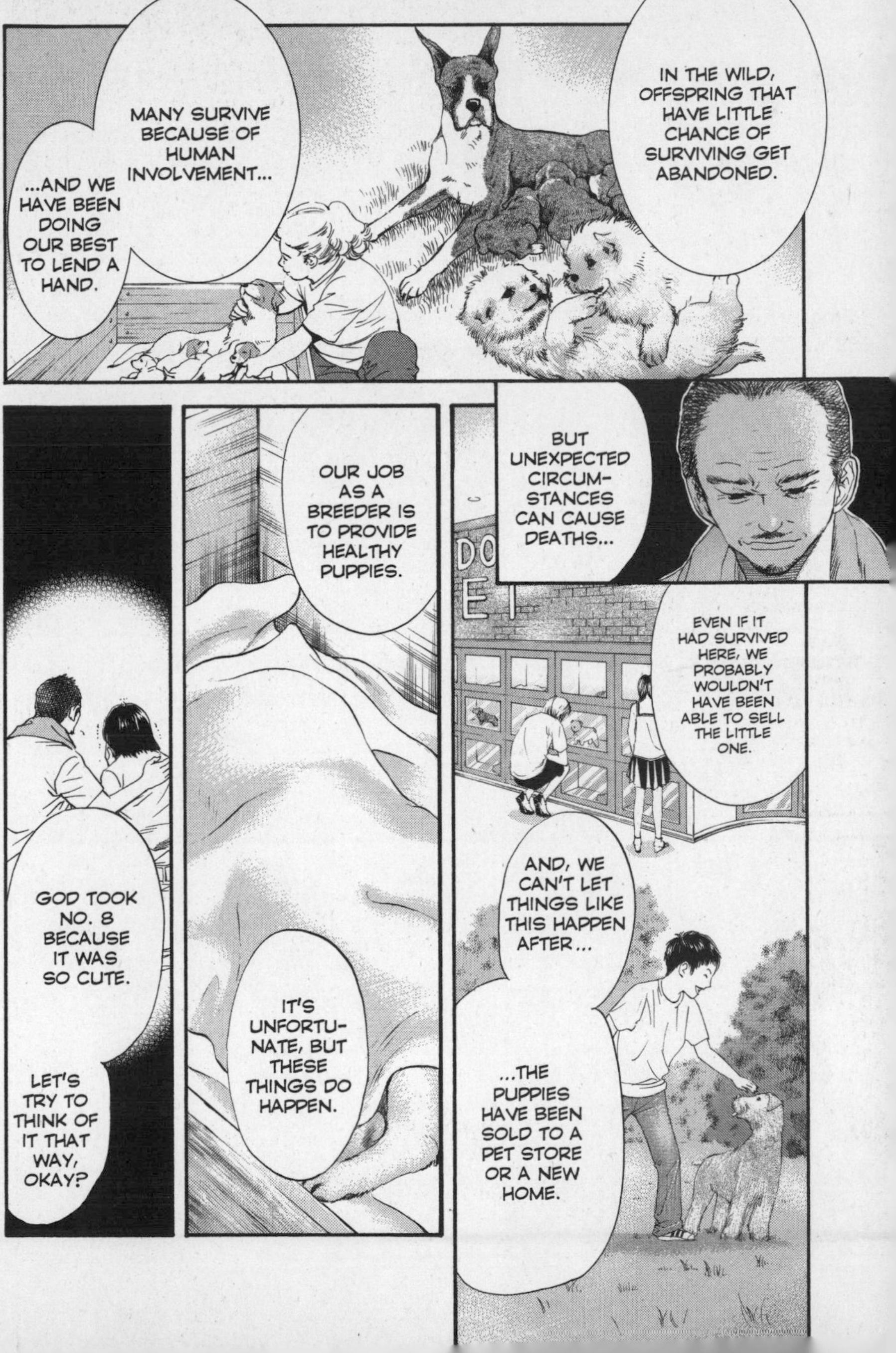
IN THE WILD, OFFSPRING THAT HAVE LITTLE CHANCE OF SURVIVING GET ABANDONED.
MANY SURVIVE BECAUSE OF HUMAN INVOLVEMENT...
...AND WE HAVE BEEN DOING OUR BEST TO LEND A HAND.
BUT UNEXPECTED CIRCUM-STANCES CAN CAUSE DEATHS...
EVEN IF IT HAD SURVIVED HERE, WE PROBABLY WOULDN'T HAVE BEEN ABLE TO SELL THE LITTLE ONE.
AND, WE CAN'T LET THINGS LIKE THIS HAPPEN AFTER...
...THE PUPPIES HAVE BEEN SOLD TO A PET STORE OR A NEW HOME.
OUR JOB AS A BREEDER IS TO PROVIDE HEALTHY PUPPIES.
IT'S UNFORTU-NATE, BUT THESE THINGS DO HAPPEN.
GOD TOOK NO. 8 BECAUSE IT WAS SO CUTE.
LET'S TRY TO THINK OF IT THAT WAY, OKAY?

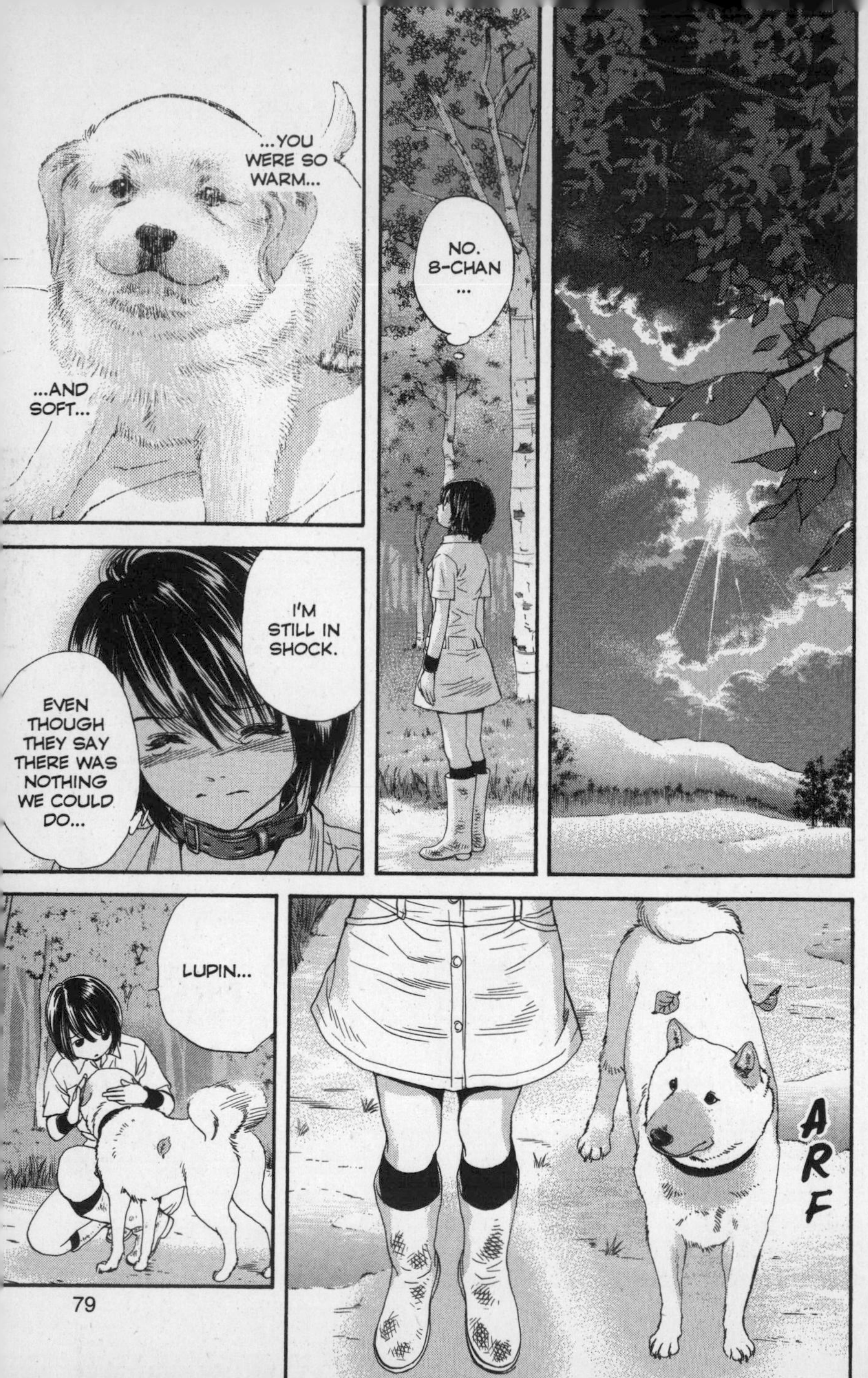
NO. 8-CHAN ...
...YOU WERE SO WARM...
...AND SOFT...
I'M STILL IN SHOCK.
EVEN THOUGH THEY SAY THERE WAS NOTHING WE COULD DO...
ARF
LUPIN...

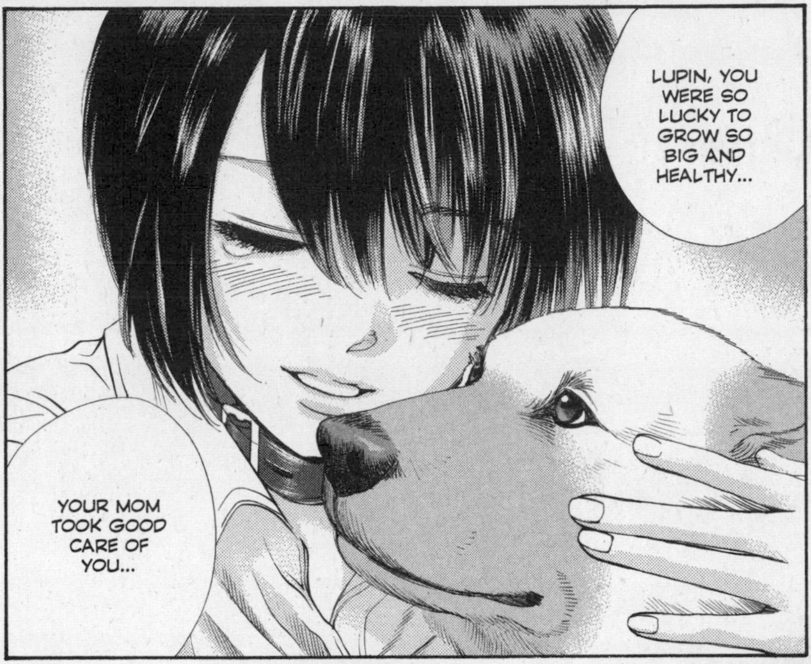
LUPIN, YOU WERE SO LUCKY TO GROW SO BIG AND HEALTHY...
YOUR MOM TOOK GOOD CARE OF YOU...

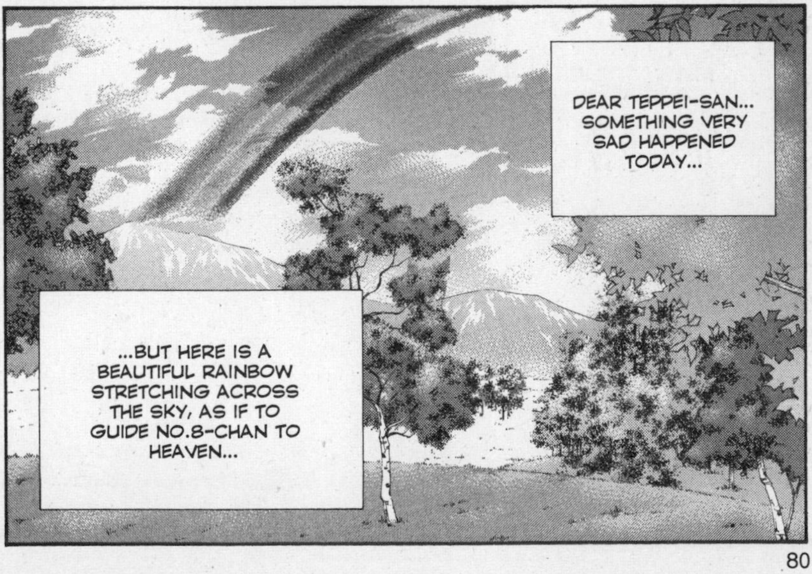
DEAR TEPPEI-SAN... SOMETHING VERY SAD HAPPENED TODAY...
...BUT HERE IS A BEAUTIFUL RAINBOW STRETCHING ACROSS THE SKY, AS IF TO GUIDE NO.8-CHAN TO HEAVEN...

CHAPTER 91: BIG NEWS

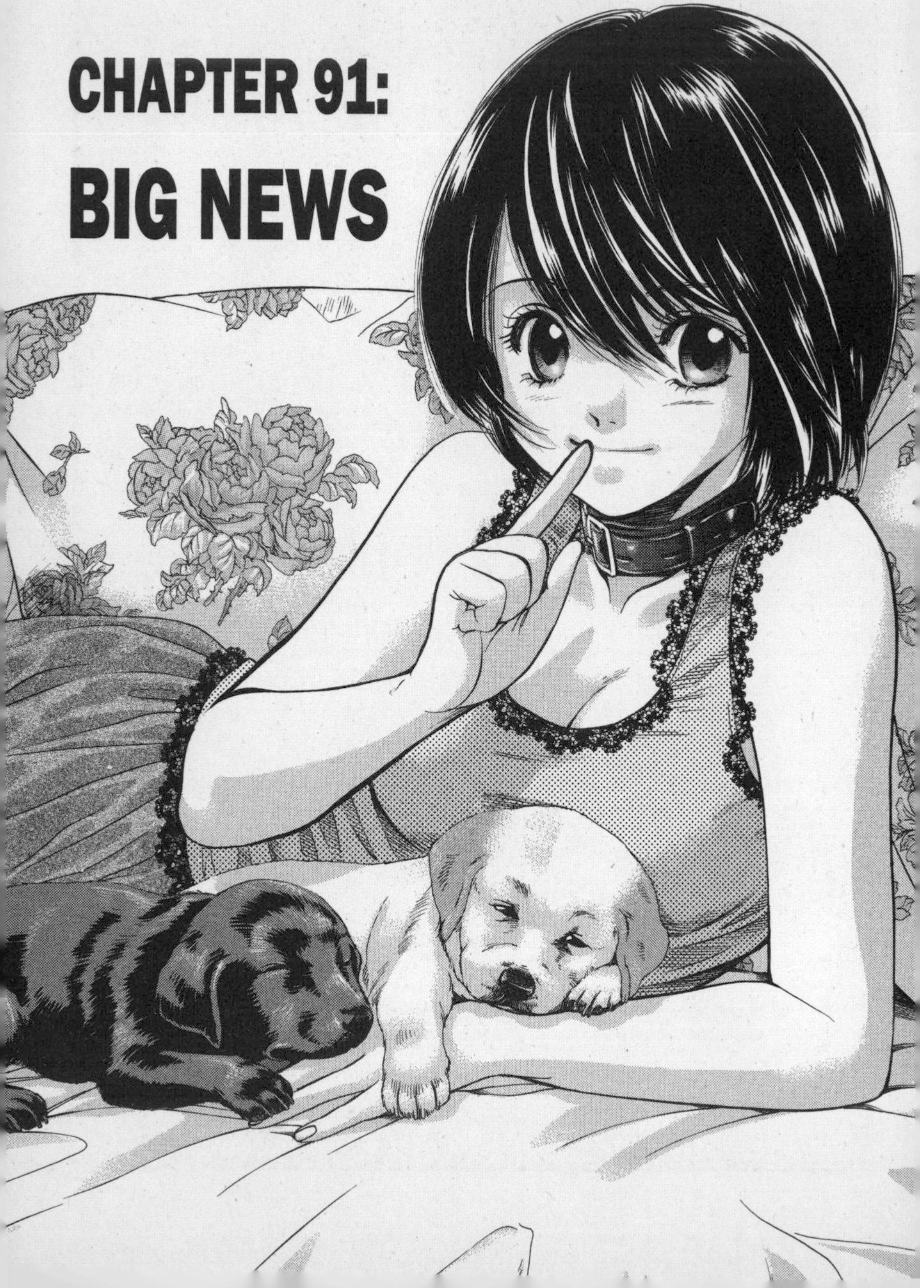

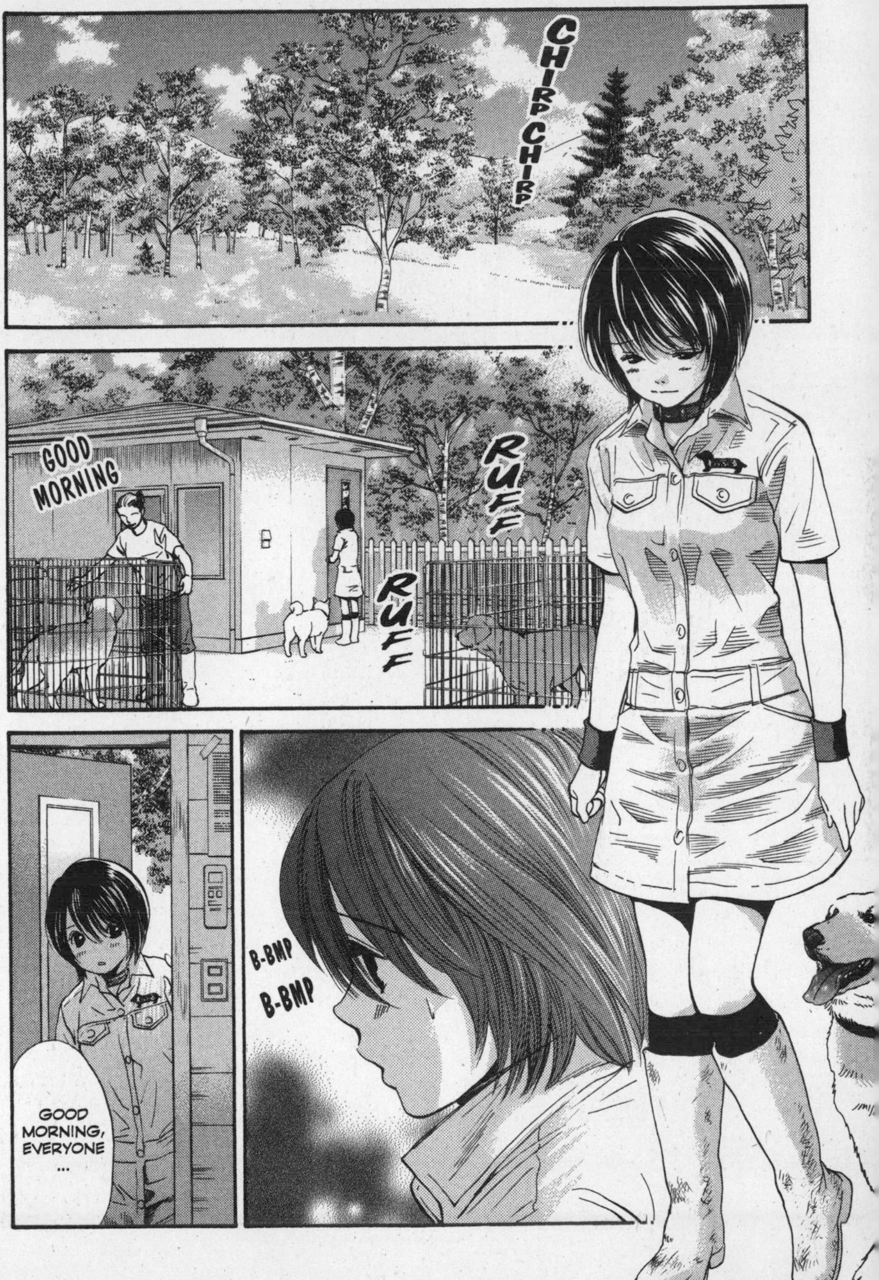
CHIRP CHIRP CHIRP
RUFF
RUFF
GOOD MORNING
B-BMP
B-BMP
GOOD MORNING, EVERYONE ...

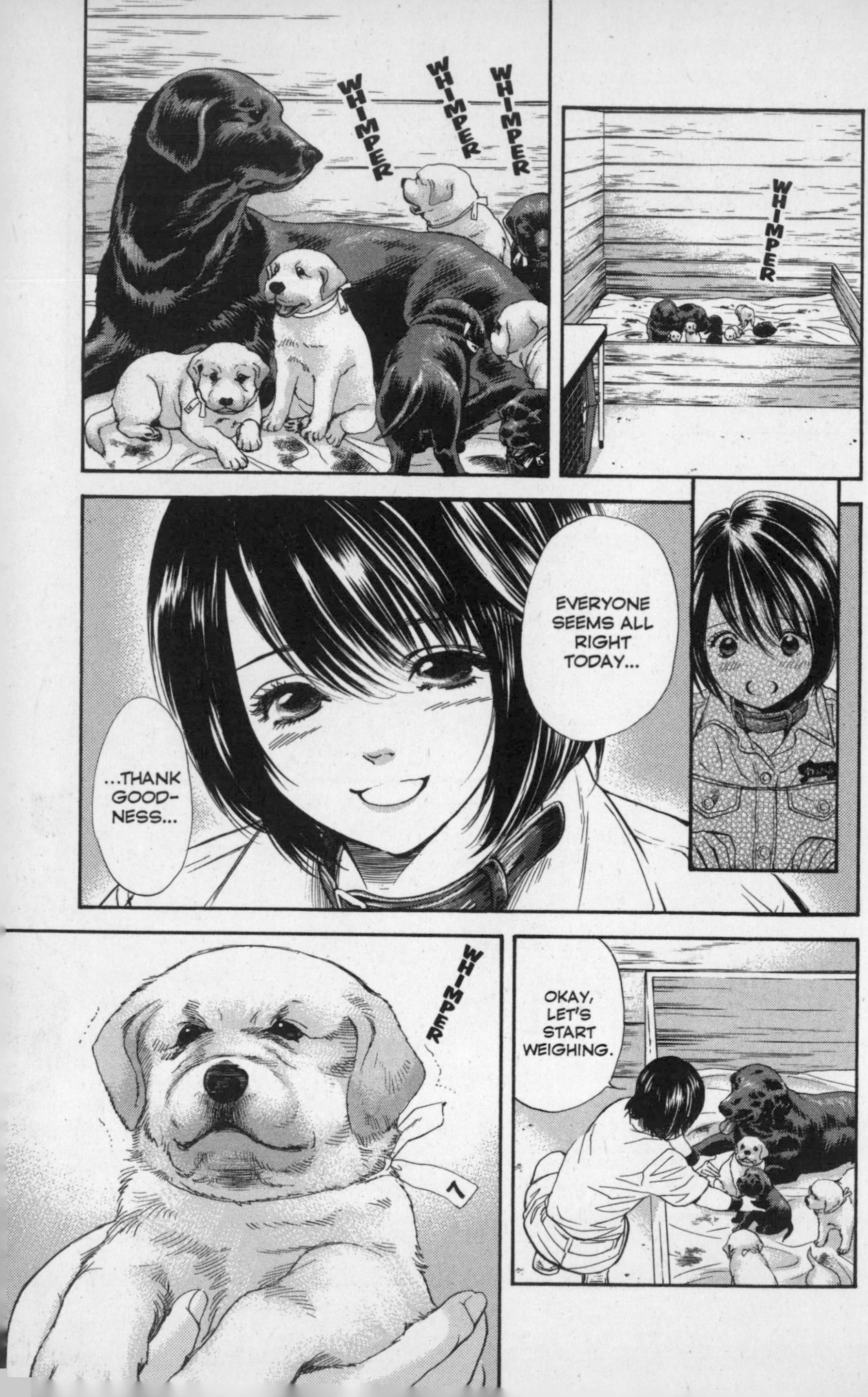
WHIMPER
WHIMPER
WHIMPER
WHIMPER
EVERYONE SEEMS ALL RIGHT TODAY...
...THANK GOODNESS...
OKAY, LET'S START WEIGHING.
WHIMPER

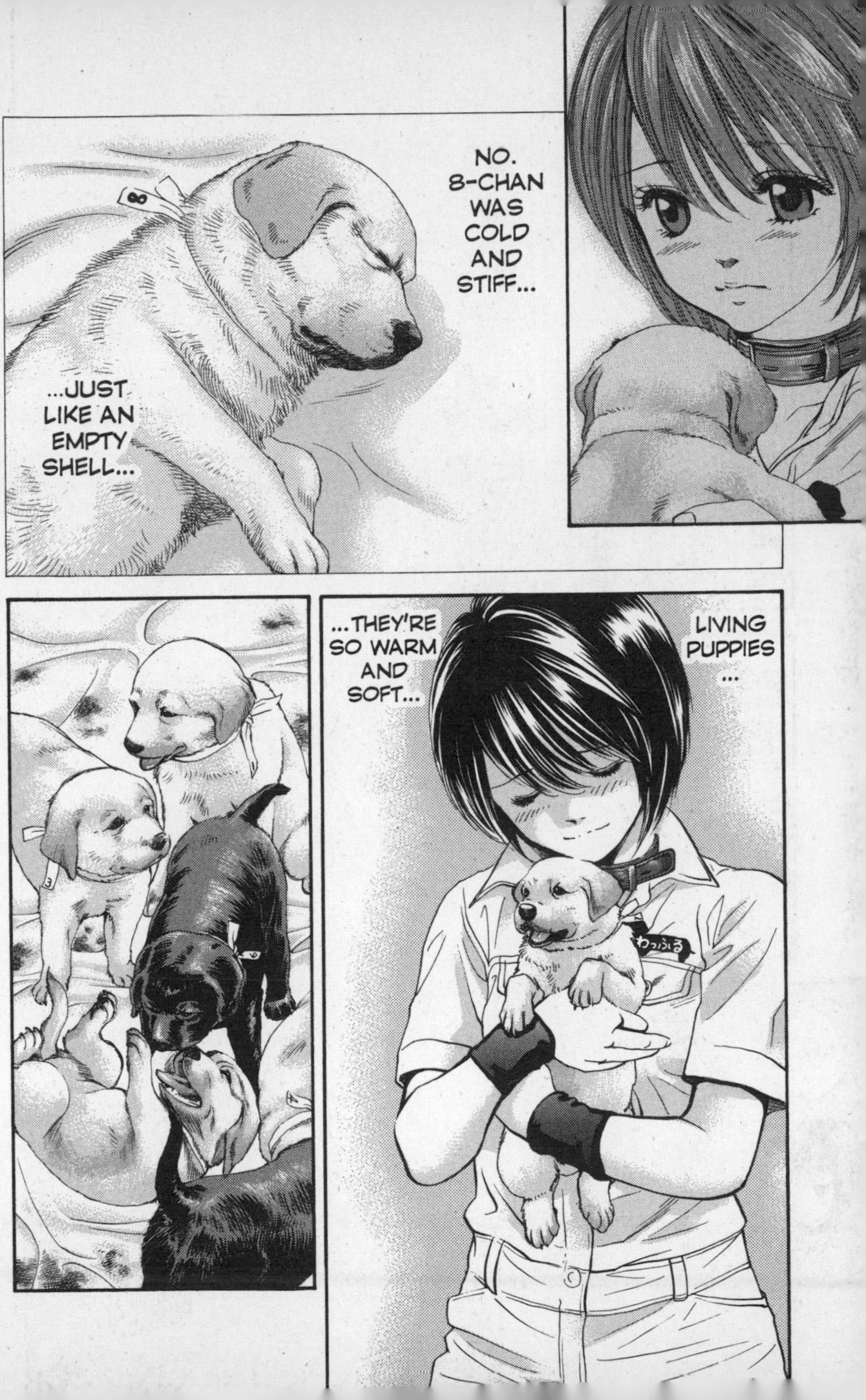
NO. 8-CHAN WAS COLD AND STIFF...
...JUST LIKE AN EMPTY SHELL...
LIVING PUPPIES ...
...THEY'RE SO WARM AND SOFT...
わっふる

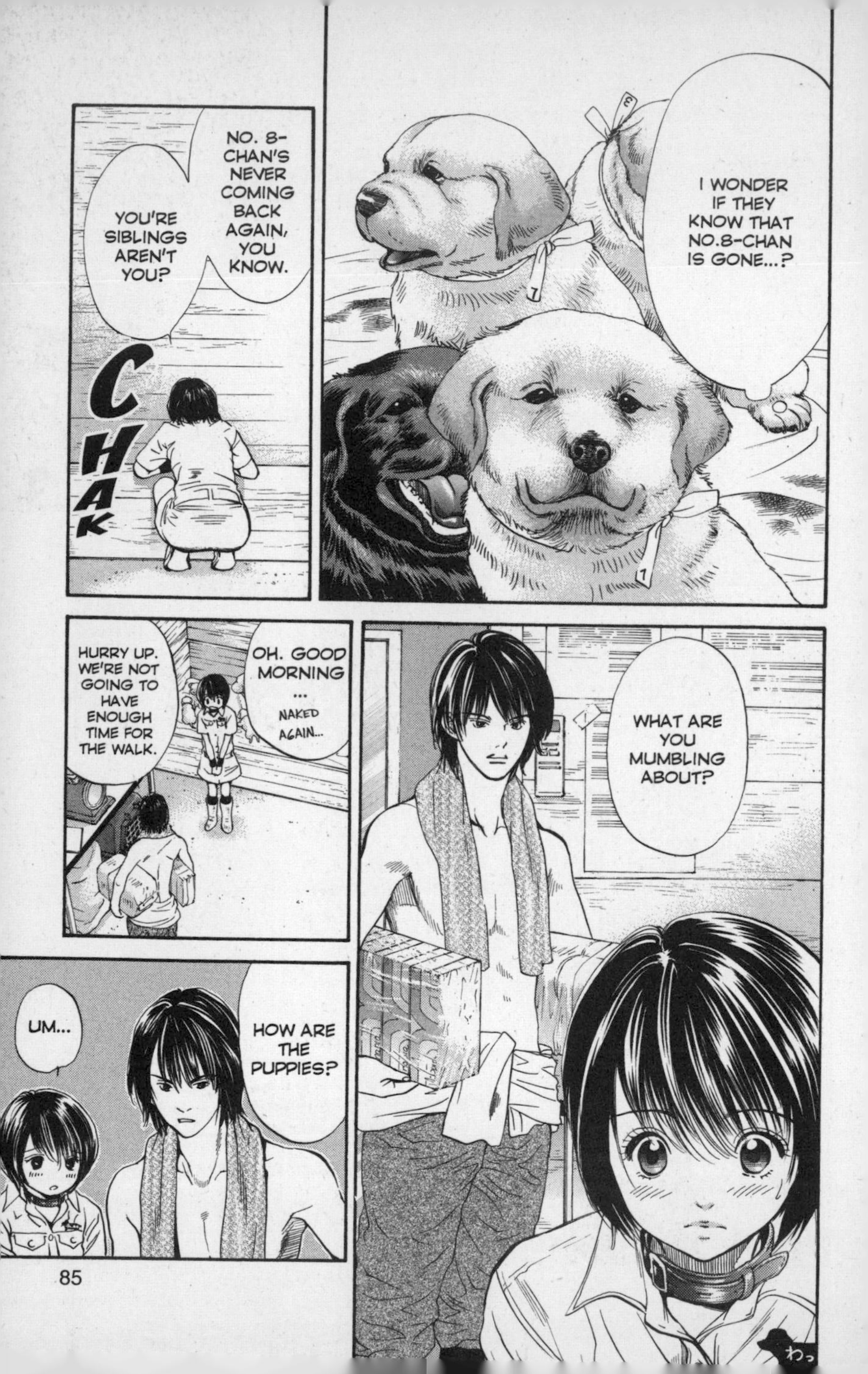
I WONDER IF THEY KNOW THAT NO.8-CHAN IS GONE...?
NO. 8-CHAN'S NEVER COMING BACK AGAIN, YOU KNOW.
YOU'RE SIBLINGS AREN'T YOU?
CHAK
WHAT ARE YOU MUMBLING ABOUT?
わっ
OH. GOOD MORNING ...
NAKED AGAIN...
HURRY UP. WE'RE NOT GOING TO HAVE ENOUGH TIME FOR THE WALK.
HOW ARE THE PUPPIES?
UM...

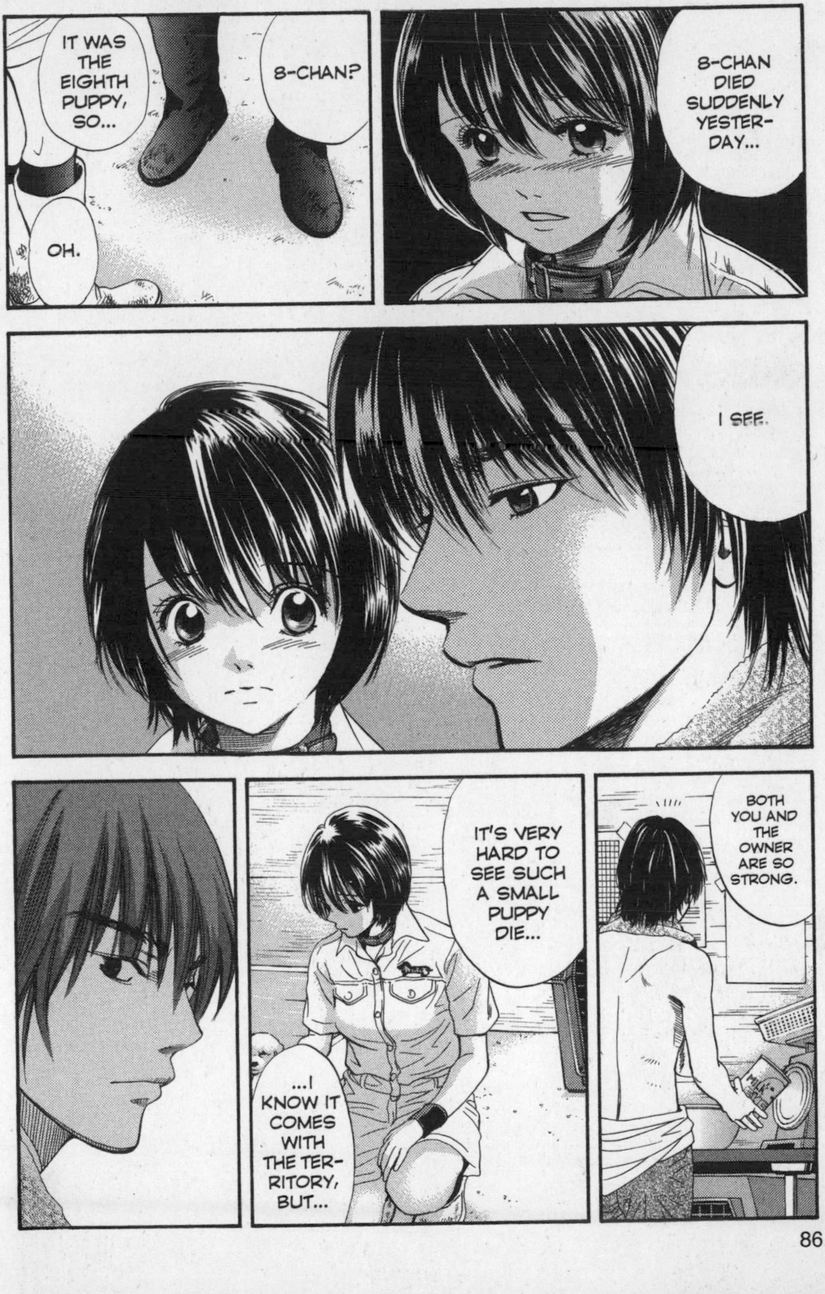
8-CHAN DIED SUDDENLY YESTER-DAY...
8-CHAN?
IT WAS THE EIGHTH PUPPY, SO...
OH.
I SEE.
BOTH YOU AND THE OWNER ARE SO STRONG.
IT'S VERY HARD TO SEE SUCH A SMALL PUPPY DIE...
...I KNOW IT COMES WITH THE TER-RITORY, BUT...

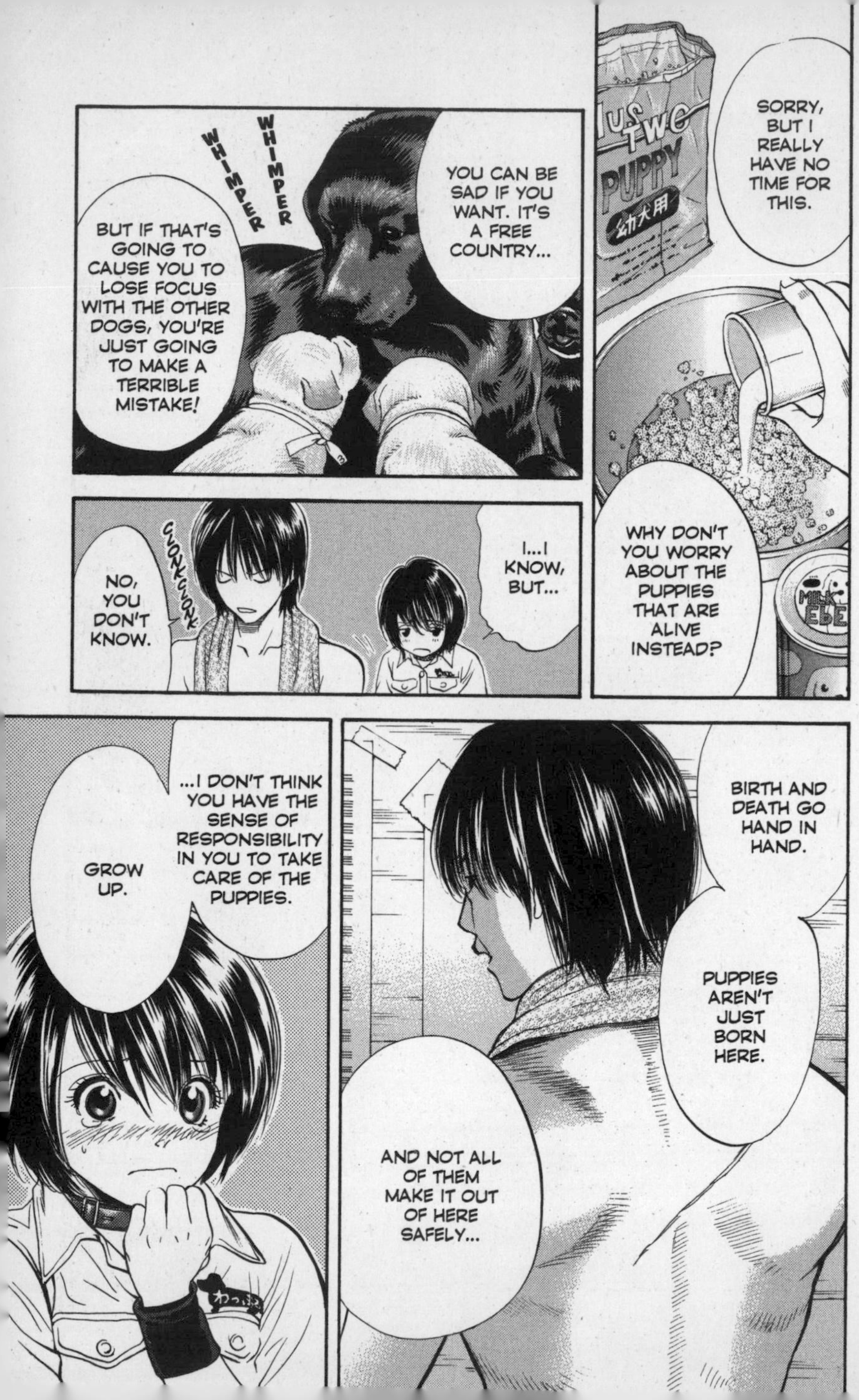
PUPPY
幼犬用
SORRY, BUT I REALLY HAVE NO TIME FOR THIS.
WHY DON'T YOU WORRY ABOUT THE PUPPIES THAT ARE ALIVE INSTEAD?
WHIMPER WHIMPER
YOU CAN BE SAD IF YOU WANT. IT'S A FREE COUNTRY...
BUT IF THAT'S GOING TO CAUSE YOU TO LOSE FOCUS WITH THE OTHER DOGS, YOU'RE JUST GOING TO MAKE A TERRIBLE MISTAKE!
I...I KNOW, BUT...
CLONK CLONK
NO, YOU DON'T KNOW.
BIRTH AND DEATH GO HAND IN HAND.
PUPPIES AREN'T JUST BORN HERE.
AND NOT ALL OF THEM MAKE IT OUT OF HERE SAFELY...
...I DON'T THINK YOU HAVE THE SENSE OF RESPONSIBILITY IN YOU TO TAKE CARE OF THE PUPPIES.
GROW UP.

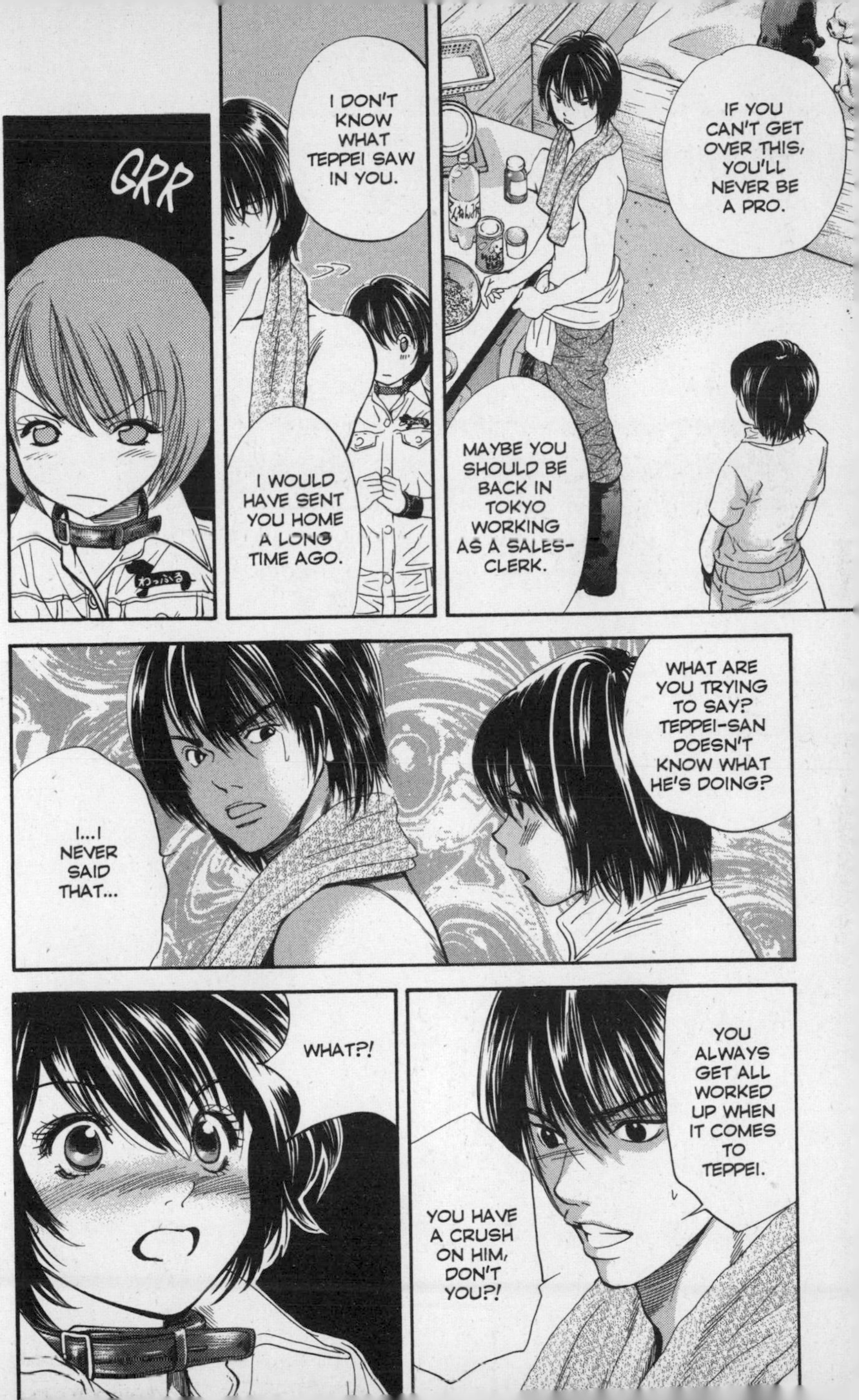
IF YOU CAN'T GET OVER THIS, YOU'LL NEVER BE A PRO.
MAYBE YOU SHOULD BE BACK IN TOKYO WORKING AS A SALES-CLERK.
I DON'T KNOW WHAT TEPPEI SAW IN YOU.
I WOULD HAVE SENT YOU HOME A LONG TIME AGO.
GRR
WHAT ARE YOU TRYING TO SAY? TEPPEI-SAN DOESN'T KNOW WHAT HE'S DOING?
I...I NEVER SAID THAT...
YOU ALWAYS GET ALL WORKED UP WHEN IT COMES TO TEPPEI.
YOU HAVE A CRUSH ON HIM, DON'T YOU?!
WHAT?!

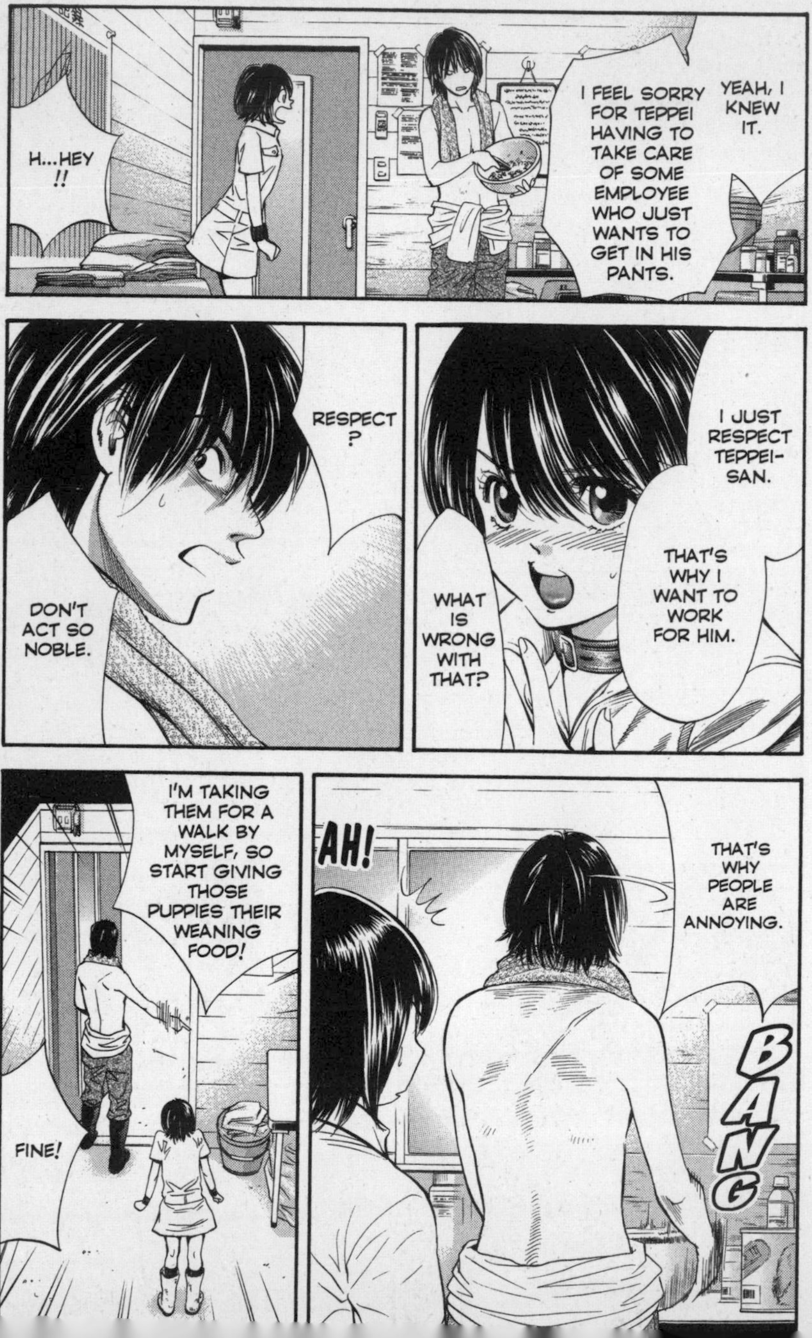
YEAH, I KNEW IT.
I FEEL SORRY FOR TEPPEI HAVING TO TAKE CARE OF SOME EMPLOYEE WHO JUST WANTS TO GET IN HIS PANTS.
H...HEY!!
I JUST RESPECT TEPPEI-SAN.
THAT'S WHY I WANT TO WORK FOR HIM.
WHAT IS WRONG WITH THAT?
RESPECT?
DON'T ACT SO NOBLE.
THAT'S WHY PEOPLE ARE ANNOYING.
AH!
BANG
I'M TAKING THEM FOR A WALK BY MYSELF, SO START GIVING THOSE PUPPIES THEIR WEANING FOOD!
FINE!

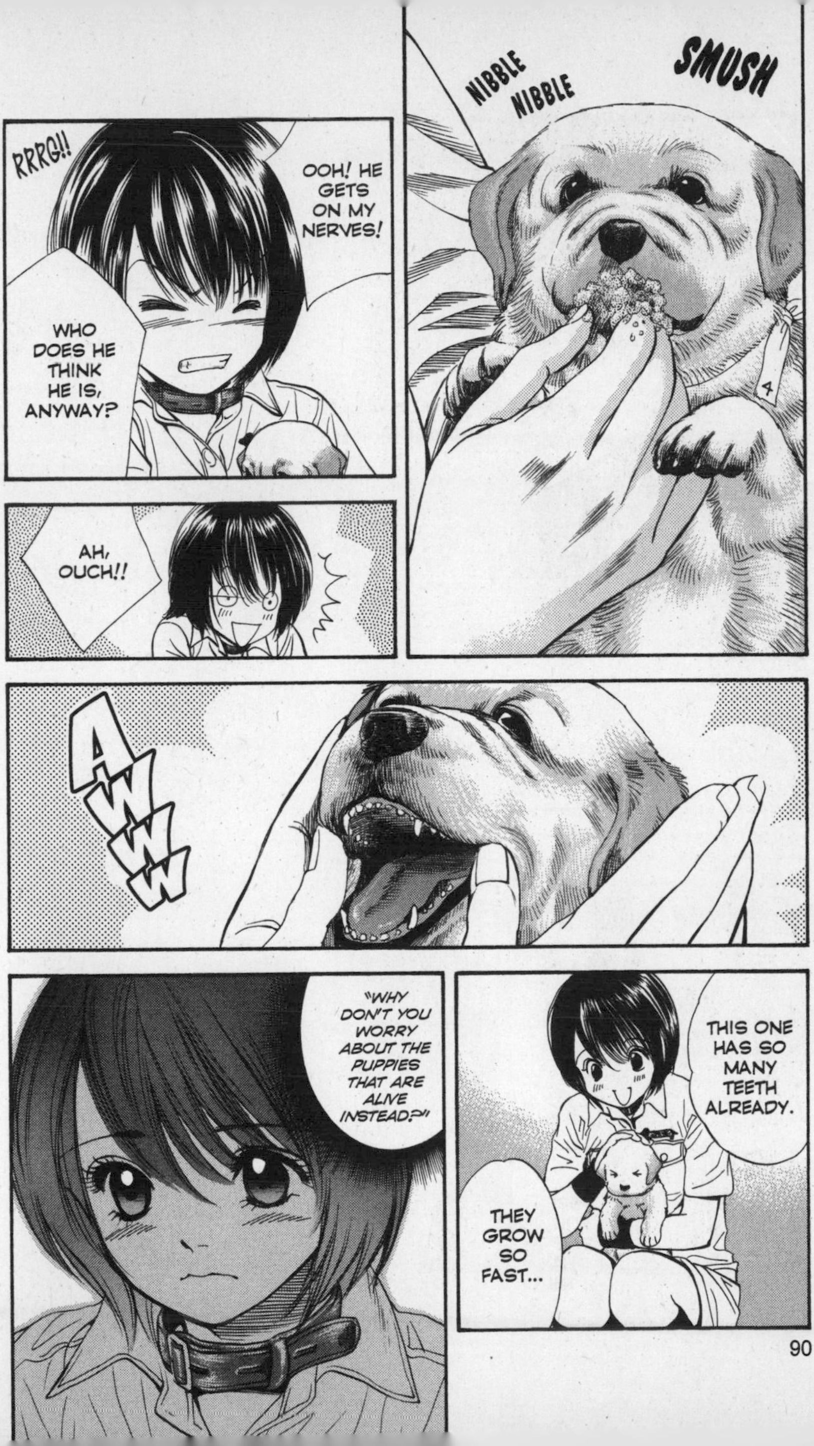
SMUSH
NIBBLE NIBBLE
OOH! HE GETS ON MY NERVES!
RRRG!!
WHO DOES HE THINK HE IS, ANYWAY?
AH, OUCH!!
AWWW
THIS ONE HAS SO MANY TEETH ALREADY.
THEY GROW SO FAST...
"WHY DON'T YOU WORRY ABOUT THE PUPPIES THAT ARE ALIVE INSTEAD?"

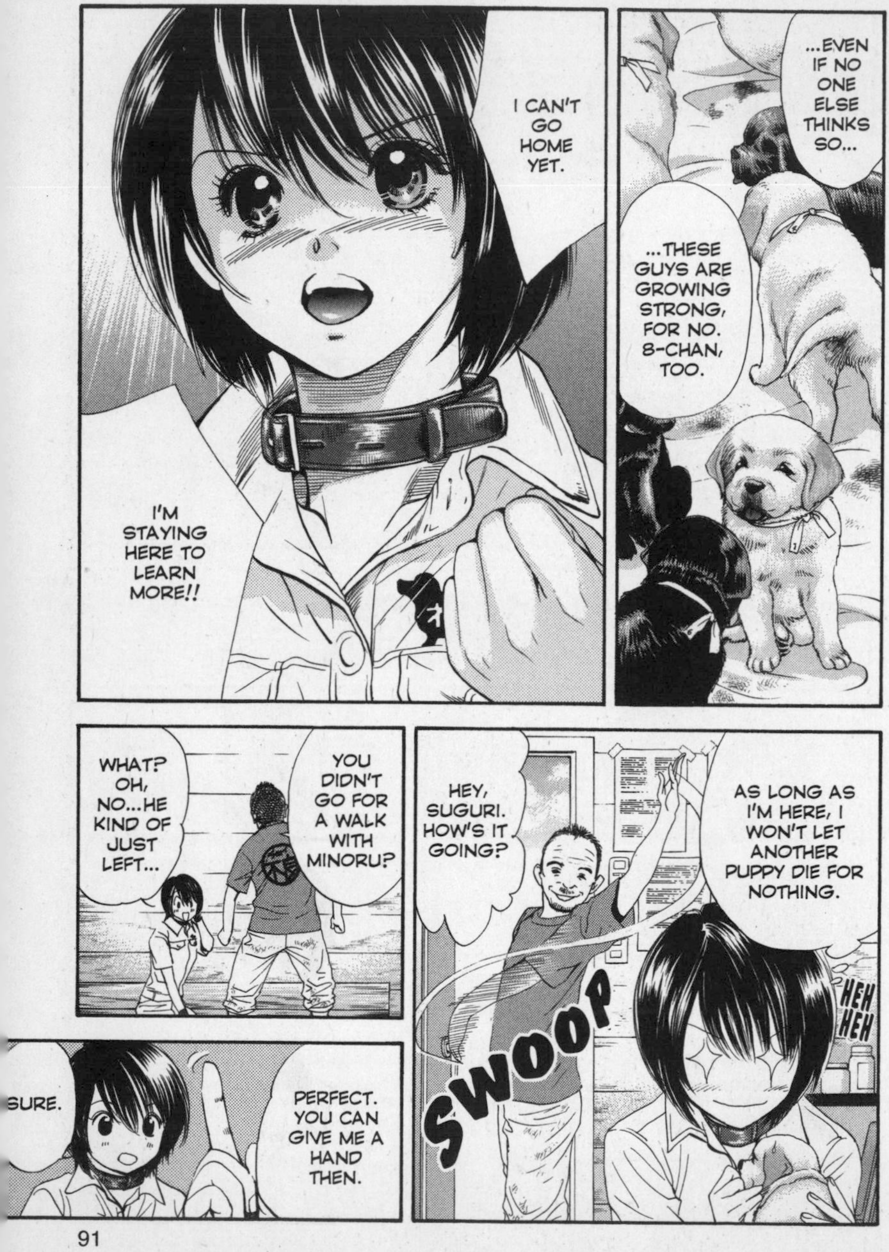
...EVEN IF NO ONE ELSE THINKS SO...
...THESE GUYS ARE GROWING STRONG, FOR NO. 8-CHAN, TOO.
I CAN'T GO HOME YET.
I'M STAYING HERE TO LEARN MORE!!
AS LONG AS I'M HERE, I WON'T LET ANOTHER PUPPY DIE FOR NOTHING.
HEH HEH
HEY, SUGURI. HOW'S IT GOING?
SWOOP
YOU DIDN'T GO FOR A WALK WITH MINORU?
WHAT? OH, NO...HE KIND OF JUST LEFT...
PERFECT. YOU CAN GIVE ME A HAND THEN.
SURE.

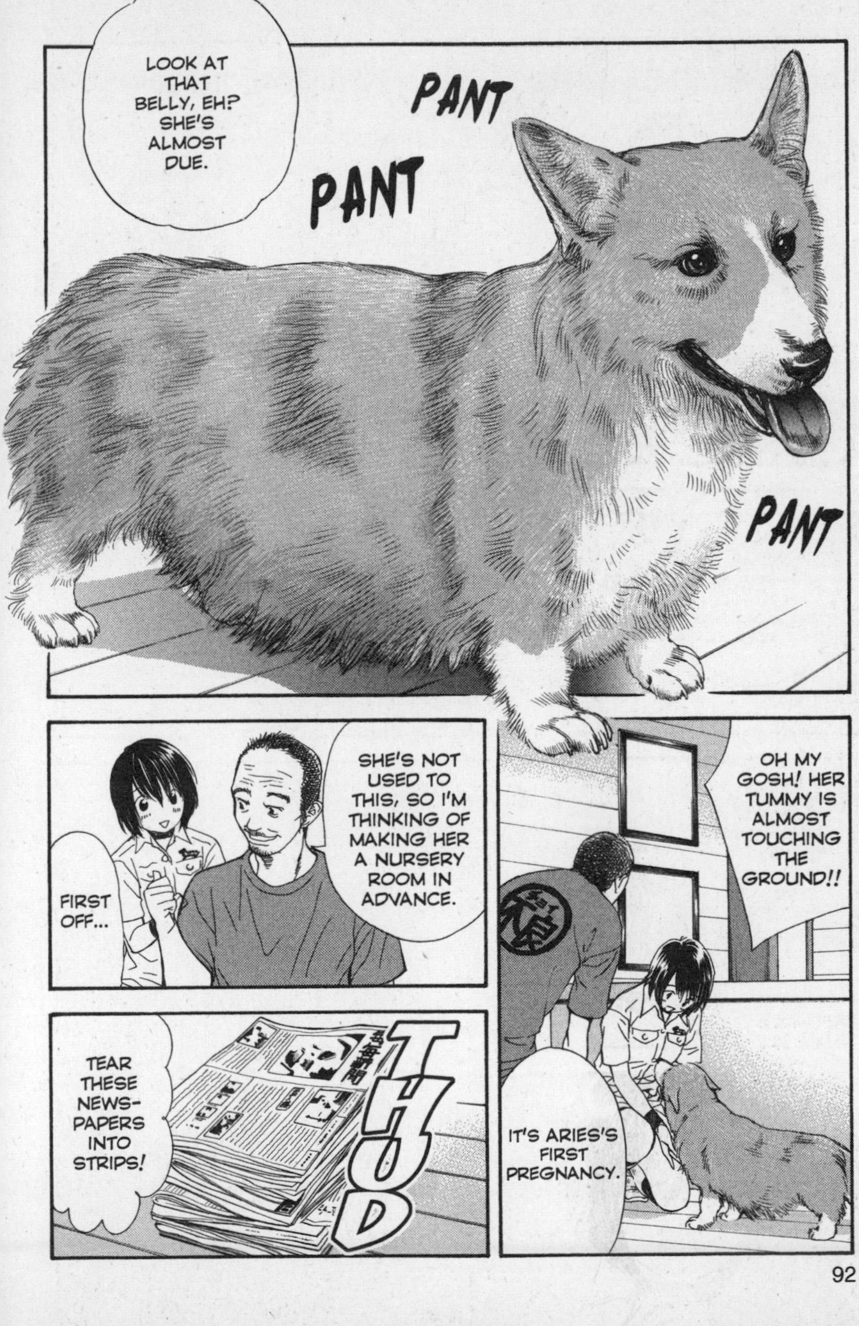
LOOK AT THAT BELLY, EH? SHE'S ALMOST DUE.
PANT
PANT
PANT
OH MY GOSH! HER TUMMY IS ALMOST TOUCHING THE GROUND!!
IT'S ARIES'S FIRST PREGNANCY.
SHE'S NOT USED TO THIS, SO I'M THINKING OF MAKING HER A NURSERY ROOM IN ADVANCE.
FIRST OFF...
THUD
TEAR THESE NEWS-PAPERS INTO STRIPS!

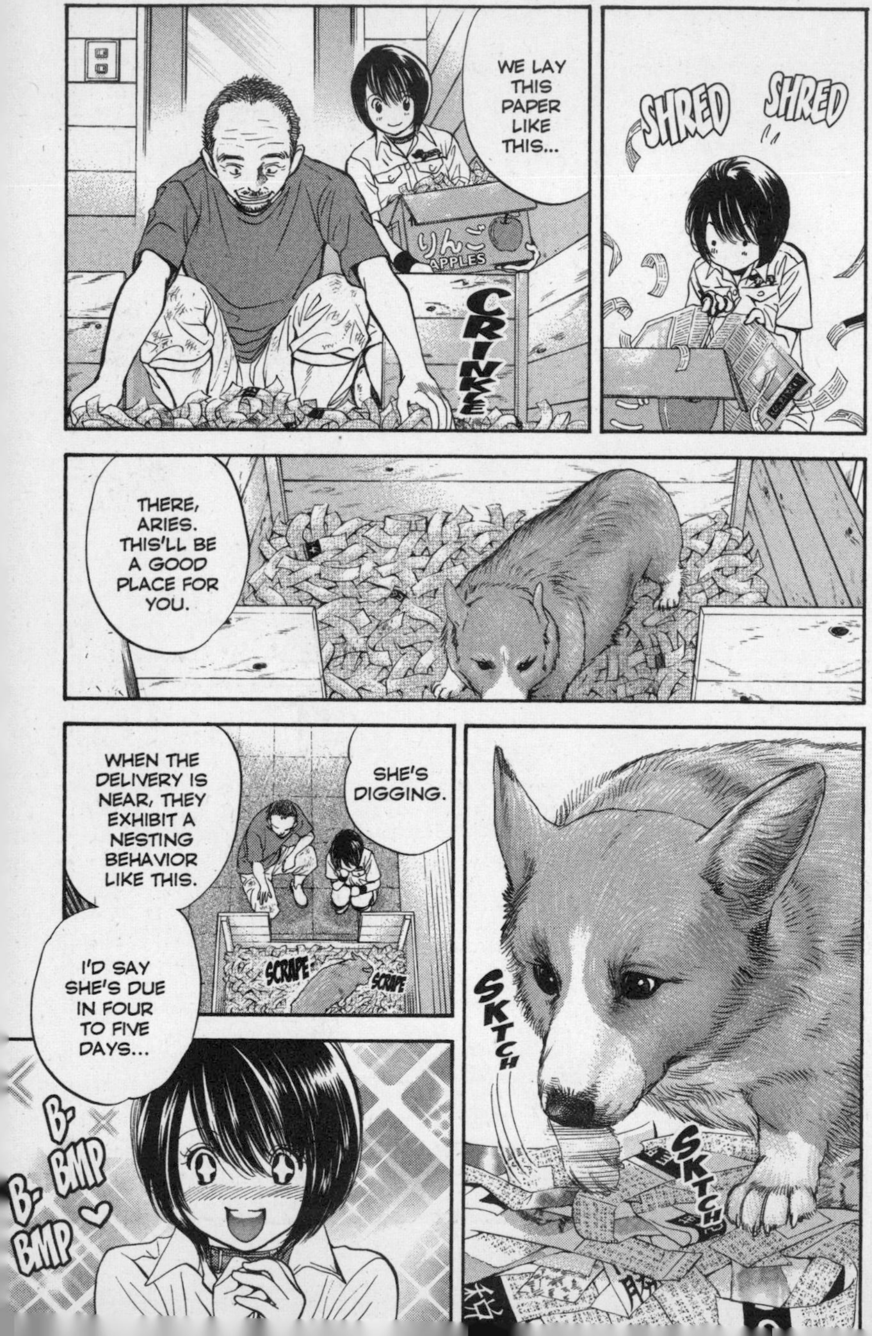
SHRED
SHRED
WE LAY THIS PAPER LIKE THIS...
りんご
APPLES
THERE, ARIES. THIS'LL BE A GOOD PLACE FOR YOU.
SKTCH
SKTCH
SHE'S DIGGING.
WHEN THE DELIVERY IS NEAR, THEY EXHIBIT A NESTING BEHAVIOR LIKE THIS.
SCRAPE
SCRAPE
I'D SAY SHE'S DUE IN FOUR TO FIVE DAYS...
B-BMP
B-BMP

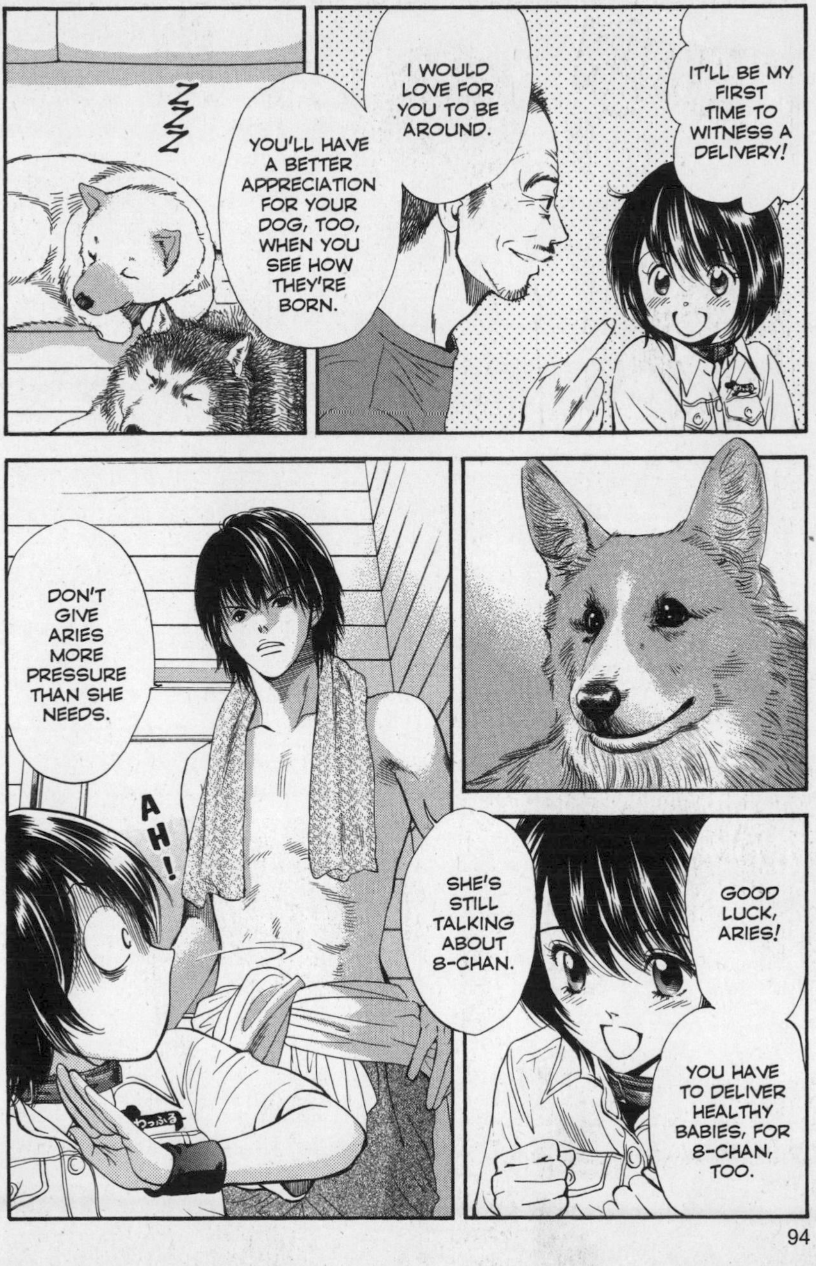
IT'LL BE MY FIRST TIME TO WITNESS A DELIVERY!
I WOULD LOVE FOR YOU TO BE AROUND.
YOU'LL HAVE A BETTER APPRECIATION FOR YOUR DOG, TOO, WHEN YOU SEE HOW THEY'RE BORN.
ZZZ
GOOD LUCK, ARIES!
YOU HAVE TO DELIVER HEALTHY BABIES, FOR 8-CHAN, TOO.
DON'T GIVE ARIES MORE PRESSURE THAN SHE NEEDS.
AH!
SHE'S STILL TALKING ABOUT 8-CHAN.

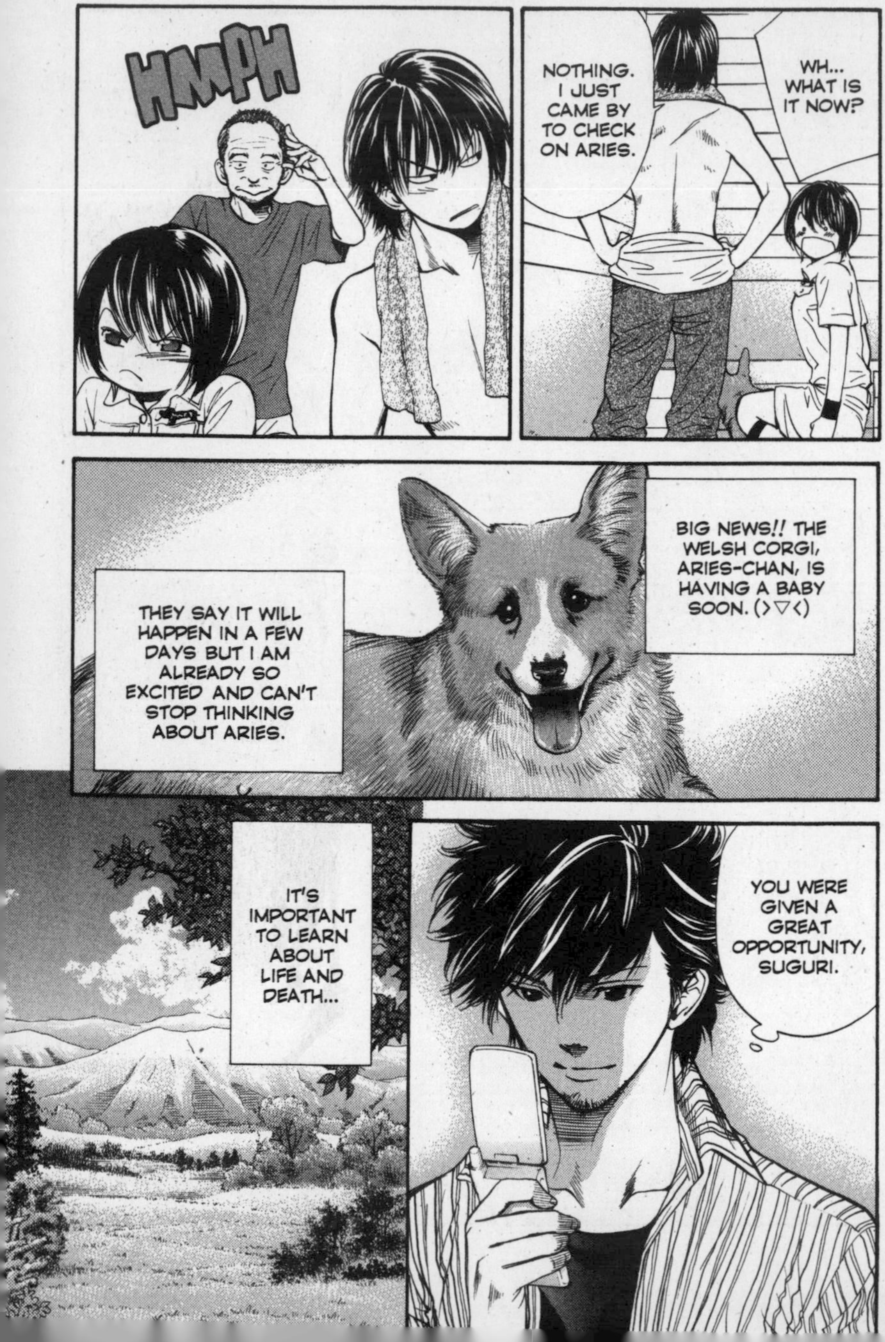
WH... WHAT IS IT NOW?
NOTHING. I JUST CAME BY TO CHECK ON ARIES.
HMPH
BIG NEWS!! THE WELSH CORGI, ARIES-CHAN, IS HAVING A BABY SOON. (>▽<)
THEY SAY IT WILL HAPPEN IN A FEW DAYS BUT I AM ALREADY SO EXCITED AND CAN'T STOP THINKING ABOUT ARIES.
YOU WERE GIVEN A GREAT OPPORTUNITY, SUGURI.
IT'S IMPORTANT TO LEARN ABOUT LIFE AND DEATH...

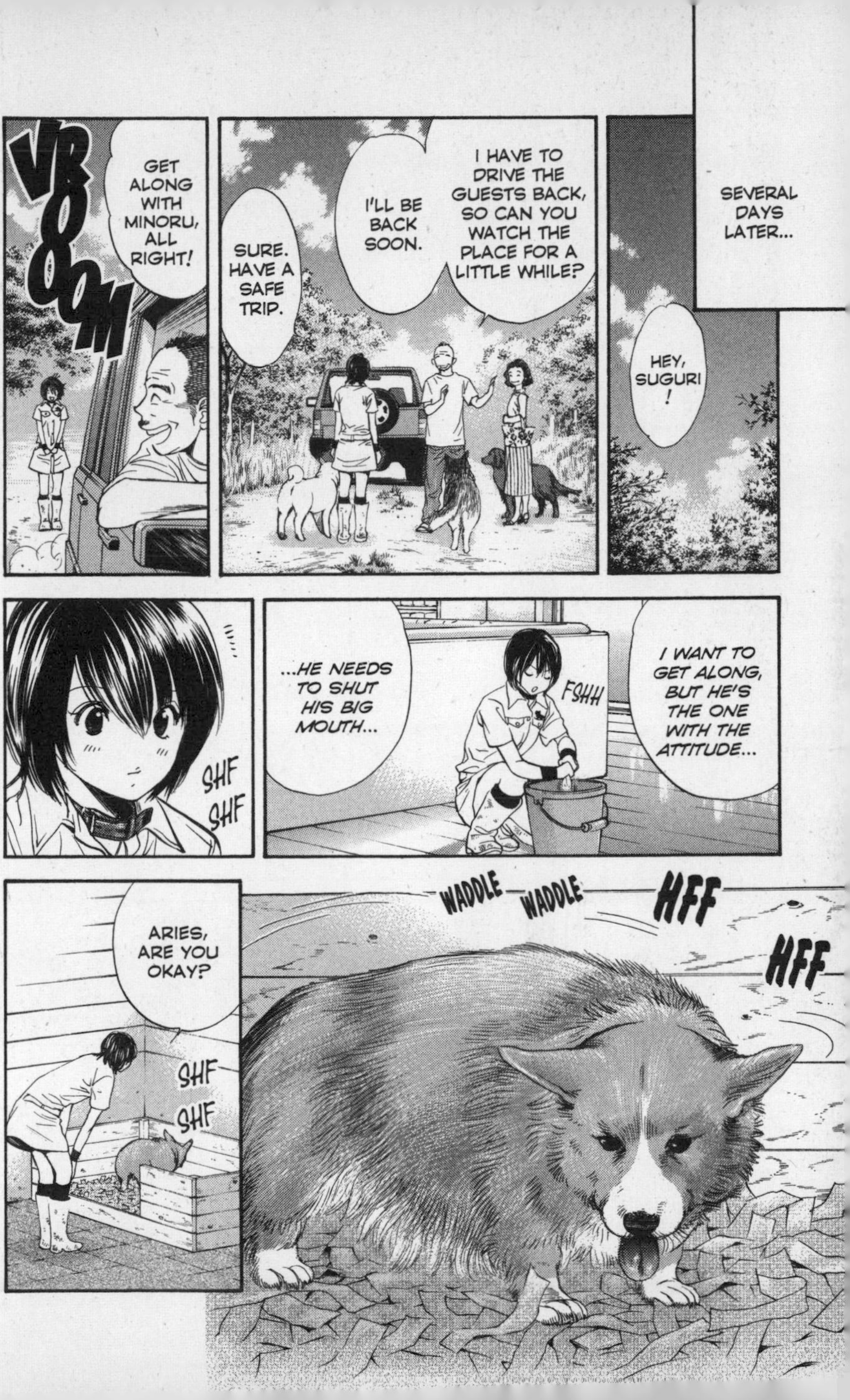
SEVERAL DAYS LATER...
HEY, SUGURI!
I HAVE TO DRIVE THE GUESTS BACK, SO CAN YOU WATCH THE PLACE FOR A LITTLE WHILE?
I'LL BE BACK SOON.
SURE. HAVE A SAFE TRIP.
GET ALONG WITH MINORU, ALL RIGHT!
VROOOM
I WANT TO GET ALONG, BUT HE'S THE ONE WITH THE ATTITUDE...
FSHH
...HE NEEDS TO SHUT HIS BIG MOUTH...
SHF SHF
WADDLE WADDLE
HFF
HFF
ARIES, ARE YOU OKAY?
SHF SHF

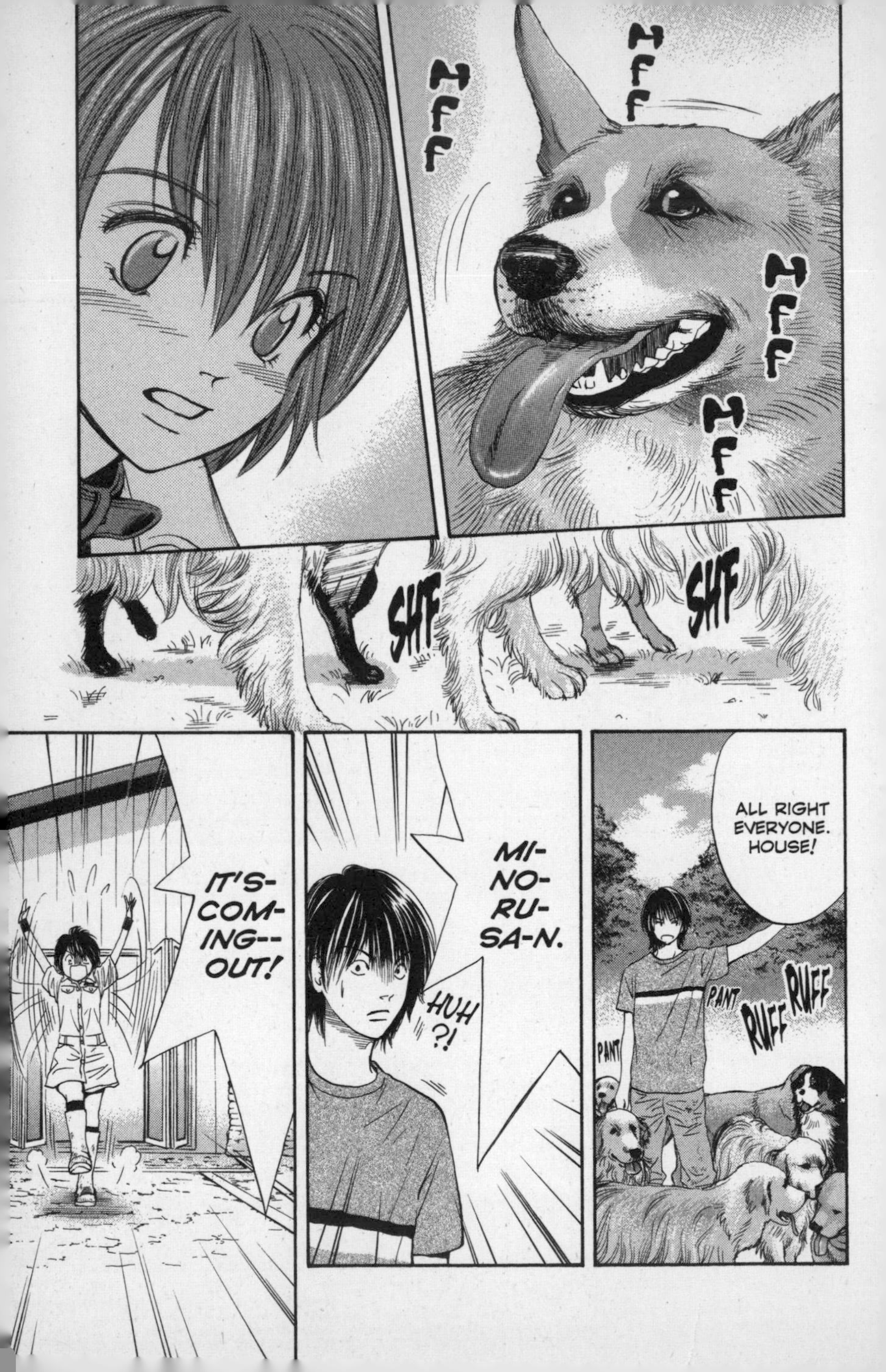
HFF HFF
HFF HFF
HFF HFF
HFF HFF
SHF
SHF
ALL RIGHT EVERYONE. HOUSE!
RUFF RUFF
PANT
RUFF
PANT
MI-NO-RU-SA-N.
HUH?!
IT'S-COMING--OUT!

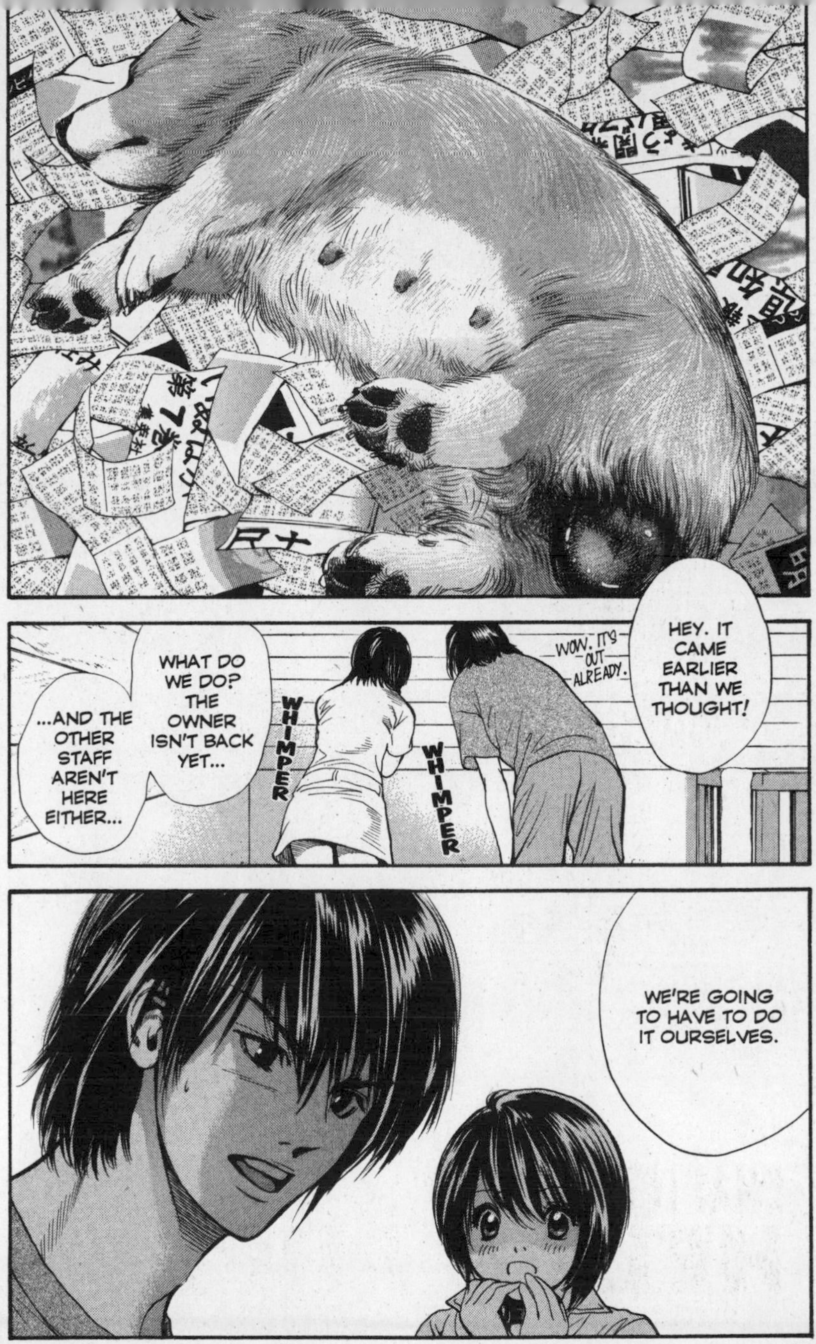

HEY. IT CAME EARLIER THAN WE THOUGHT!
WOW. IT'S OUT ALREADY.
WHIMPER
WHIMPER
WHAT DO WE DO? THE OWNER ISN'T BACK YET...
...AND THE OTHER STAFF AREN'T HERE EITHER...
WE'RE GOING TO HAVE TO DO IT OURSELVES.

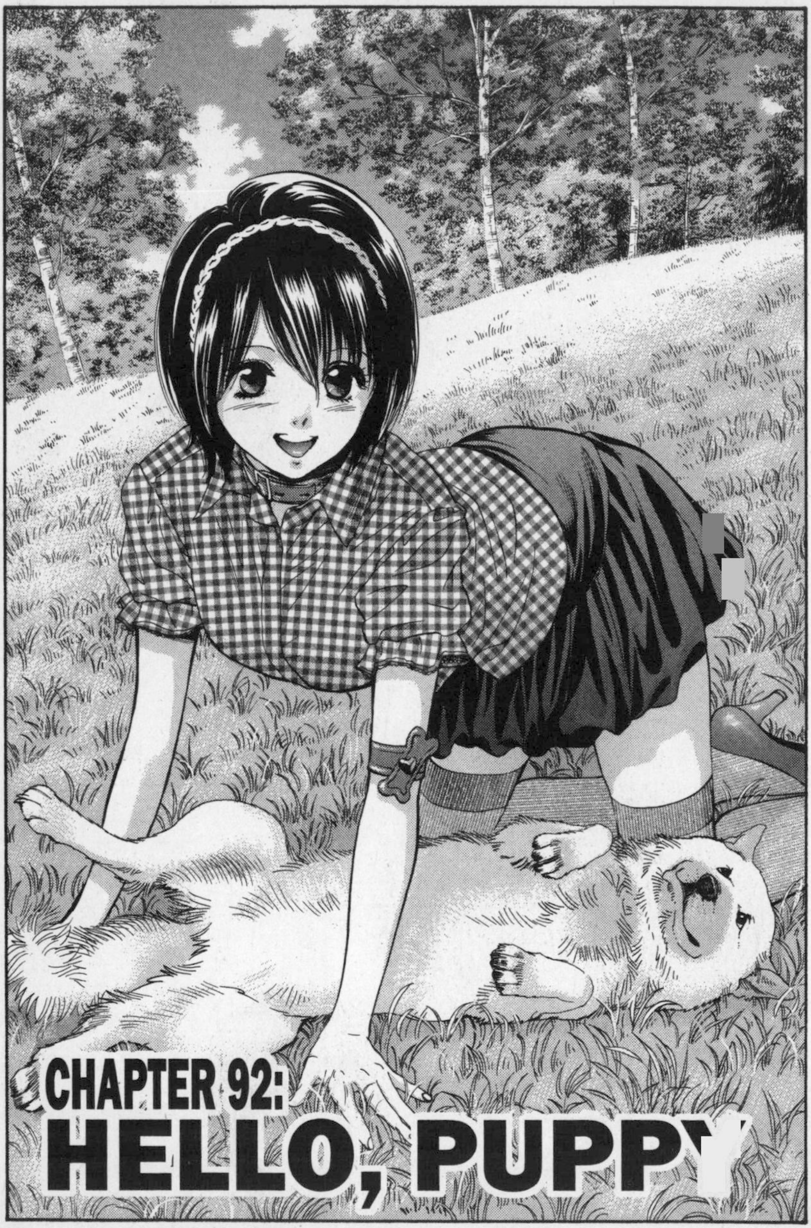
CHAPTER 92:
HELLO, PUPPY

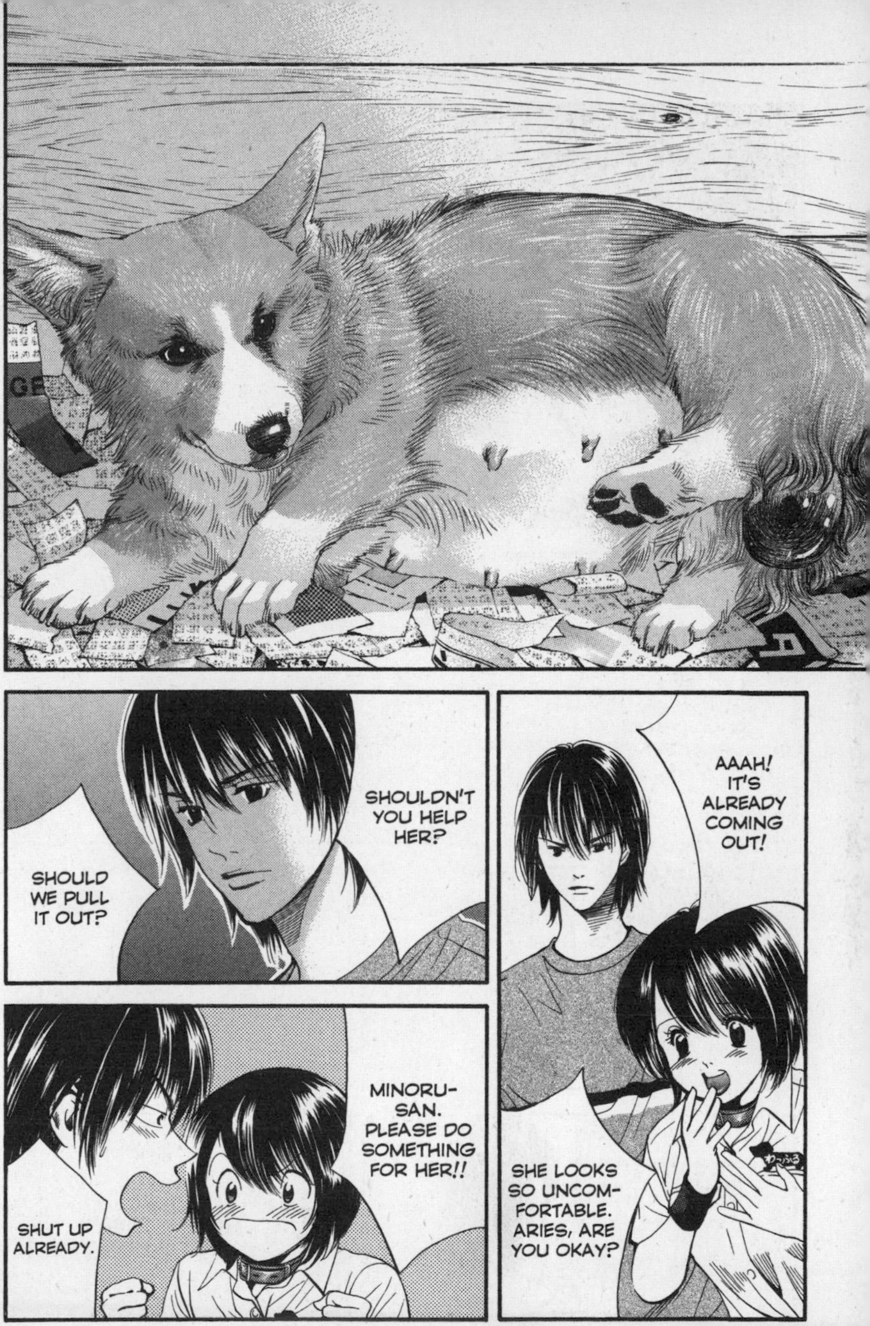
AAAH! IT'S ALREADY COMING OUT!
SHE LOOKS SO UNCOMFORTABLE. ARIES, ARE YOU OKAY?
SHOULDN'T YOU HELP HER?
SHOULD WE PULL IT OUT?
MINORU-SAN. PLEASE DO SOMETHING FOR HER!!
SHUT UP ALREADY.

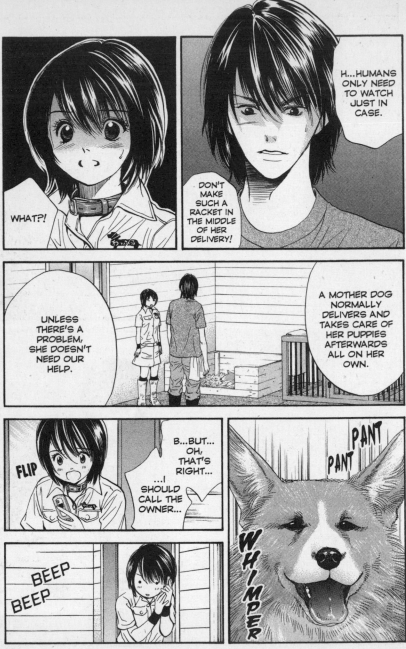

H...HUMANS ONLY NEED TO WATCH JUST IN CASE.
DON'T MAKE SUCH A RACKET IN THE MIDDLE OF HER DELIVERY!
WHAT?!
A MOTHER DOG NORMALLY DELIVERS AND TAKES CARE OF HER PUPPIES AFTERWARDS ALL ON HER OWN.
UNLESS THERE'S A PROBLEM, SHE DOESN'T NEED OUR HELP.
PANT
PANT
WHIMPER
B...BUT... OH, THAT'S RIGHT...
...I SHOULD CALL THE OWNER...
FLIP
BEEP
BEEP

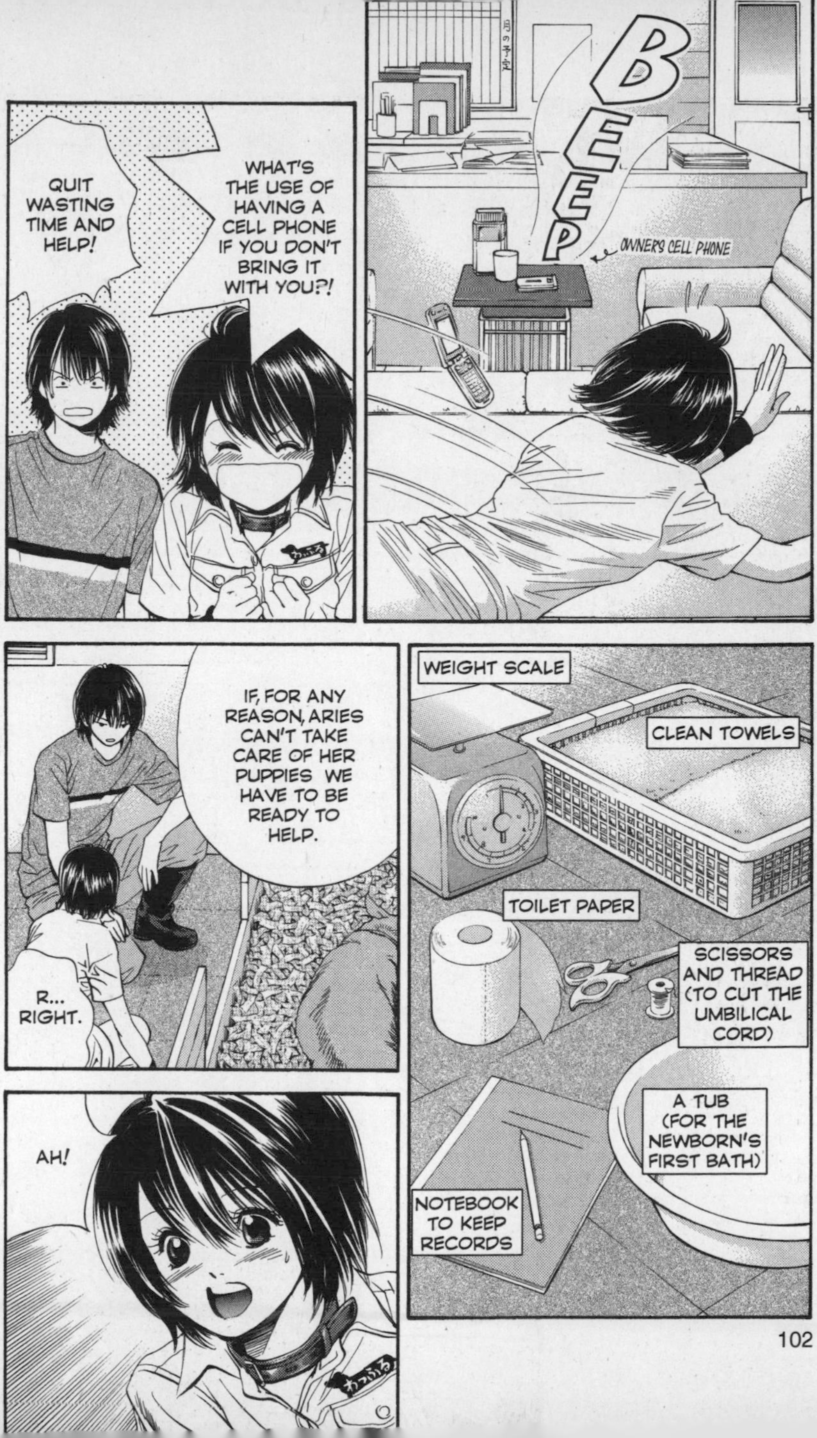
BEEP
OWNER'S CELL PHONE
WHAT'S THE USE OF HAVING A CELL PHONE IF YOU DON'T BRING IT WITH YOU?!
QUIT WASTING TIME AND HELP!
WEIGHT SCALE
CLEAN TOWELS
TOILET PAPER
SCISSORS AND THREAD (TO CUT THE UMBILICAL CORD)
A TUB (FOR THE NEWBORN'S FIRST BATH)
NOTEBOOK TO KEEP RECORDS
IF, FOR ANY REASON, ARIES CAN'T TAKE CARE OF HER PUPPIES WE HAVE TO BE READY TO HELP.
R... RIGHT.
AH!

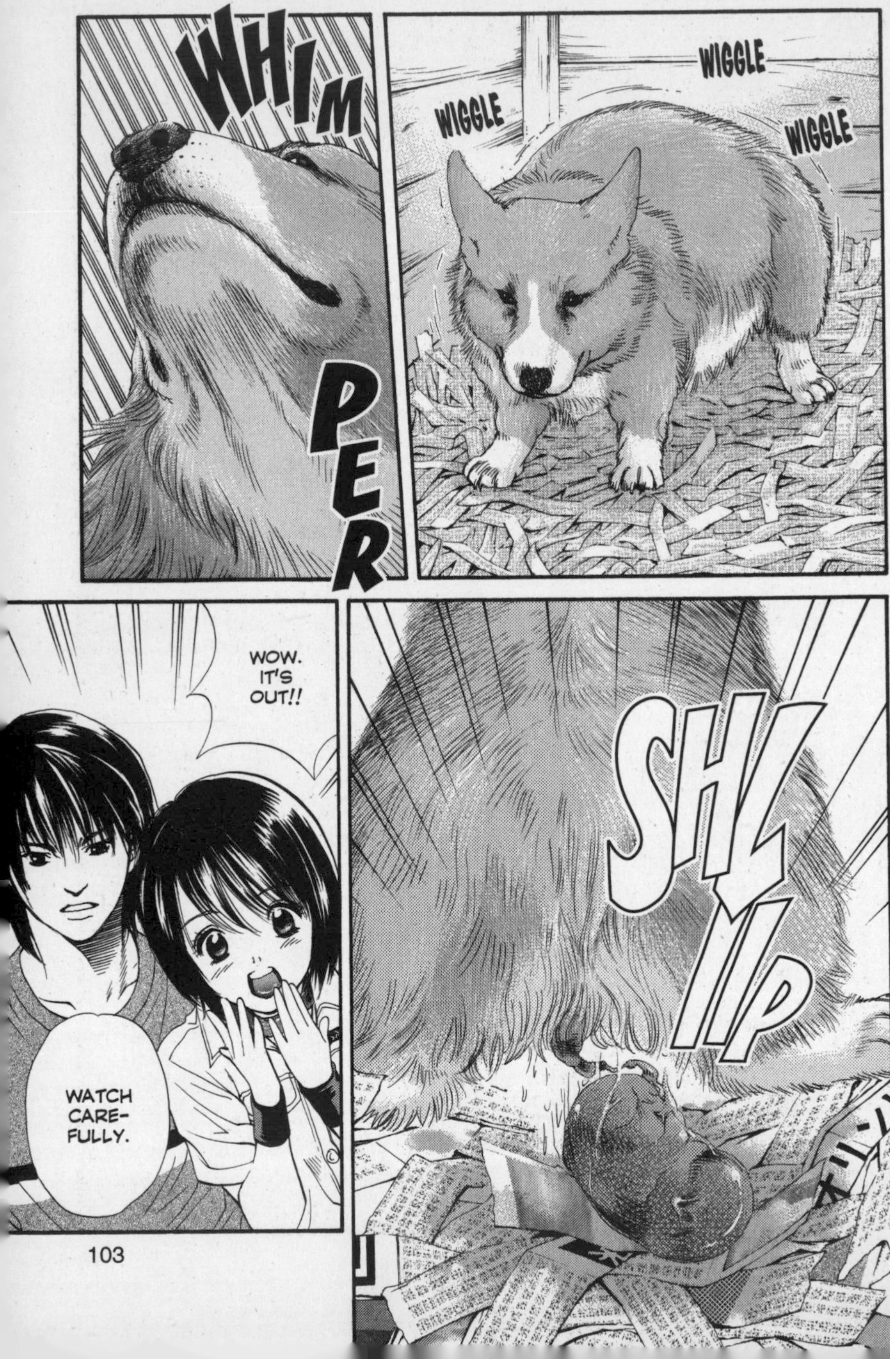
WIGGLE
WIGGLE
WIGGLE
WHIMPER
SHLUP
WOW. IT'S OUT!!
WATCH CARE-FULLY.

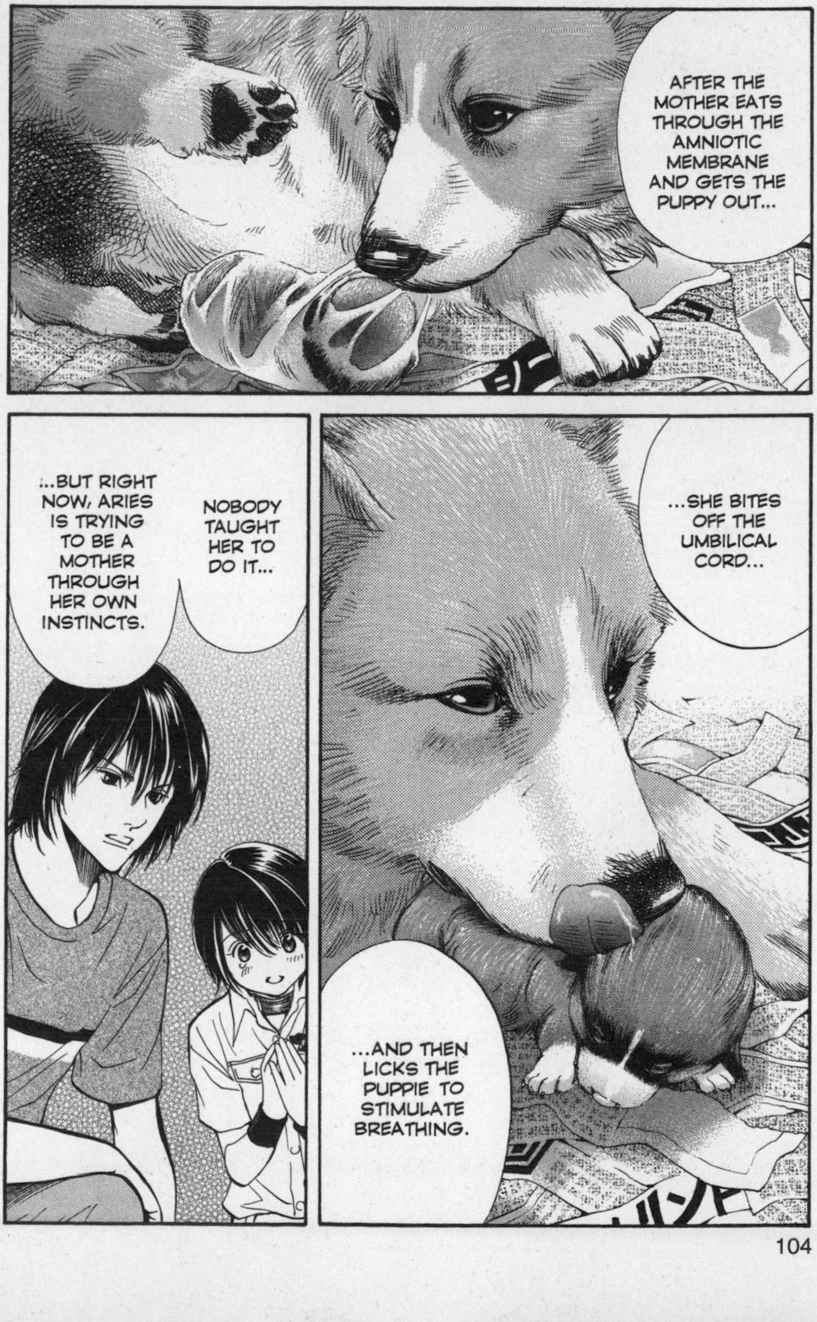
AFTER THE MOTHER EATS THROUGH THE AMNIOTIC MEMBRANE AND GETS THE PUPPY OUT...
...SHE BITES OFF THE UMBILICAL CORD...
...AND THEN LICKS THE PUPPIE TO STIMULATE BREATHING.
NOBODY TAUGHT HER TO DO IT...
...BUT RIGHT NOW, ARIES IS TRYING TO BE A MOTHER THROUGH HER OWN INSTINCTS.

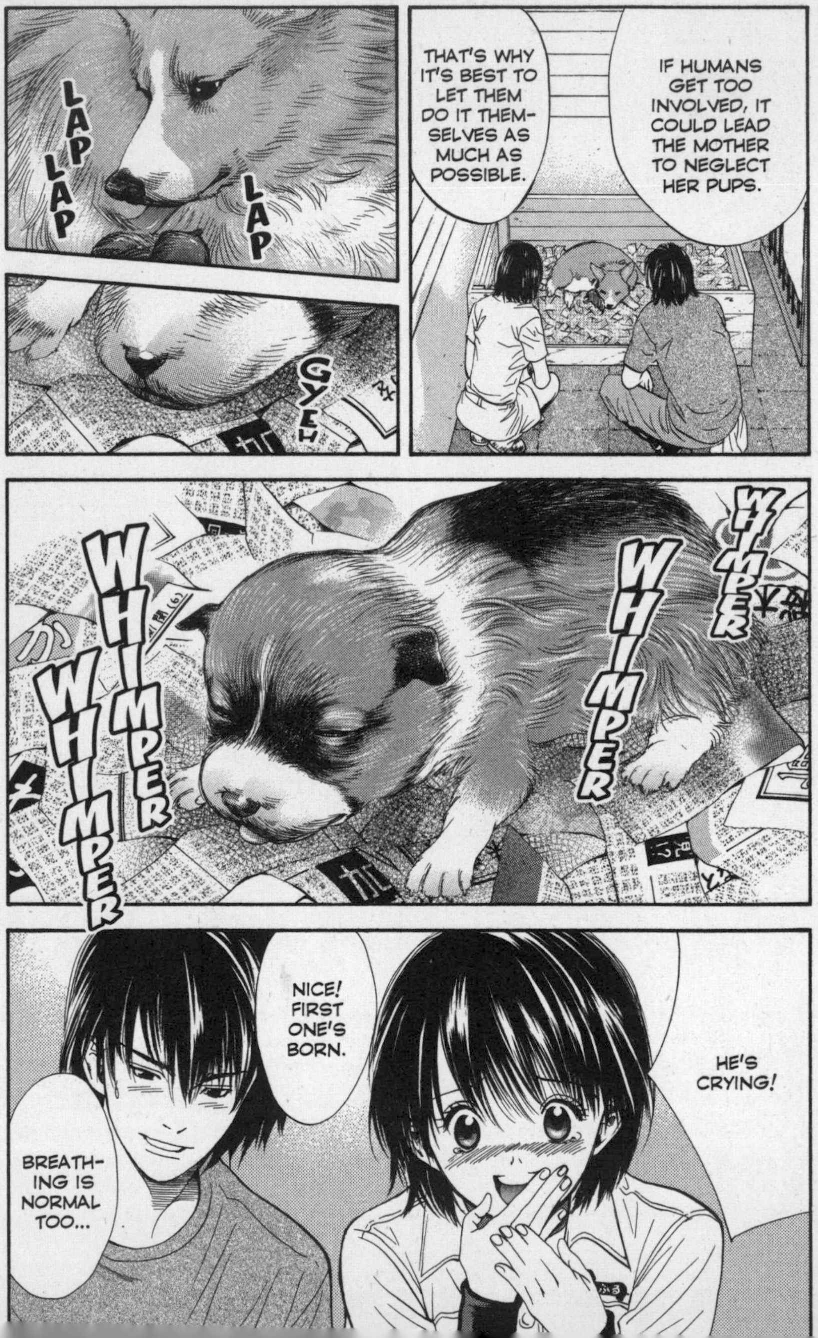
IF HUMANS GET TOO INVOLVED, IT COULD LEAD THE MOTHER TO NEGLECT HER PUPS.
THAT'S WHY IT'S BEST TO LET THEM DO IT THEMSELVES AS MUCH AS POSSIBLE.
LAP
LAP
LAP
GYEH
WHIMPER
WHIMPER
WHIMPER
WHIMPER
HE'S CRYING!
NICE! FIRST ONE'S BORN.
BREATHING IS NORMAL TOO...

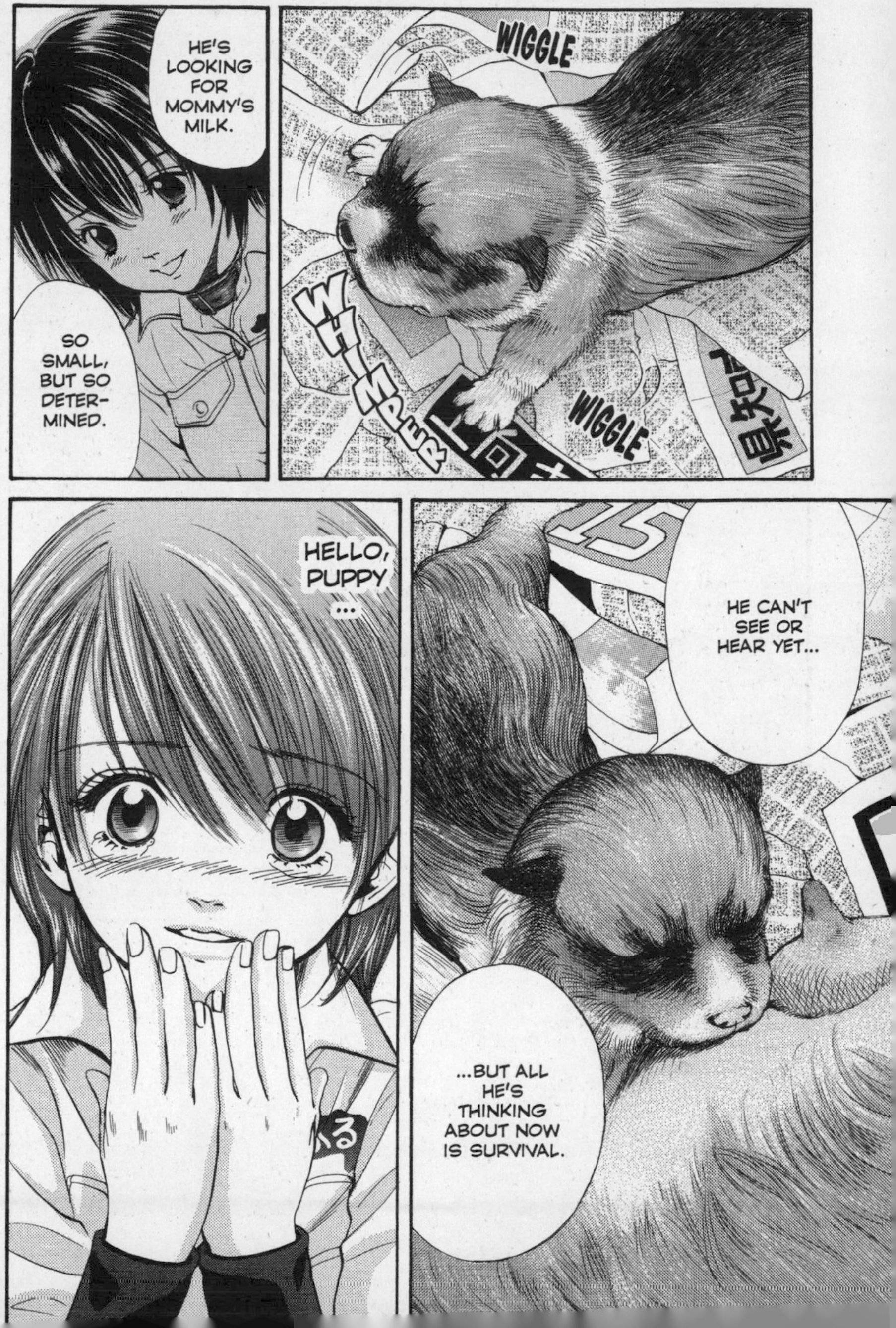
WIGGLE
WIGGLE
WHIMPER
HE'S LOOKING FOR MOMMY'S MILK.
SO SMALL, BUT SO DETERMINED.
HE CAN'T SEE OR HEAR YET...
...BUT ALL HE'S THINKING ABOUT NOW IS SURVIVAL.
HELLO, PUPPY ...

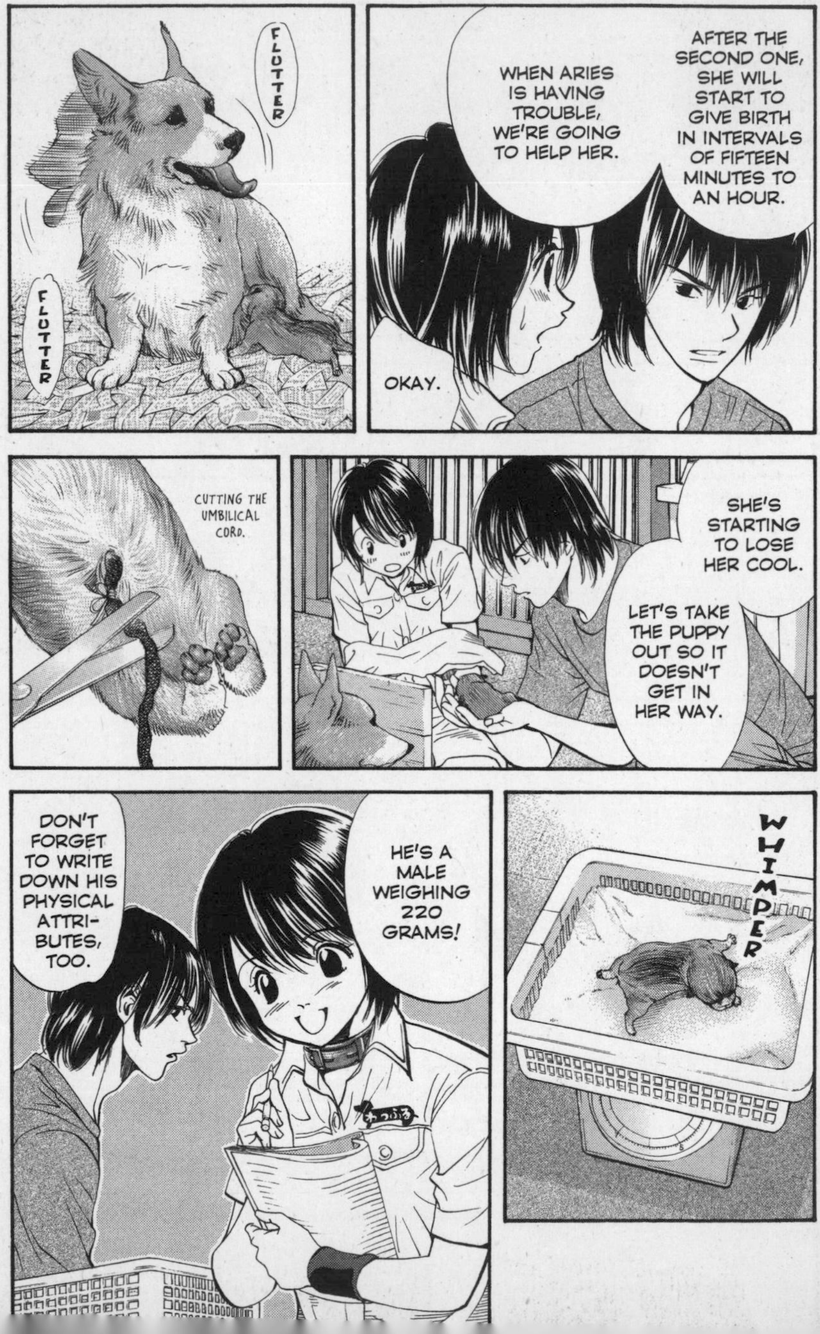
AFTER THE SECOND ONE, SHE WILL START TO GIVE BIRTH IN INTERVALS OF FIFTEEN MINUTES TO AN HOUR.
WHEN ARIES IS HAVING TROUBLE, WE'RE GOING TO HELP HER.
OKAY.
FLUTTER
FLUTTER
SHE'S STARTING TO LOSE HER COOL.
LET'S TAKE THE PUPPY OUT SO IT DOESN'T GET IN HER WAY.
CUTTING THE UMBILICAL CORD.
WHIMPER
HE'S A MALE WEIGHING 220 GRAMS!
DON'T FORGET TO WRITE DOWN HIS PHYSICAL ATTRI-BUTES, TOO.

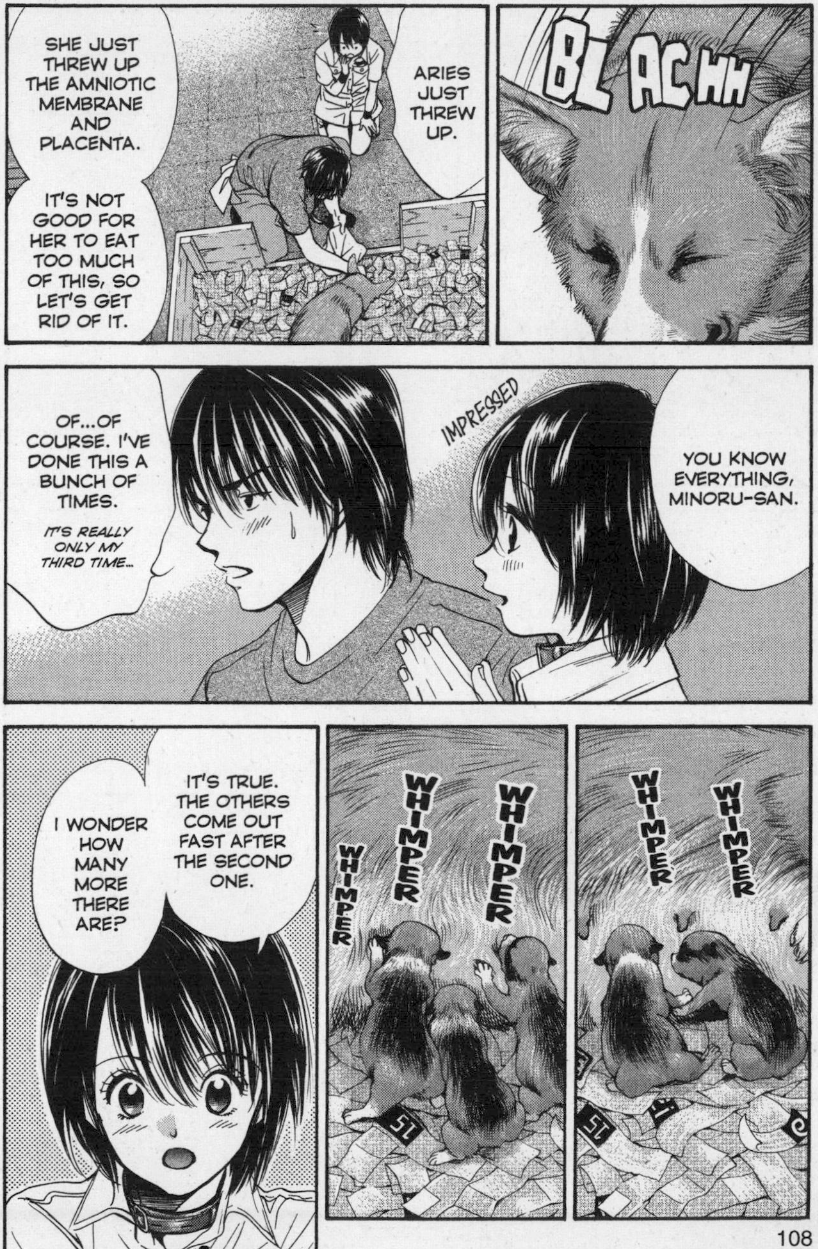
BLACHH
ARIES JUST THREW UP.
SHE JUST THREW UP THE AMNIOTIC MEMBRANE AND PLACENTA.
IT'S NOT GOOD FOR HER TO EAT TOO MUCH OF THIS, SO LET'S GET RID OF IT.
YOU KNOW EVERYTHING, MINORU-SAN.
IMPRESSED
OF...OF COURSE. I'VE DONE THIS A BUNCH OF TIMES.
IT'S REALLY ONLY MY THIRD TIME...
WHIMPER
WHIMPER
WHIMPER
WHIMPER
WHIMPER
IT'S TRUE. THE OTHERS COME OUT FAST AFTER THE SECOND ONE.
I WONDER HOW MANY MORE THERE ARE?

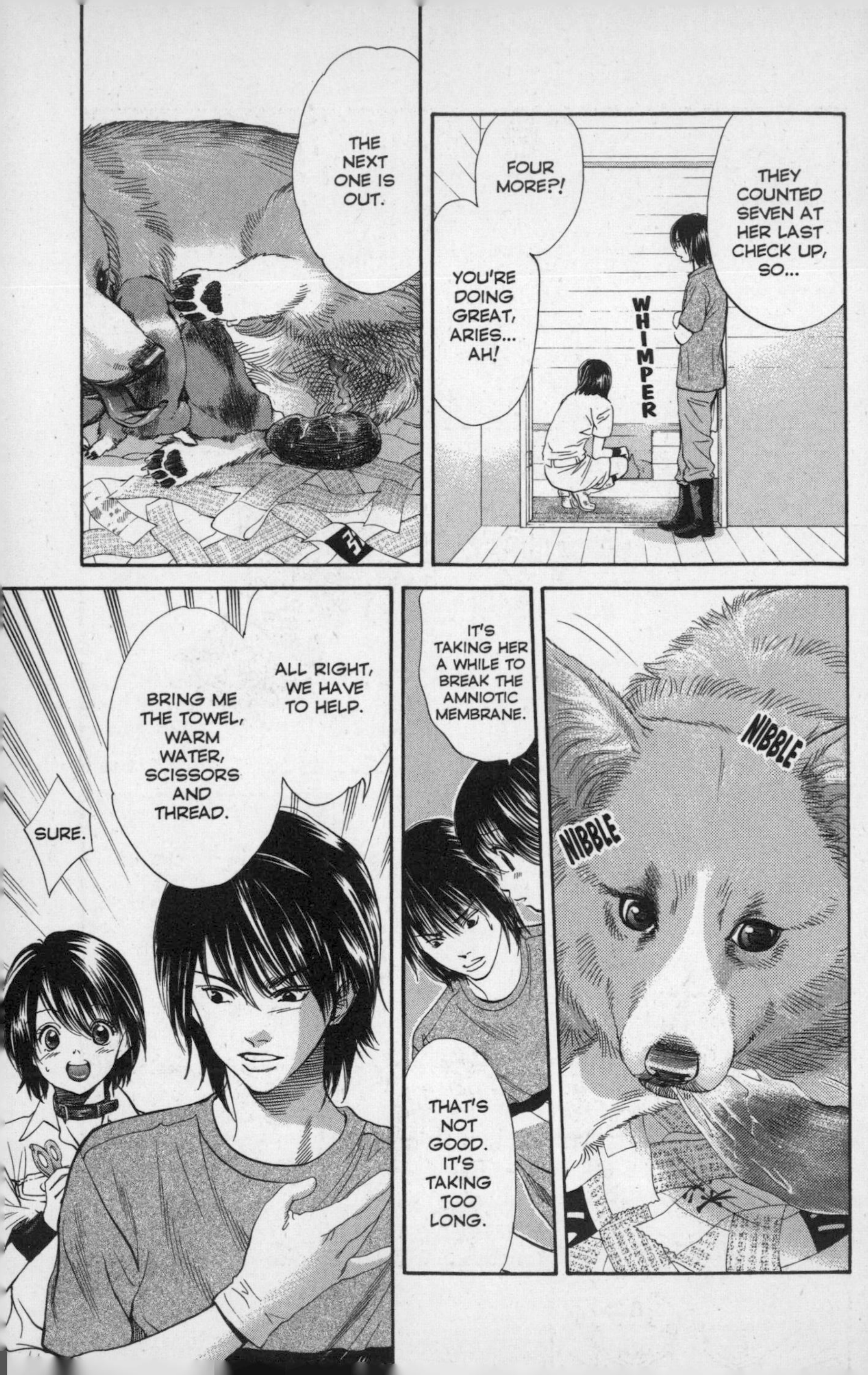
THEY COUNTED SEVEN AT HER LAST CHECK UP, SO...
FOUR MORE?!
YOU'RE DOING GREAT, ARIES... AH!
WHIMPER
THE NEXT ONE IS OUT.
NIBBLE
NIBBLE
IT'S TAKING HER A WHILE TO BREAK THE AMNIOTIC MEMBRANE.
THAT'S NOT GOOD. IT'S TAKING TOO LONG.
ALL RIGHT, WE HAVE TO HELP.
BRING ME THE TOWEL, WARM WATER, SCISSORS AND THREAD.
SURE.

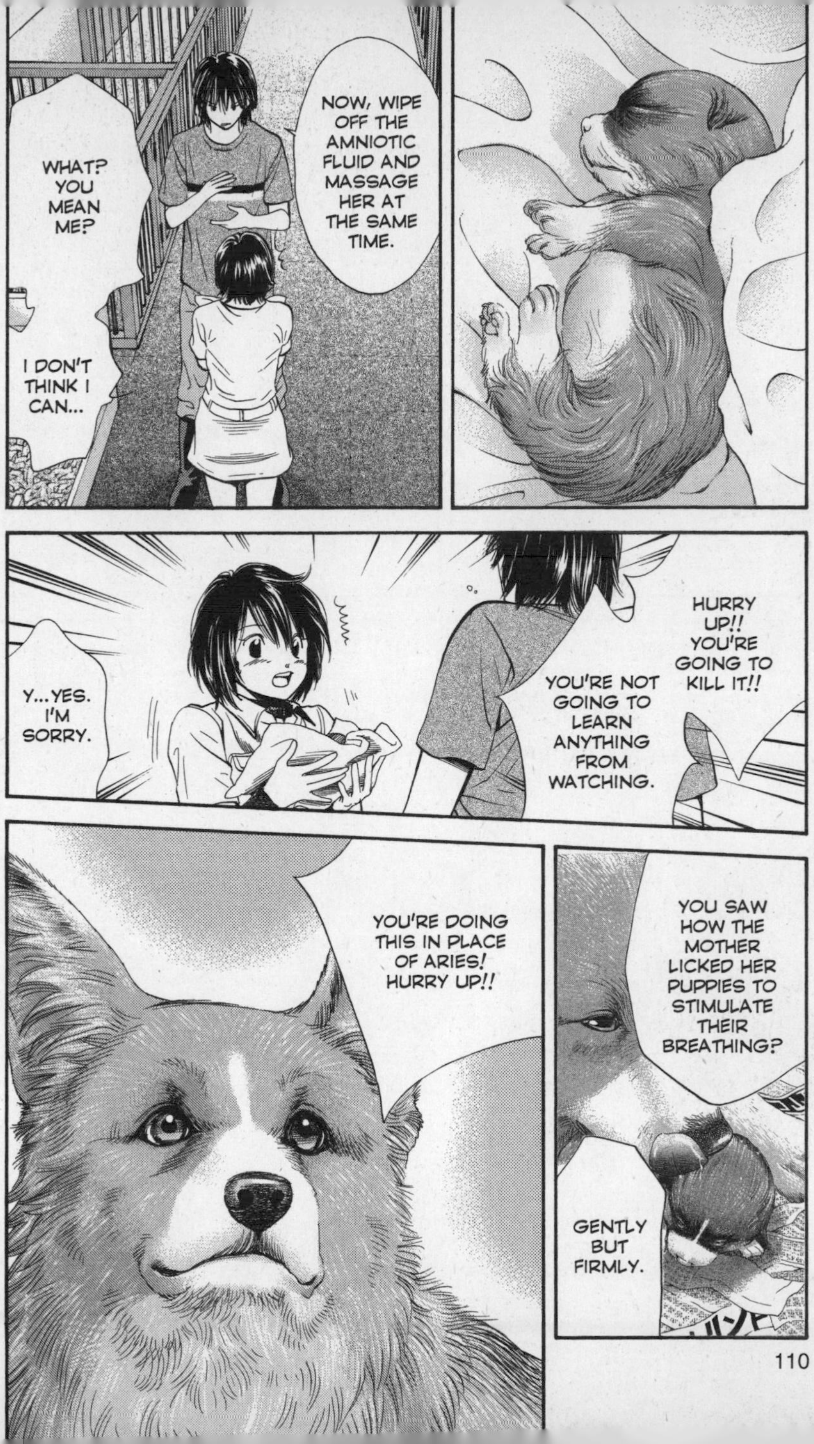
NOW, WIPE OFF THE AMNIOTIC FLUID AND MASSAGE HER AT THE SAME TIME.
WHAT? YOU MEAN ME?
I DON'T THINK I CAN...
HURRY UP!! YOU'RE GOING TO KILL IT!!
YOU'RE NOT GOING TO LEARN ANYTHING FROM WATCHING.
Y...YES. I'M SORRY.
YOU SAW HOW THE MOTHER LICKED HER PUPPIES TO STIMULATE THEIR BREATHING?
GENTLY BUT FIRMLY.
YOU'RE DOING THIS IN PLACE OF ARIES! HURRY UP!!

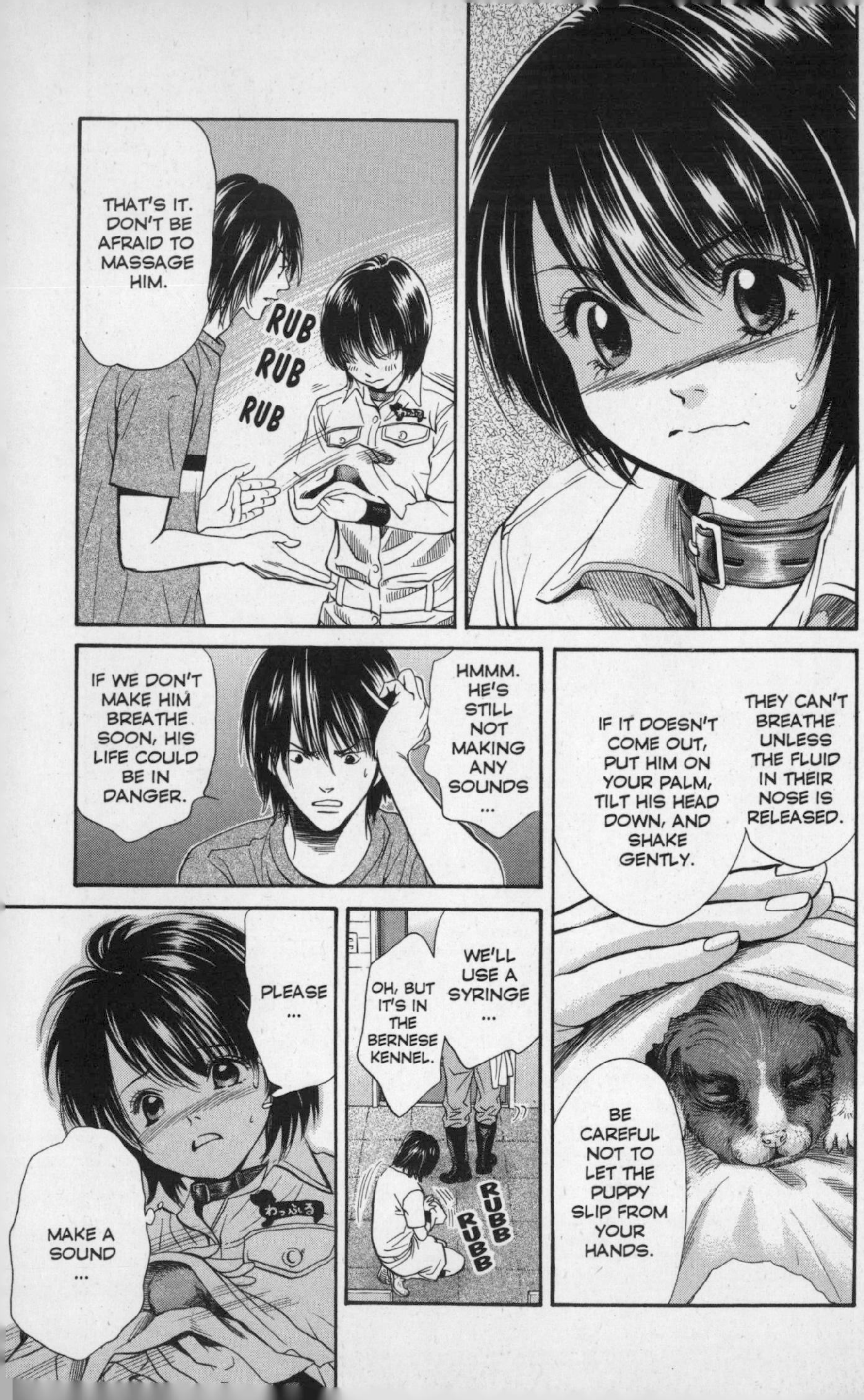
THAT'S IT. DON'T BE AFRAID TO MASSAGE HIM.
RUB RUB RUB
THEY CAN'T BREATHE UNLESS THE FLUID IN THEIR NOSE IS RELEASED.
IF IT DOESN'T COME OUT, PUT HIM ON YOUR PALM, TILT HIS HEAD DOWN, AND SHAKE GENTLY.
BE CAREFUL NOT TO LET THE PUPPY SLIP FROM YOUR HANDS.
HMMM. HE'S STILL NOT MAKING ANY SOUNDS ...
IF WE DON'T MAKE HIM BREATHE SOON, HIS LIFE COULD BE IN DANGER.
WE'LL USE A SYRINGE ...
OH, BUT IT'S IN THE BERNESE KENNEL.
RUBB RUBB
PLEASE ...
MAKE A SOUND ...

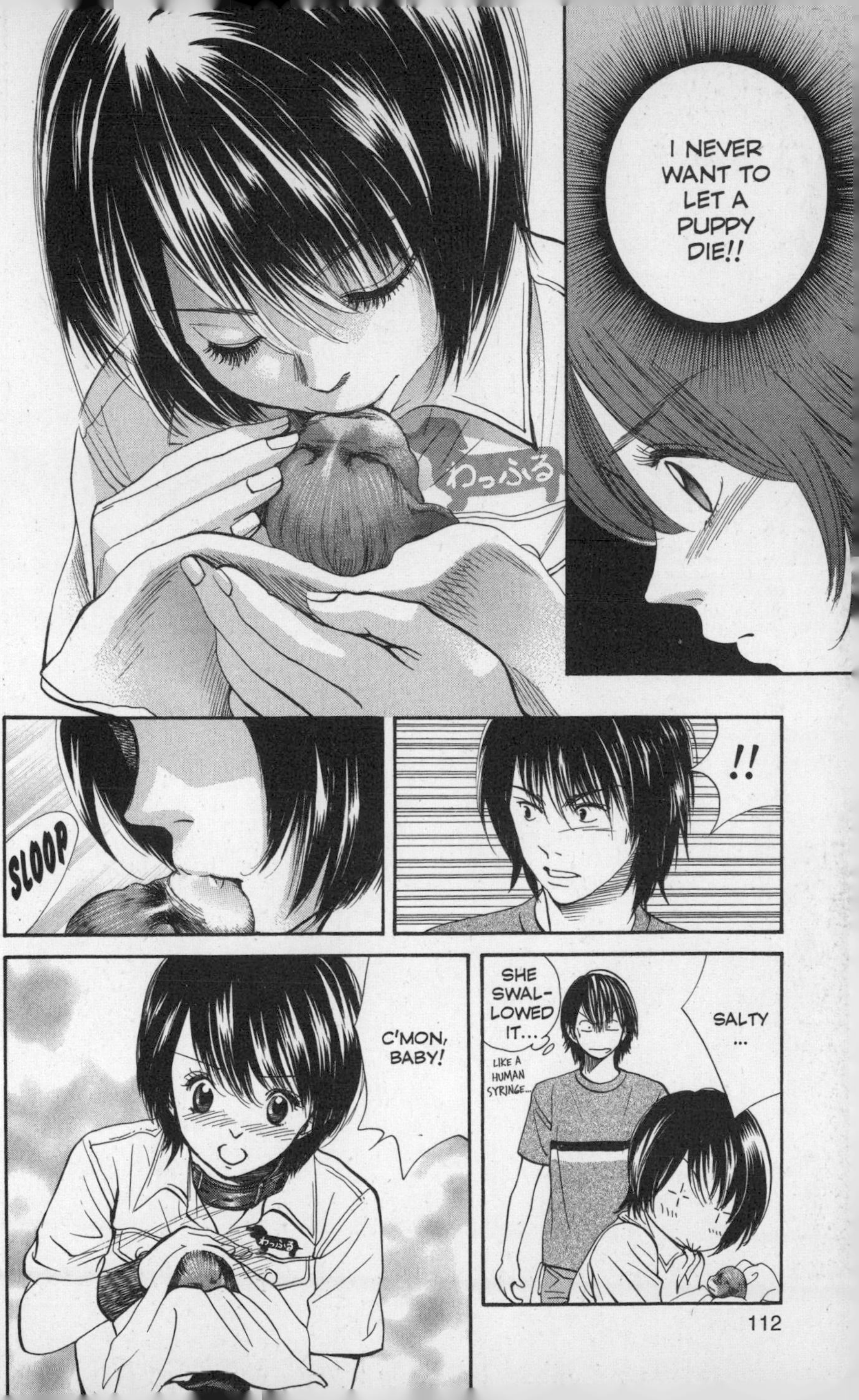
I NEVER WANT TO LET A PUPPY DIE!!
わっふる
!!
SLOOP
SALTY ...
SHE SWAL-LOWED IT...
LIKE A HUMAN SYRINGE...
C'MON, BABY!
わっふる

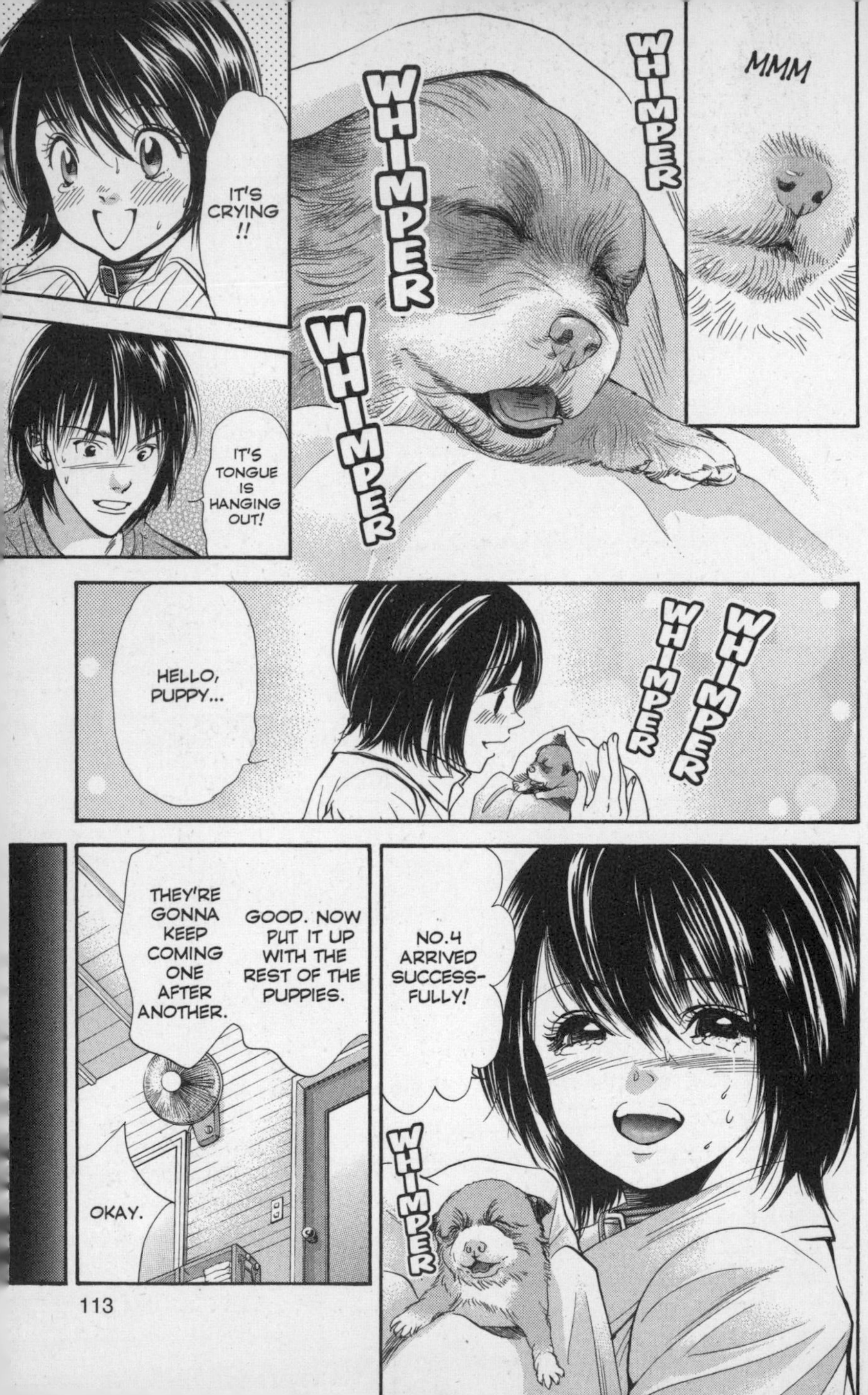
MMM
WHIMPER
WHIMPER
WHIMPER
IT'S CRYING !!
IT'S TONGUE IS HANGING OUT!
WHIMPER
WHIMPER
HELLO, PUPPY...
NO.4 ARRIVED SUCCESS-FULLY!
WHIMPER
GOOD. NOW PUT IT UP WITH THE REST OF THE PUPPIES.
THEY'RE GONNA KEEP COMING ONE AFTER ANOTHER.
OKAY.

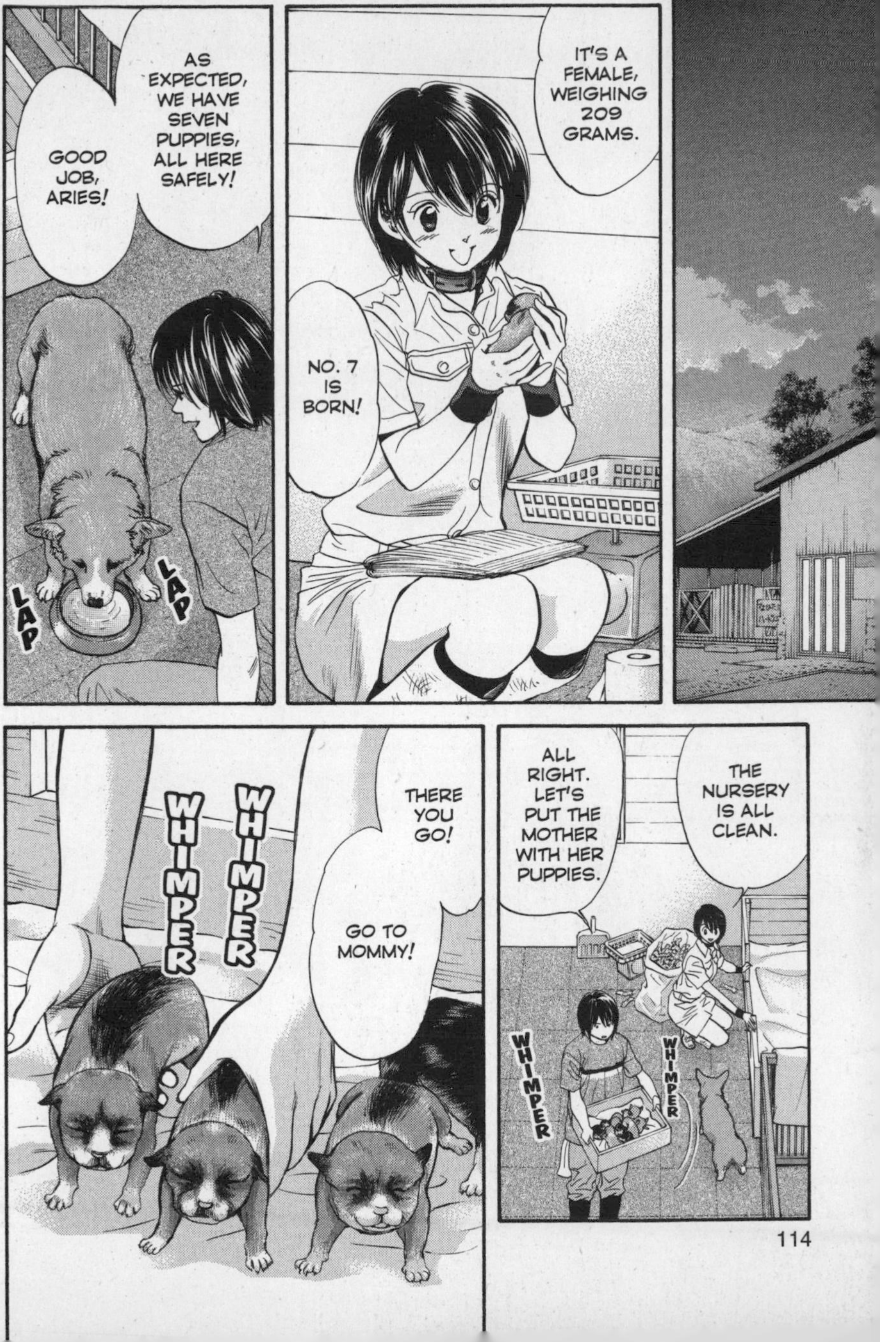
IT'S A FEMALE, WEIGHING 209 GRAMS.
NO. 7 IS BORN!
AS EXPECTED, WE HAVE SEVEN PUPPIES, ALL HERE SAFELY!
GOOD JOB, ARIES!
LAP
LAP
THE NURSERY IS ALL CLEAN.
ALL RIGHT. LET'S PUT THE MOTHER WITH HER PUPPIES.
WHIMPER
WHIMPER
THERE YOU GO!
GO TO MOMMY!
WHIMPER
WHIMPER

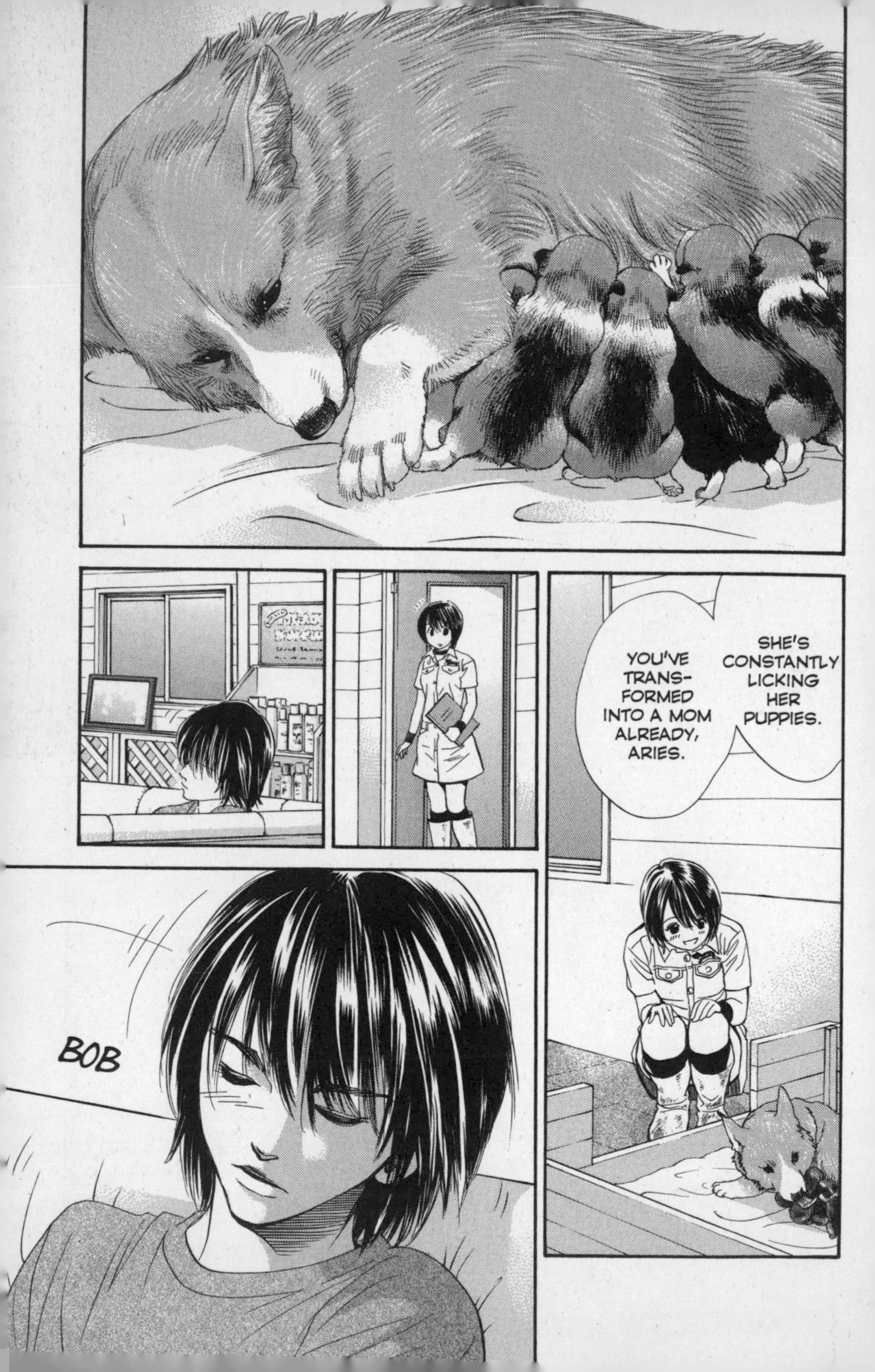
SHE'S CONSTANTLY LICKING HER PUPPIES.
YOU'VE TRANS-FORMED INTO A MOM ALREADY, ARIES.
BOB

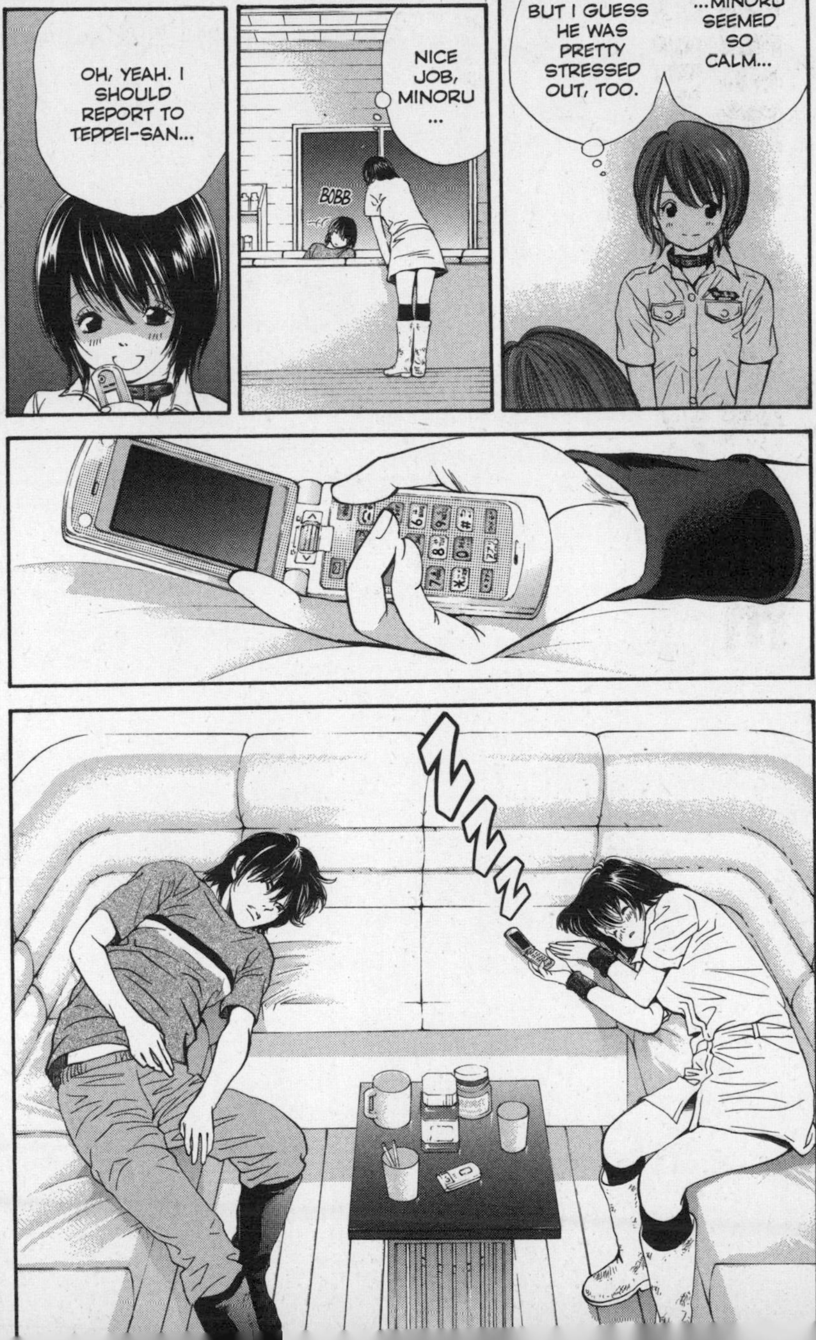
...MINORU SEEMED SO CALM...
BUT I GUESS HE WAS PRETTY STRESSED OUT, TOO.
NICE JOB, MINORU ...
BOBB
OH, YEAH. I SHOULD REPORT TO TEPPEI-SAN...

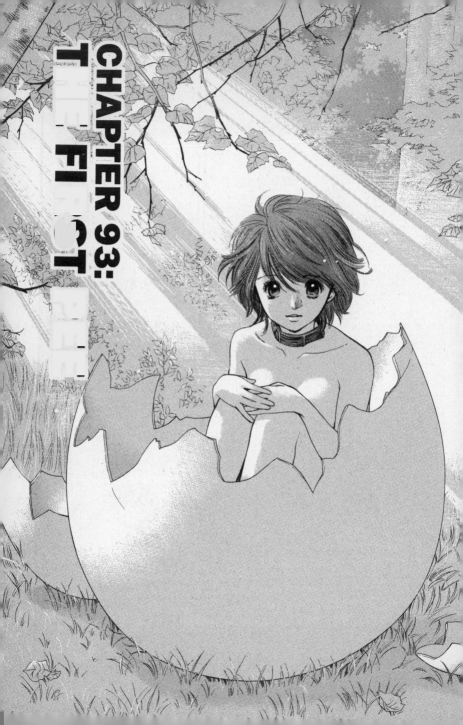

CHAPTER 93: THE FIRST LIE

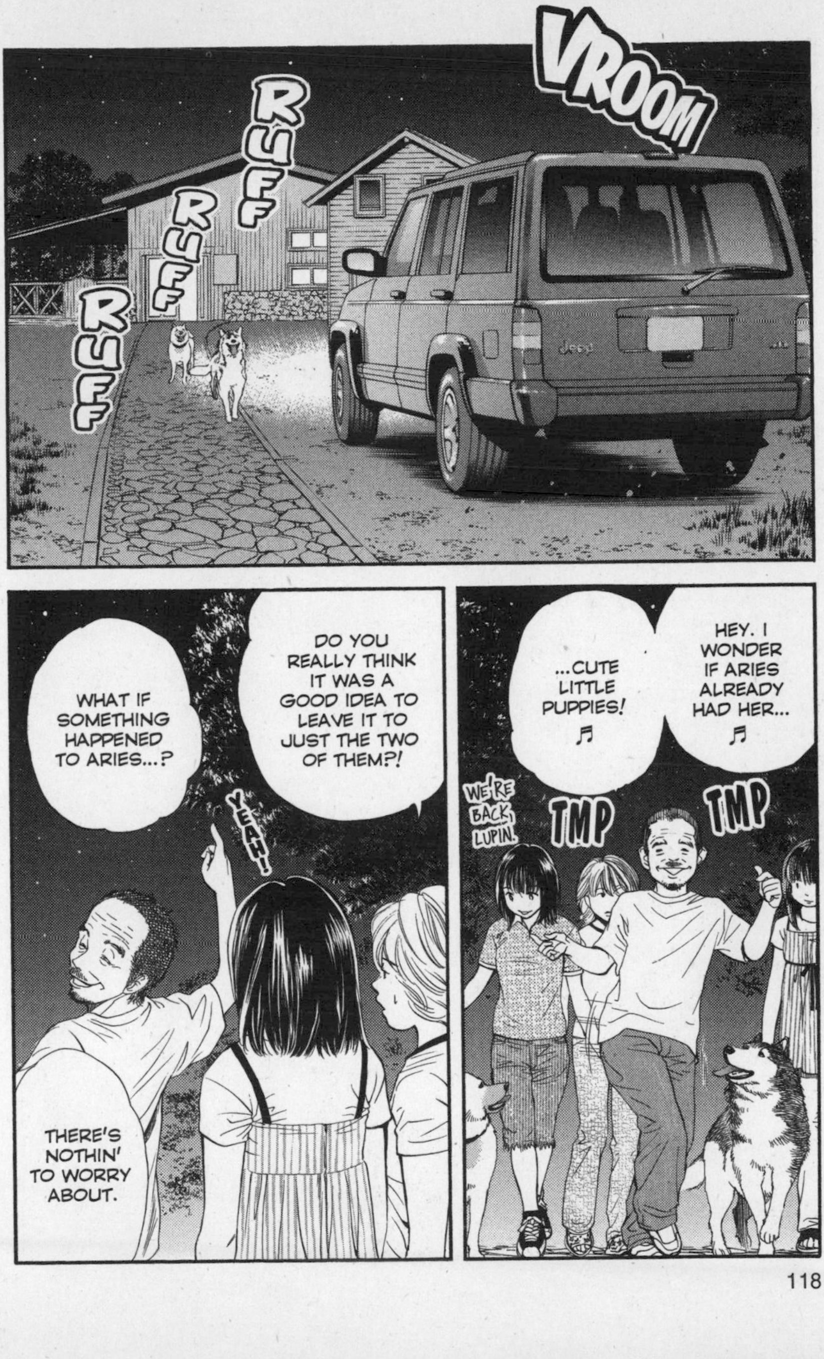
VROOM
RUFF
RUFF
RUFF
HEY. I WONDER IF ARIES ALREADY HAD HER... ♬
...CUTE LITTLE PUPPIES! ♬
TMP
TMP
WE'RE BACK, LUPIN.
DO YOU REALLY THINK IT WAS A GOOD IDEA TO LEAVE IT TO JUST THE TWO OF THEM?!
WHAT IF SOMETHING HAPPENED TO ARIES...?
YEAH!
THERE'S NOTHIN' TO WORRY ABOUT.

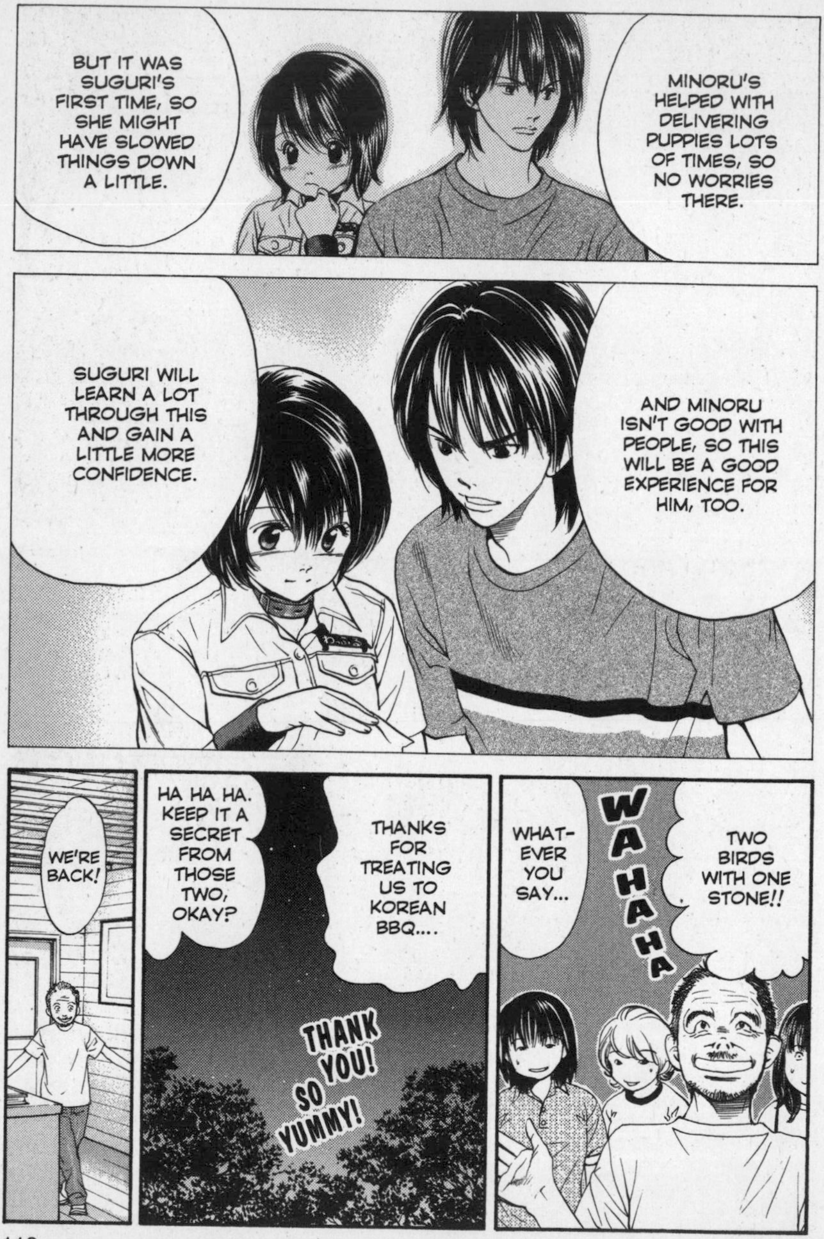
MINORU'S HELPED WITH DELIVERING PUPPIES LOTS OF TIMES, SO NO WORRIES THERE.
BUT IT WAS SUGURI'S FIRST TIME, SO SHE MIGHT HAVE SLOWED THINGS DOWN A LITTLE.
AND MINORU ISN'T GOOD WITH PEOPLE, SO THIS WILL BE A GOOD EXPERIENCE FOR HIM, TOO.
SUGURI WILL LEARN A LOT THROUGH THIS AND GAIN A LITTLE MORE CONFIDENCE.
TWO BIRDS WITH ONE STONE!!
WAHAHAHA
WHAT-EVER YOU SAY...
THANKS FOR TREATING US TO KOREAN BBQ....
HA HA HA. KEEP IT A SECRET FROM THOSE TWO, OKAY?
THANK YOU!
SO YUMMY!
WE'RE BACK!

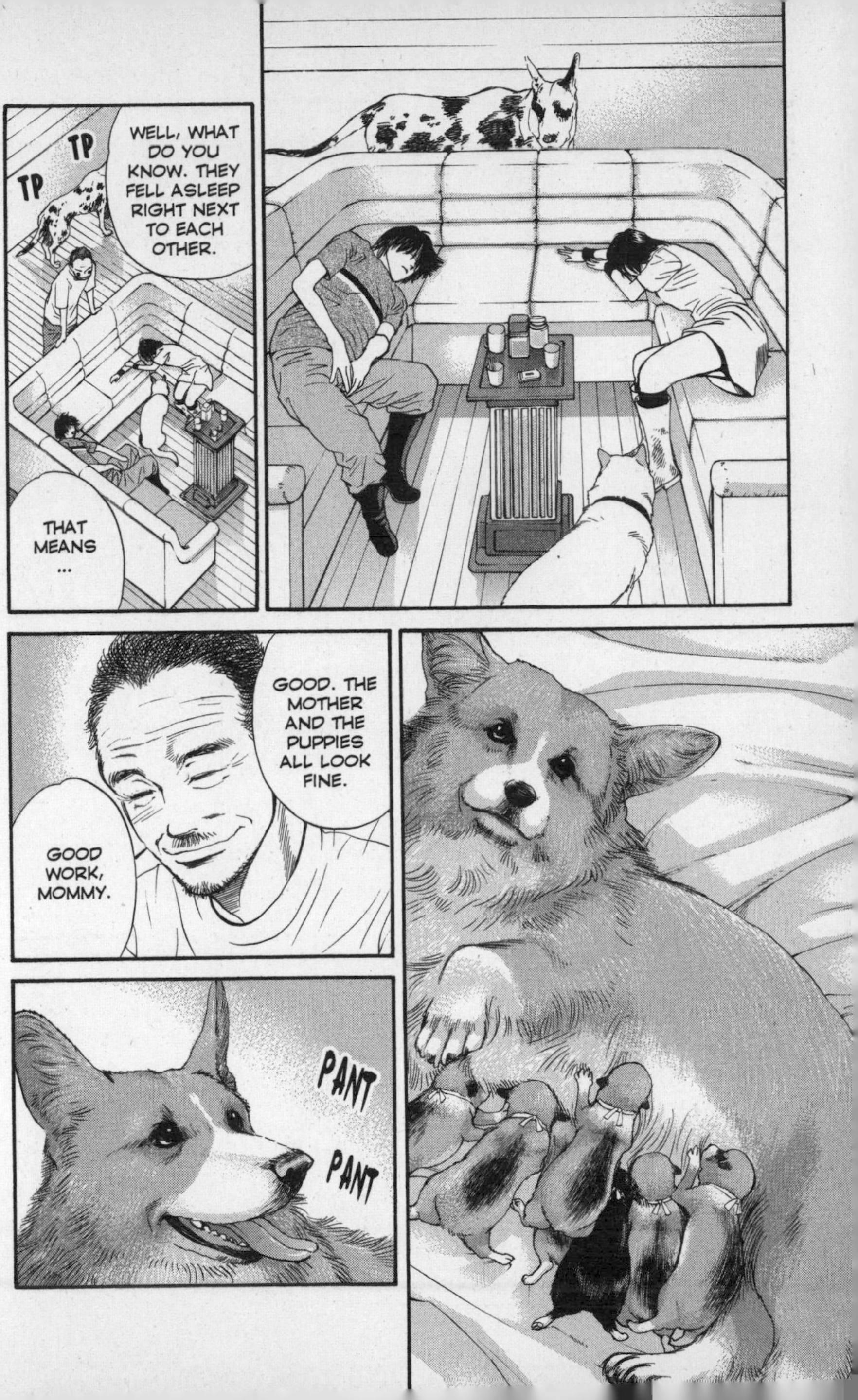
TP
TP
WELL, WHAT DO YOU KNOW. THEY FELL ASLEEP RIGHT NEXT TO EACH OTHER.
THAT MEANS ...
GOOD. THE MOTHER AND THE PUPPIES ALL LOOK FINE.
GOOD WORK, MOMMY.
PANT
PANT

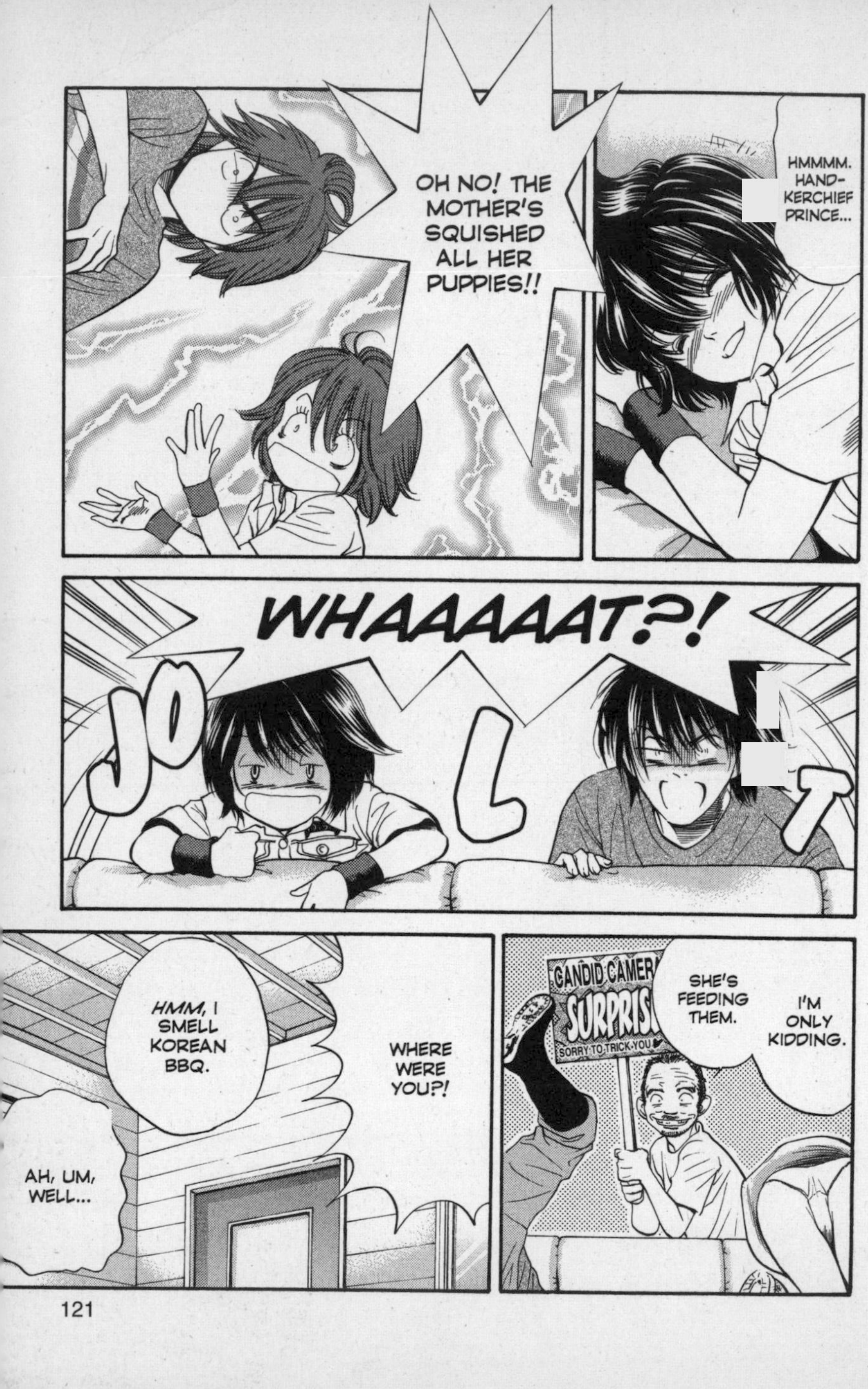
HMMMM. HAND-KERCHIEF PRINCE...
OH NO! THE MOTHER'S SQUISHED ALL HER PUPPIES!!
WHAAAAAT?!
JO
L
T
CANDID CAMER
SURPRIS
SORRY TO TRICK YOU
SHE'S FEEDING THEM.
I'M ONLY KIDDING.
WHERE WERE YOU?!
AH, UM, WELL...
HMM, I SMELL KOREAN BBQ.

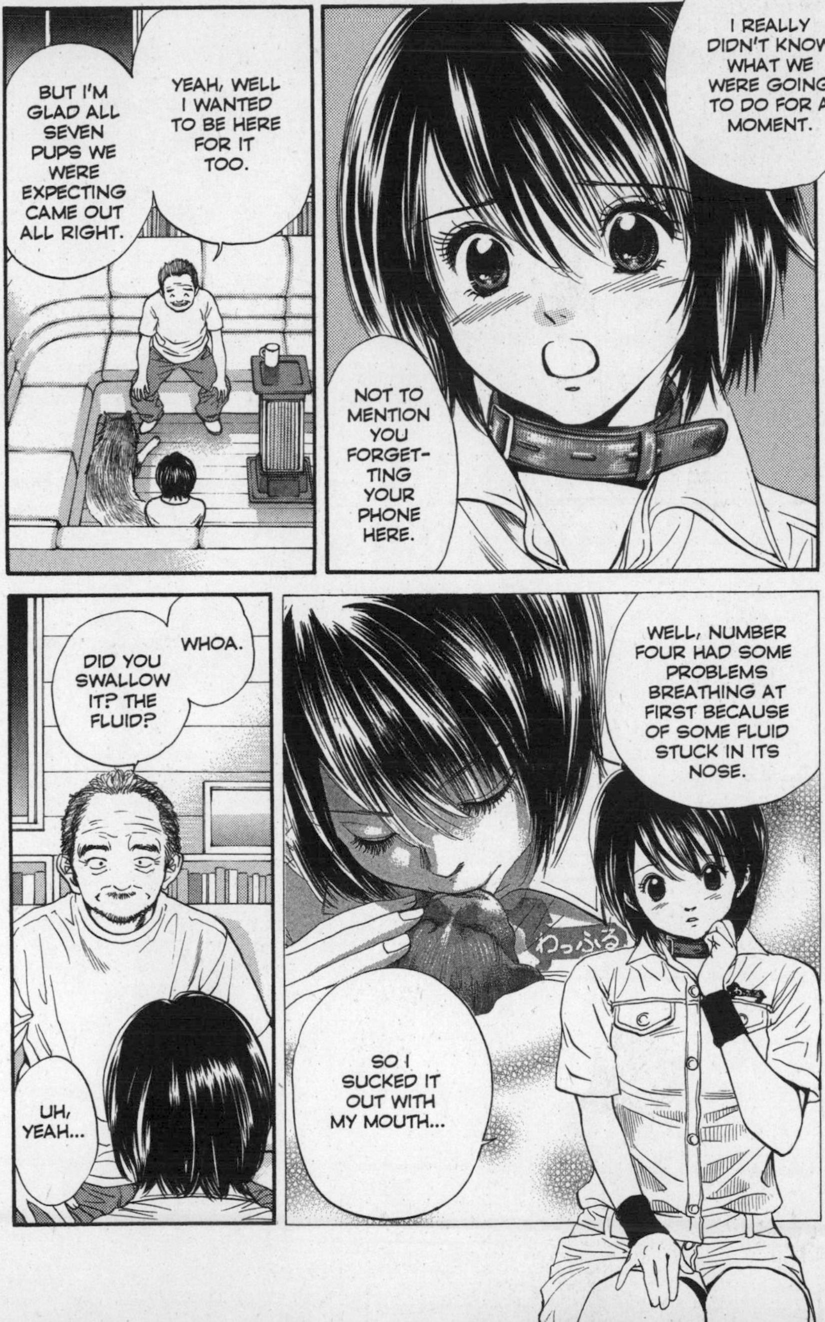
I REALLY DIDN'T KNOW WHAT WE WERE GOING TO DO FOR A MOMENT.
NOT TO MENTION YOU FORGETTING YOUR PHONE HERE.
YEAH, WELL I WANTED TO BE HERE FOR IT TOO.
BUT I'M GLAD ALL SEVEN PUPS WE WERE EXPECTING CAME OUT ALL RIGHT.
WELL, NUMBER FOUR HAD SOME PROBLEMS BREATHING AT FIRST BECAUSE OF SOME FLUID STUCK IN ITS NOSE.
わっふる
SO I SUCKED IT OUT WITH MY MOUTH...
WHOA.
DID YOU SWALLOW IT? THE FLUID?
UH, YEAH...

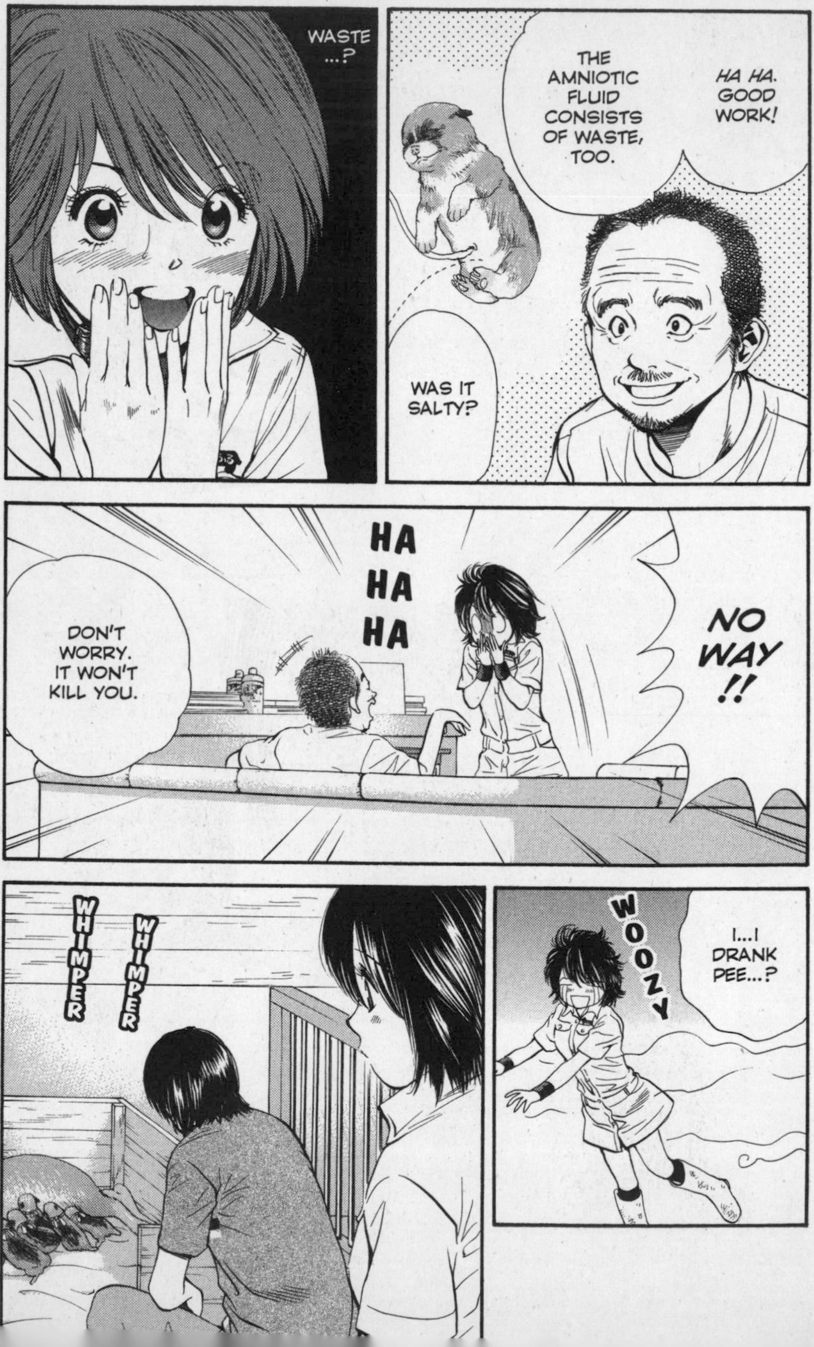
HA HA. GOOD WORK!
THE AMNIOTIC FLUID CONSISTS OF WASTE, TOO.
WAS IT SALTY?
WASTE ...?
NO WAY !!
HA HA HA
DON'T WORRY. IT WON'T KILL YOU.
I...I DRANK PEE...?
WOOZY
WHIMPER
WHIMPER

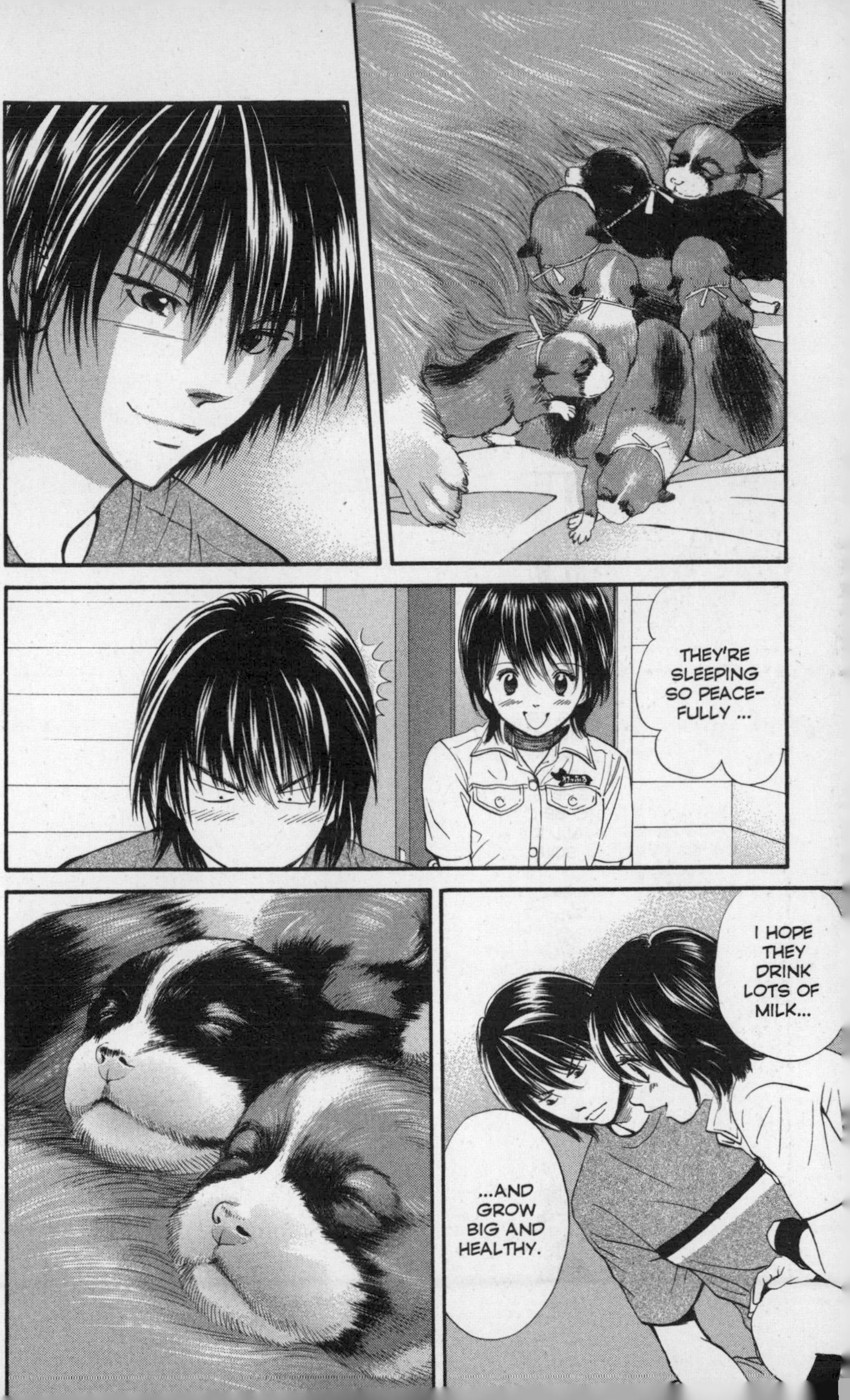
THEY'RE SLEEPING SO PEACE-FULLY ...
I HOPE THEY DRINK LOTS OF MILK...
...AND GROW BIG AND HEALTHY.

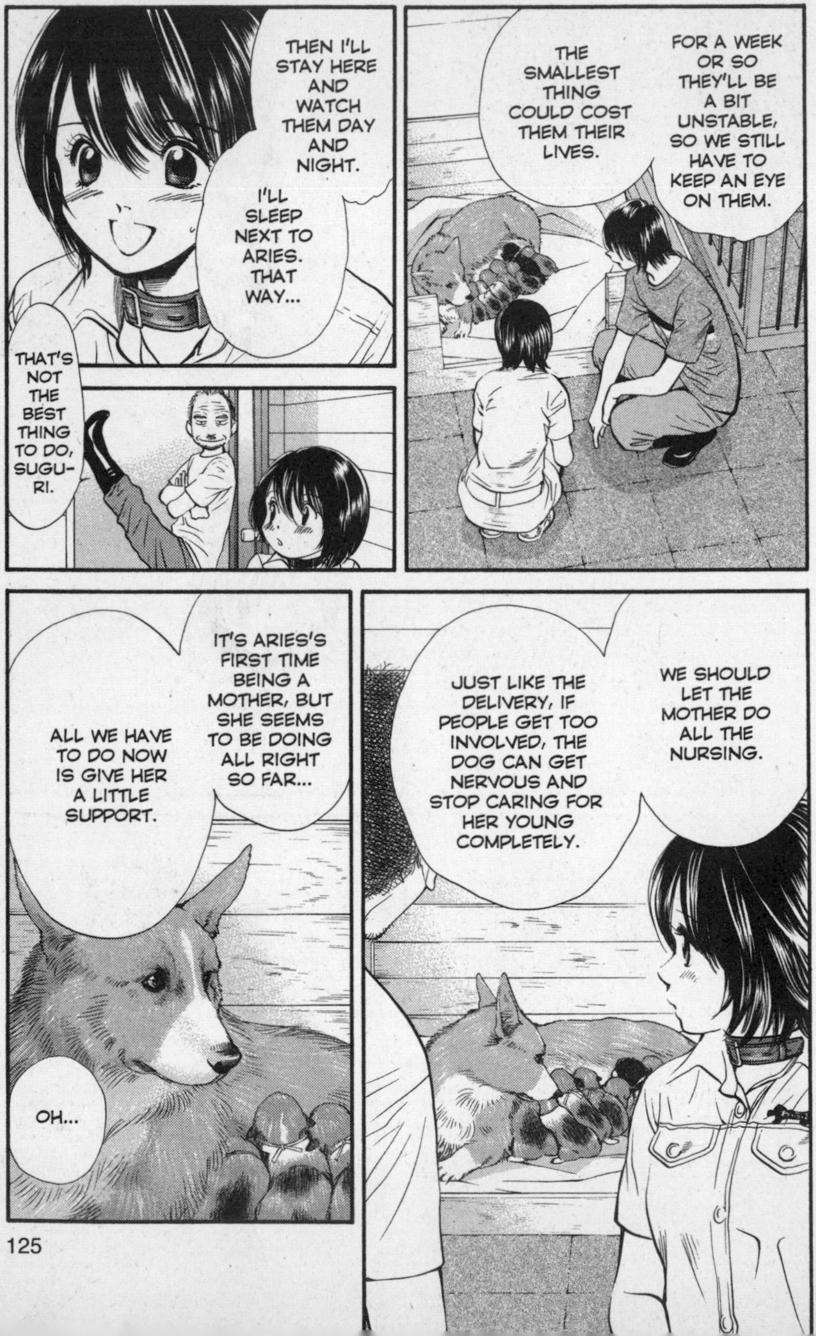

FOR A WEEK OR SO THEY'LL BE A BIT UNSTABLE, SO WE STILL HAVE TO KEEP AN EYE ON THEM.
THE SMALLEST THING COULD COST THEM THEIR LIVES.
THEN I'LL STAY HERE AND WATCH THEM DAY AND NIGHT.
I'LL SLEEP NEXT TO ARIES. THAT WAY...
THAT'S NOT THE BEST THING TO DO, SUGURI.
WE SHOULD LET THE MOTHER DO ALL THE NURSING.
JUST LIKE THE DELIVERY, IF PEOPLE GET TOO INVOLVED, THE DOG CAN GET NERVOUS AND STOP CARING FOR HER YOUNG COMPLETELY.
IT'S ARIES'S FIRST TIME BEING A MOTHER, BUT SHE SEEMS TO BE DOING ALL RIGHT SO FAR...
ALL WE HAVE TO DO NOW IS GIVE HER A LITTLE SUPPORT.
OH...

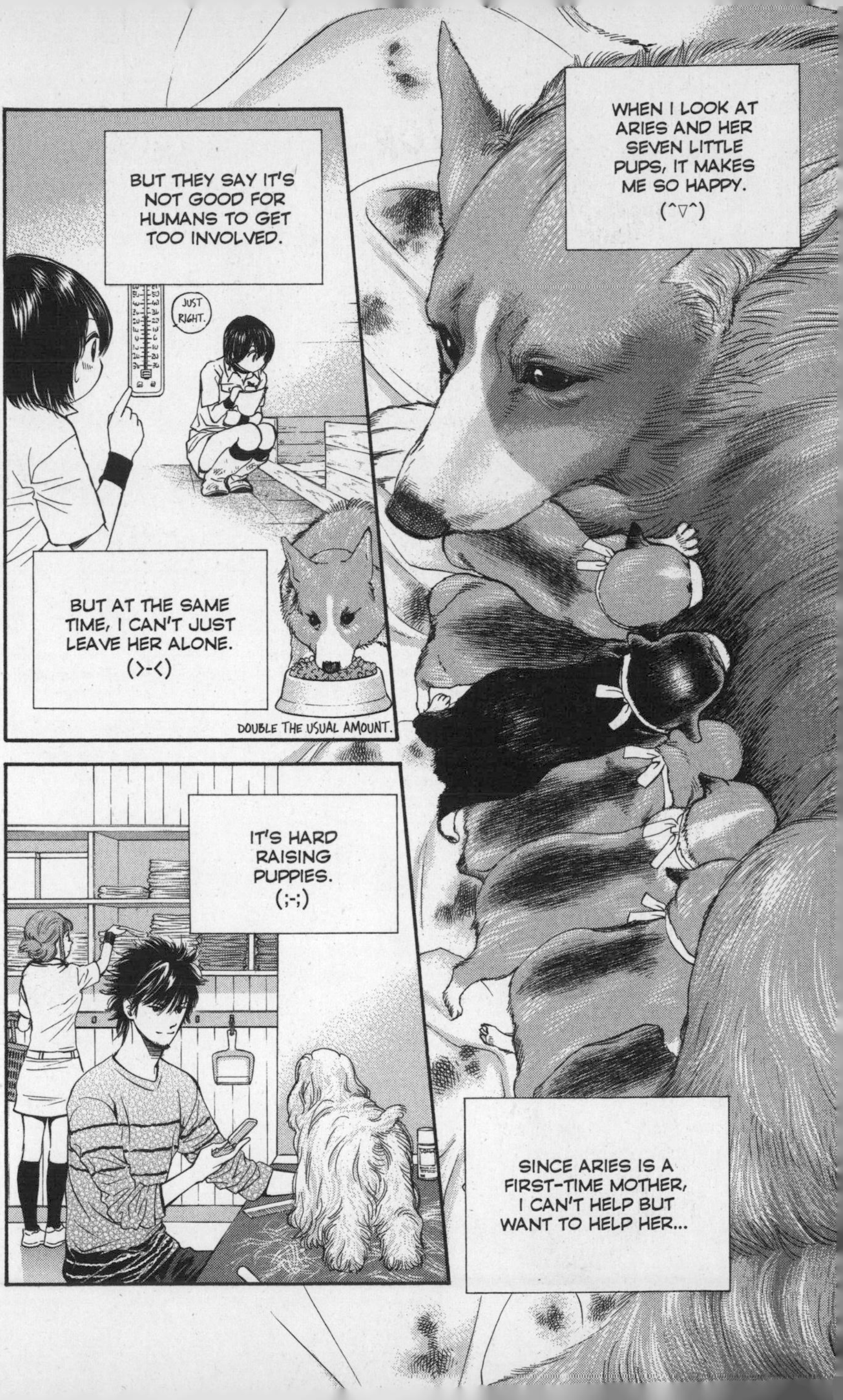
WHEN I LOOK AT ARIES AND HER SEVEN LITTLE PUPS, IT MAKES ME SO HAPPY. (^▽^)
SINCE ARIES IS A FIRST-TIME MOTHER, I CAN'T HELP BUT WANT TO HELP HER...
BUT THEY SAY IT'S NOT GOOD FOR HUMANS TO GET TOO INVOLVED.
JUST RIGHT.
BUT AT THE SAME TIME, I CAN'T JUST LEAVE HER ALONE. (>-<)
DOUBLE THE USUAL AMOUNT.
IT'S HARD RAISING PUPPIES. (;-;)

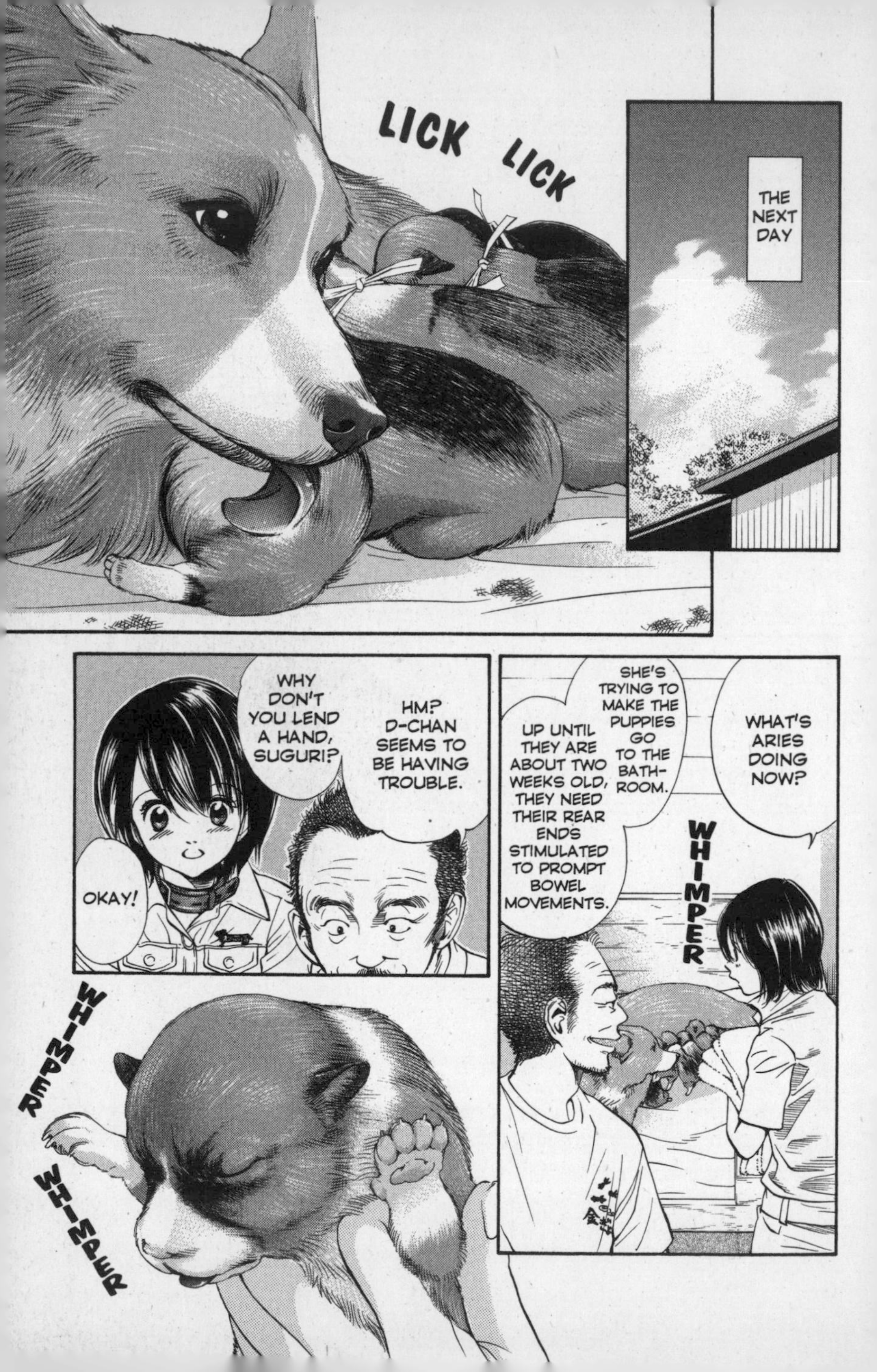
THE NEXT DAY
LICK LICK
WHAT'S ARIES DOING NOW?
SHE'S TRYING TO MAKE THE PUPPIES GO TO THE BATHROOM.
UP UNTIL THEY ARE ABOUT TWO WEEKS OLD, THEY NEED THEIR REAR ENDS STIMULATED TO PROMPT BOWEL MOVEMENTS.
WHIMPER
HM? D-CHAN SEEMS TO BE HAVING TROUBLE.
WHY DON'T YOU LEND A HAND, SUGURI?
OKAY!
WHIMPER
WHIMPER

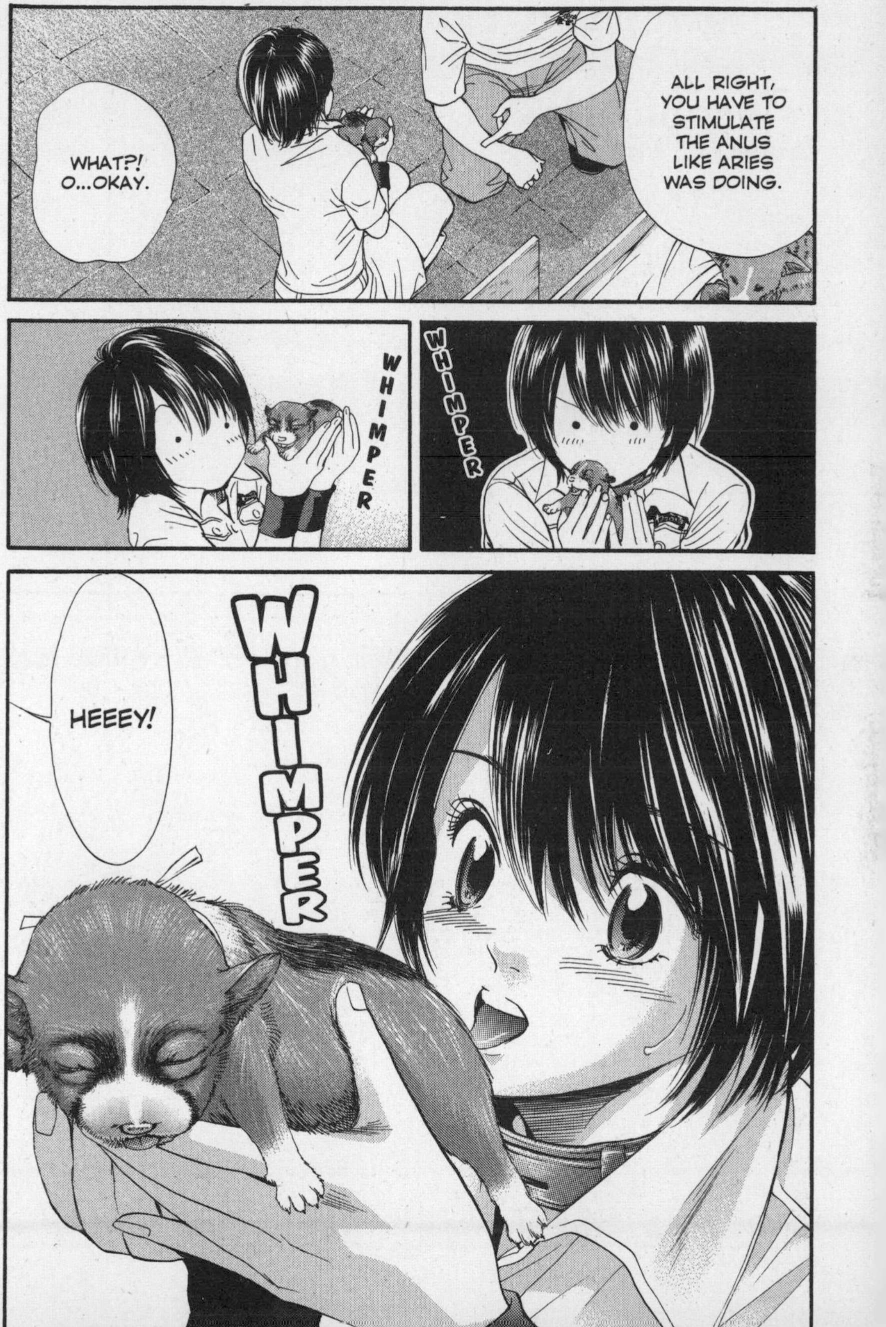
ALL RIGHT, YOU HAVE TO STIMULATE THE ANUS LIKE ARIES WAS DOING.
WHAT?! O...OKAY.
WHIMPER
WHIMPER
WHIMPER
HEEEY!

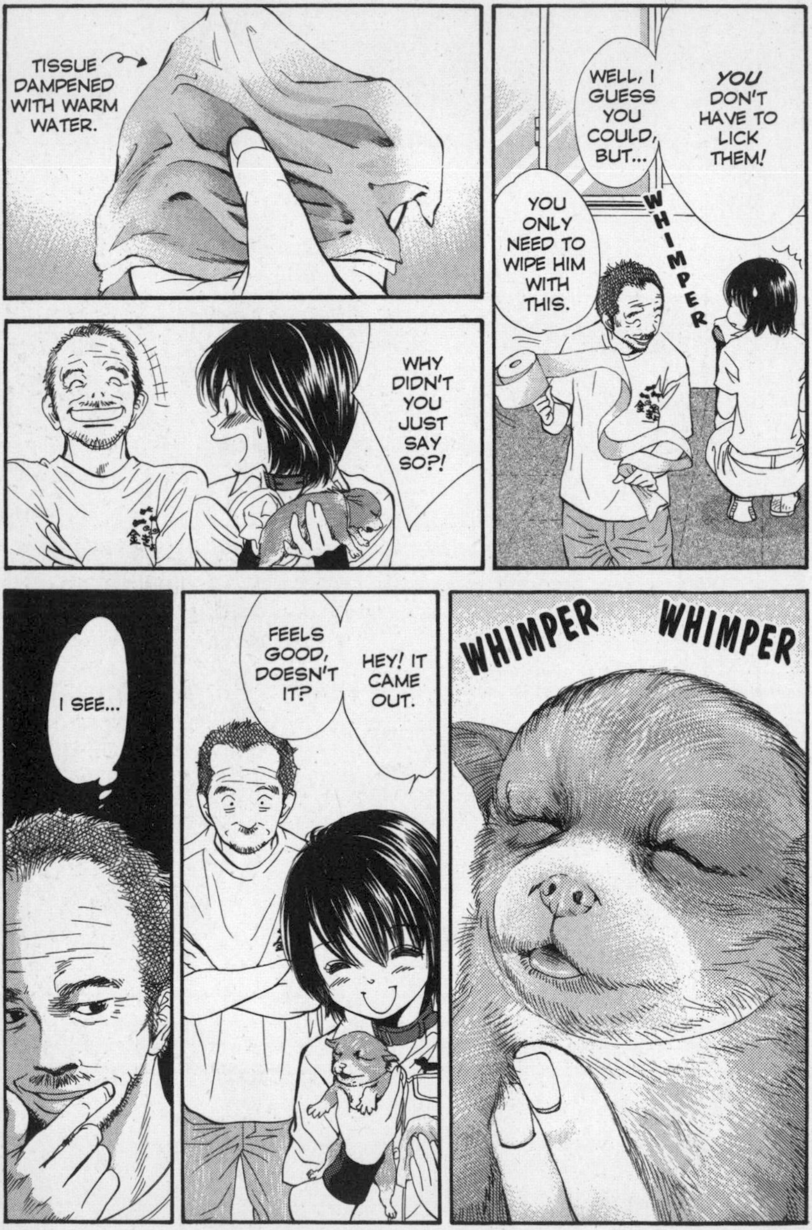
YOU DON'T HAVE TO LICK THEM!
WELL, I GUESS YOU COULD, BUT...
WHIMPER
YOU ONLY NEED TO WIPE HIM WITH THIS.
TISSUE DAMPENED WITH WARM WATER.
WHY DIDN'T YOU JUST SAY SO?!
WHIMPER WHIMPER
HEY! IT CAME OUT.
FEELS GOOD, DOESN'T IT?
I SEE...

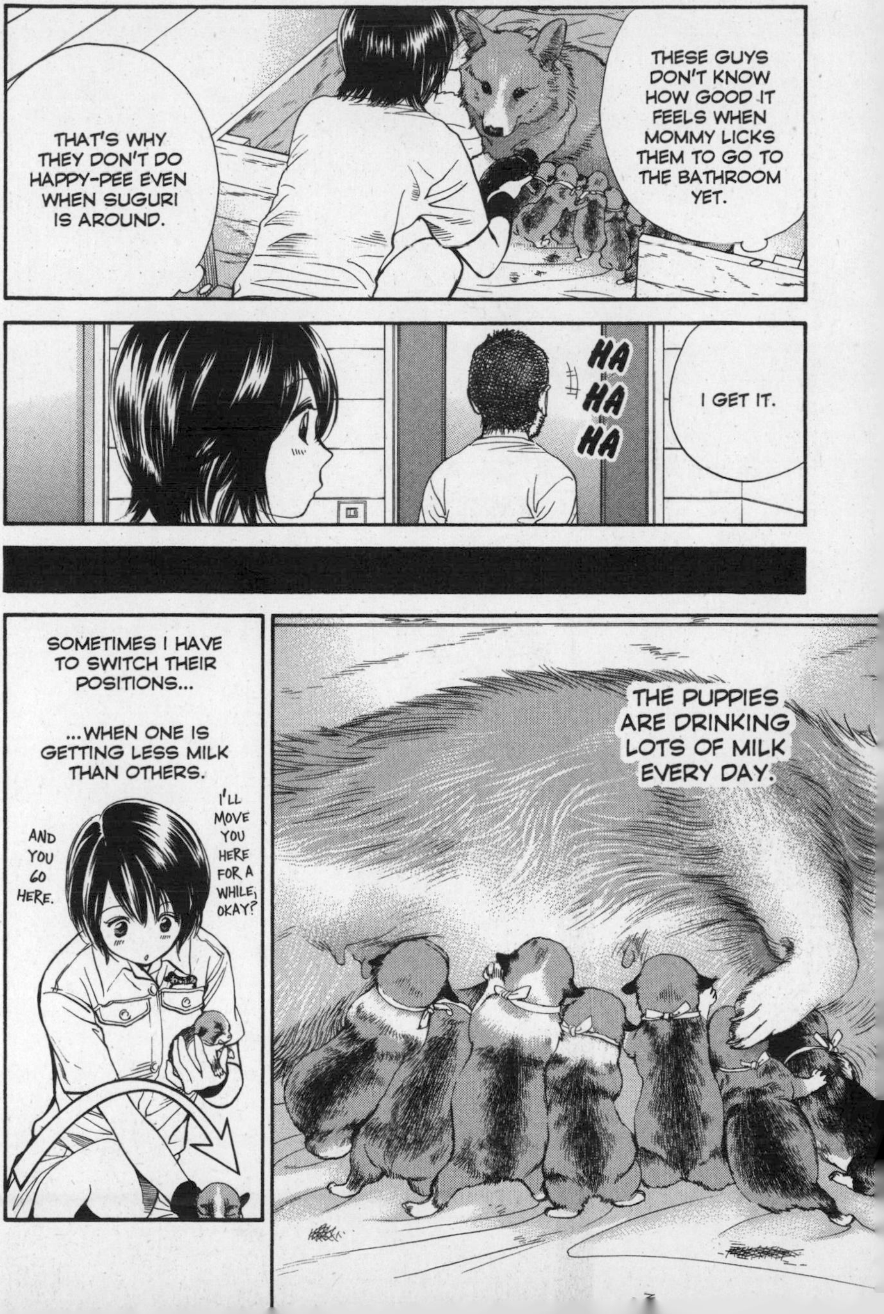
THESE GUYS DON'T KNOW HOW GOOD IT FEELS WHEN MOMMY LICKS THEM TO GO TO THE BATHROOM YET.
THAT'S WHY THEY DON'T DO HAPPY-PEE EVEN WHEN SUGURI IS AROUND.
I GET IT.
HA HA HA
THE PUPPIES ARE DRINKING LOTS OF MILK EVERY DAY.
SOMETIMES I HAVE TO SWITCH THEIR POSITIONS...
...WHEN ONE IS GETTING LESS MILK THAN OTHERS.
I'LL MOVE YOU HERE FOR A WHILE, OKAY?
AND YOU GO HERE.

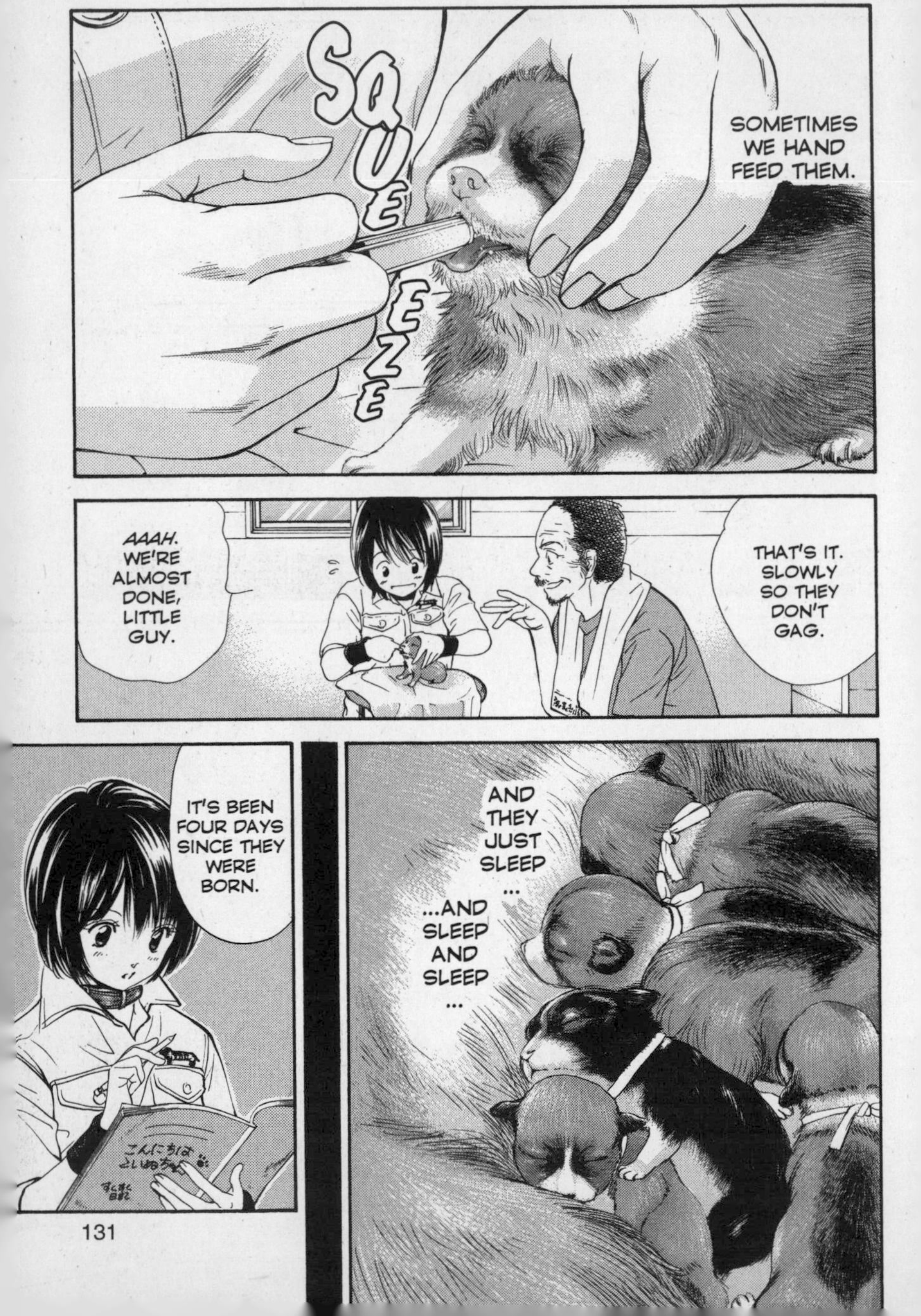
SQUEEZE
SOMETIMES WE HAND FEED THEM.
THAT'S IT. SLOWLY SO THEY DON'T GAG.
AAAH. WE'RE ALMOST DONE, LITTLE GUY.
AND THEY JUST SLEEP ...
...AND SLEEP AND SLEEP ...
IT'S BEEN FOUR DAYS SINCE THEY WERE BORN.

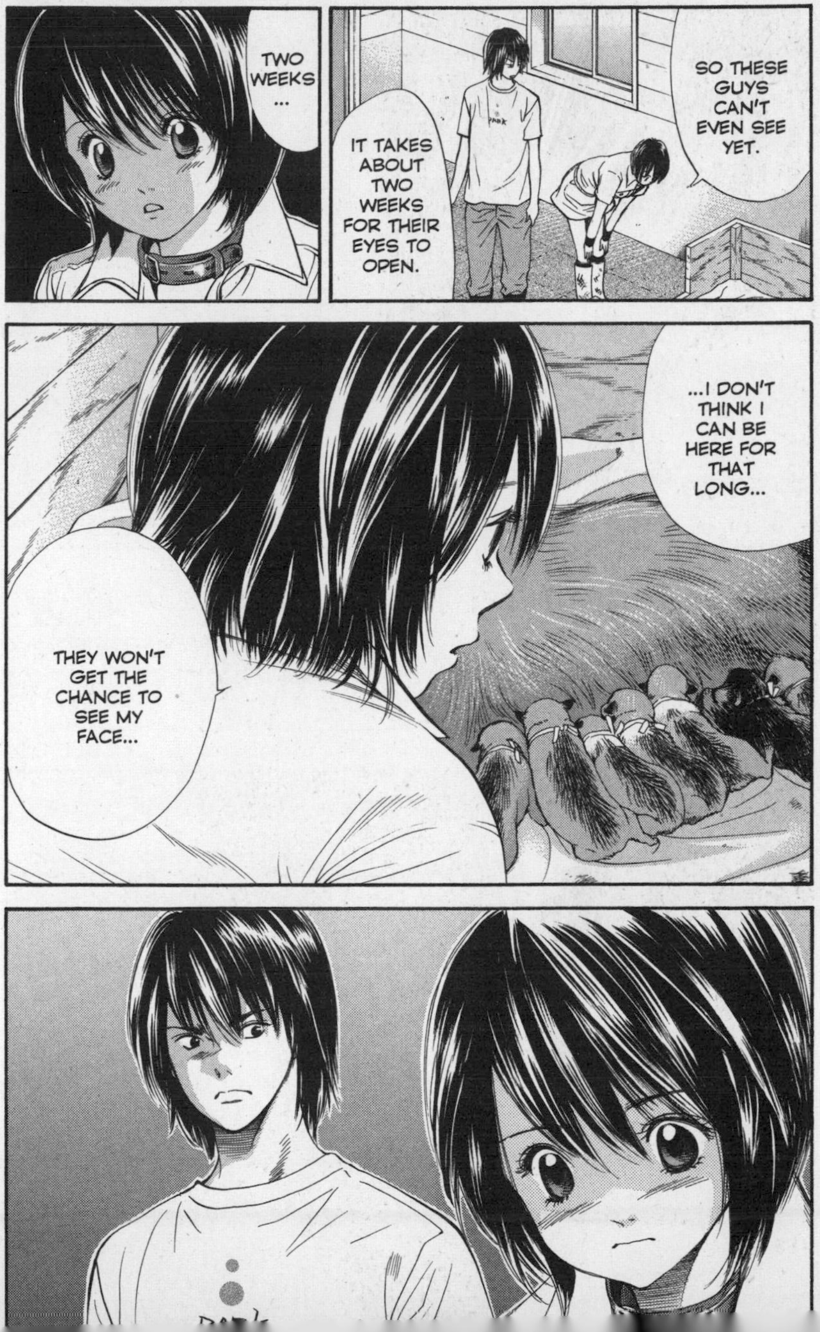
SO THESE GUYS CAN'T EVEN SEE YET.
IT TAKES ABOUT TWO WEEKS FOR THEIR EYES TO OPEN.
TWO WEEKS ...
...I DON'T THINK I CAN BE HERE FOR THAT LONG...
THEY WON'T GET THE CHANCE TO SEE MY FACE...

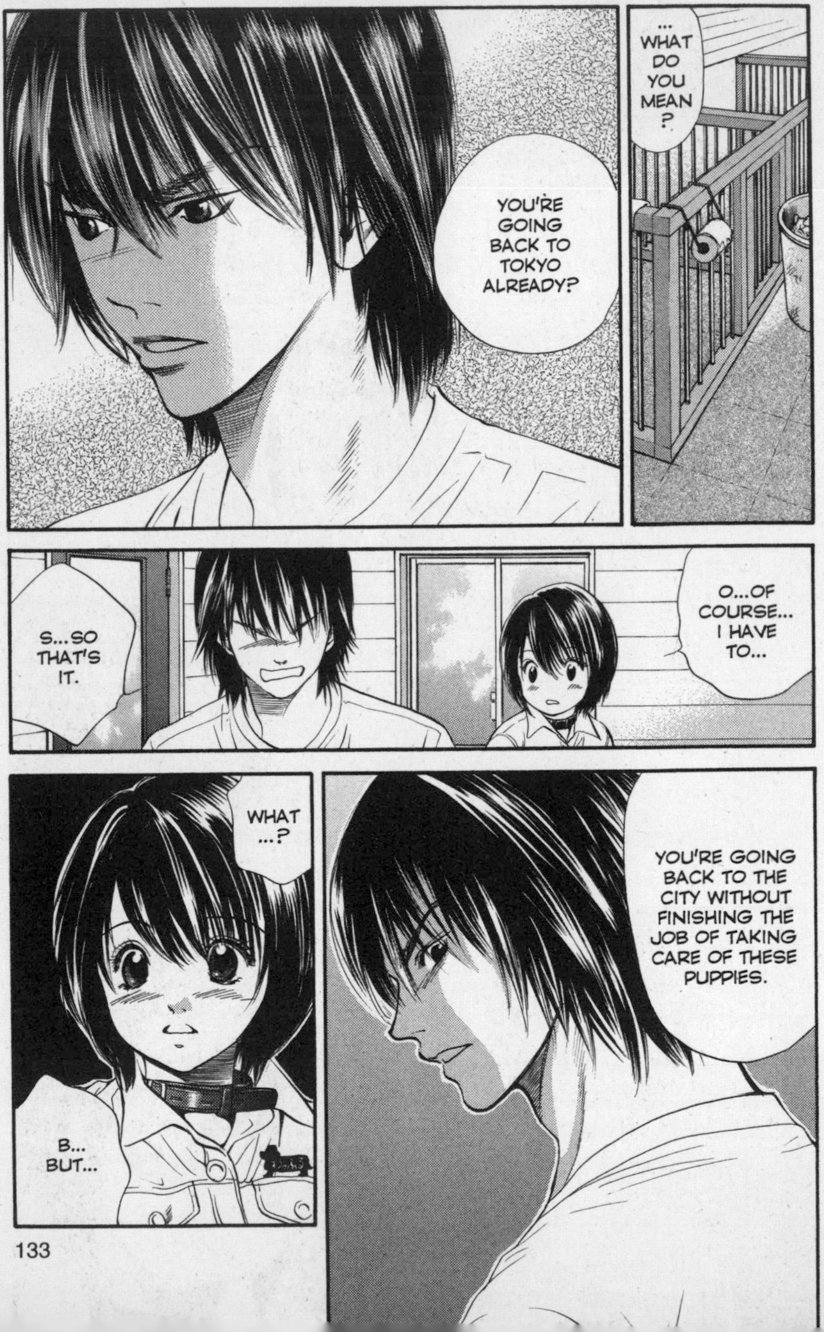
... WHAT DO YOU MEAN?
YOU'RE GOING BACK TO TOKYO ALREADY?
O...OF COURSE... I HAVE TO...
S...SO THAT'S IT.
YOU'RE GOING BACK TO THE CITY WITHOUT FINISHING THE JOB OF TAKING CARE OF THESE PUPPIES.
WHAT ...?
B... BUT...

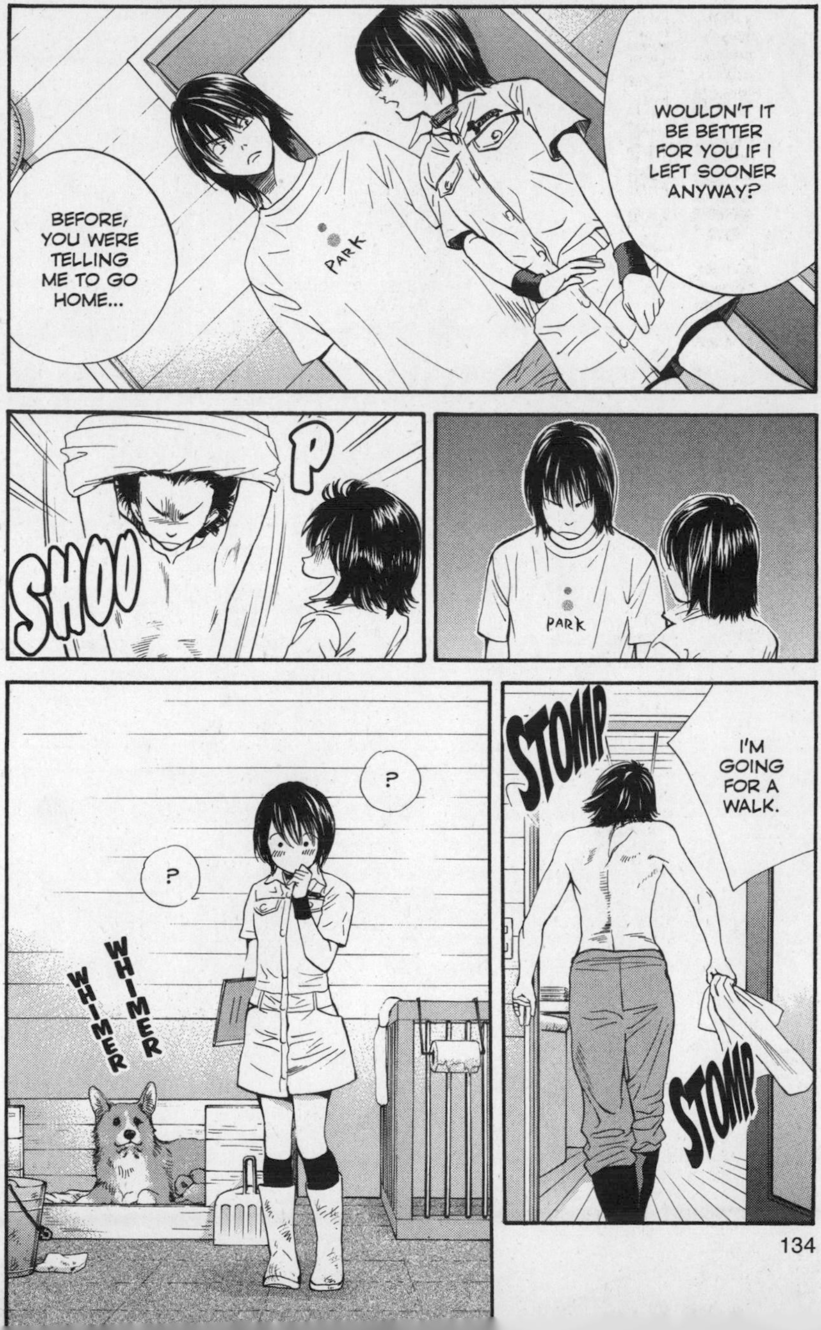
WOULDN'T IT BE BETTER FOR YOU IF I LEFT SOONER ANYWAY?
PARK
BEFORE, YOU WERE TELLING ME TO GO HOME...
PARK
P
SHOO
I'M GOING FOR A WALK.
STOMP
STOMP
?
?
WHIMPER
WHIMPER

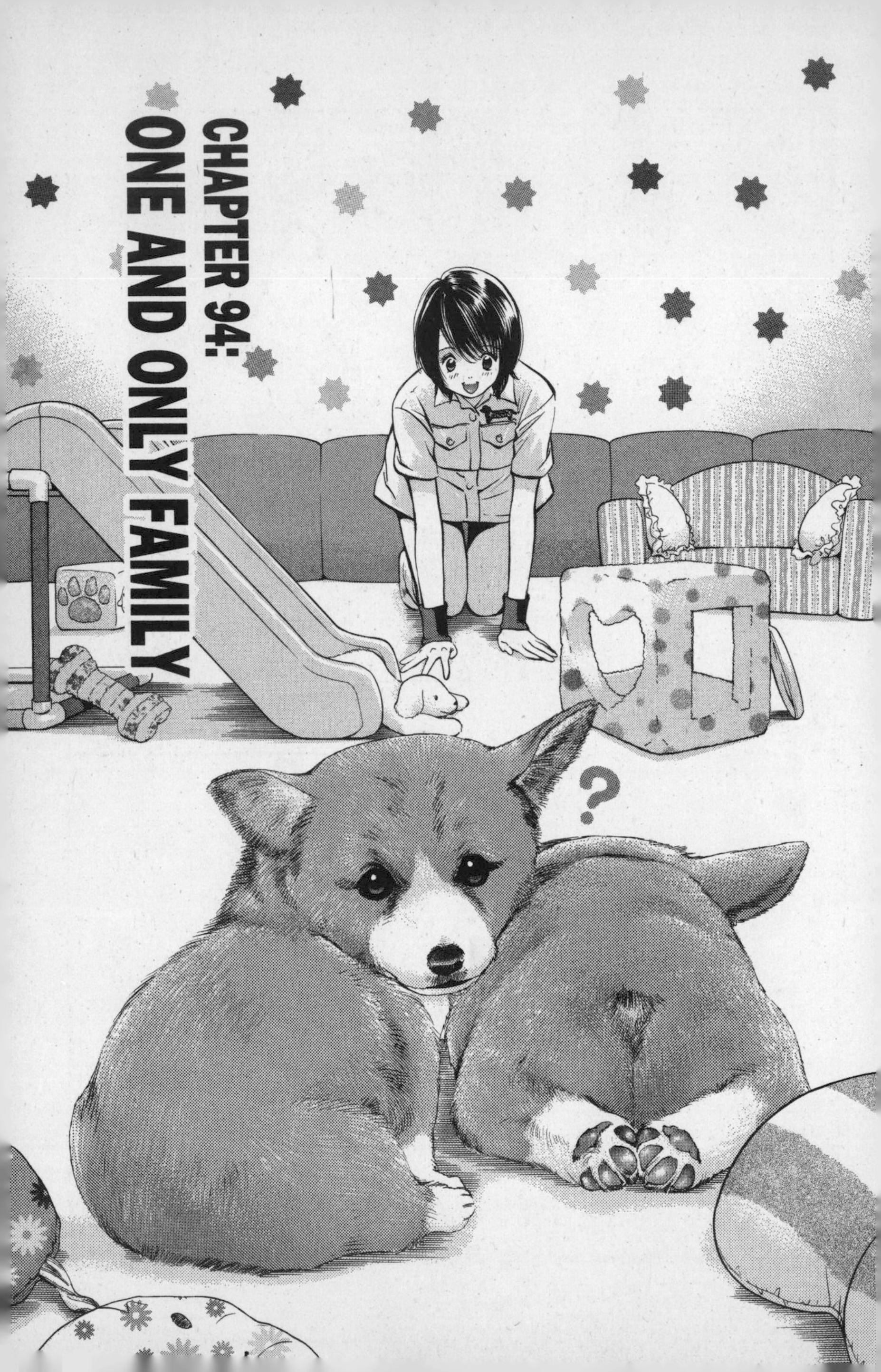
CHAPTER 94:
ONE AND ONLY FAMILY
?

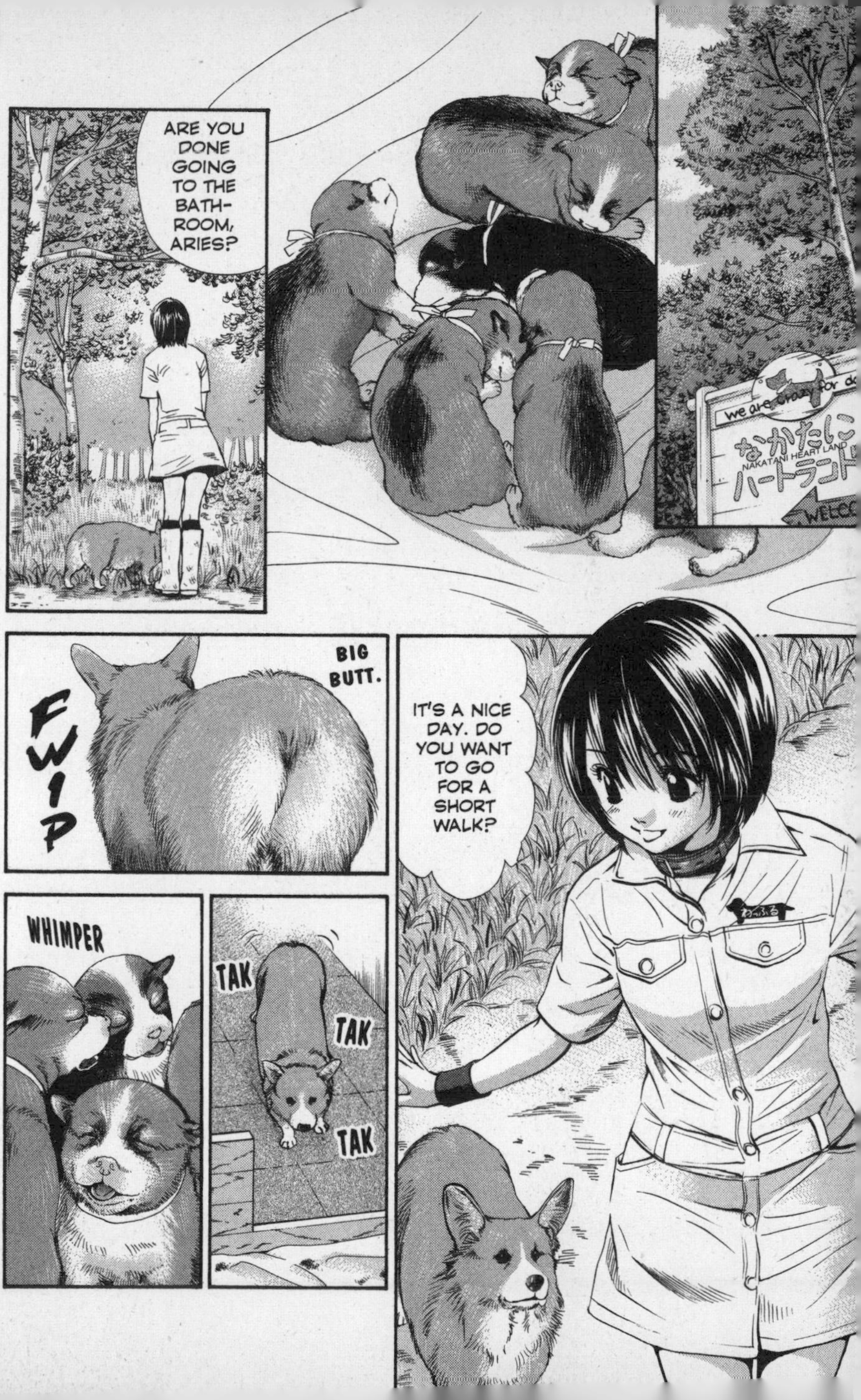
なかたに
NAKATANI HEART LAND
ARE YOU DONE GOING TO THE BATH-ROOM, ARIES?
IT'S A NICE DAY. DO YOU WANT TO GO FOR A SHORT WALK?
BIG BUTT.
FWIP
TAK
TAK
TAK
WHIMPER

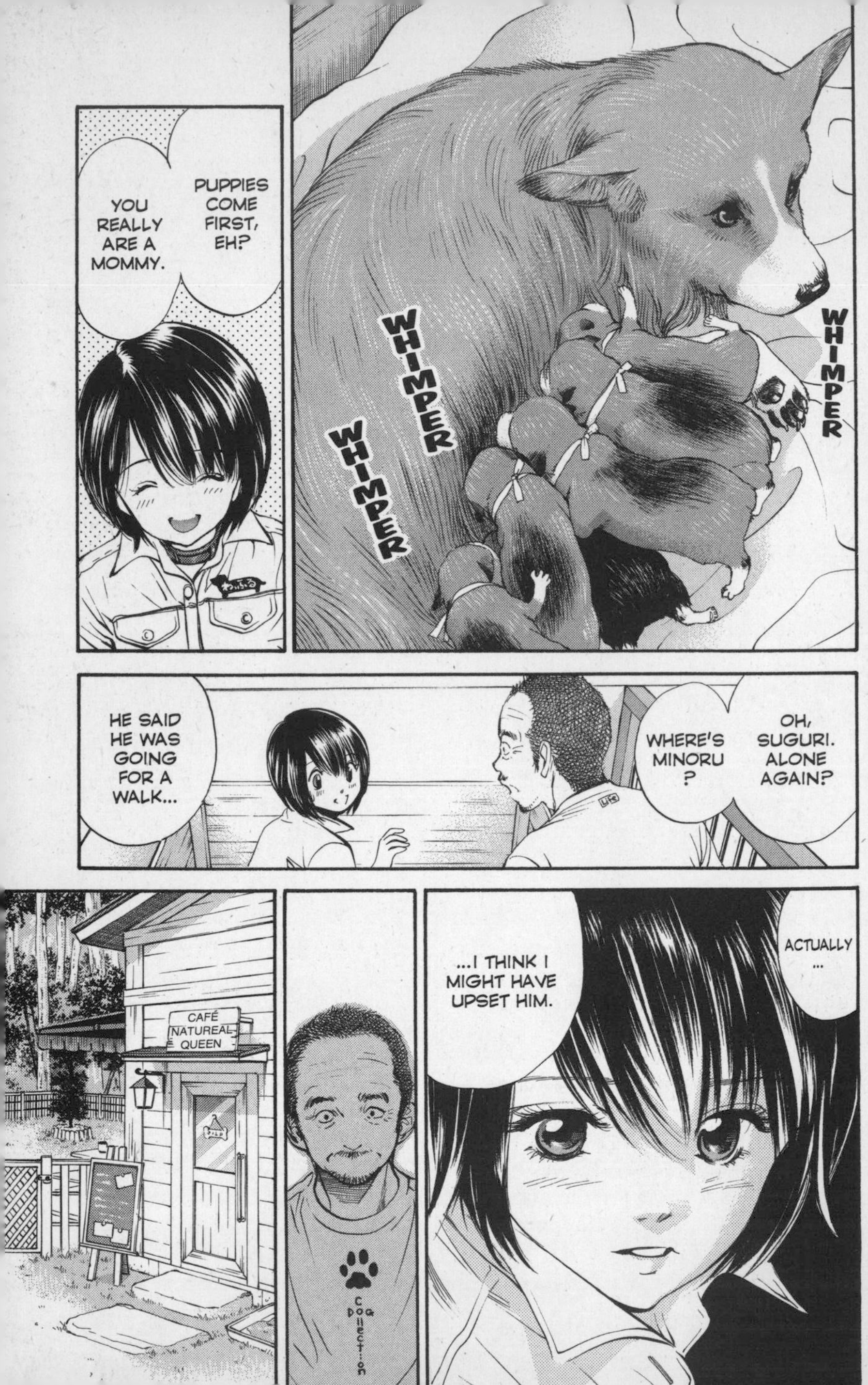
WHIMPER
WHIMPER
WHIMPER
PUPPIES COME FIRST, EH?
YOU REALLY ARE A MOMMY.
OH, SUGURI. ALONE AGAIN?
WHERE'S MINORU?
HE SAID HE WAS GOING FOR A WALK...
ACTUALLY...
...I THINK I MIGHT HAVE UPSET HIM.
CAFÉ NATUREAL QUEEN

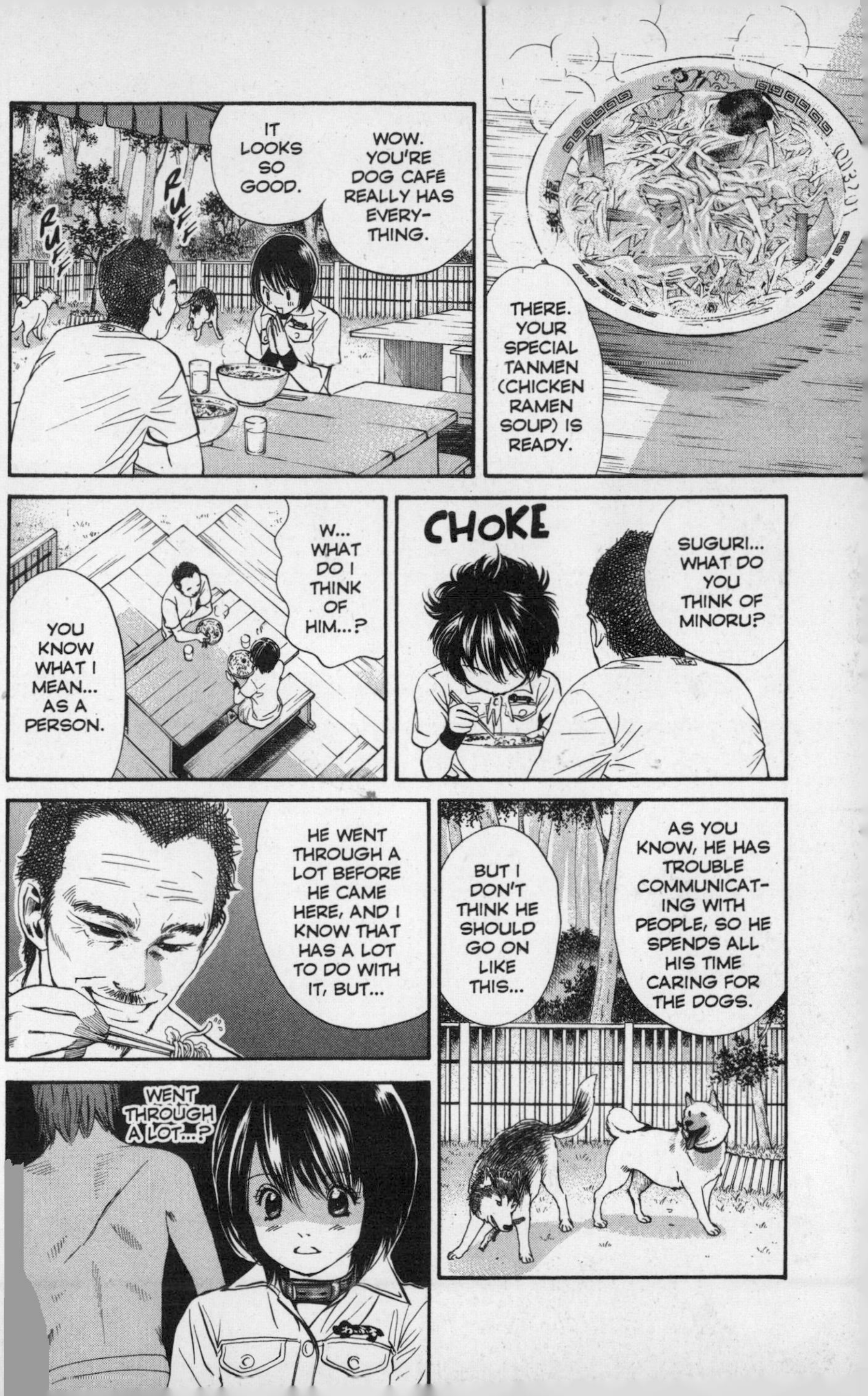
THERE. YOUR SPECIAL TANMEN (CHICKEN RAMEN SOUP) IS READY.
WOW. YOU'RE DOG CAFÉ REALLY HAS EVERYTHING.
IT LOOKS SO GOOD.
RUFF
RUFF
SUGURI... WHAT DO YOU THINK OF MINORU?
CHOKE
W... WHAT DO I THINK OF HIM...?
YOU KNOW WHAT I MEAN... AS A PERSON.
AS YOU KNOW, HE HAS TROUBLE COMMUNICATING WITH PEOPLE, SO HE SPENDS ALL HIS TIME CARING FOR THE DOGS.
BUT I DON'T THINK HE SHOULD GO ON LIKE THIS...
HE WENT THROUGH A LOT BEFORE HE CAME HERE, AND I KNOW THAT HAS A LOT TO DO WITH IT, BUT...
WENT THROUGH A LOT...?

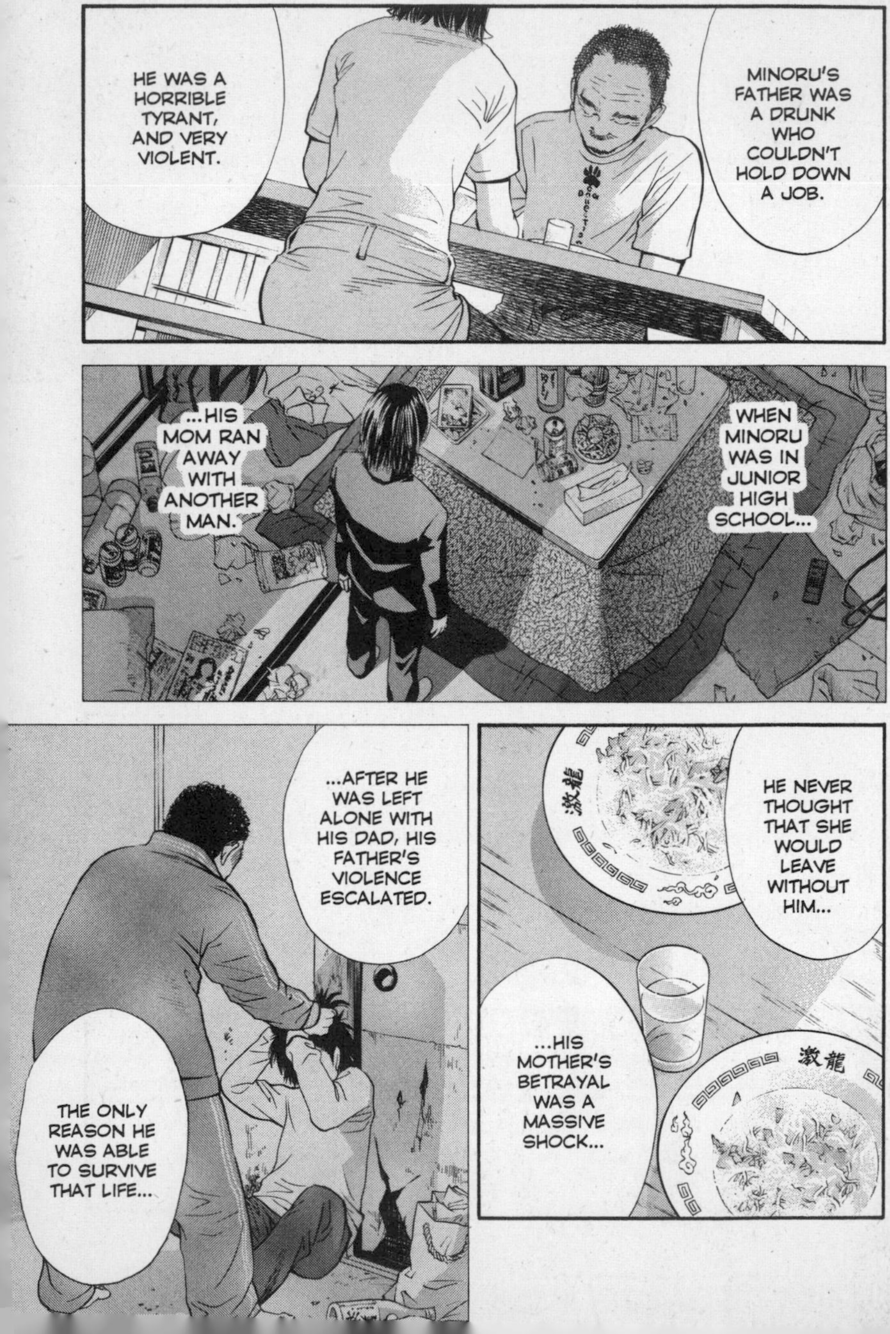
MINORU'S FATHER WAS A DRUNK WHO COULDN'T HOLD DOWN A JOB.
HE WAS A HORRIBLE TYRANT, AND VERY VIOLENT.
WHEN MINORU WAS IN JUNIOR HIGH SCHOOL...
...HIS MOM RAN AWAY WITH ANOTHER MAN.
HE NEVER THOUGHT THAT SHE WOULD LEAVE WITHOUT HIM...
...HIS MOTHER'S BETRAYAL WAS A MASSIVE SHOCK...
...AFTER HE WAS LEFT ALONE WITH HIS DAD, HIS FATHER'S VIOLENCE ESCALATED.
THE ONLY REASON HE WAS ABLE TO SURVIVE THAT LIFE...

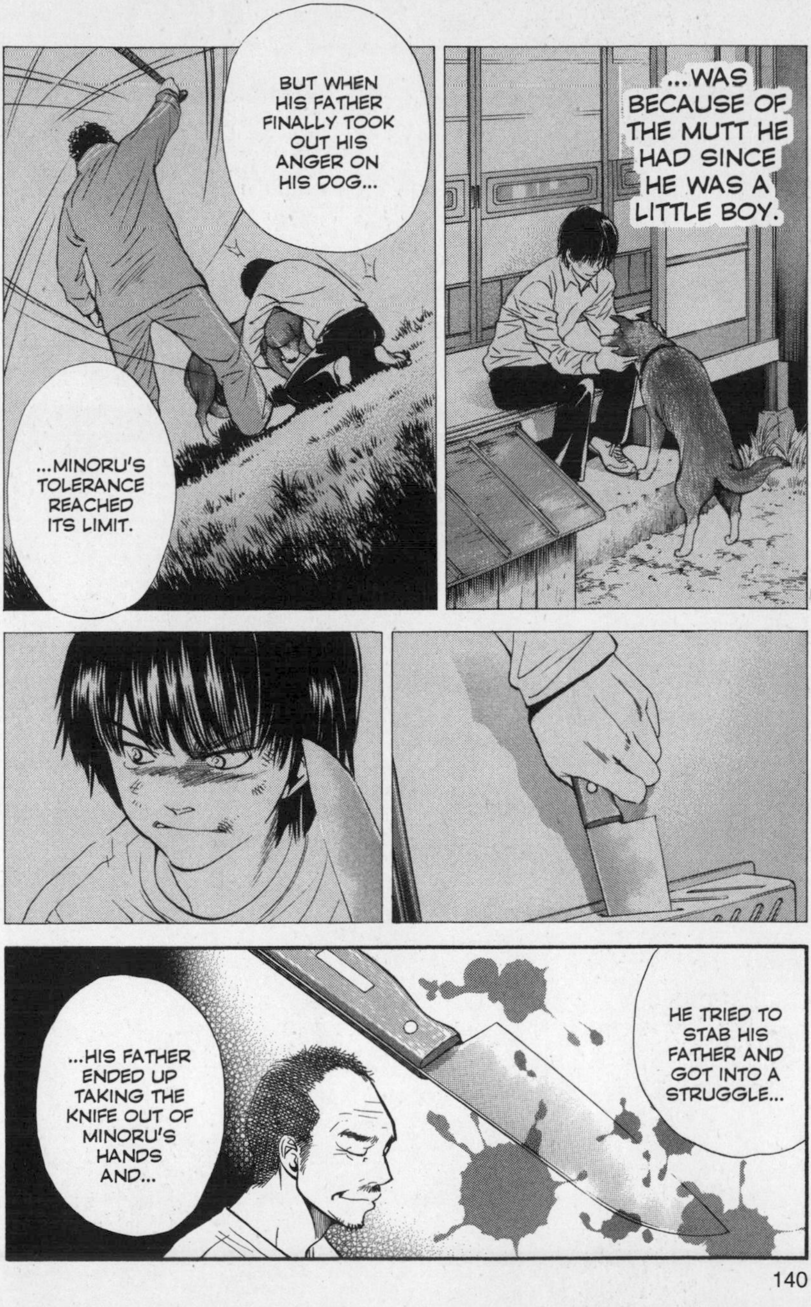
...WAS BECAUSE OF THE MUTT HE HAD SINCE HE WAS A LITTLE BOY.
BUT WHEN HIS FATHER FINALLY TOOK OUT HIS ANGER ON HIS DOG...
...MINORU'S TOLERANCE REACHED ITS LIMIT.
HE TRIED TO STAB HIS FATHER AND GOT INTO A STRUGGLE...
...HIS FATHER ENDED UP TAKING THE KNIFE OUT OF MINORU'S HANDS AND...

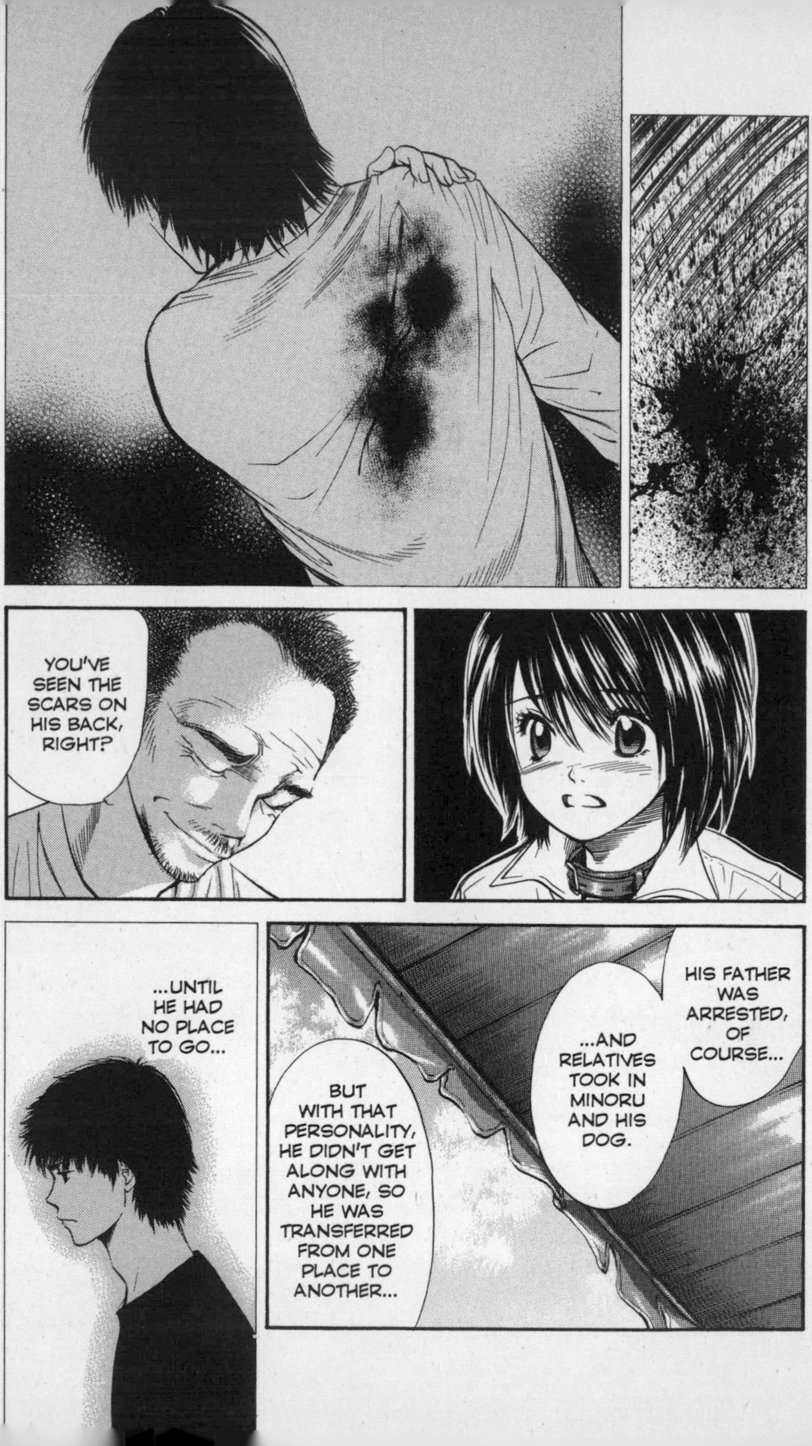
YOU'VE SEEN THE SCARS ON HIS BACK, RIGHT?
HIS FATHER WAS ARRESTED, OF COURSE...
...AND RELATIVES TOOK IN MINORU AND HIS DOG.
BUT WITH THAT PERSONALITY, HE DIDN'T GET ALONG WITH ANYONE, SO HE WAS TRANSFERRED FROM ONE PLACE TO ANOTHER...
...UNTIL HE HAD NO PLACE TO GO...

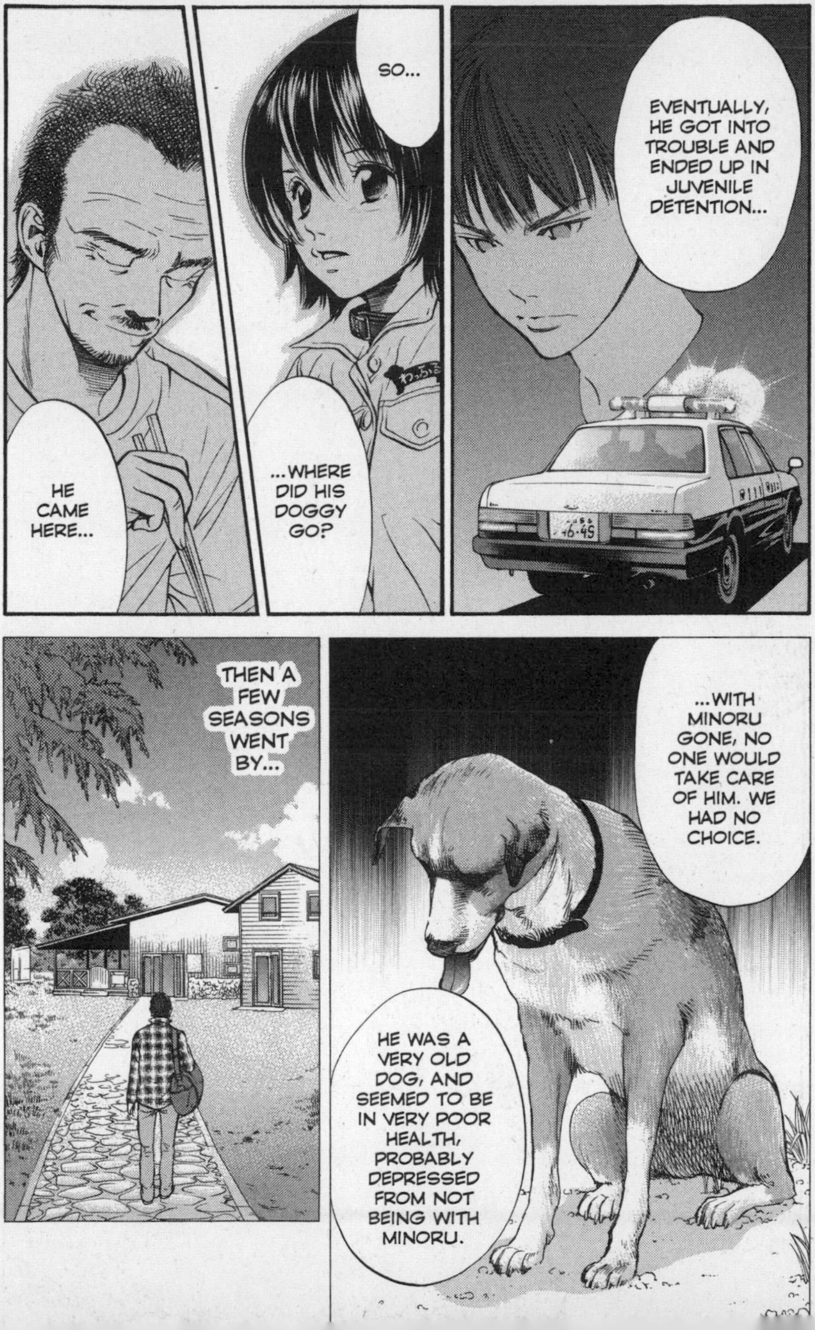
EVENTUALLY, HE GOT INTO TROUBLE AND ENDED UP IN JUVENILE DETENTION...
SO...
...WHERE DID HIS DOGGY GO?
HE CAME HERE...
...WITH MINORU GONE, NO ONE WOULD TAKE CARE OF HIM. WE HAD NO CHOICE.
HE WAS A VERY OLD DOG, AND SEEMED TO BE IN VERY POOR HEALTH, PROBABLY DEPRESSED FROM NOT BEING WITH MINORU.
THEN A FEW SEASONS WENT BY...

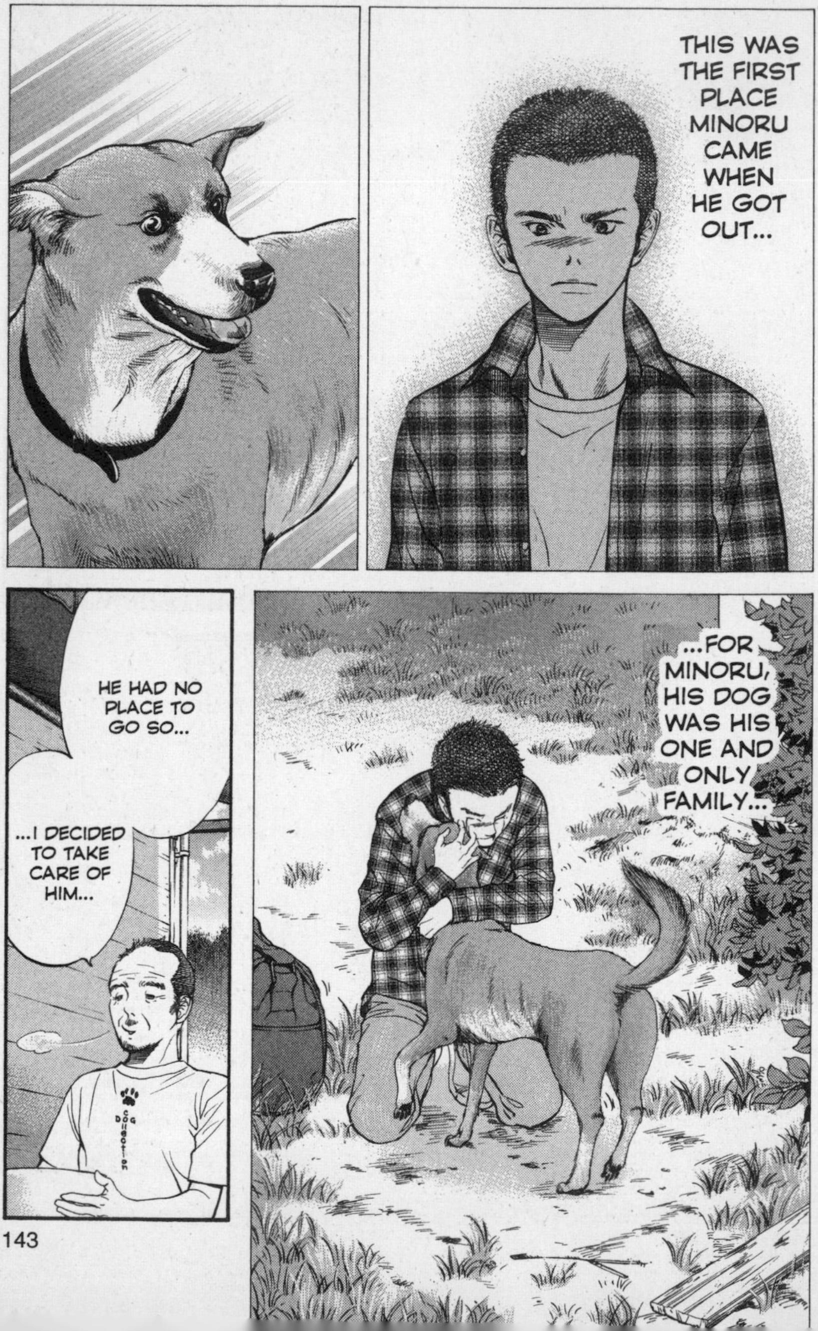
THIS WAS THE FIRST PLACE MINORU CAME WHEN HE GOT OUT...
...FOR MINORU, HIS DOG WAS HIS ONE AND ONLY FAMILY...
HE HAD NO PLACE TO GO SO...
...I DECIDED TO TAKE CARE OF HIM...

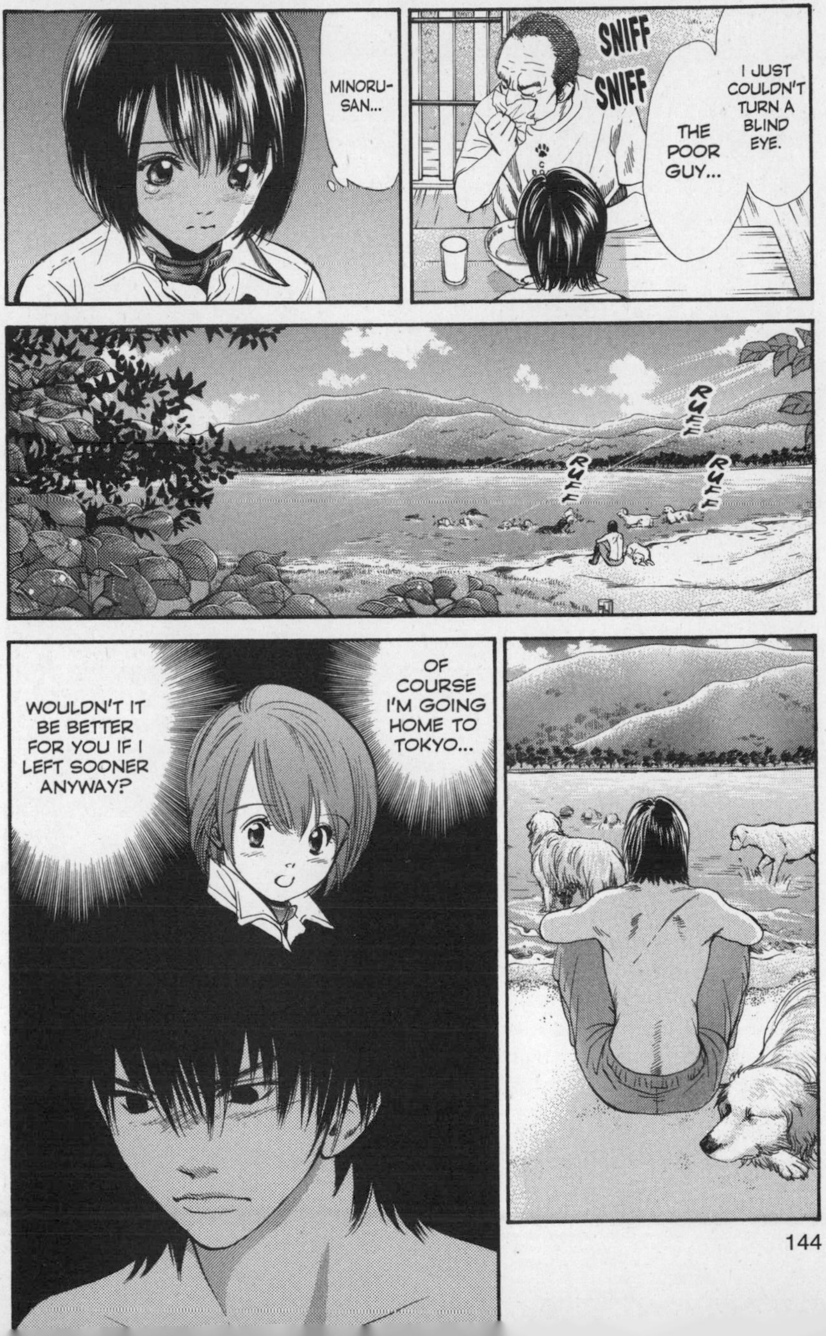
SNIFF
SNIFF
I JUST COULDN'T TURN A BLIND EYE.
THE POOR GUY...
MINORU-SAN...
RUFF
RUFF
RUFF
OF COURSE I'M GOING HOME TO TOKYO...
WOULDN'T IT BE BETTER FOR YOU IF I LEFT SOONER ANYWAY?

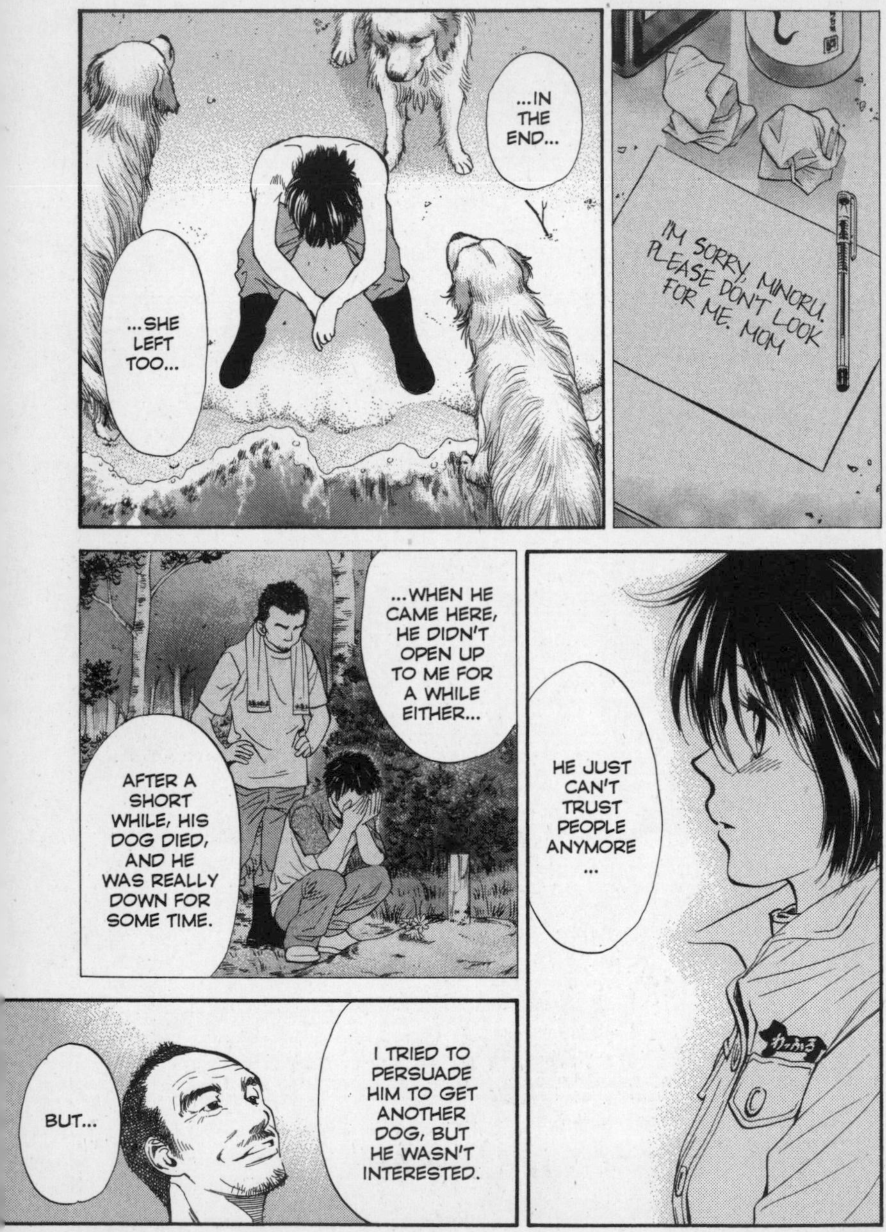
I'M SORRY, MINORU. PLEASE DON'T LOOK FOR ME. MOM
...IN THE END...
...SHE LEFT TOO...
HE JUST CAN'T TRUST PEOPLE ANYMORE ...
...WHEN HE CAME HERE, HE DIDN'T OPEN UP TO ME FOR A WHILE EITHER...
AFTER A SHORT WHILE, HIS DOG DIED, AND HE WAS REALLY DOWN FOR SOME TIME.
I TRIED TO PERSUADE HIM TO GET ANOTHER DOG, BUT HE WASN'T INTERESTED.
BUT...

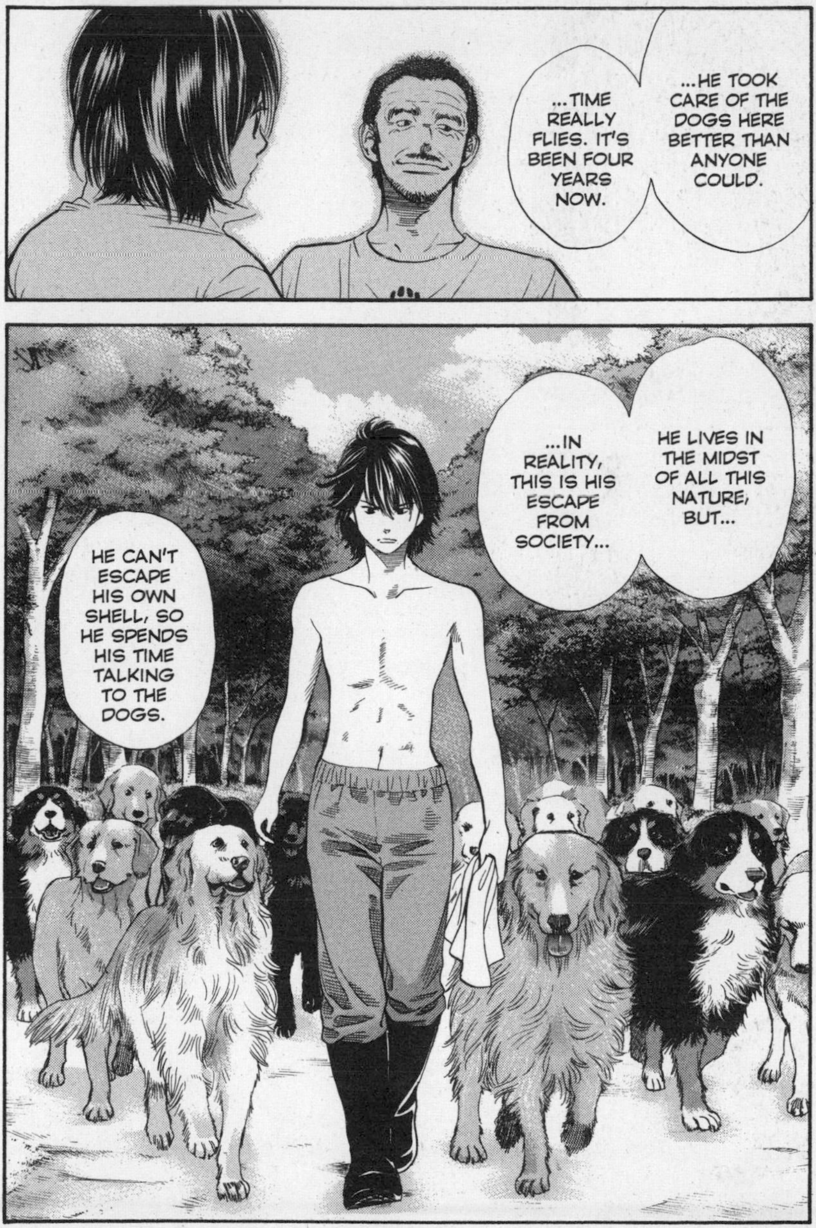
...HE TOOK CARE OF THE DOGS HERE BETTER THAN ANYONE COULD.
...TIME REALLY FLIES. IT'S BEEN FOUR YEARS NOW.
HE LIVES IN THE MIDST OF ALL THIS NATURE, BUT...
...IN REALITY, THIS IS HIS ESCAPE FROM SOCIETY...
HE CAN'T ESCAPE HIS OWN SHELL, SO HE SPENDS HIS TIME TALKING TO THE DOGS.

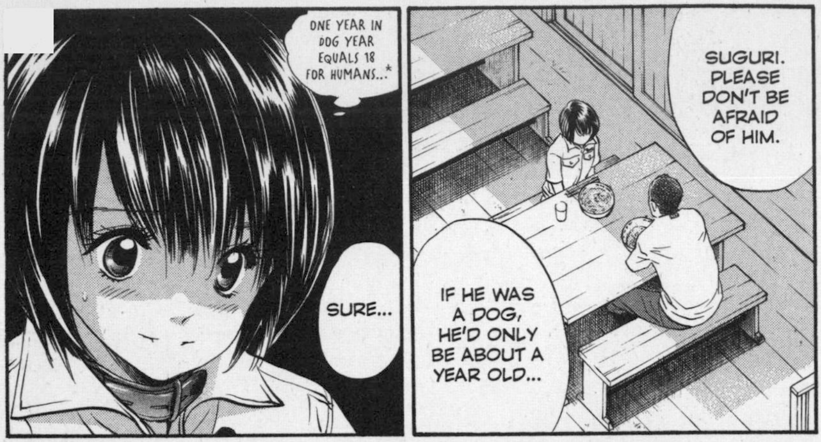
SUGURI. PLEASE DON'T BE AFRAID OF HIM.
IF HE WAS A DOG, HE'D ONLY BE ABOUT A YEAR OLD...
ONE YEAR IN DOG YEAR EQUALS 18 FOR HUMANS...*
SURE...
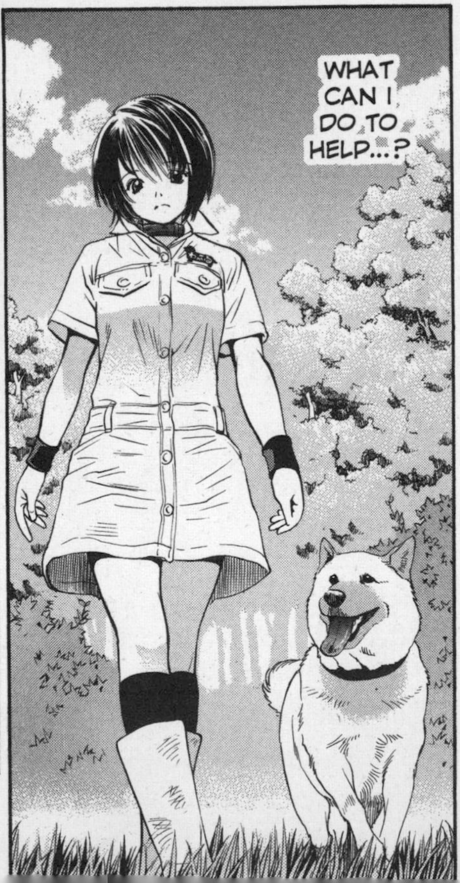
WHAT CAN I DO TO HELP...?
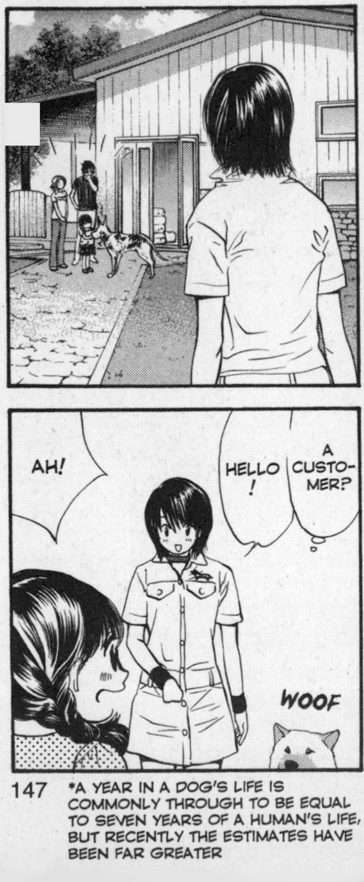
A CUSTOMER?
HELLO!
AH!
WOOF

*A YEAR IN A DOG'S LIFE IS COMMONLY THROUGH TO BE EQUAL TO SEVEN YEARS OF A HUMAN'S LIFE, BUT RECENTLY THE ESTIMATES HAVE BEEN FAR GREATER

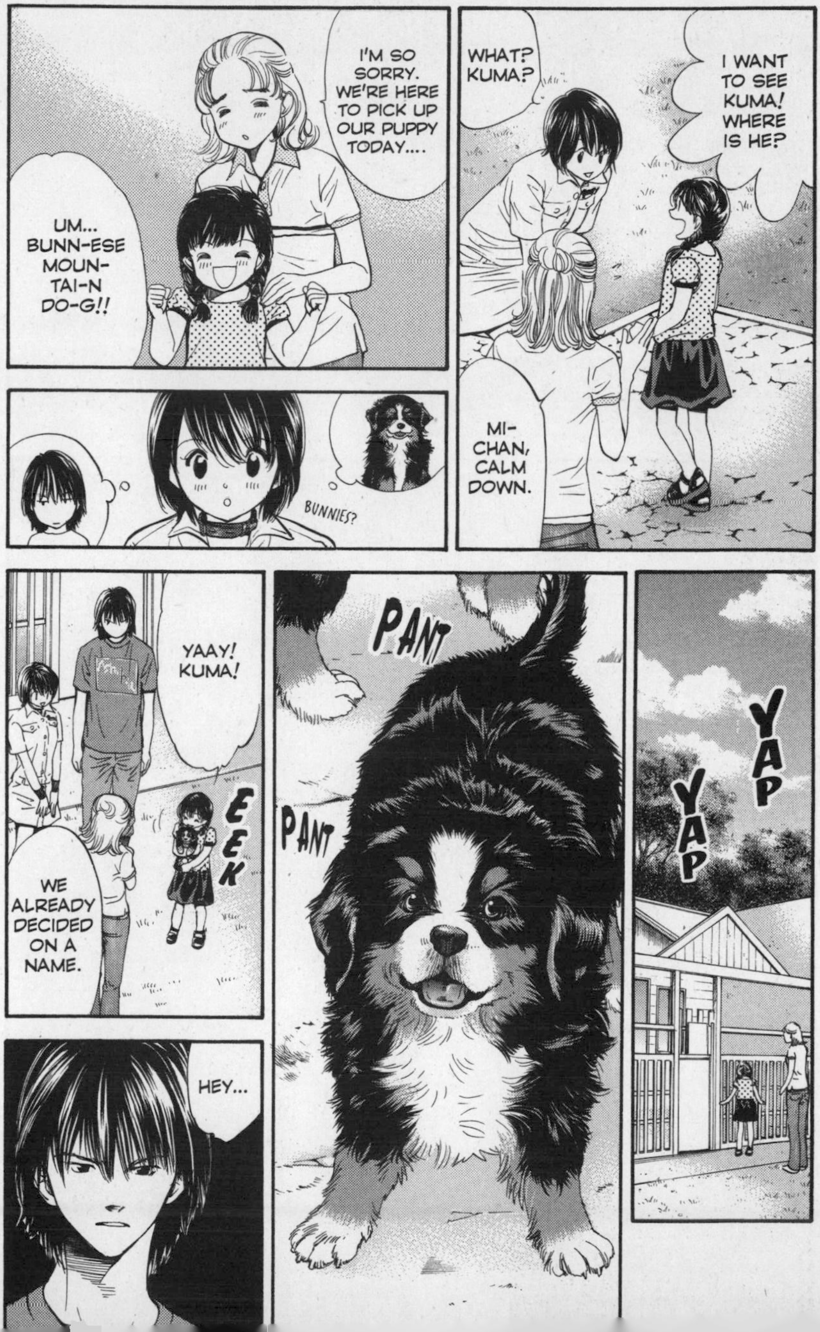
I WANT TO SEE KUMA! WHERE IS HE?
WHAT? KUMA?
MI-CHAN, CALM DOWN.
I'M SO SORRY. WE'RE HERE TO PICK UP OUR PUPPY TODAY....
UM... BUNN-ESE MOUN-TAI-N DO-G!!
BUNNIES?
YAP
YAP
PANT
PANT
YAAY! KUMA!
EEK
WE ALREADY DECIDED ON A NAME.
HEY...

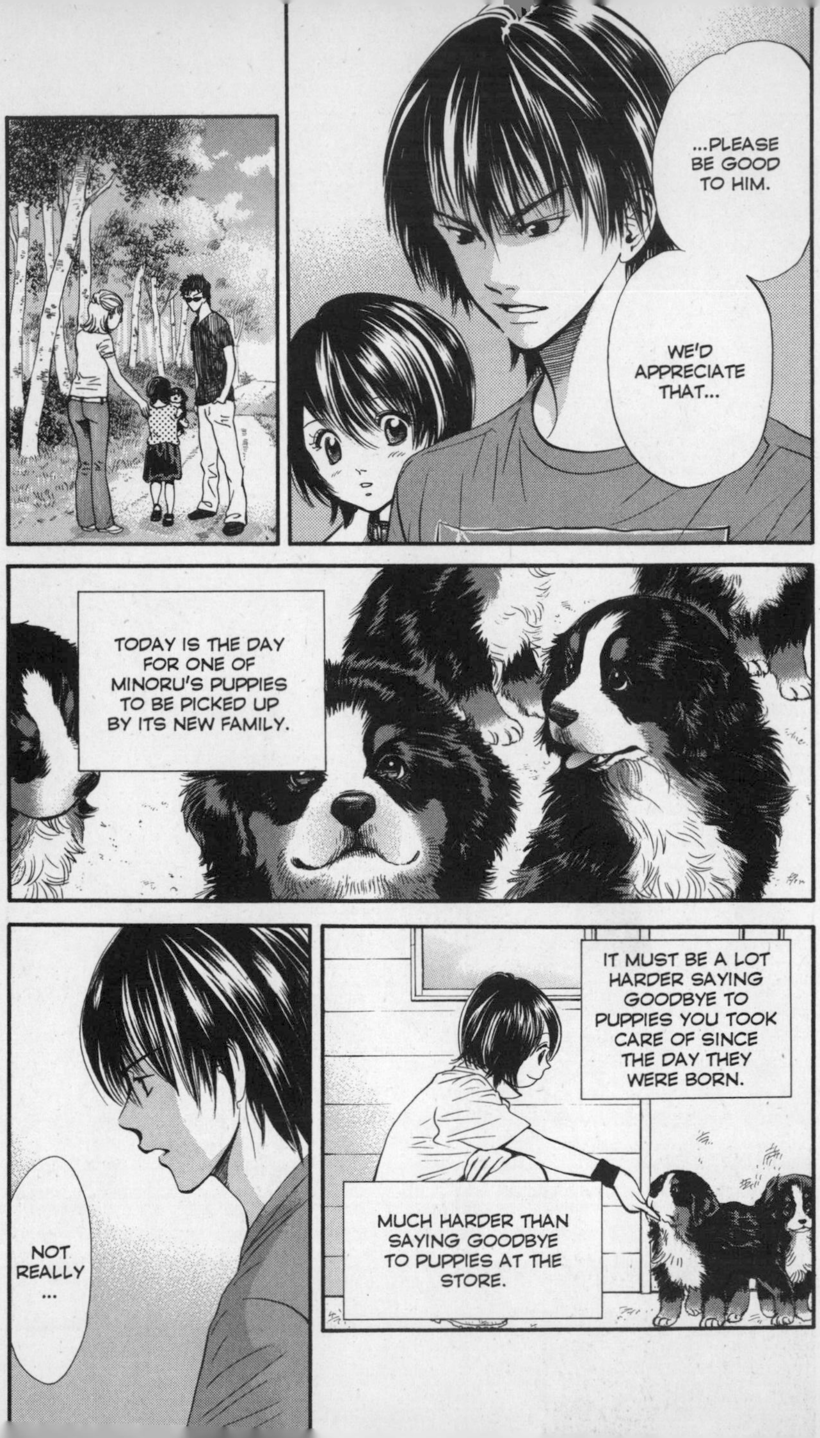
...PLEASE BE GOOD TO HIM.
WE'D APPRECIATE THAT...
TODAY IS THE DAY FOR ONE OF MINORU'S PUPPIES TO BE PICKED UP BY ITS NEW FAMILY.
IT MUST BE A LOT HARDER SAYING GOODBYE TO PUPPIES YOU TOOK CARE OF SINCE THE DAY THEY WERE BORN.
MUCH HARDER THAN SAYING GOODBYE TO PUPPIES AT THE STORE.
NOT REALLY ...

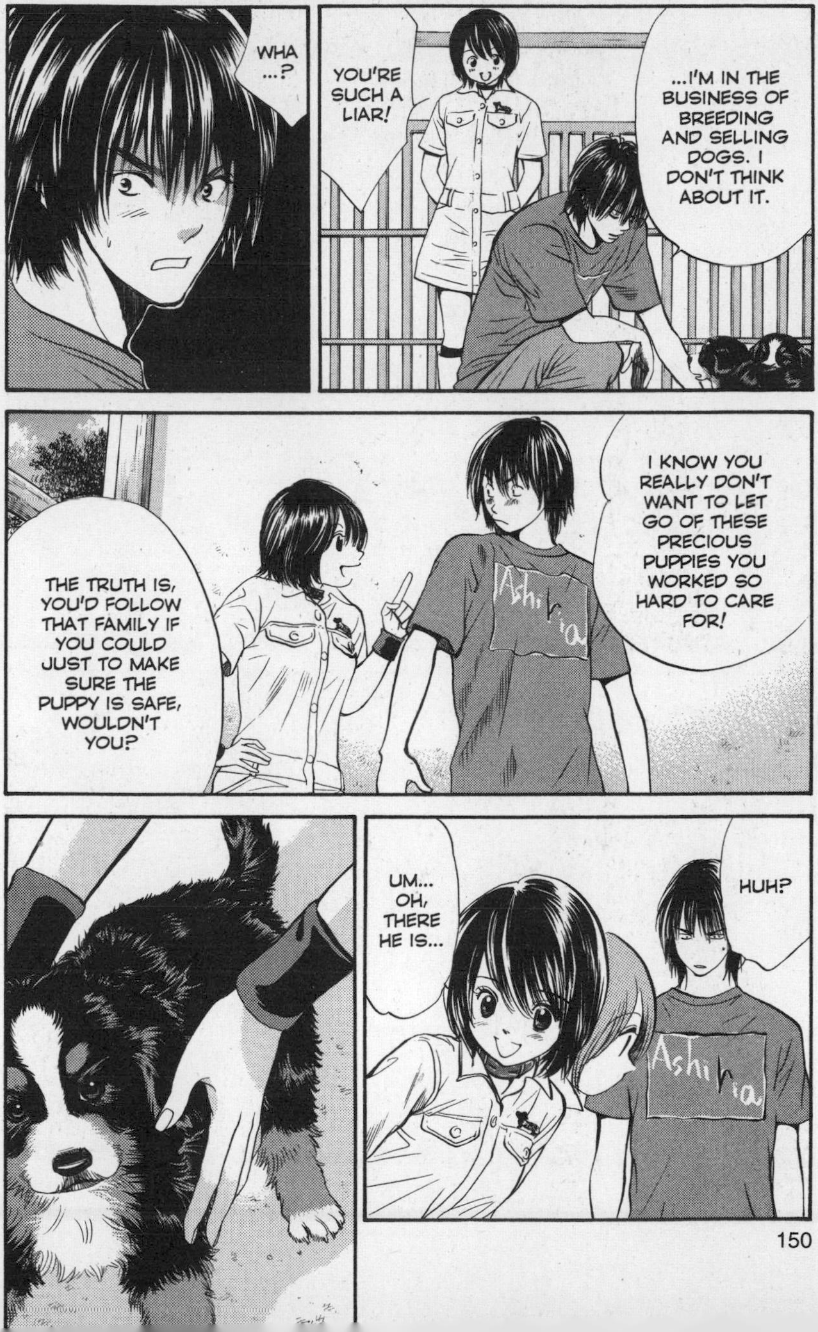
...I'M IN THE BUSINESS OF BREEDING AND SELLING DOGS. I DON'T THINK ABOUT IT.
YOU'RE SUCH A LIAR!
WHA ...?
I KNOW YOU REALLY DON'T WANT TO LET GO OF THESE PRECIOUS PUPPIES YOU WORKED SO HARD TO CARE FOR!
THE TRUTH IS, YOU'D FOLLOW THAT FAMILY IF YOU COULD JUST TO MAKE SURE THE PUPPY IS SAFE, WOULDN'T YOU?
HUH?
UM... OH, THERE HE IS...

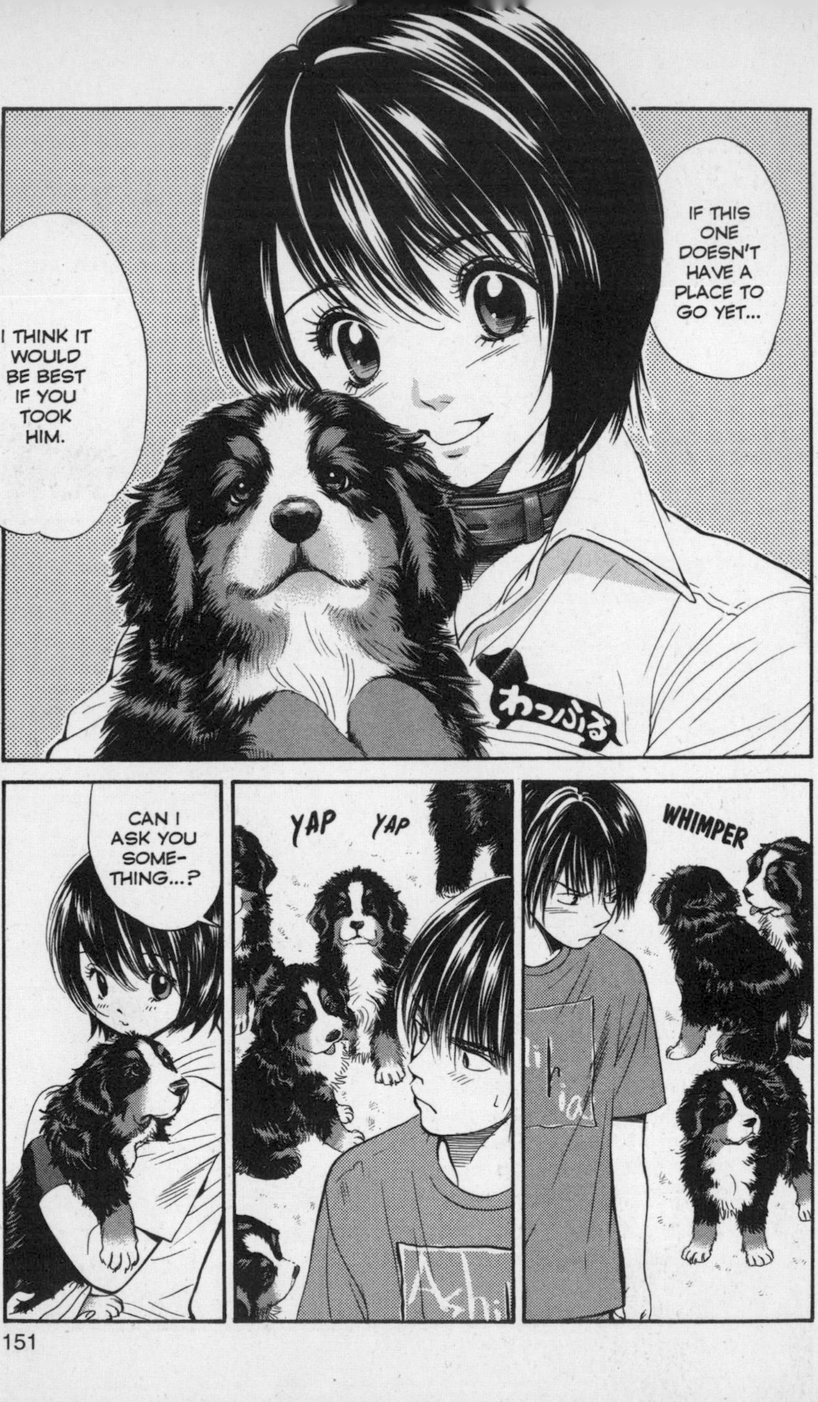
IF THIS ONE DOESN'T HAVE A PLACE TO GO YET...
I THINK IT WOULD BE BEST IF YOU TOOK HIM.
わっぷる
WHIMPER
YAP YAP
CAN I ASK YOU SOME-THING...?

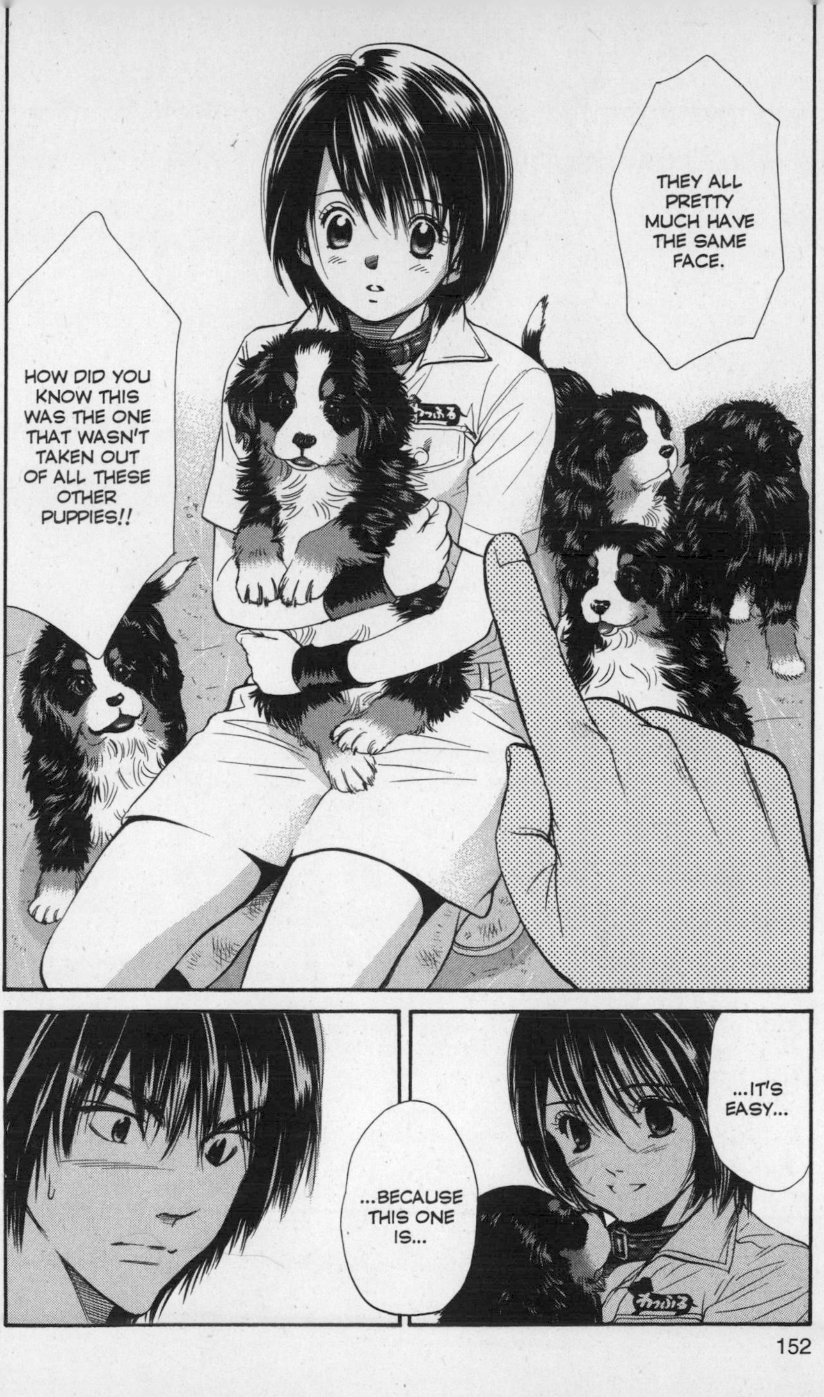
THEY ALL PRETTY MUCH HAVE THE SAME FACE.
HOW DID YOU KNOW THIS WAS THE ONE THAT WASN'T TAKEN OUT OF ALL THESE OTHER PUPPIES!!
...IT'S EASY...
...BECAUSE THIS ONE IS...

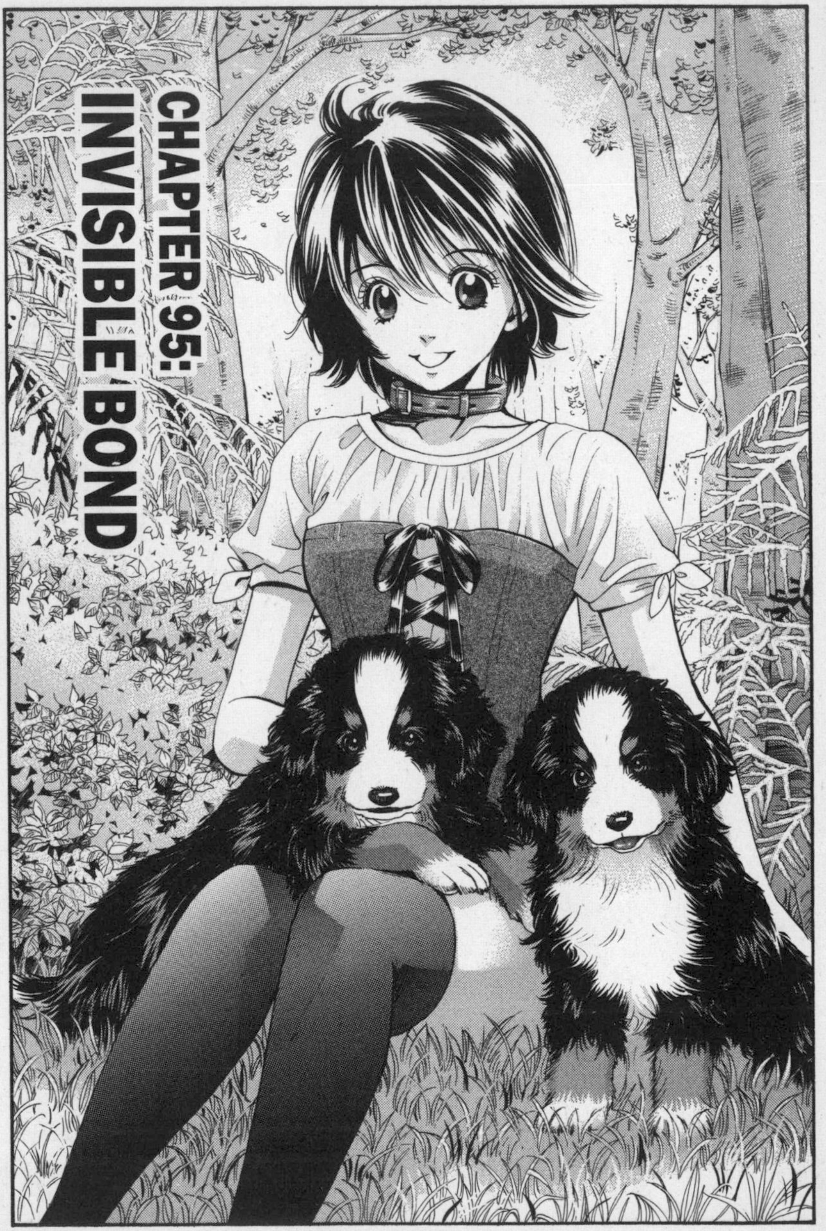
CHAPTER 95:
INVISIBLE BOND

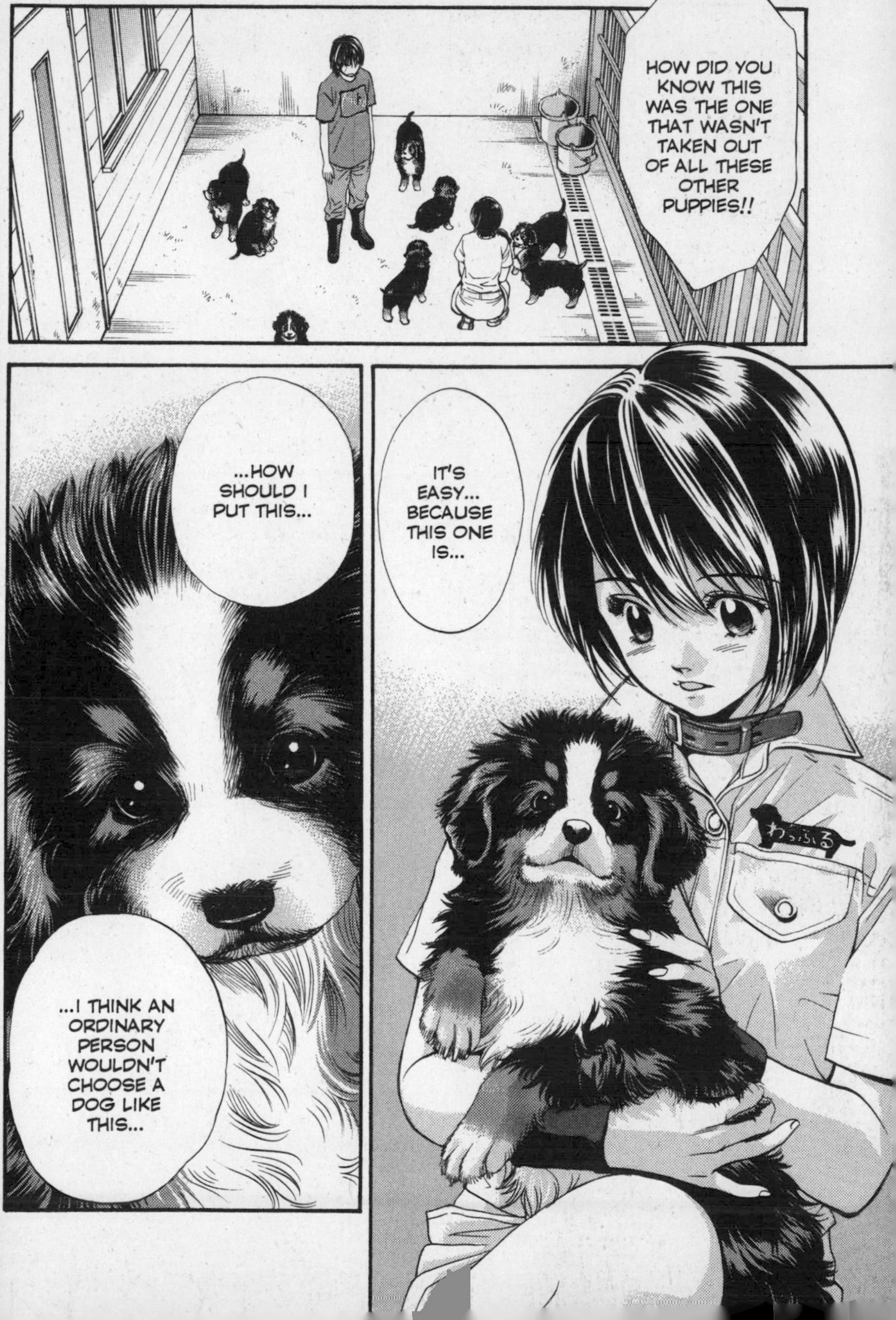
HOW DID YOU KNOW THIS WAS THE ONE THAT WASN'T TAKEN OUT OF ALL THESE OTHER PUPPIES!!
IT'S EASY... BECAUSE THIS ONE IS...
わっふる
...HOW SHOULD I PUT THIS...
...I THINK AN ORDINARY PERSON WOULDN'T CHOOSE A DOG LIKE THIS...

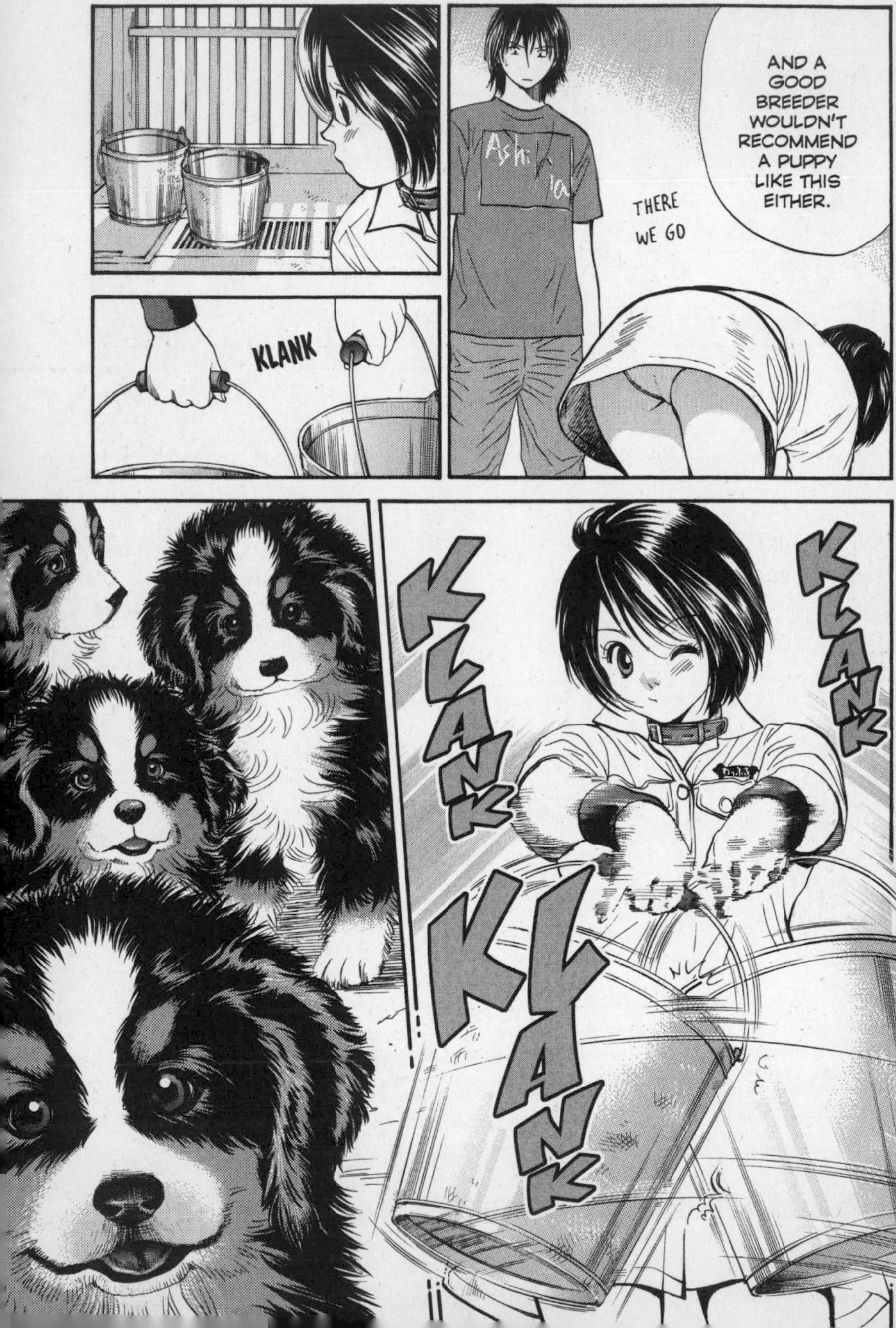
AND A GOOD BREEDER WOULDN'T RECOMMEND A PUPPY LIKE THIS EITHER.
THERE WE GO
KLANK
KLANK
KLANK
KLANK

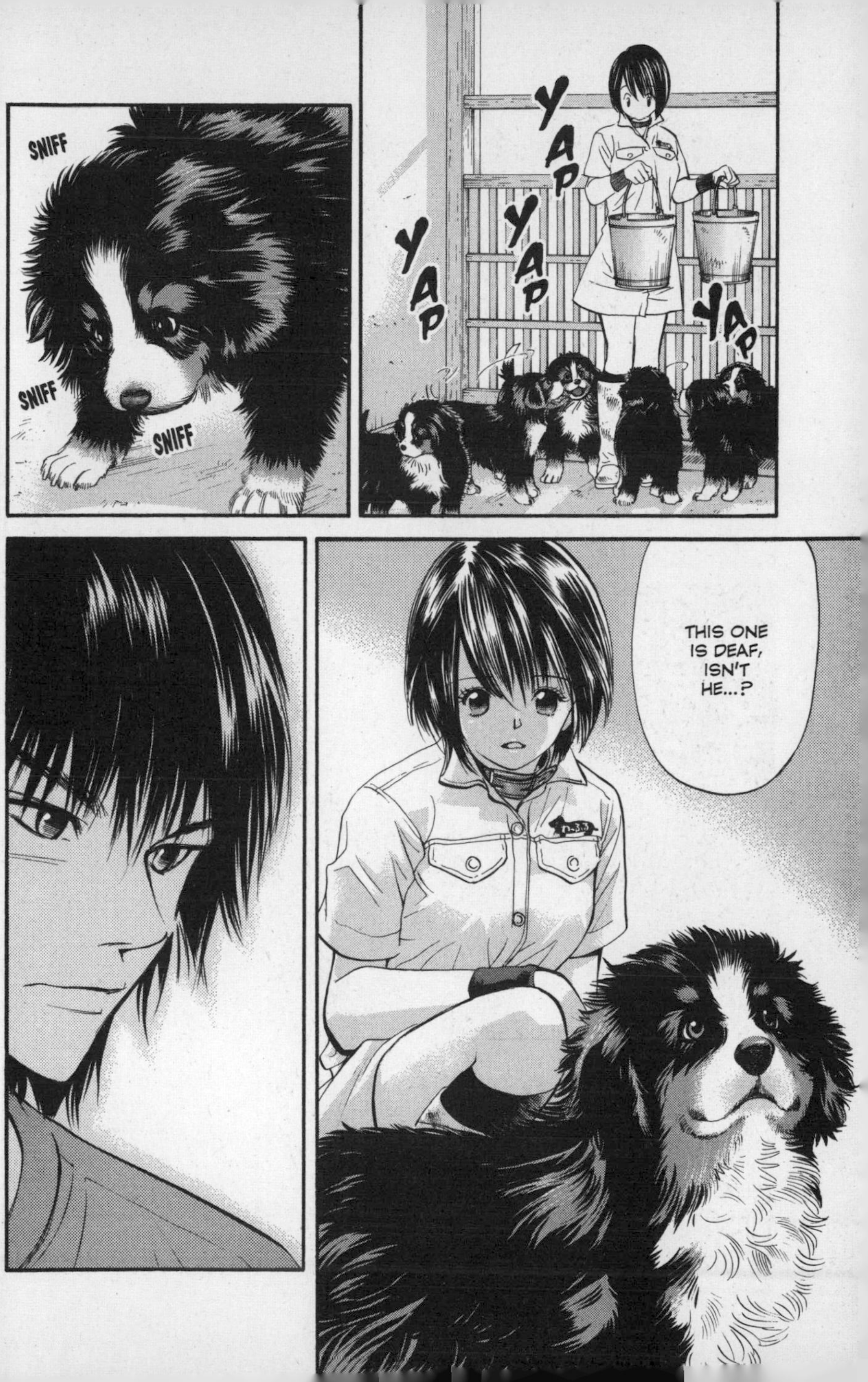
YAP YAP
YAP YAP
YAP YAP
YAP YAP
SNIFF
SNIFF
SNIFF
THIS ONE IS DEAF, ISN'T HE...?

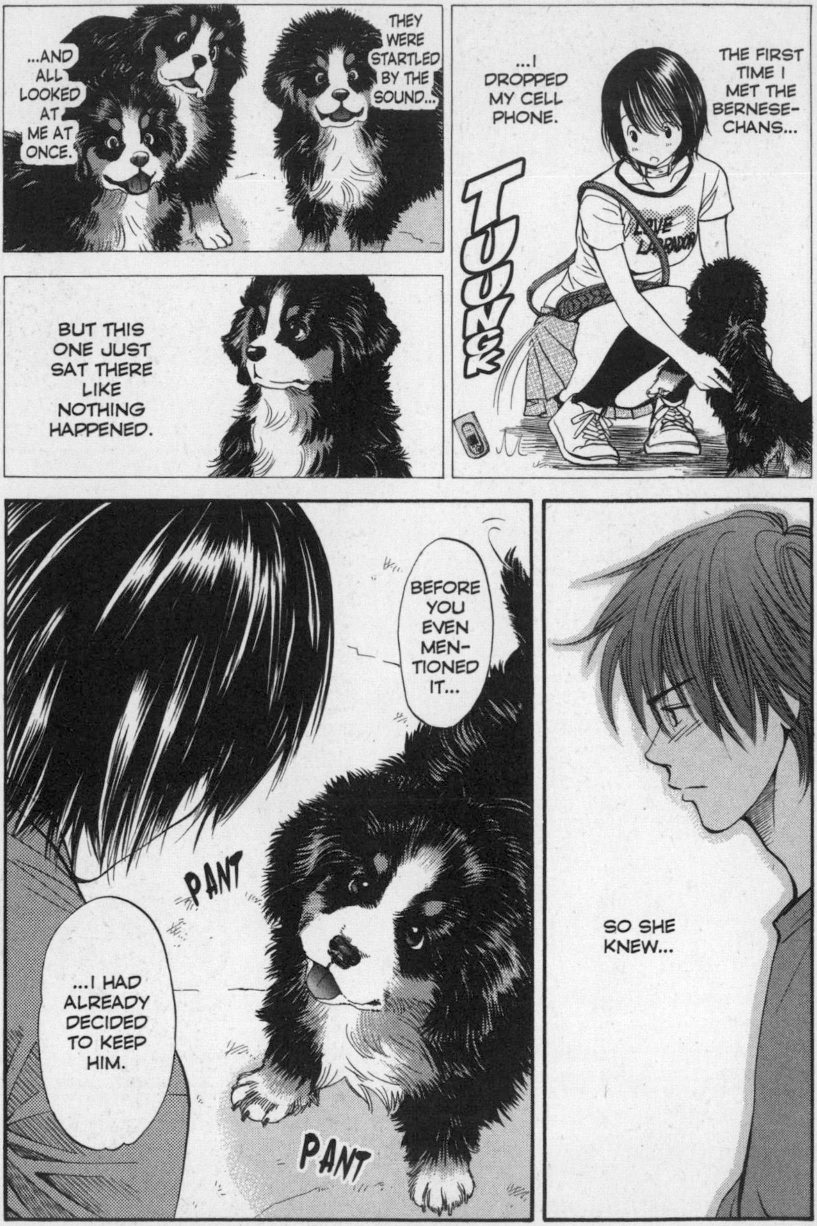
THE FIRST TIME I MET THE BERNESE-CHANS...
...I DROPPED MY CELL PHONE.
TUUUNGK
THEY WERE STARTLED BY THE SOUND...
...AND ALL LOOKED AT ME AT ONCE.
BUT THIS ONE JUST SAT THERE LIKE NOTHING HAPPENED.
SO SHE KNEW...
BEFORE YOU EVEN MENTIONED IT...
PANT
...I HAD ALREADY DECIDED TO KEEP HIM.
PANT

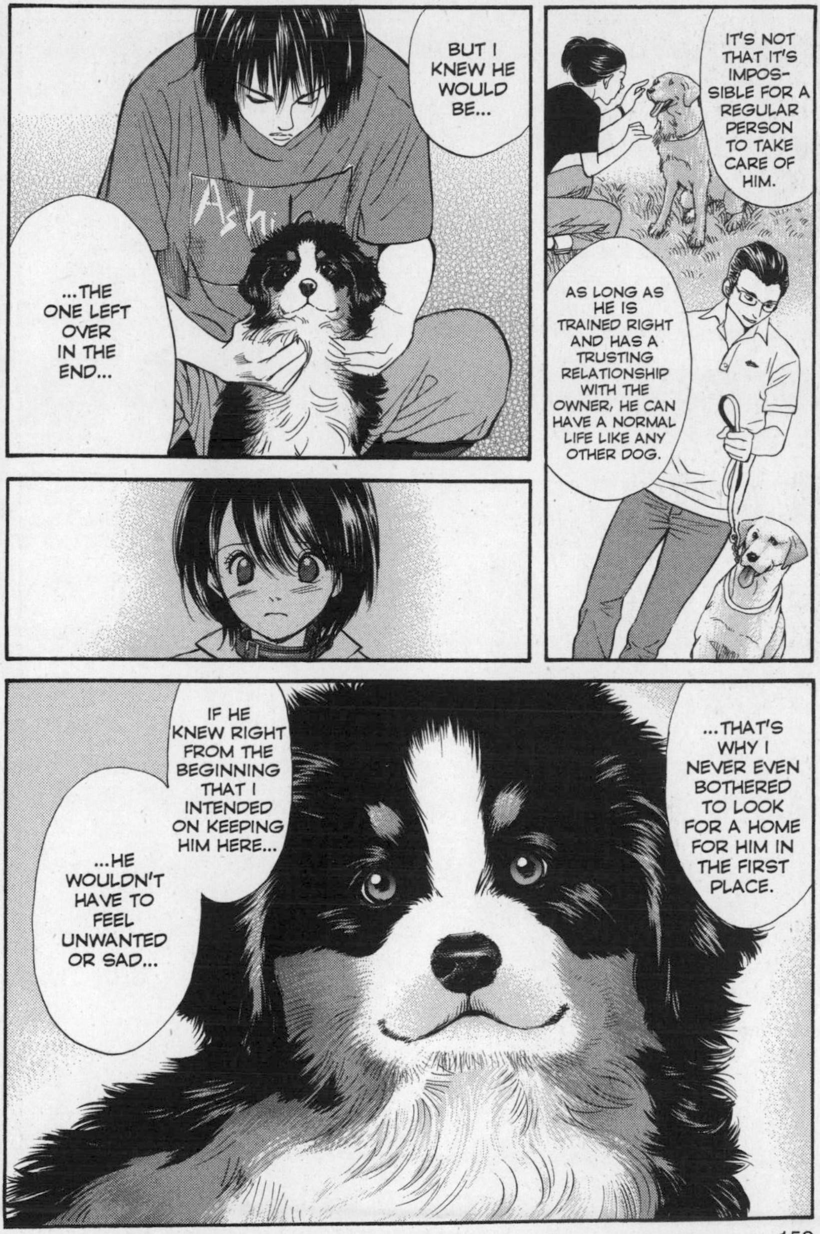
IT'S NOT THAT IT'S IMPOSSIBLE FOR A REGULAR PERSON TO TAKE CARE OF HIM.
AS LONG AS HE IS TRAINED RIGHT AND HAS A TRUSTING RELATIONSHIP WITH THE OWNER, HE CAN HAVE A NORMAL LIFE LIKE ANY OTHER DOG.
BUT I KNEW HE WOULD BE...
...THE ONE LEFT OVER IN THE END...
...THAT'S WHY I NEVER EVEN BOTHERED TO LOOK FOR A HOME FOR HIM IN THE FIRST PLACE.
IF HE KNEW RIGHT FROM THE BEGINNING THAT I INTENDED ON KEEPING HIM HERE...
...HE WOULDN'T HAVE TO FEEL UNWANTED OR SAD...

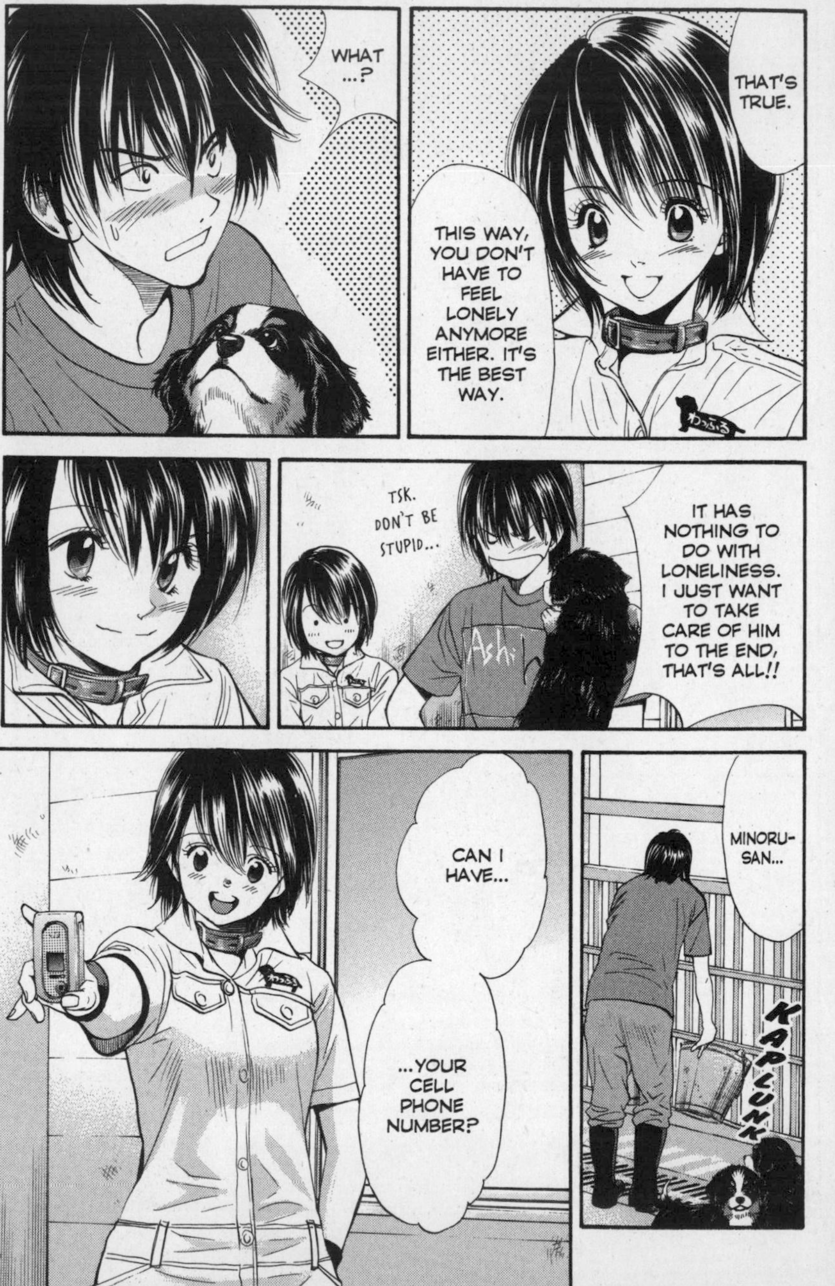
THAT'S TRUE.
THIS WAY, YOU DON'T HAVE TO FEEL LONELY ANYMORE EITHER. IT'S THE BEST WAY.
WHAT ...?
IT HAS NOTHING TO DO WITH LONELINESS. I JUST WANT TO TAKE CARE OF HIM TO THE END, THAT'S ALL!!
TSK. DON'T BE STUPID...
MINORU-SAN...
KAPLUNK
CAN I HAVE...
...YOUR CELL PHONE NUMBER?

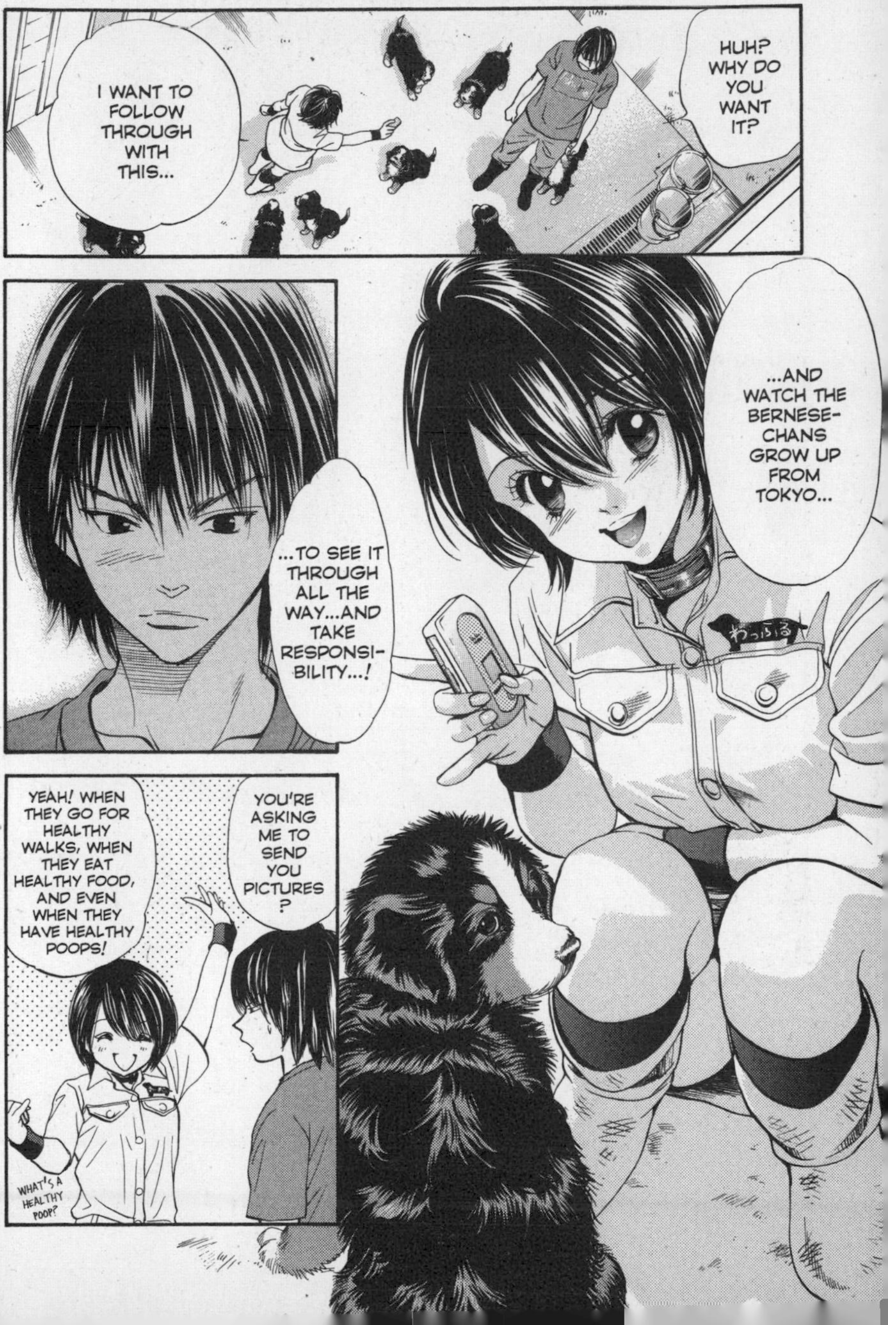
HUH? WHY DO YOU WANT IT?
I WANT TO FOLLOW THROUGH WITH THIS...
...TO SEE IT THROUGH ALL THE WAY...AND TAKE RESPONSIBILITY...!
...AND WATCH THE BERNESE-CHANS GROW UP FROM TOKYO...
YOU'RE ASKING ME TO SEND YOU PICTURES?
YEAH! WHEN THEY GO FOR HEALTHY WALKS, WHEN THEY EAT HEALTHY FOOD, AND EVEN WHEN THEY HAVE HEALTHY POOPS!
WHAT'S A HEALTHY POOP?

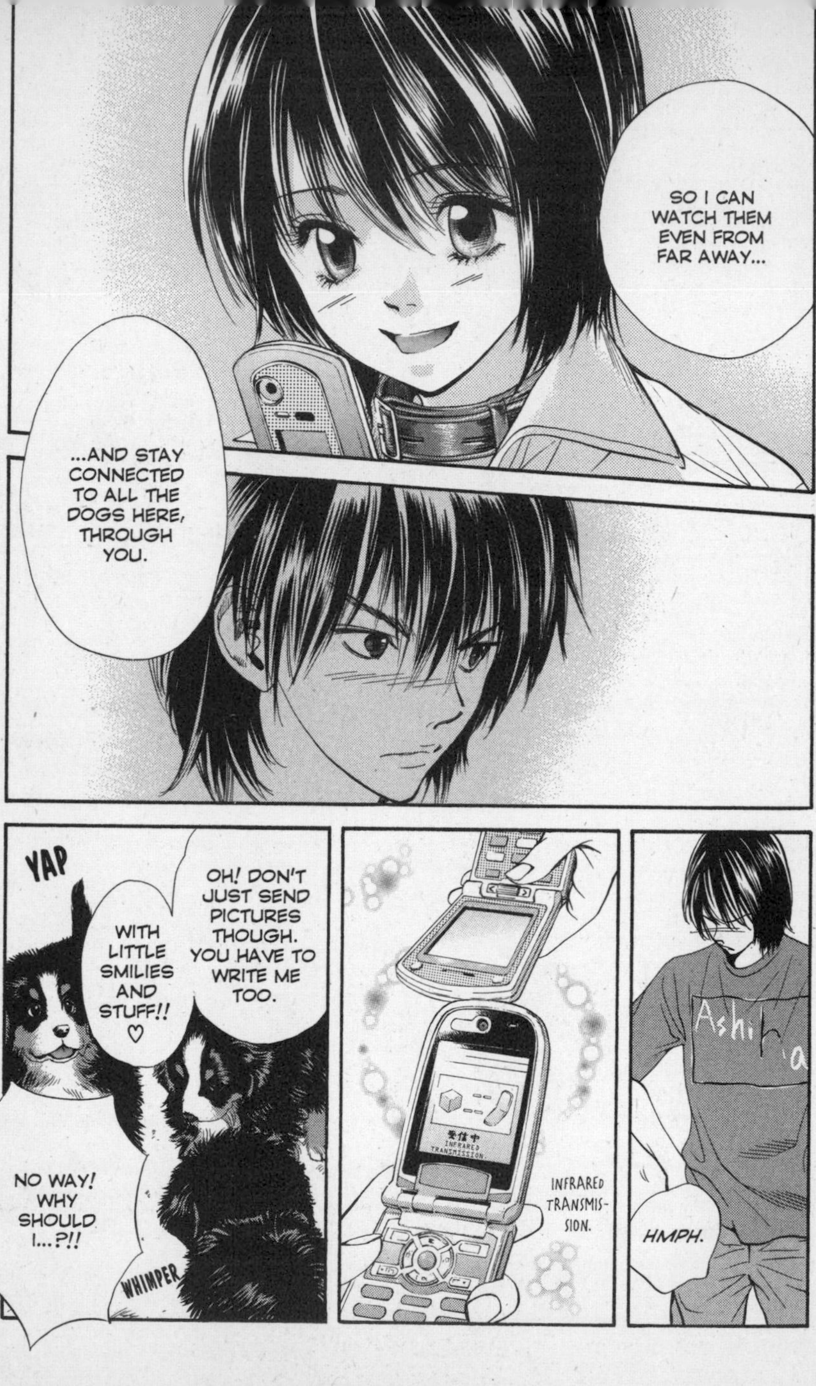
SO I CAN WATCH THEM EVEN FROM FAR AWAY...
...AND STAY CONNECTED TO ALL THE DOGS HERE, THROUGH YOU.
HMPH.
受信中
INFRARED TRANSMISSION.
INFRARED TRANSMIS-SION.
OH! DON'T JUST SEND PICTURES THOUGH. YOU HAVE TO WRITE ME TOO.
WITH LITTLE SMILIES AND STUFF!! ♡
YAP
NO WAY! WHY SHOULD I...?!!
WHIMPER

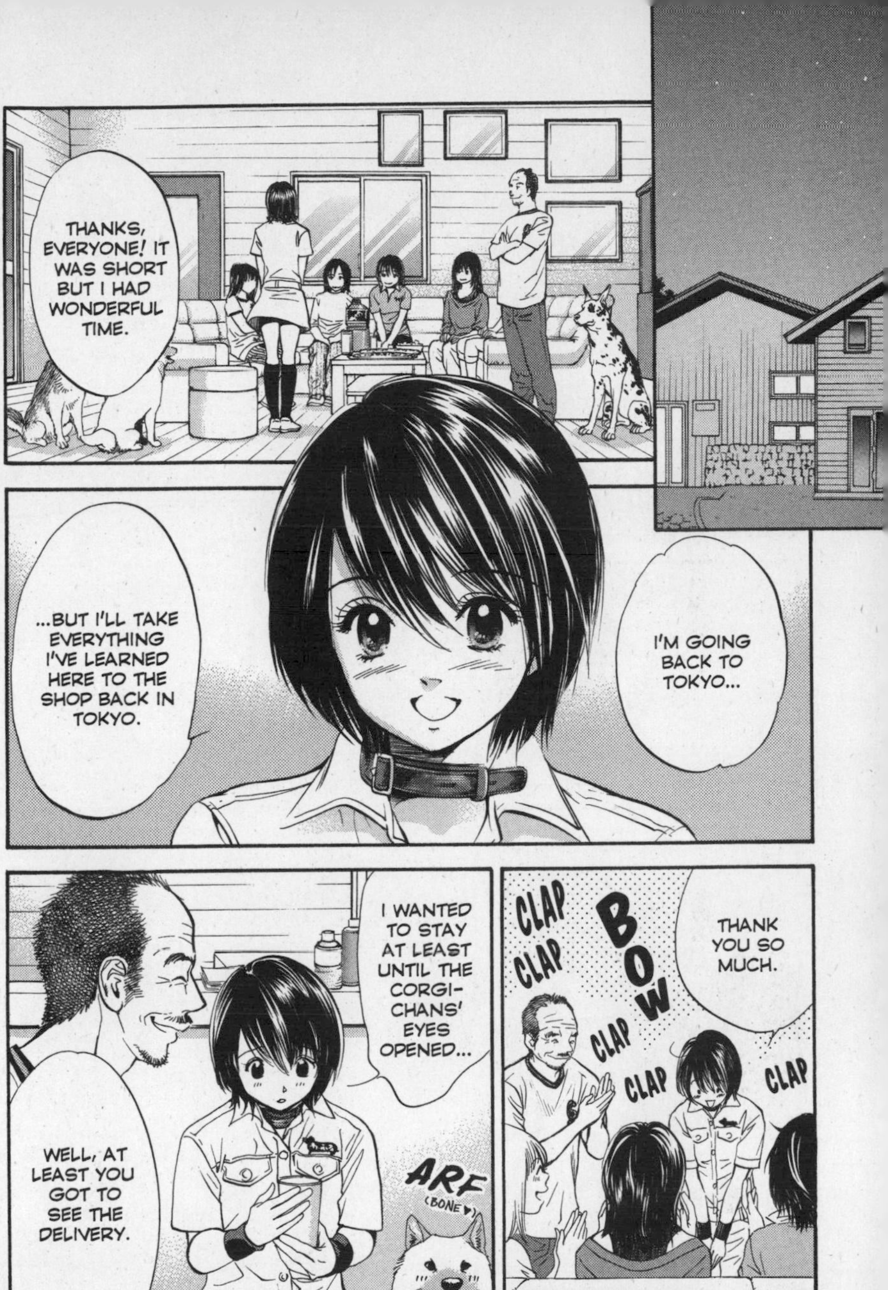
THANKS, EVERYONE! IT WAS SHORT BUT I HAD WONDERFUL TIME.
I'M GOING BACK TO TOKYO...
...BUT I'LL TAKE EVERYTHING I'VE LEARNED HERE TO THE SHOP BACK IN TOKYO.
THANK YOU SO MUCH.
BOW
CLAP CLAP
CLAP
CLAP
CLAP
I WANTED TO STAY AT LEAST UNTIL THE CORGI-CHANS' EYES OPENED...
WELL, AT LEAST YOU GOT TO SEE THE DELIVERY.
ARF
(BONE▸)

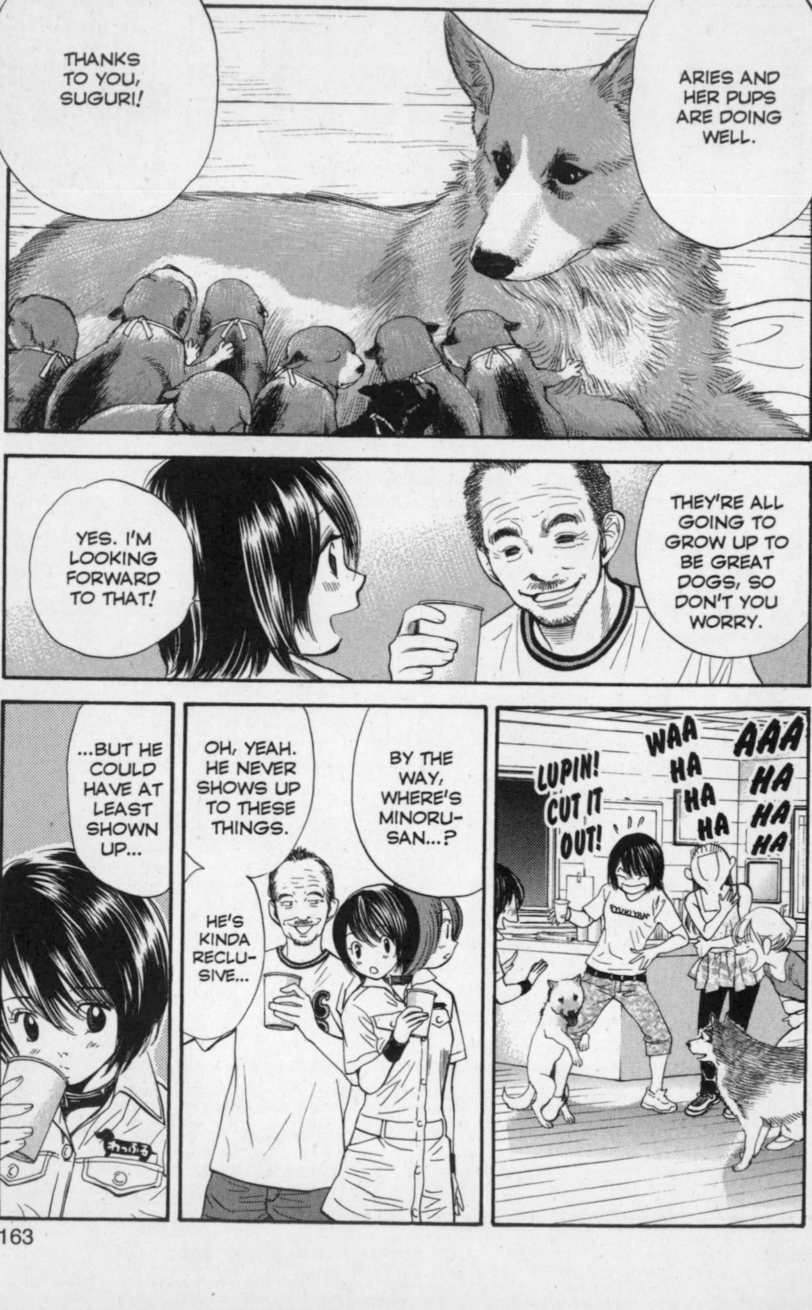
ARIES AND HER PUPS ARE DOING WELL.
THANKS TO YOU, SUGURI!
THEY'RE ALL GOING TO GROW UP TO BE GREAT DOGS, SO DON'T YOU WORRY.
YES. I'M LOOKING FORWARD TO THAT!
AAA HA HA HA
WAA HA HA HA
LUPIN! CUT IT OUT!
BY THE WAY, WHERE'S MINORU-SAN...?
OH, YEAH. HE NEVER SHOWS UP TO THESE THINGS.
HE'S KINDA RECLUSIVE...
...BUT HE COULD HAVE AT LEAST SHOWN UP...

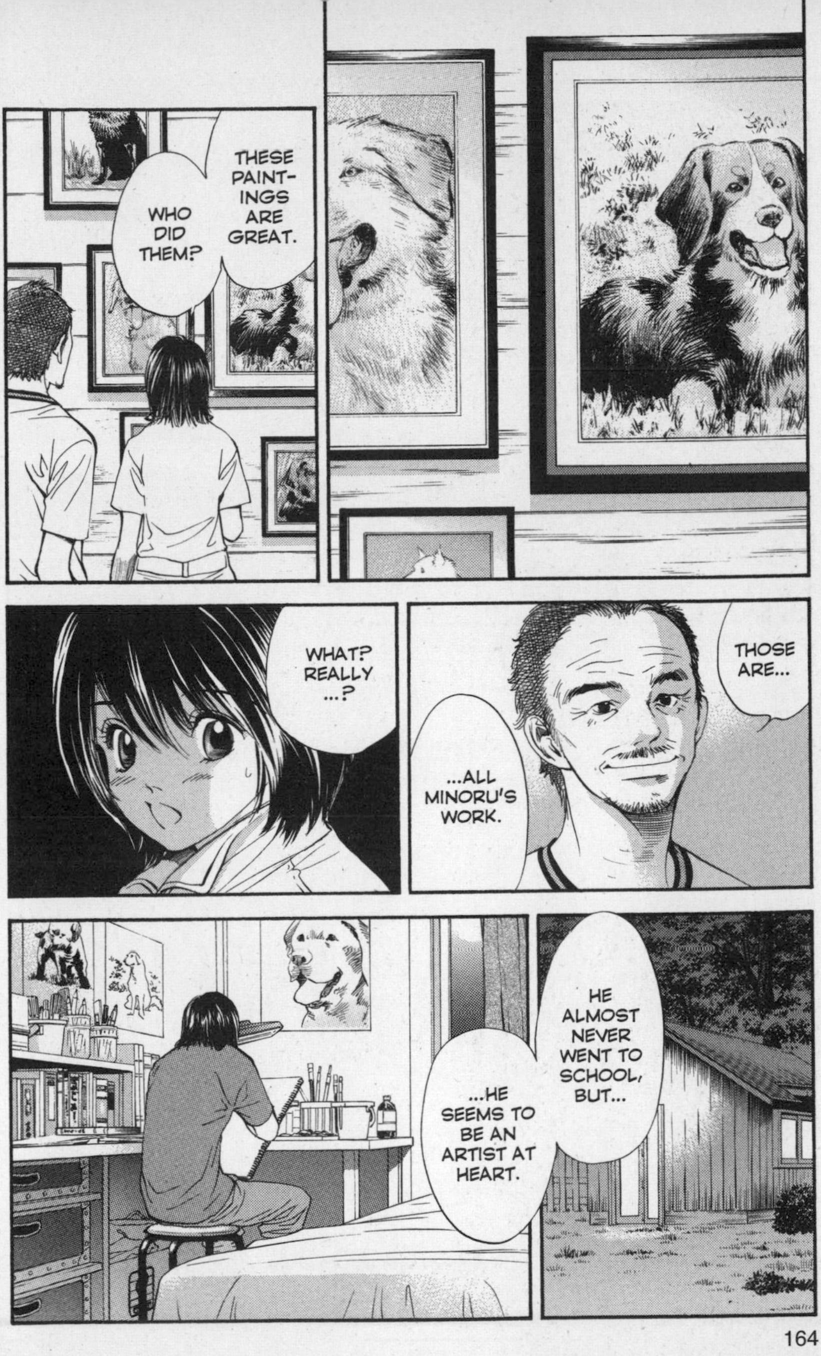
THESE PAINT- INGS ARE GREAT.
WHO DID THEM?
THOSE ARE...
...ALL MINORU'S WORK.
WHAT? REALLY ...?
HE ALMOST NEVER WENT TO SCHOOL, BUT...
...HE SEEMS TO BE AN ARTIST AT HEART.

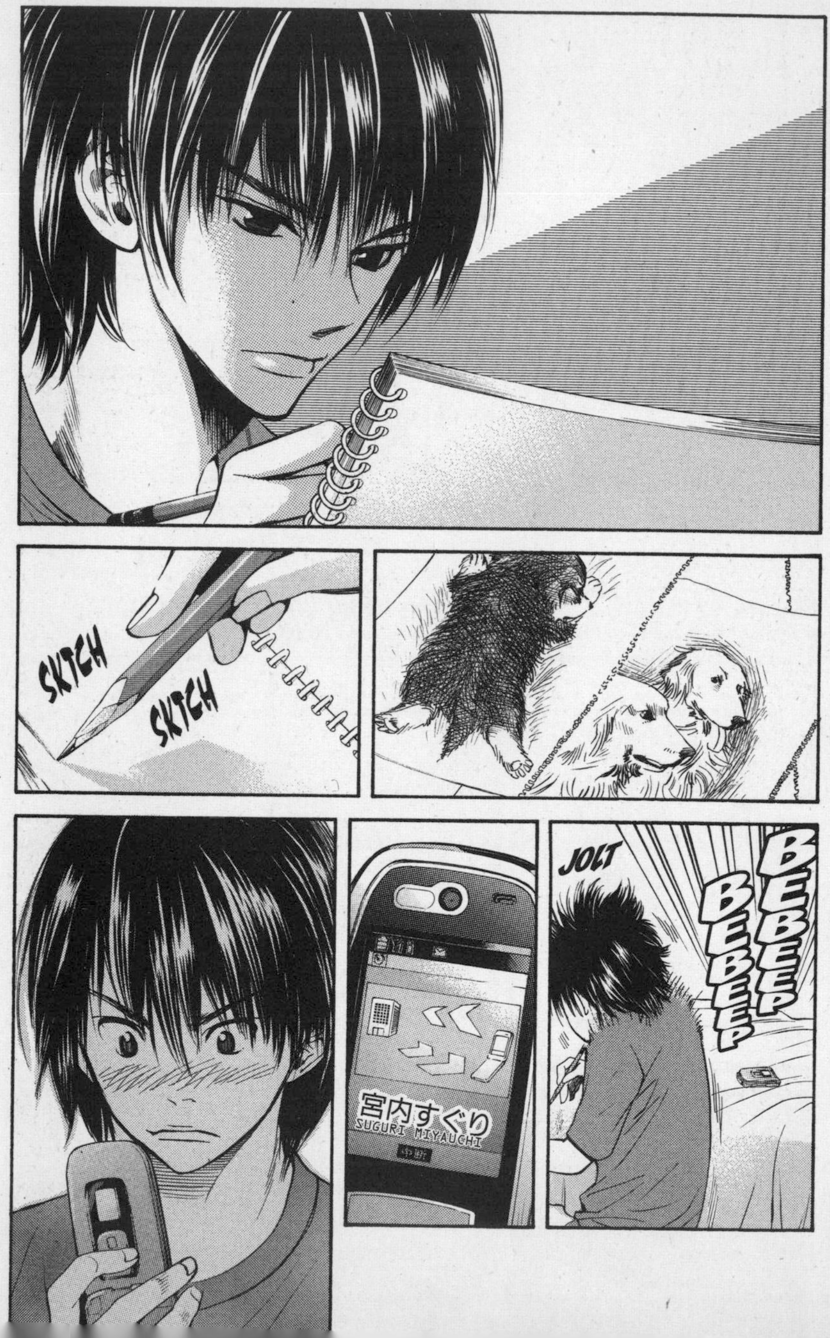
SKTCH
SKTCH
BEBEBEP
BEBEBEP
JOLT
宮内すぐり
SUGURI MIYAUCHI

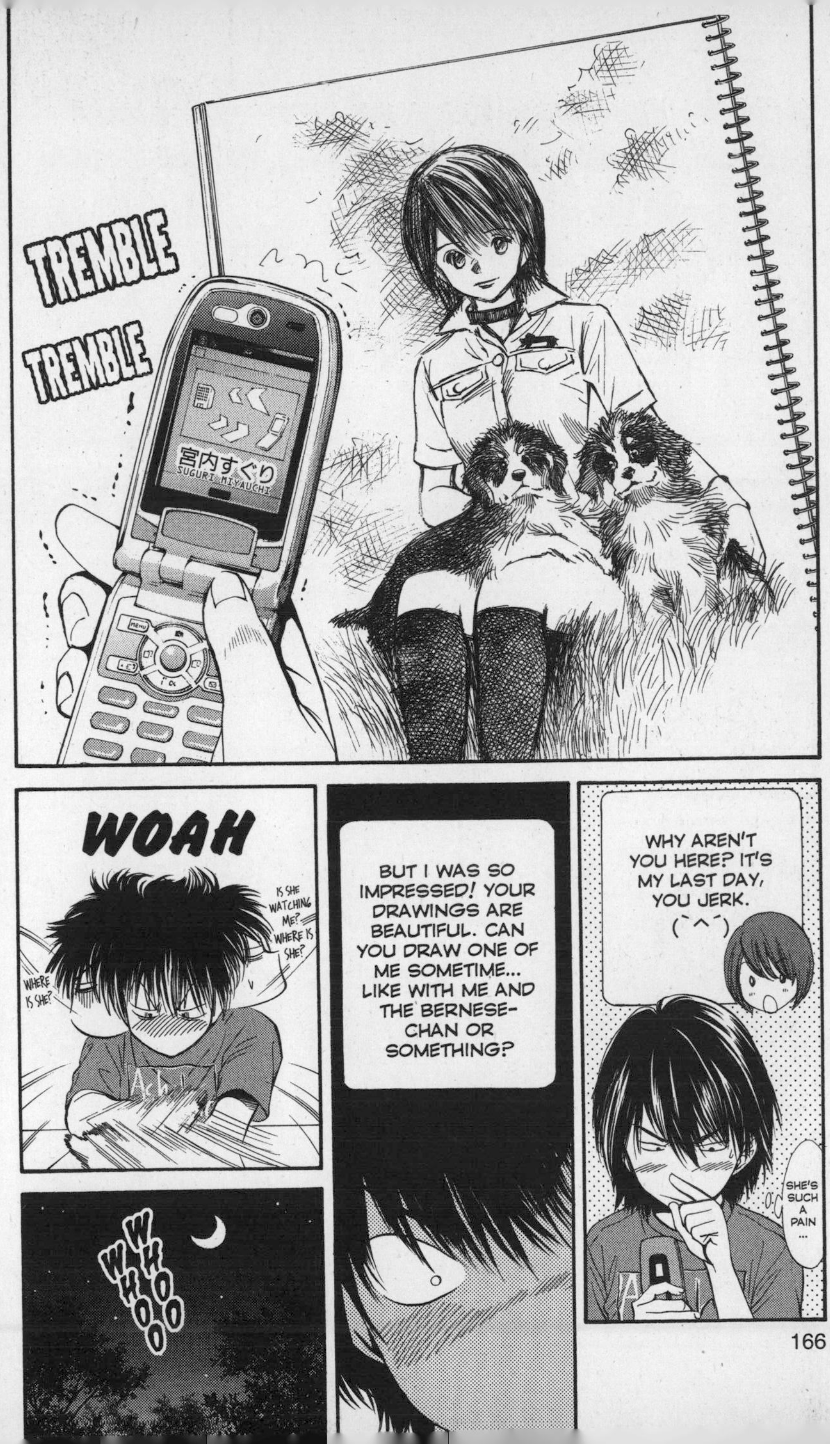
TREMBLE
TREMBLE
宮内すぐり
SUGURI MIYAUCHI
WHY AREN'T YOU HERE? IT'S MY LAST DAY, YOU JERK. (ˆ^ˆ)
SHE'S SUCH A PAIN...
BUT I WAS SO IMPRESSED! YOUR DRAWINGS ARE BEAUTIFUL. CAN YOU DRAW ONE OF ME SOMETIME... LIKE WITH ME AND THE BERNESE-CHAN OR SOMETHING?
WOAH
IS SHE WATCHING ME? WHERE IS SHE?
WHERE IS SHE?
WHOOO
WHOOO

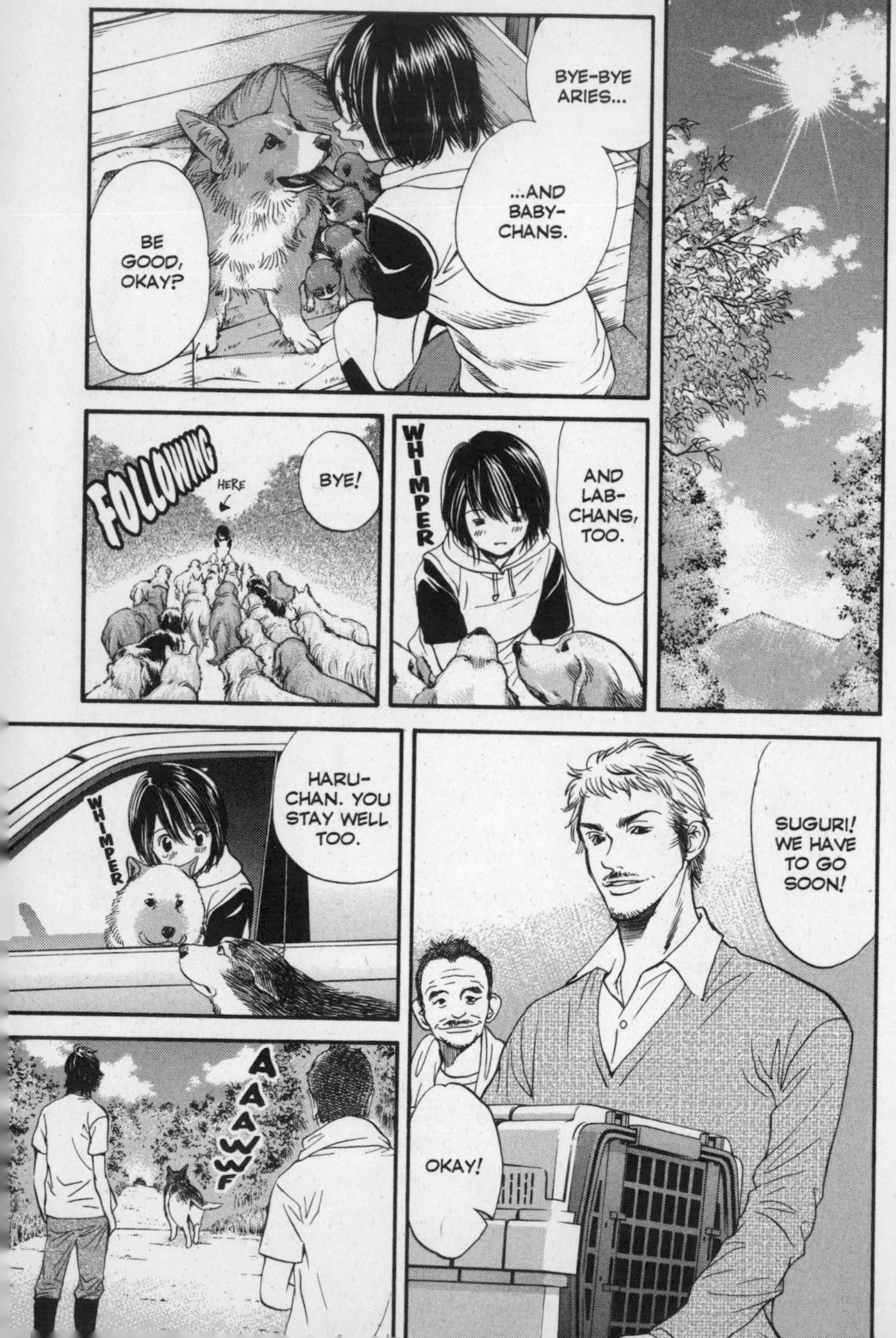
BYE-BYE ARIES...
...AND BABY-CHANS.
BE GOOD, OKAY?
WHIMPER
AND LAB-CHANS, TOO.
FOLLOWING
HERE
BYE!
SUGURI! WE HAVE TO GO SOON!
OKAY!
WHIMPER
HARU-CHAN. YOU STAY WELL TOO.
AAAAWWF

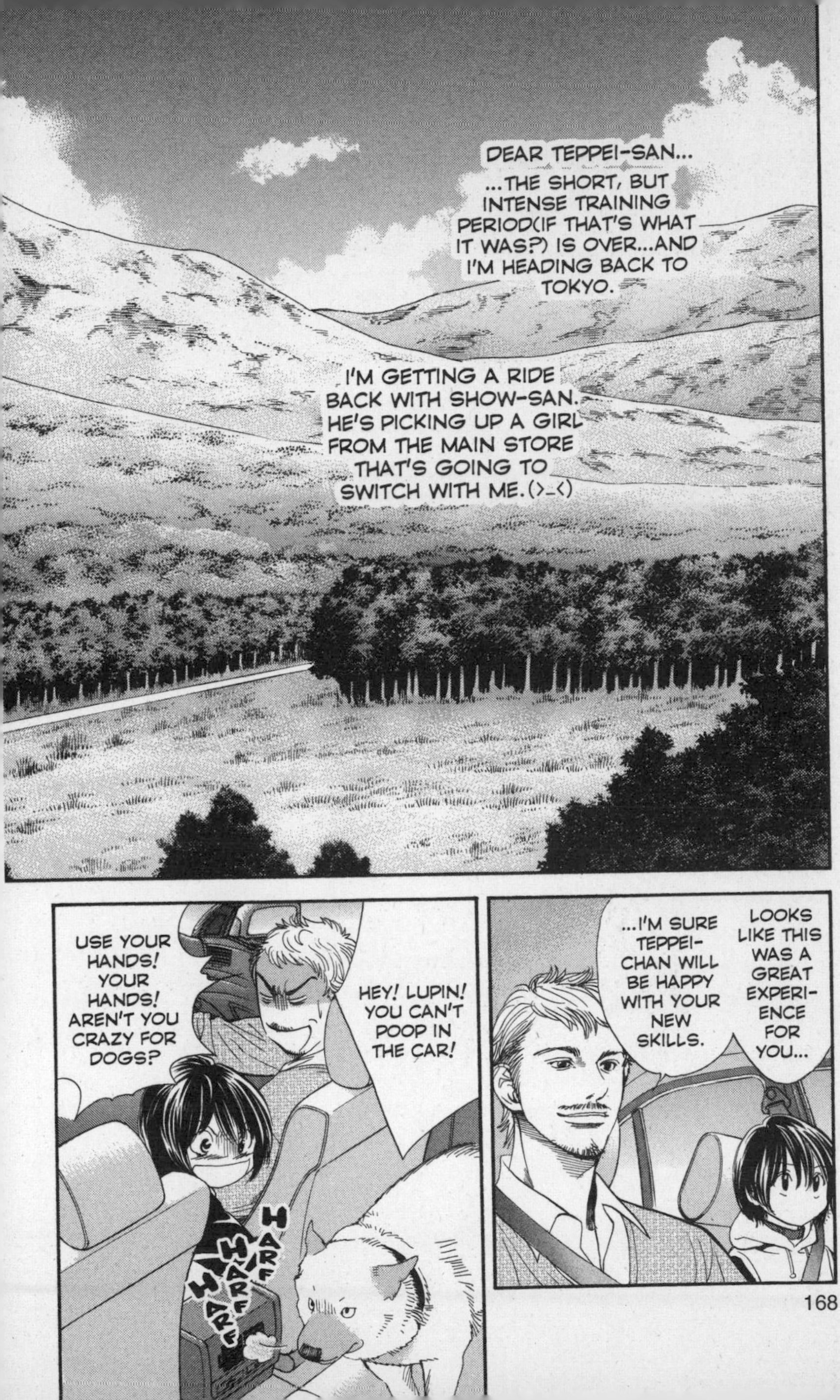
DEAR TEPPEI-SAN...
...THE SHORT, BUT INTENSE TRAINING PERIOD(IF THAT'S WHAT IT WAS?) IS OVER...AND I'M HEADING BACK TO TOKYO.
I'M GETTING A RIDE BACK WITH SHOW-SAN. HE'S PICKING UP A GIRL FROM THE MAIN STORE THAT'S GOING TO SWITCH WITH ME. (>_<)
LOOKS LIKE THIS WAS A GREAT EXPERIENCE FOR YOU...
...I'M SURE TEPPEI-CHAN WILL BE HAPPY WITH YOUR NEW SKILLS.
HEY! LUPIN! YOU CAN'T POOP IN THE CAR!
USE YOUR HANDS! YOUR HANDS! AREN'T YOU CRAZY FOR DOGS?
HARF HARF
HARF HARF
HARF

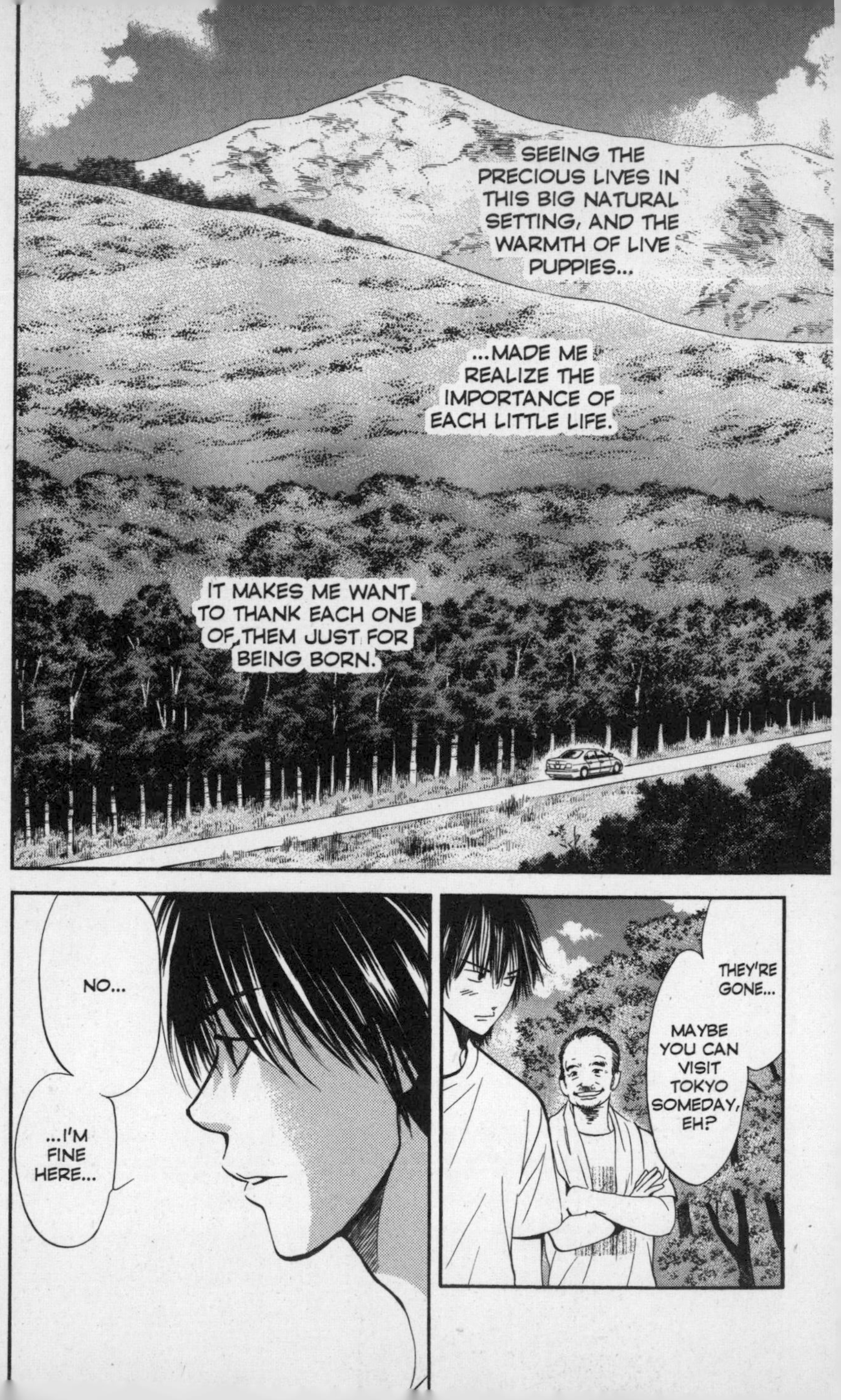
SEEING THE PRECIOUS LIVES IN THIS BIG NATURAL SETTING, AND THE WARMTH OF LIVE PUPPIES...
...MADE ME REALIZE THE IMPORTANCE OF EACH LITTLE LIFE.
IT MAKES ME WANT TO THANK EACH ONE OF THEM JUST FOR BEING BORN.
THEY'RE GONE...
MAYBE YOU CAN VISIT TOKYO SOMEDAY, EH?
NO...
...I'M FINE HERE...

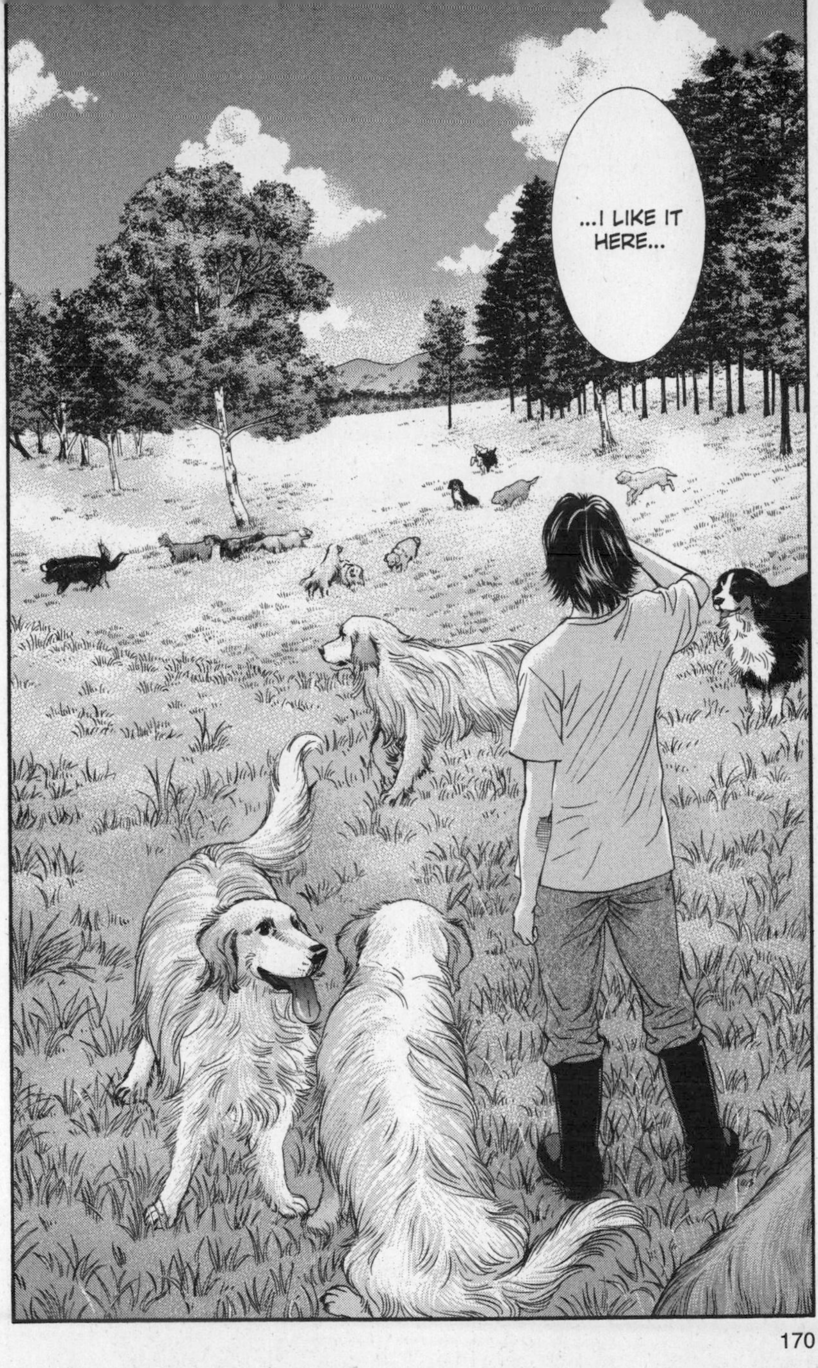
...I LIKE IT HERE...

CHAPTER 96: I WANT ONE MORE

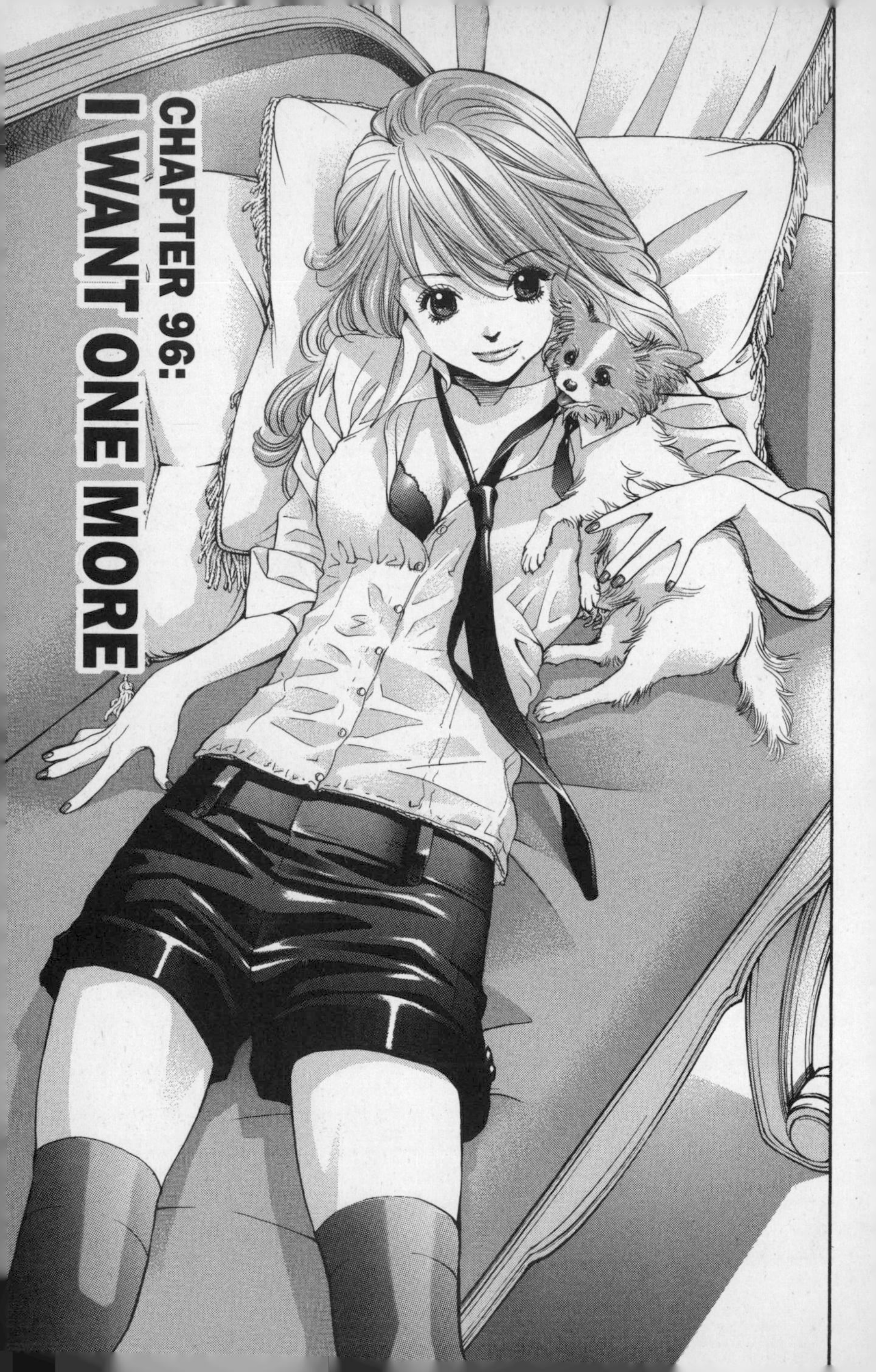

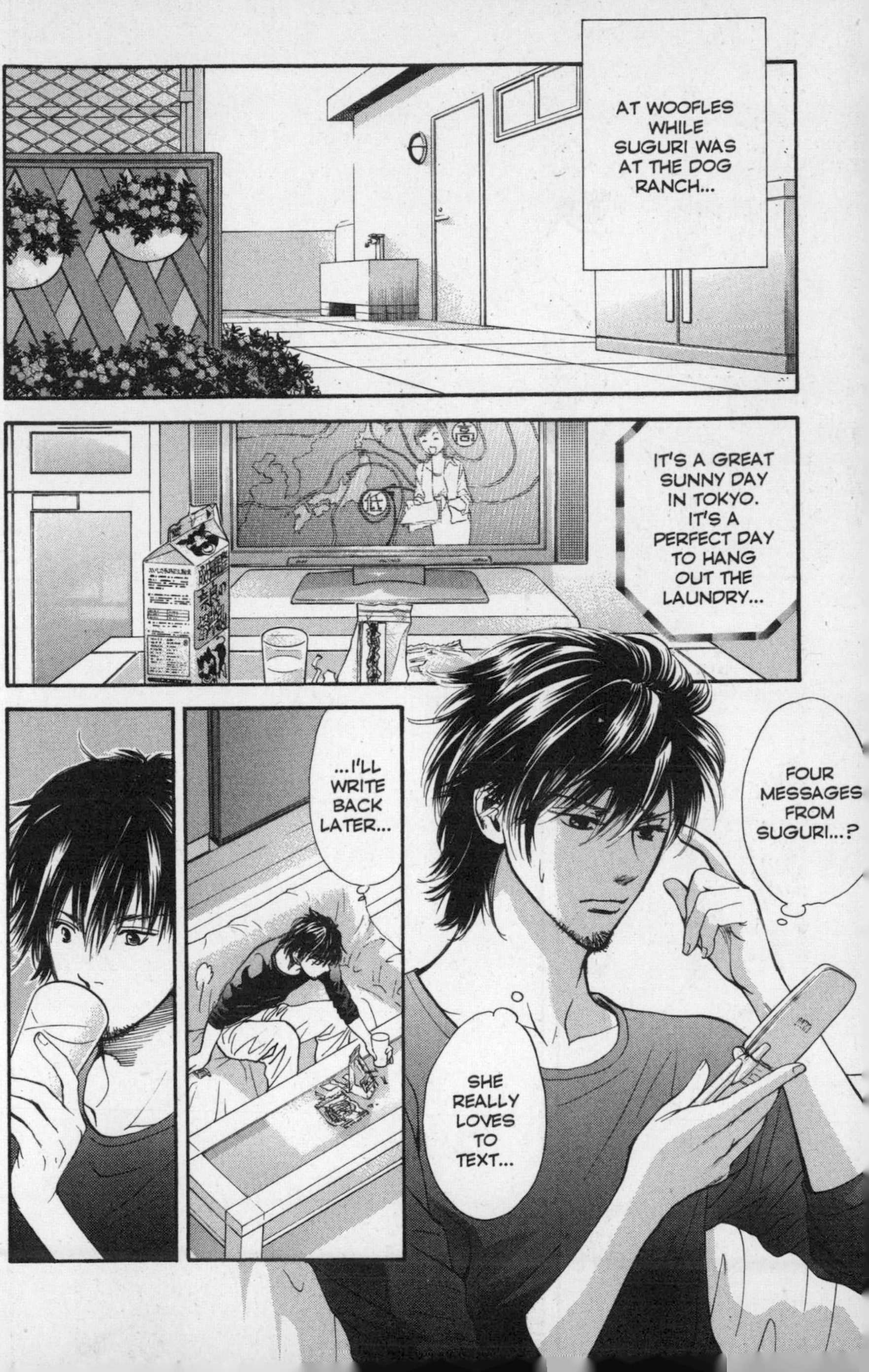
AT WOOFLES WHILE SUGURI WAS AT THE DOG RANCH...
IT'S A GREAT SUNNY DAY IN TOKYO. IT'S A PERFECT DAY TO HANG OUT THE LAUNDRY...
FOUR MESSAGES FROM SUGURI...?
SHE REALLY LOVES TO TEXT...
...I'LL WRITE BACK LATER...

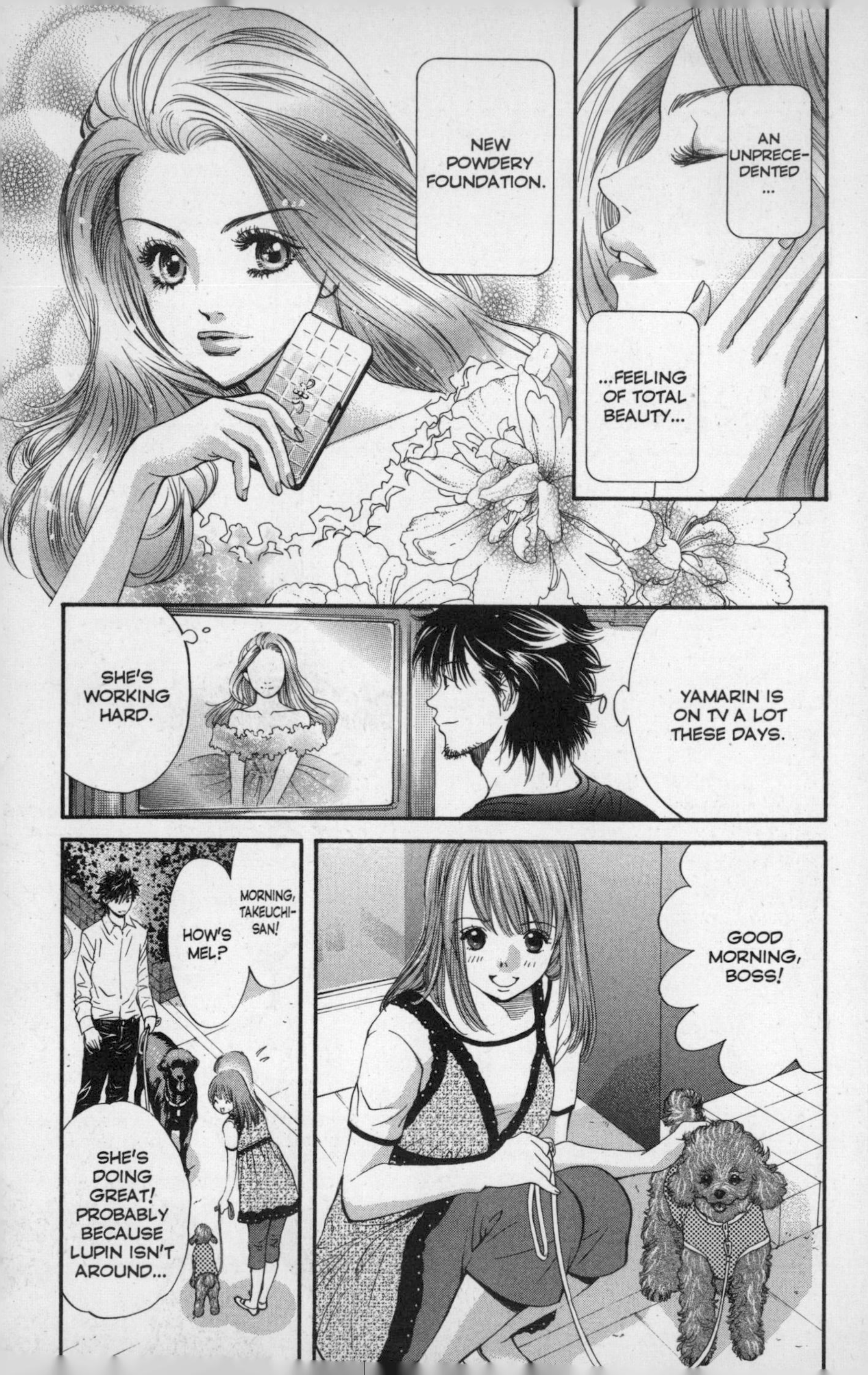
AN UNPRECEDENTED...
...FEELING OF TOTAL BEAUTY...
NEW POWDERY FOUNDATION.
YAMARIN IS ON TV A LOT THESE DAYS.
SHE'S WORKING HARD.
GOOD MORNING, BOSS!
MORNING, TAKEUCHI-SAN!
HOW'S MEL?
SHE'S DOING GREAT! PROBABLY BECAUSE LUPIN ISN'T AROUND...

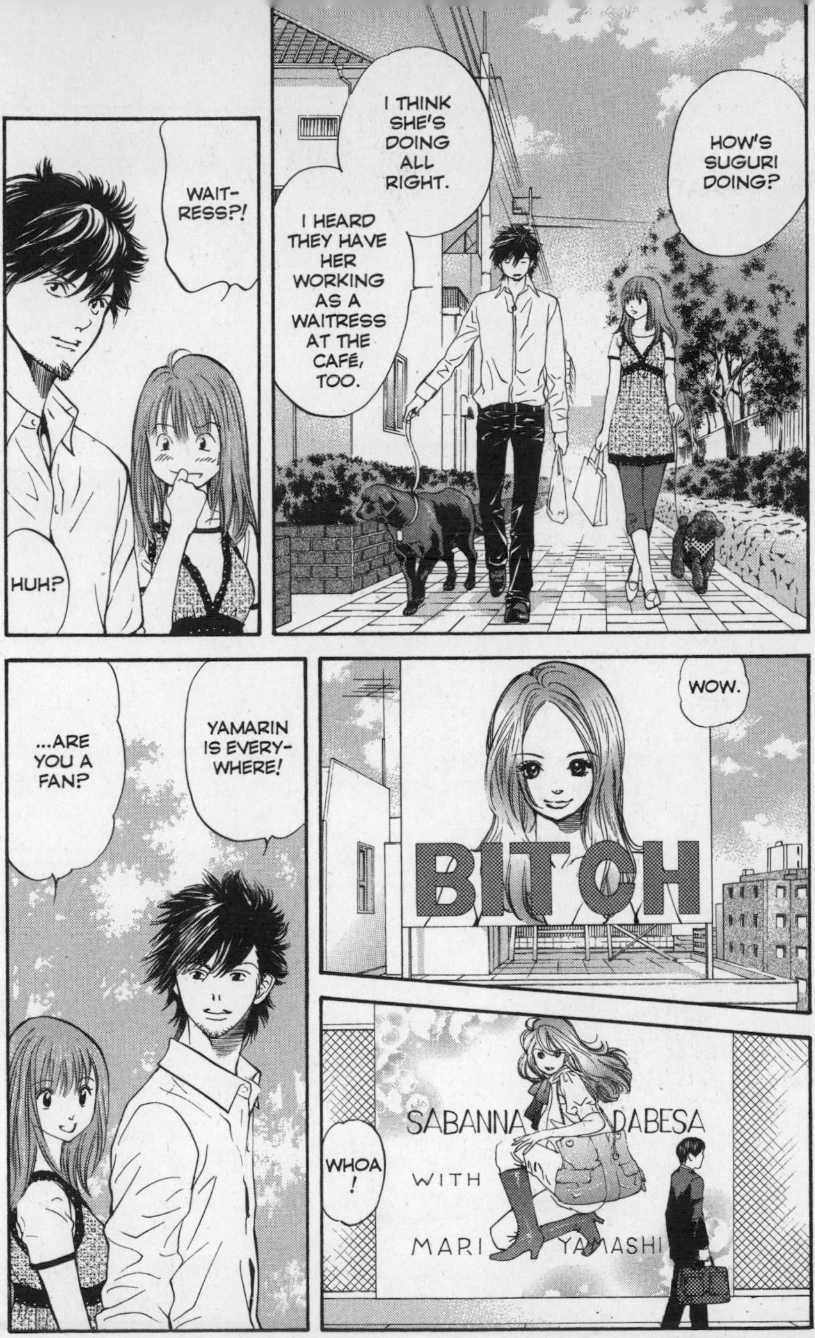
HOW'S SUGURI DOING?
I THINK SHE'S DOING ALL RIGHT.
I HEARD THEY HAVE HER WORKING AS A WAITRESS AT THE CAFÉ, TOO.
WAIT-RESS?!
HUH?
WOW.
BITCH
WHOA!
SABANNA DABESA
WITH
MARI YAMASHI
YAMARIN IS EVERY-WHERE!
...ARE YOU A FAN?

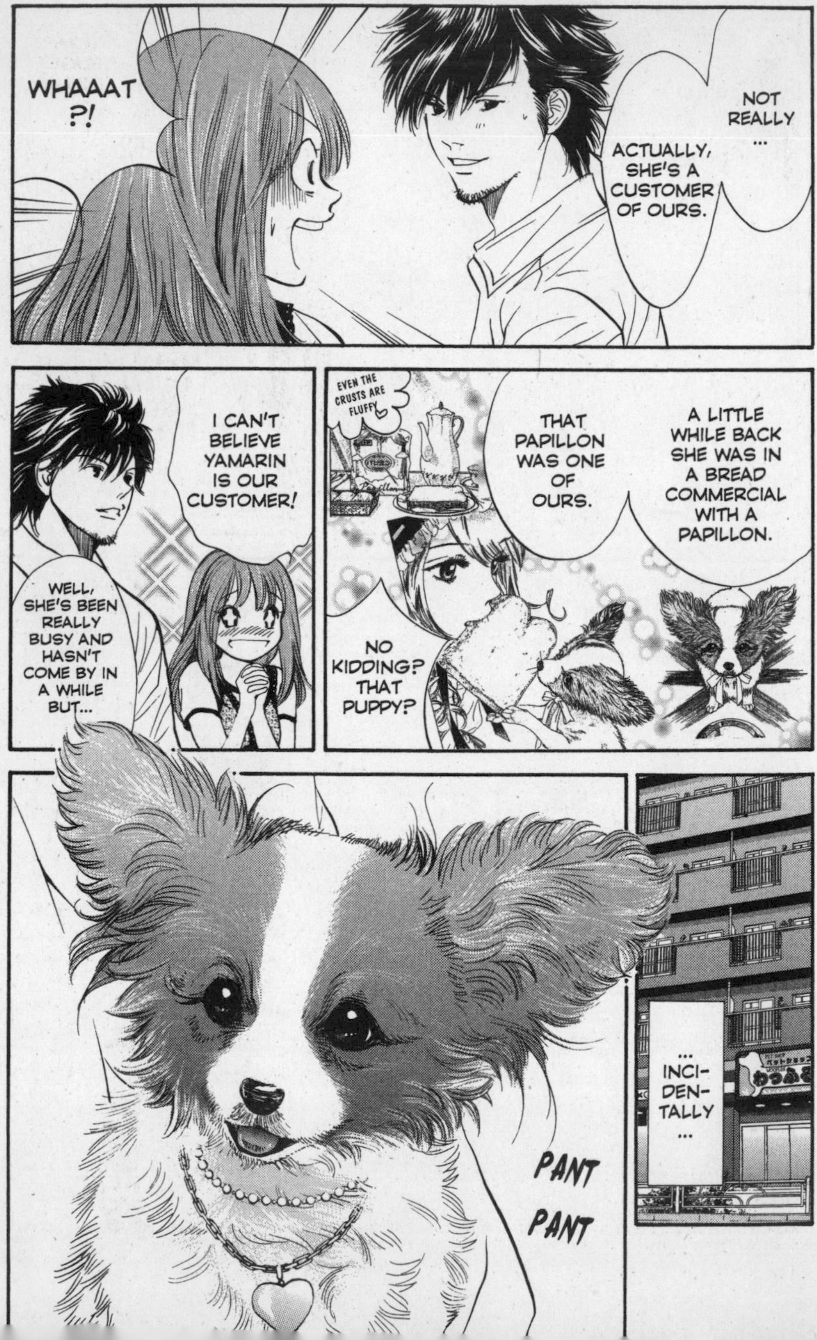
NOT REALLY ...
ACTUALLY, SHE'S A CUSTOMER OF OURS.
WHAAAT ?!
A LITTLE WHILE BACK SHE WAS IN A BREAD COMMERCIAL WITH A PAPILLON.
THAT PAPILLON WAS ONE OF OURS.
EVEN THE CRUSTS ARE FLUFFY
NO KIDDING? THAT PUPPY?
I CAN'T BELIEVE YAMARIN IS OUR CUSTOMER!
WELL, SHE'S BEEN REALLY BUSY AND HASN'T COME BY IN A WHILE BUT...
... INCI-DEN-TALLY ...
PANT
PANT

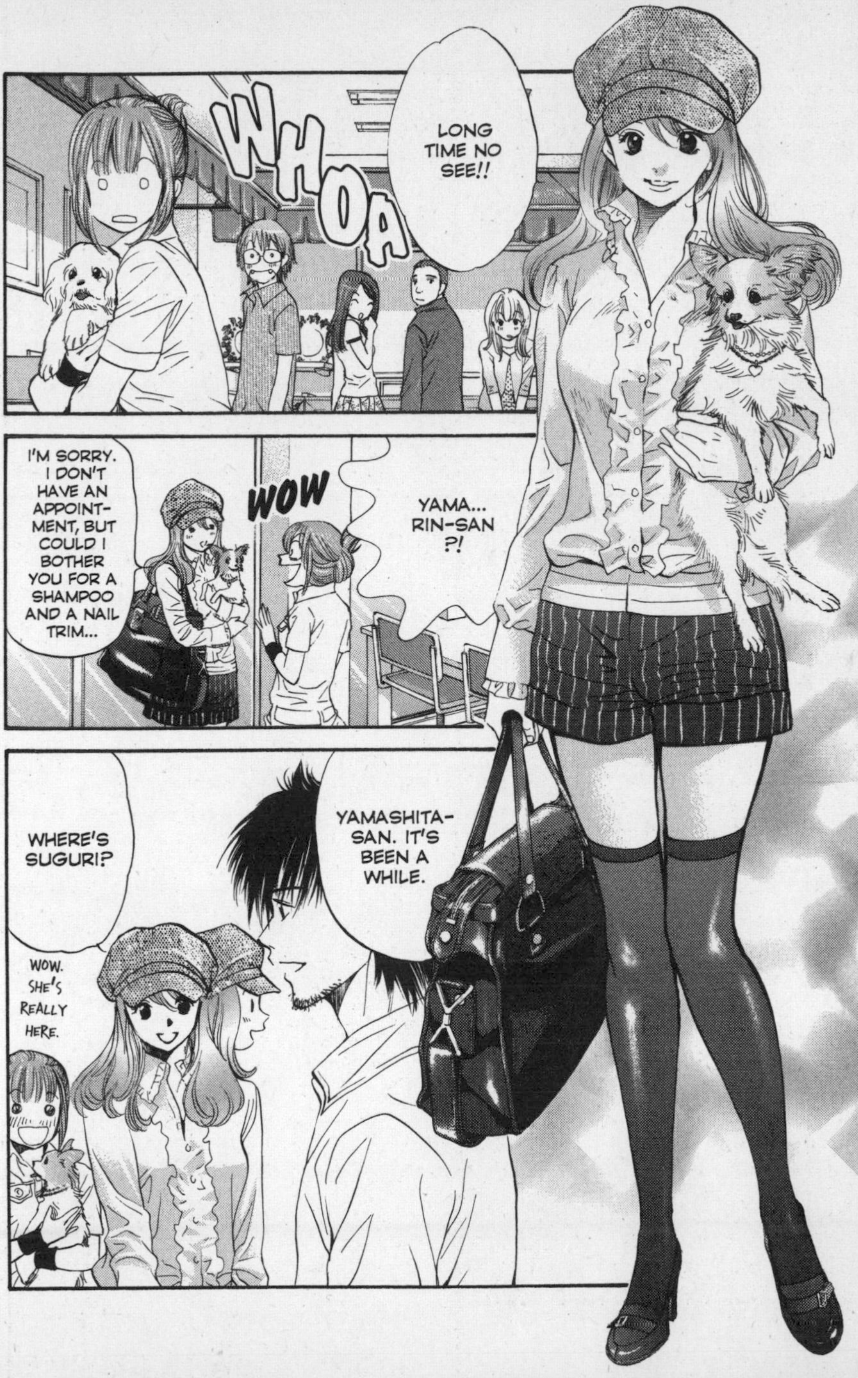
LONG TIME NO SEE!!
WHOA
YAMA... RIN-SAN?!
WOW
I'M SORRY. I DON'T HAVE AN APPOINT-MENT, BUT COULD I BOTHER YOU FOR A SHAMPOO AND A NAIL TRIM...
YAMASHITA-SAN. IT'S BEEN A WHILE.
WHERE'S SUGURI?
WOW. SHE'S REALLY HERE.

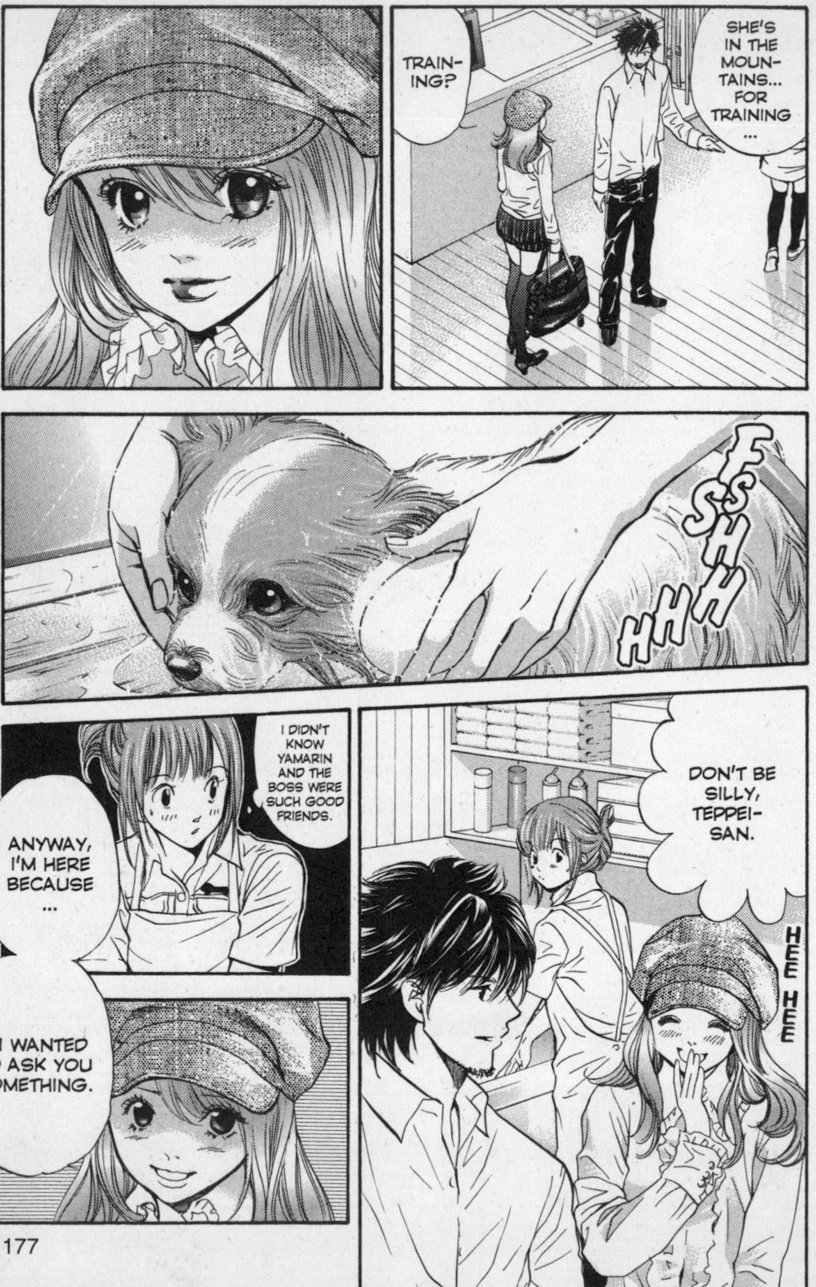
SHE'S IN THE MOUNTAINS... FOR TRAINING ...
TRAINING?
FSSHHHHH
DON'T BE SILLY, TEPPEI-SAN.
HEE HEE
I DIDN'T KNOW YAMARIN AND THE BOSS WERE SUCH GOOD FRIENDS.
ANYWAY, I'M HERE BECAUSE ...
...I WANTED TO ASK YOU SOMETHING.

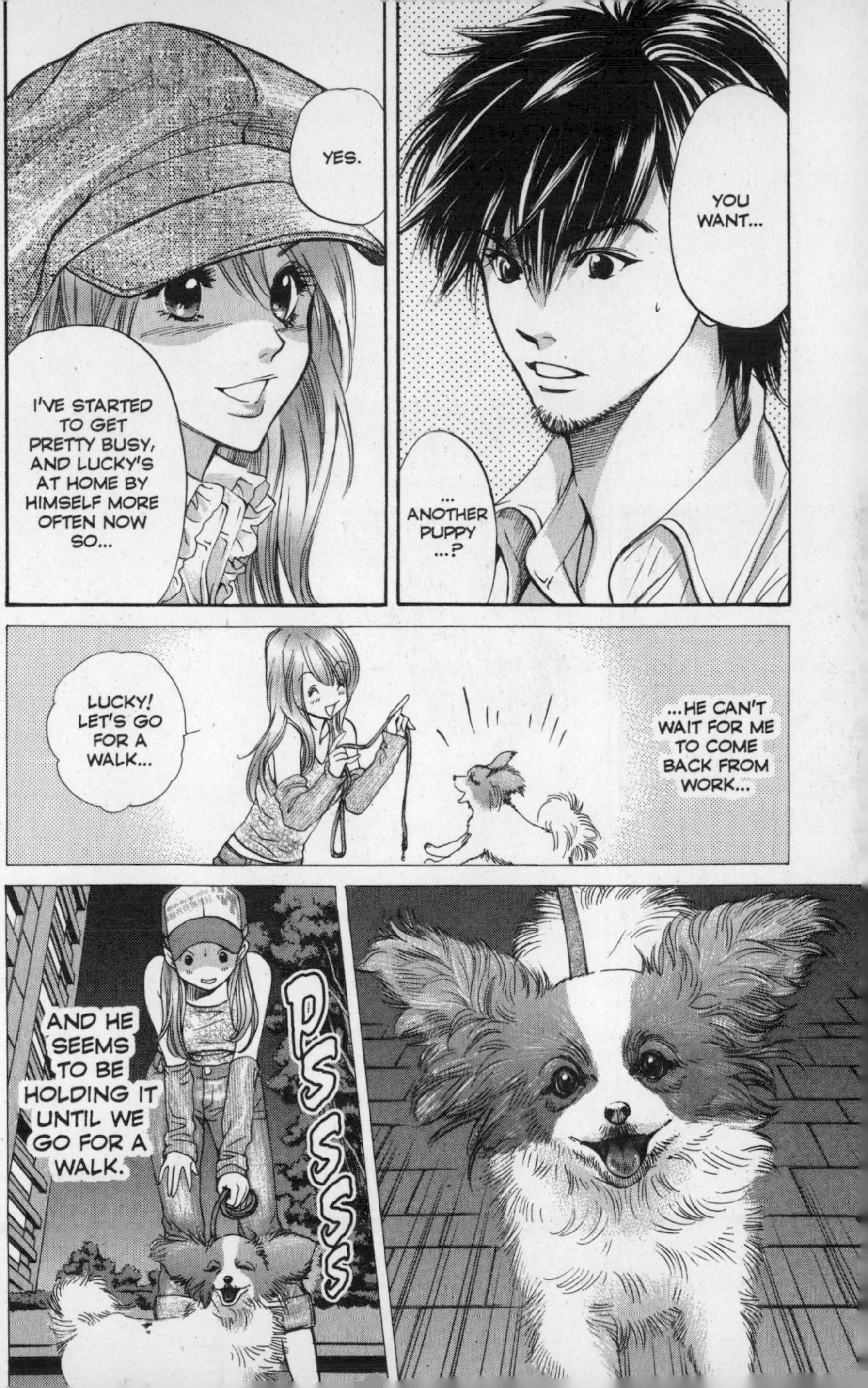
YOU WANT...
... ANOTHER PUPPY ...?
YES.
I'VE STARTED TO GET PRETTY BUSY, AND LUCKY'S AT HOME BY HIMSELF MORE OFTEN NOW SO...
...HE CAN'T WAIT FOR ME TO COME BACK FROM WORK...
LUCKY! LET'S GO FOR A WALK...
PSSSS
AND HE SEEMS TO BE HOLDING IT UNTIL WE GO FOR A WALK.

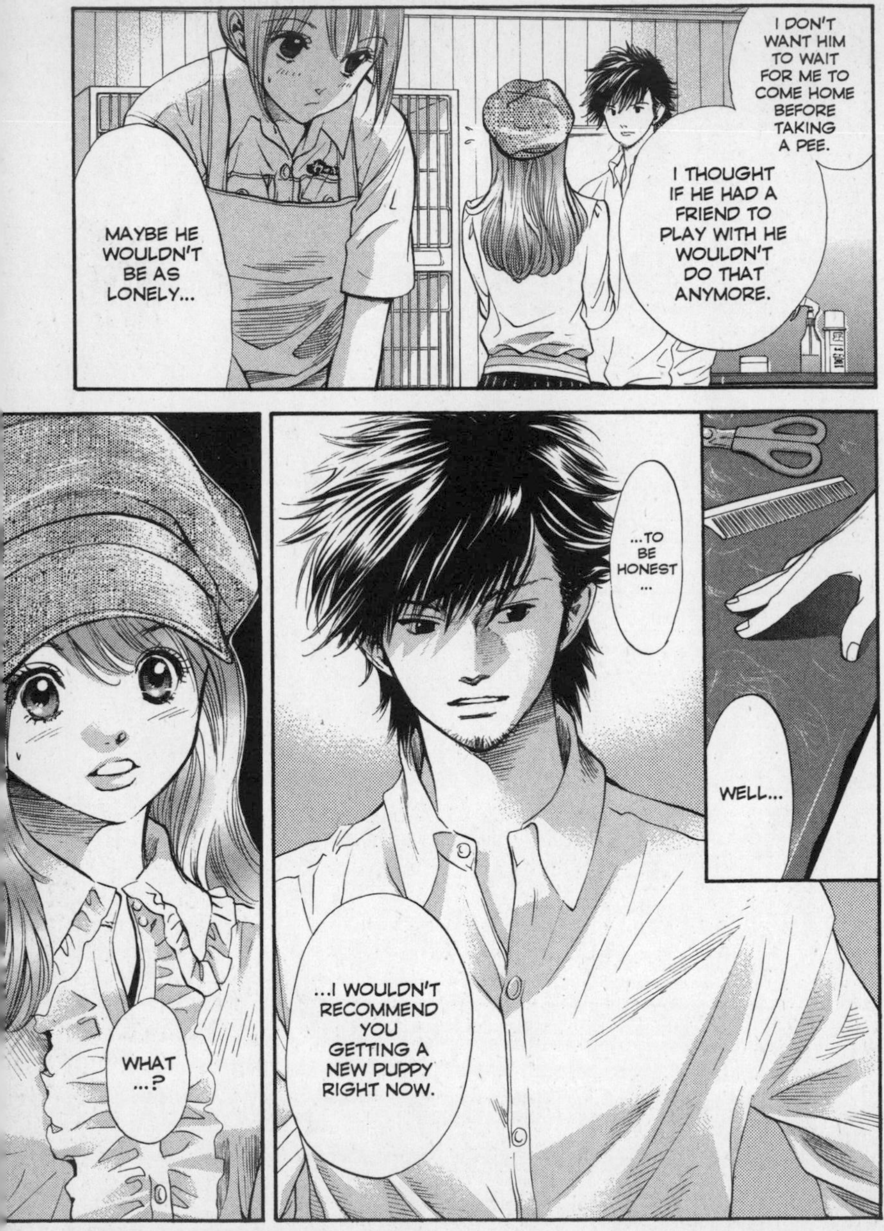
I DON'T WANT HIM TO WAIT FOR ME TO COME HOME BEFORE TAKING A PEE.
I THOUGHT IF HE HAD A FRIEND TO PLAY WITH HE WOULDN'T DO THAT ANYMORE.
MAYBE HE WOULDN'T BE AS LONELY...
WELL...
...TO BE HONEST ...
...I WOULDN'T RECOMMEND YOU GETTING A NEW PUPPY RIGHT NOW.
WHAT ...?

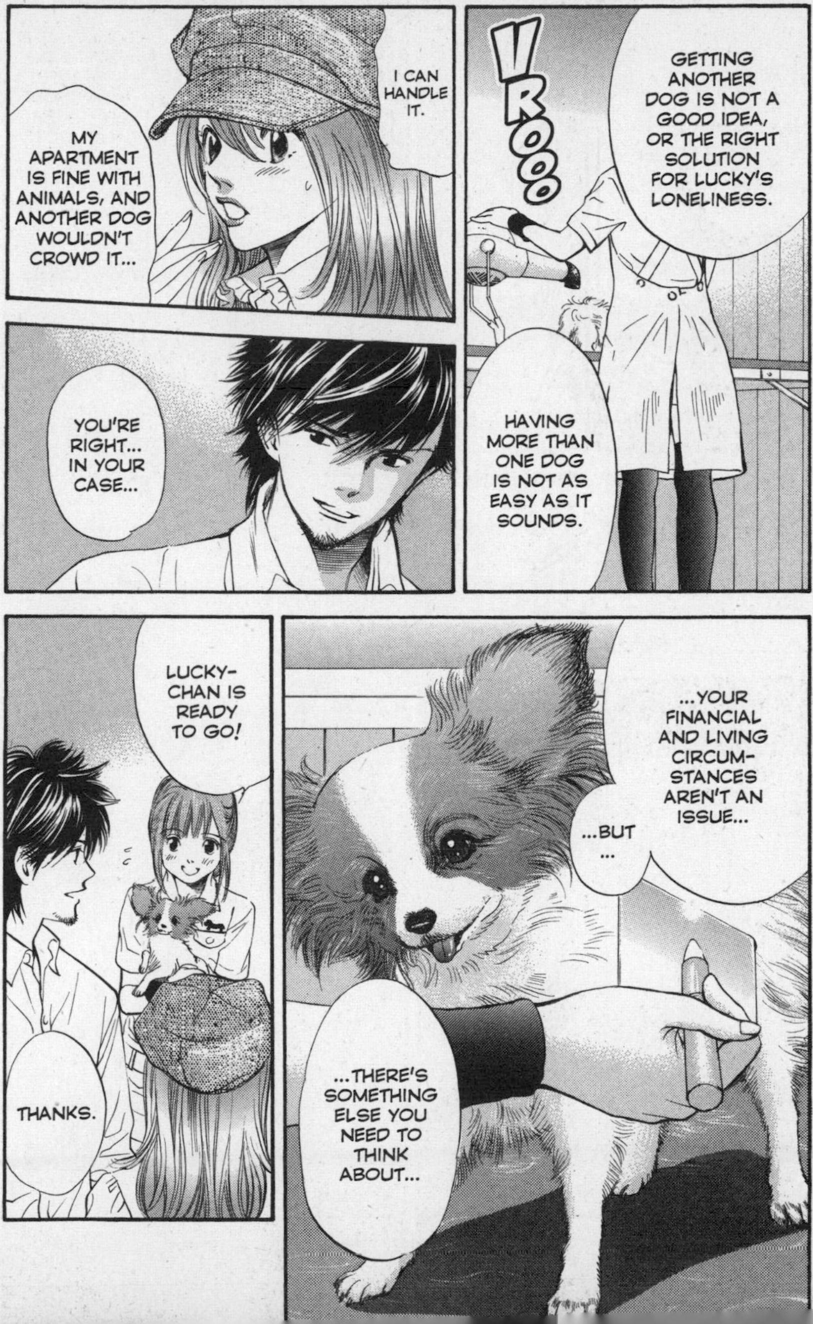
VROOO
GETTING ANOTHER DOG IS NOT A GOOD IDEA, OR THE RIGHT SOLUTION FOR LUCKY'S LONELINESS.
HAVING MORE THAN ONE DOG IS NOT AS EASY AS IT SOUNDS.
I CAN HANDLE IT.
MY APARTMENT IS FINE WITH ANIMALS, AND ANOTHER DOG WOULDN'T CROWD IT...
YOU'RE RIGHT... IN YOUR CASE...
...YOUR FINANCIAL AND LIVING CIRCUM-STANCES AREN'T AN ISSUE...
...BUT ...
...THERE'S SOMETHING ELSE YOU NEED TO THINK ABOUT...
LUCKY-CHAN IS READY TO GO!
THANKS.

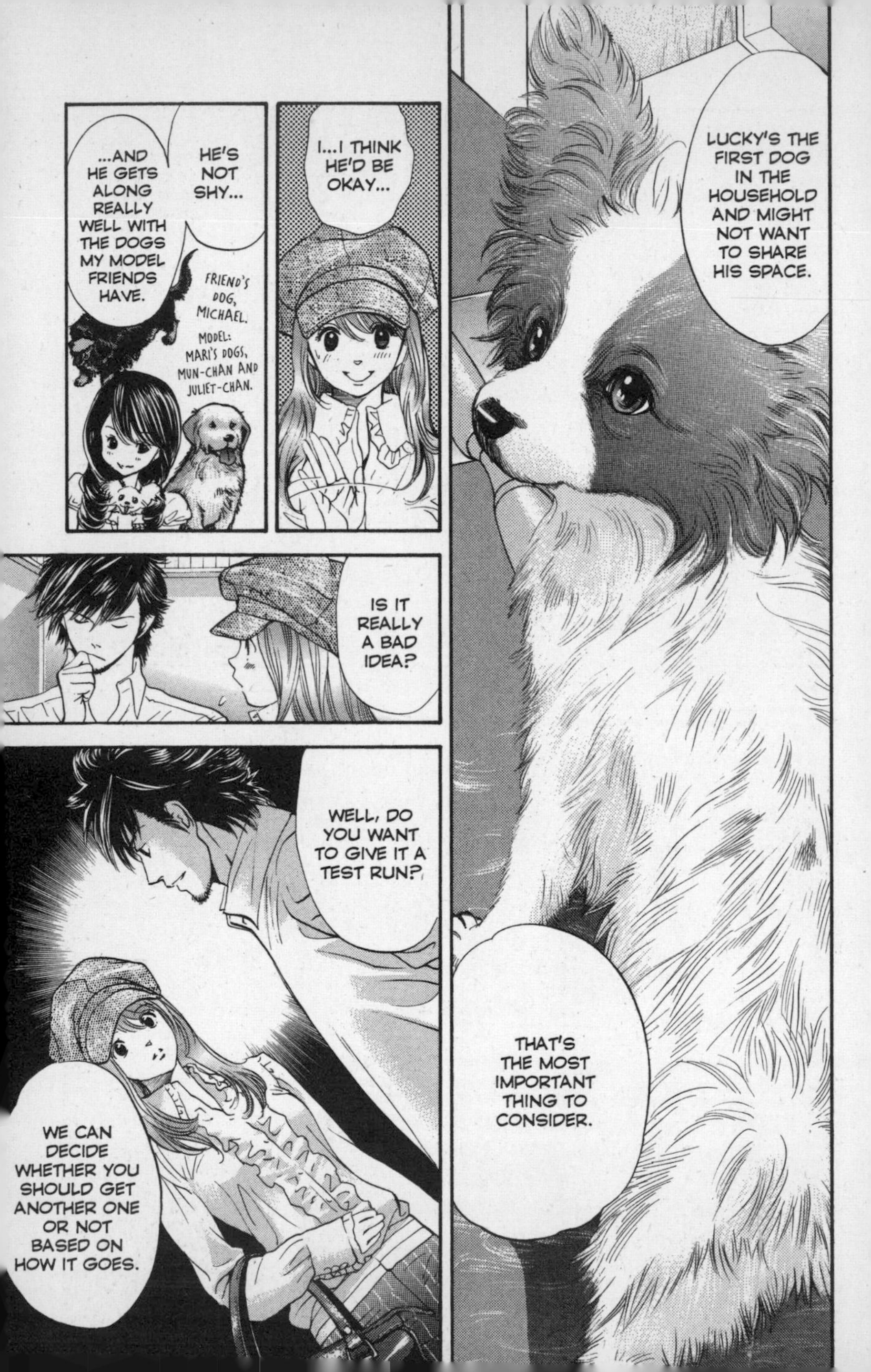
LUCKY'S THE FIRST DOG IN THE HOUSEHOLD AND MIGHT NOT WANT TO SHARE HIS SPACE.
THAT'S THE MOST IMPORTANT THING TO CONSIDER.
I...I THINK HE'D BE OKAY...
HE'S NOT SHY...
...AND HE GETS ALONG REALLY WELL WITH THE DOGS MY MODEL FRIENDS HAVE.
FRIEND'S DOG, MICHAEL.
MODEL: MARI'S DOGS, MUN-CHAN AND JULIET-CHAN.
IS IT REALLY A BAD IDEA?
WELL, DO YOU WANT TO GIVE IT A TEST RUN?
WE CAN DECIDE WHETHER YOU SHOULD GET ANOTHER ONE OR NOT BASED ON HOW IT GOES.

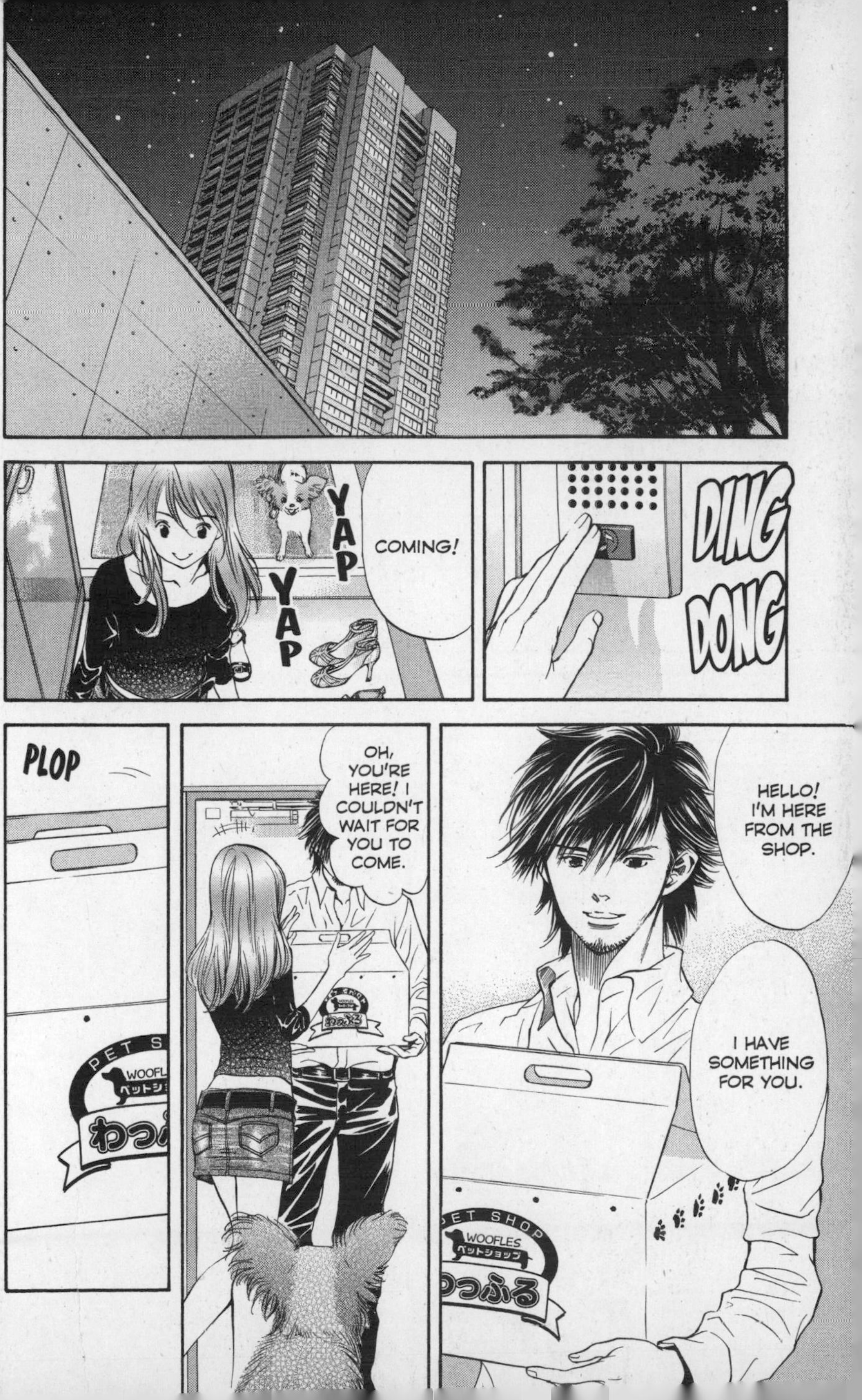
DING DONG
COMING!
YAP YAP
YAP YAP
HELLO! I'M HERE FROM THE SHOP.
I HAVE SOMETHING FOR YOU.
PET SHOP
WOOFLES
ペットショップ
わっふる
OH, YOU'RE HERE! I COULDN'T WAIT FOR YOU TO COME.
PLOP

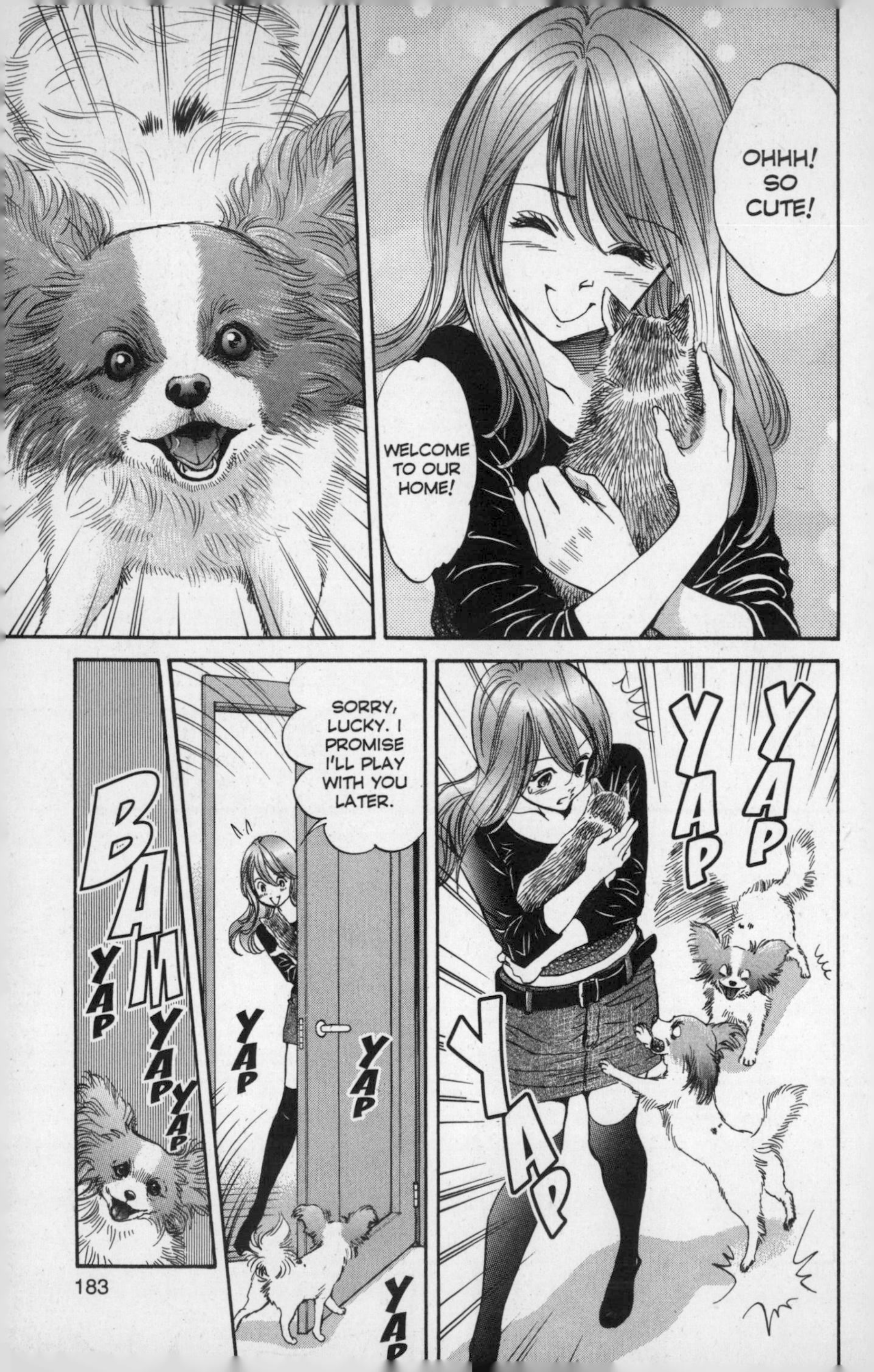
OHHH! SO CUTE!
WELCOME TO OUR HOME!
YAP
YAP
YAP
YAP
YAP
SORRY, LUCKY. I PROMISE I'LL PLAY WITH YOU LATER.
YAP
YAP
YAP
BAM
YAP
YAP
YAP
YAP

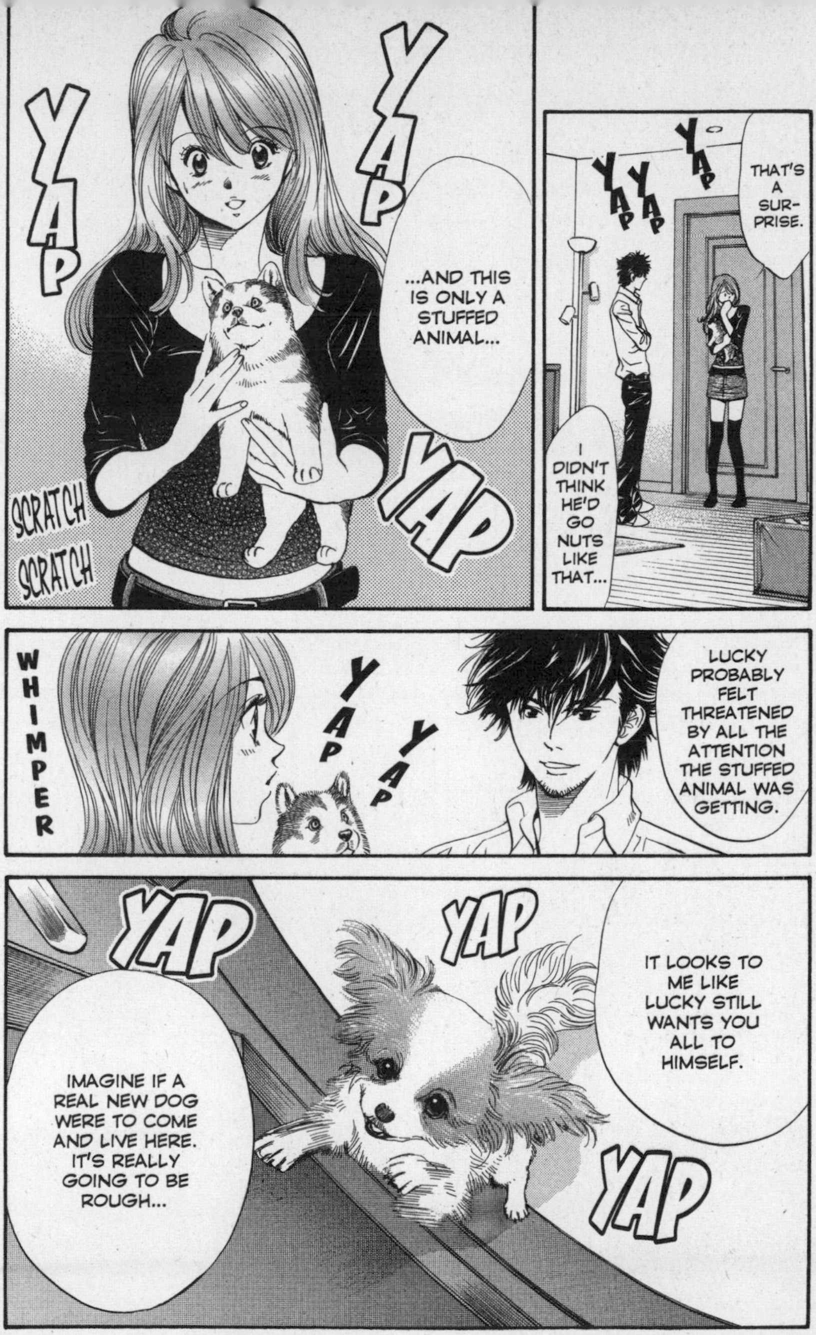
THAT'S A SUR-PRISE.
YAP
YAP
YAP
I DIDN'T THINK HE'D GO NUTS LIKE THAT...
YAP
...AND THIS IS ONLY A STUFFED ANIMAL...
YAP
YAP
SCRATCH SCRATCH
LUCKY PROBABLY FELT THREATENED BY ALL THE ATTENTION THE STUFFED ANIMAL WAS GETTING.
YAP
YAP
WHIMPER
IT LOOKS TO ME LIKE LUCKY STILL WANTS YOU ALL TO HIMSELF.
YAP
YAP
IMAGINE IF A REAL NEW DOG WERE TO COME AND LIVE HERE. IT'S REALLY GOING TO BE ROUGH...
YAP

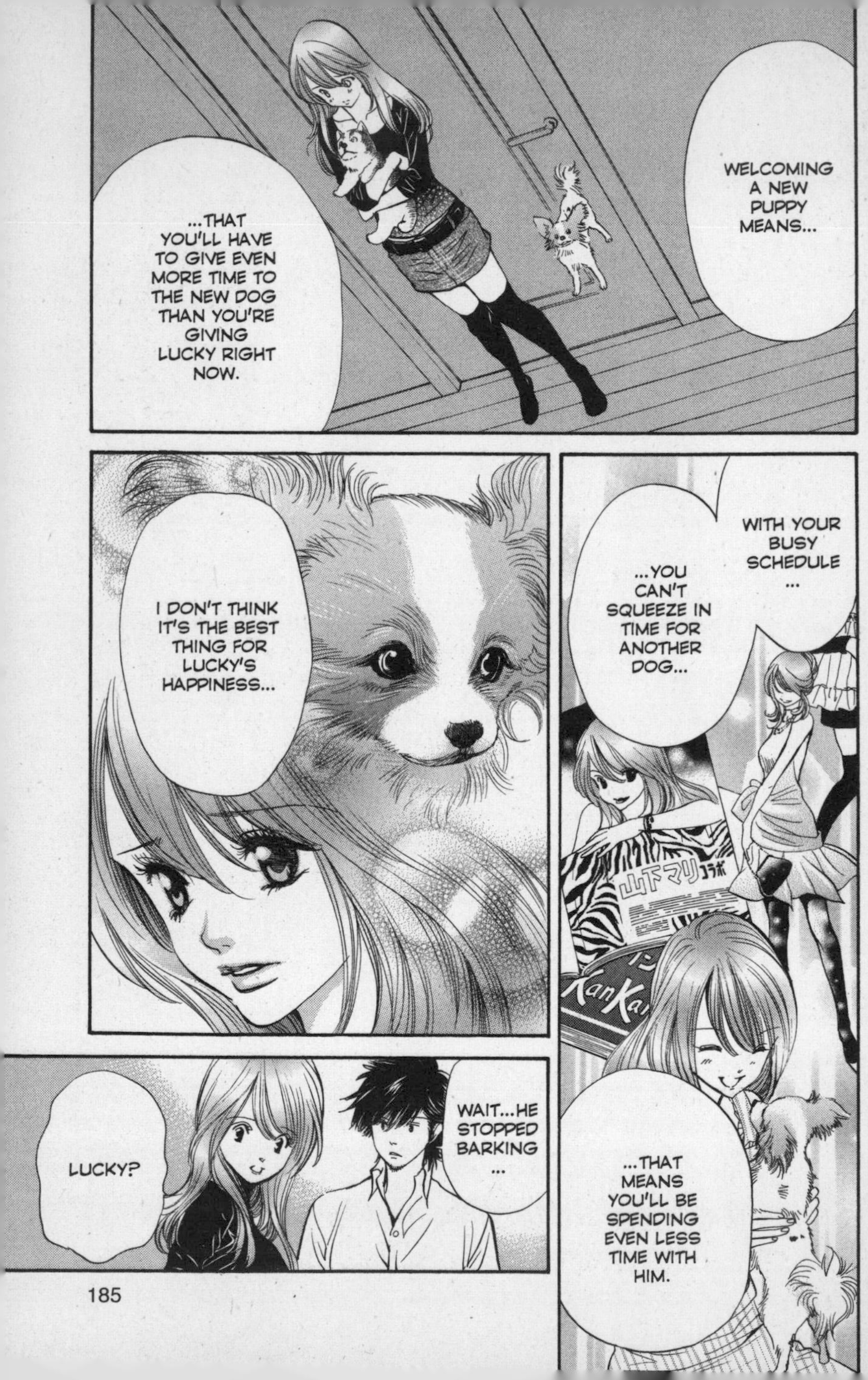
WELCOMING A NEW PUPPY MEANS...
...THAT YOU'LL HAVE TO GIVE EVEN MORE TIME TO THE NEW DOG THAN YOU'RE GIVING LUCKY RIGHT NOW.
WITH YOUR BUSY SCHEDULE ...
...YOU CAN'T SQUEEZE IN TIME FOR ANOTHER DOG...
...THAT MEANS YOU'LL BE SPENDING EVEN LESS TIME WITH HIM.
I DON'T THINK IT'S THE BEST THING FOR LUCKY'S HAPPINESS...
WAIT...HE STOPPED BARKING ...
LUCKY?

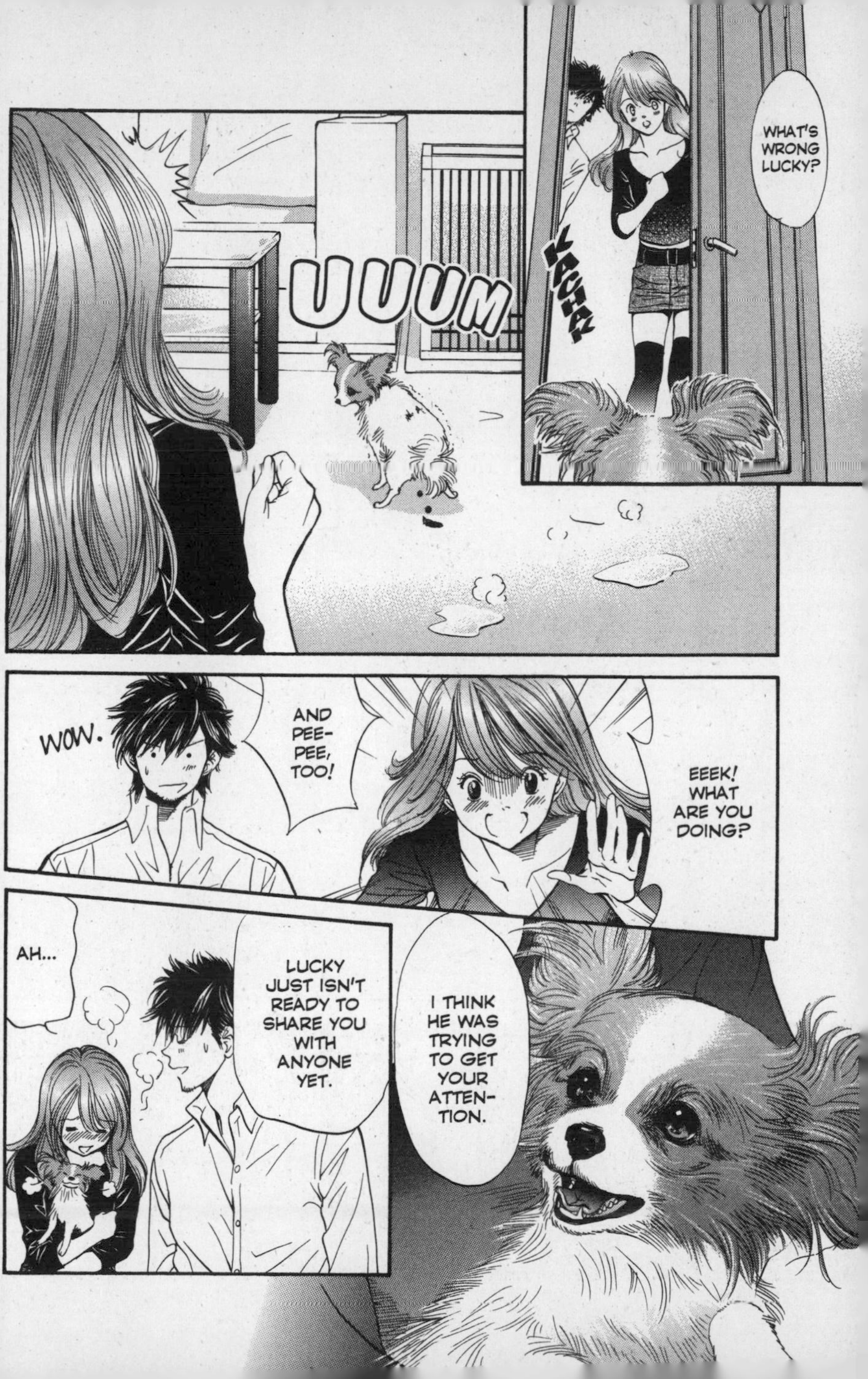
WHAT'S WRONG LUCKY?
KACHA
UUUM
EEEK! WHAT ARE YOU DOING?
AND PEE-PEE, TOO!
WOW.
I THINK HE WAS TRYING TO GET YOUR ATTENTION.
LUCKY JUST ISN'T READY TO SHARE YOU WITH ANYONE YET.
AH...

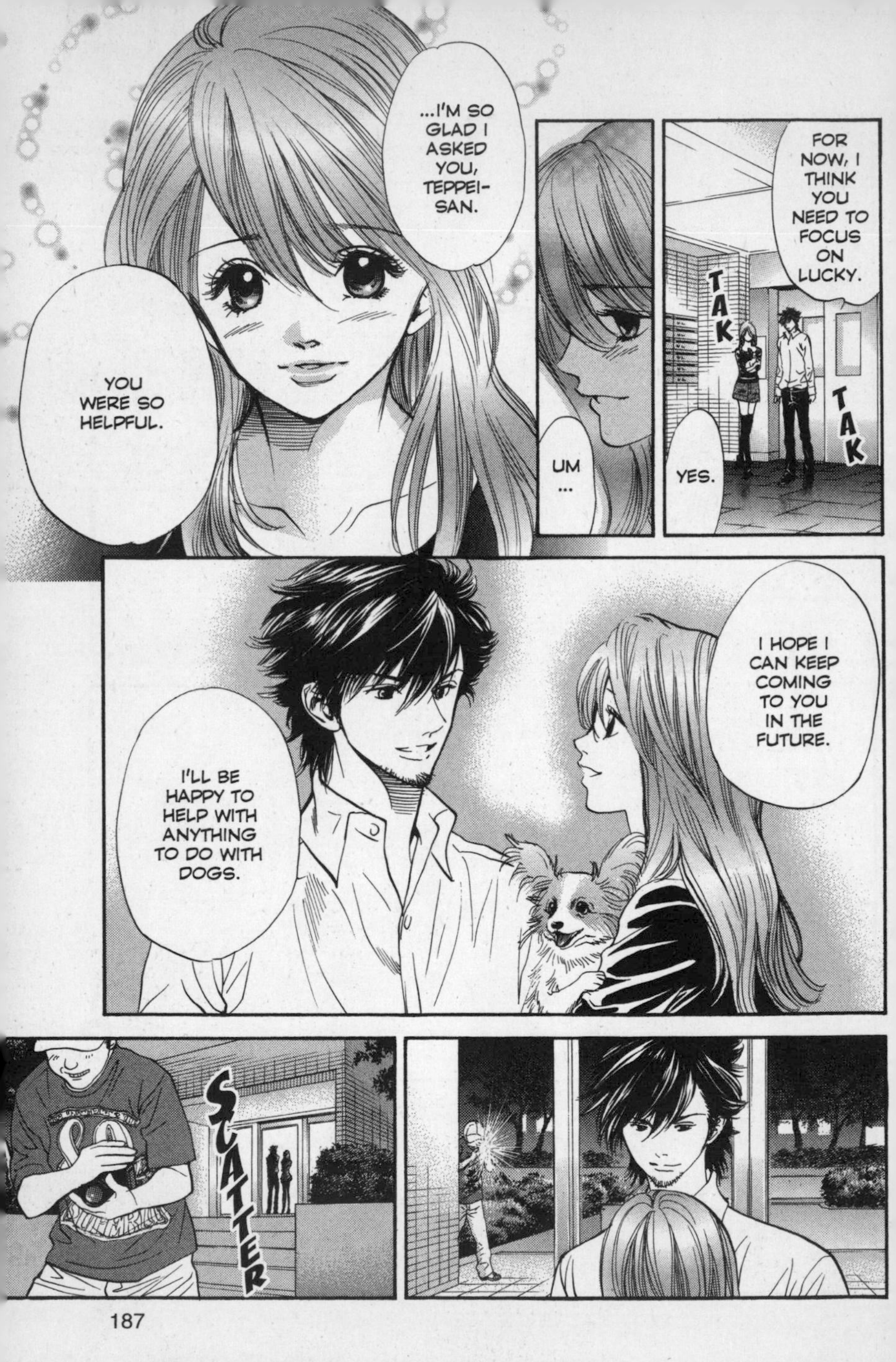
FOR NOW, I THINK YOU NEED TO FOCUS ON LUCKY.
TAK
TAK
YES.
UM ...
...I'M SO GLAD I ASKED YOU, TEPPEI-SAN.
YOU WERE SO HELPFUL.
I HOPE I CAN KEEP COMING TO YOU IN THE FUTURE.
I'LL BE HAPPY TO HELP WITH ANYTHING TO DO WITH DOGS.
SCATTER

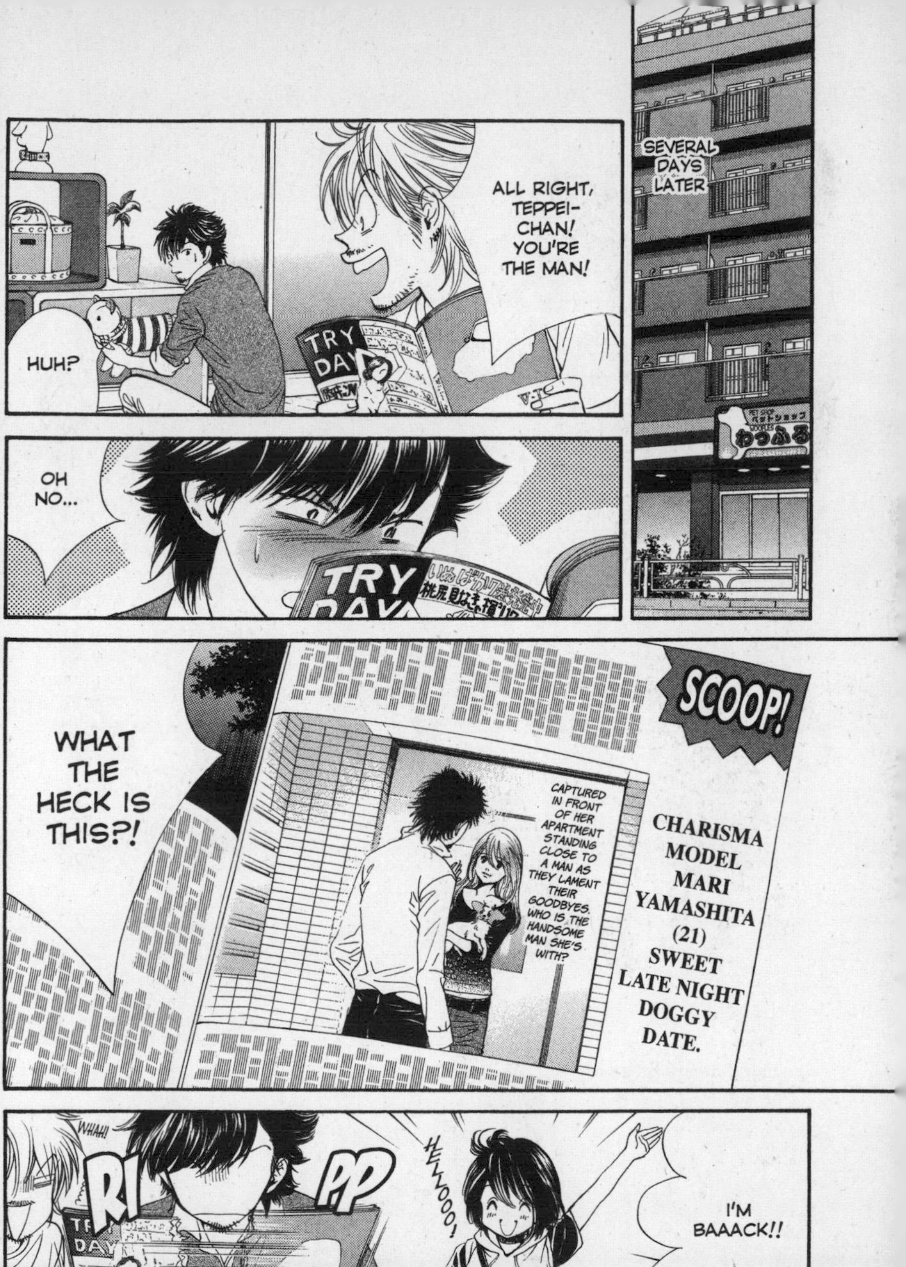

SEVERAL DAYS LATER
ALL RIGHT, TEPPEI-CHAN! YOU'RE THE MAN!
HUH?
OH NO...
SCOOP!
CHARISMA MODEL MARI YAMASHITA (21) SWEET LATE NIGHT DOGGY DATE.
CAPTURED IN FRONT OF HER APARTMENT STANDING CLOSE TO A MAN AS THEY LAMENT THEIR GOODBYES. WHO IS THE HANDSOME MAN SHE'S WITH?
WHAT THE HECK IS THIS?!
I'M BAAACK!!
HELLOOO!
RIPP
WHAH!

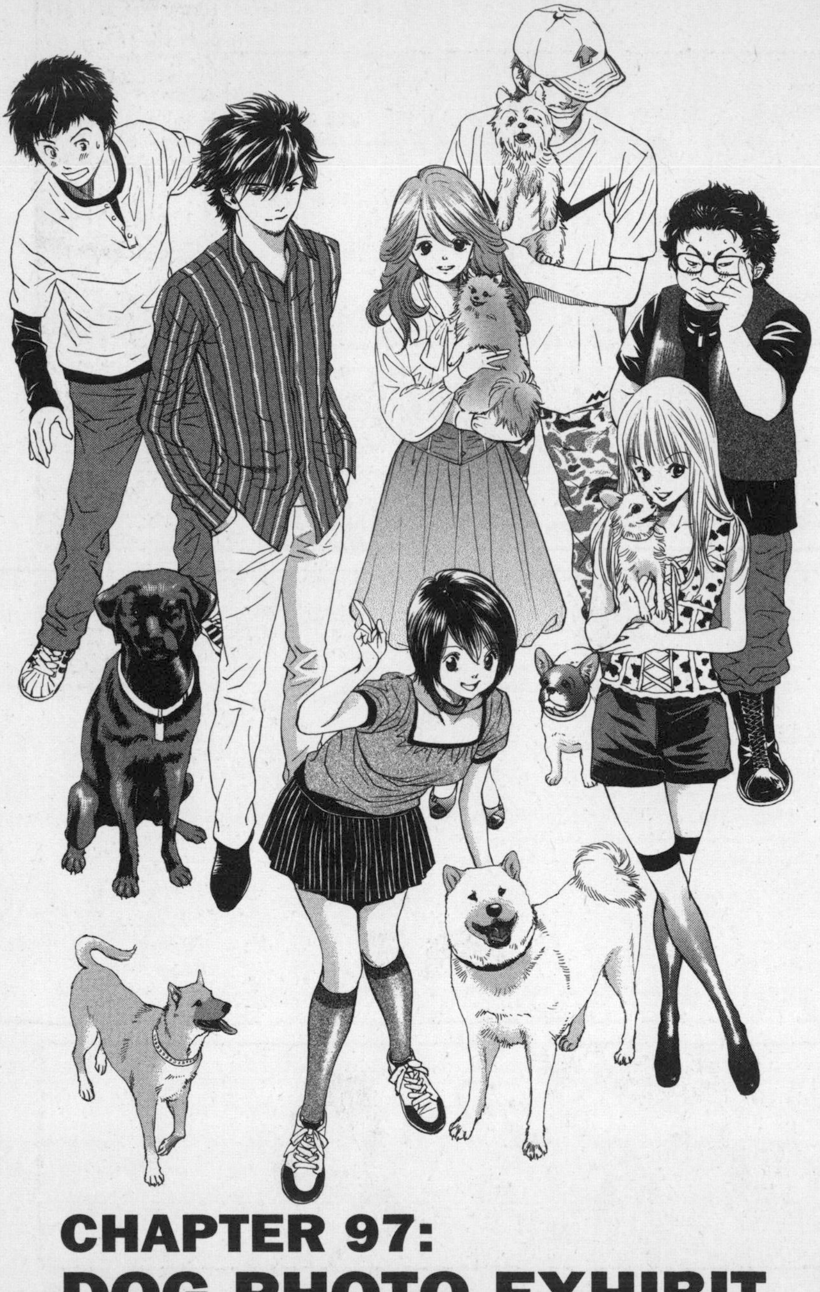

CHAPTER 97:
DOG PHOTO EXHIBIT

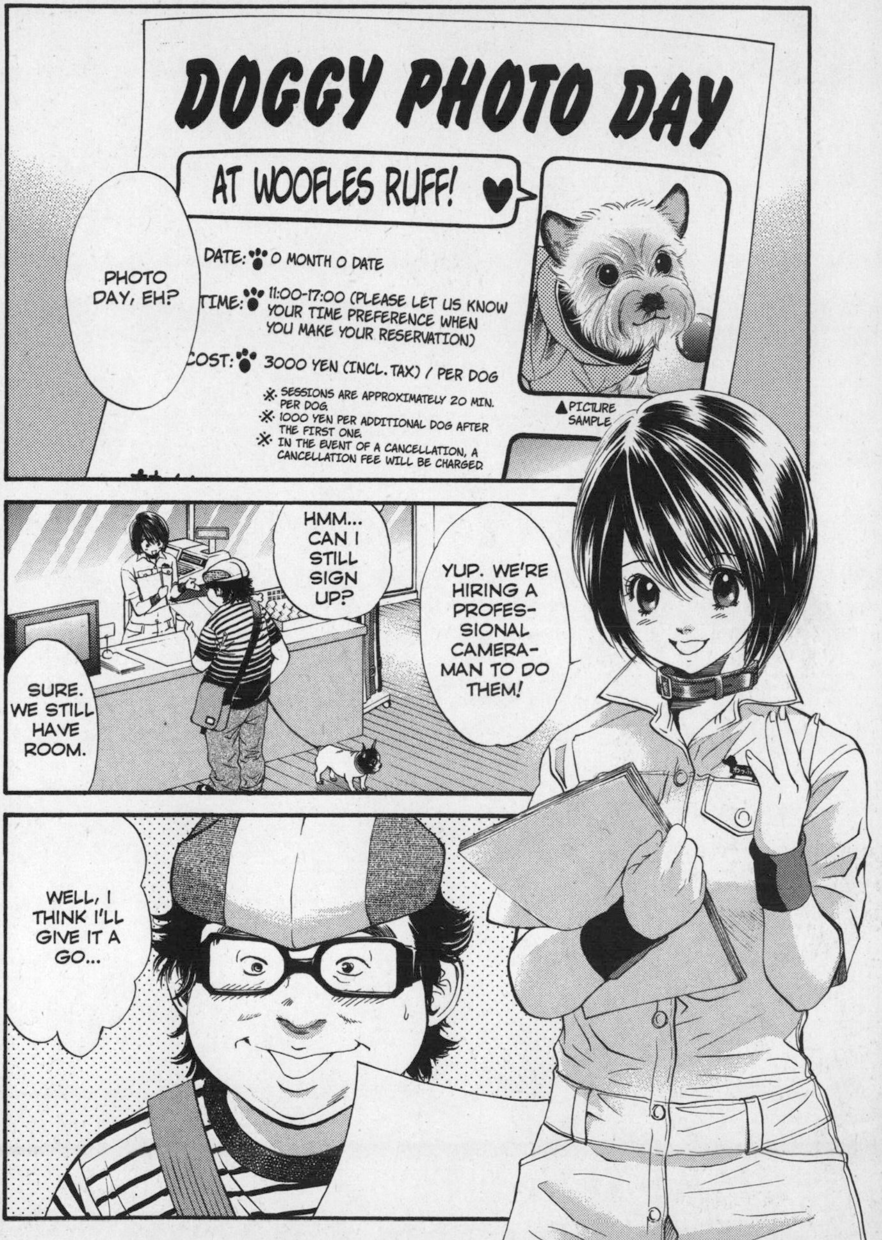
DOGGY PHOTO DAY
AT WOOFLES RUFF!
DATE: O MONTH O DATE
TIME: 11:00-17:00 (PLEASE LET US KNOW YOUR TIME PREFERENCE WHEN YOU MAKE YOUR RESERVATION)
COST: 3000 YEN (INCL. TAX) / PER DOG
※ SESSIONS ARE APPROXIMATELY 20 MIN. PER DOG.
※ 1000 YEN PER ADDITIONAL DOG AFTER THE FIRST ONE.
※ IN THE EVENT OF A CANCELLATION, A CANCELLATION FEE WILL BE CHARGED.
▲PICTURE SAMPLE
PHOTO DAY, EH?
YUP. WE'RE HIRING A PROFESSIONAL CAMERAMAN TO DO THEM!
HMM... CAN I STILL SIGN UP?
SURE. WE STILL HAVE ROOM.
WELL, I THINK I'LL GIVE IT A GO...

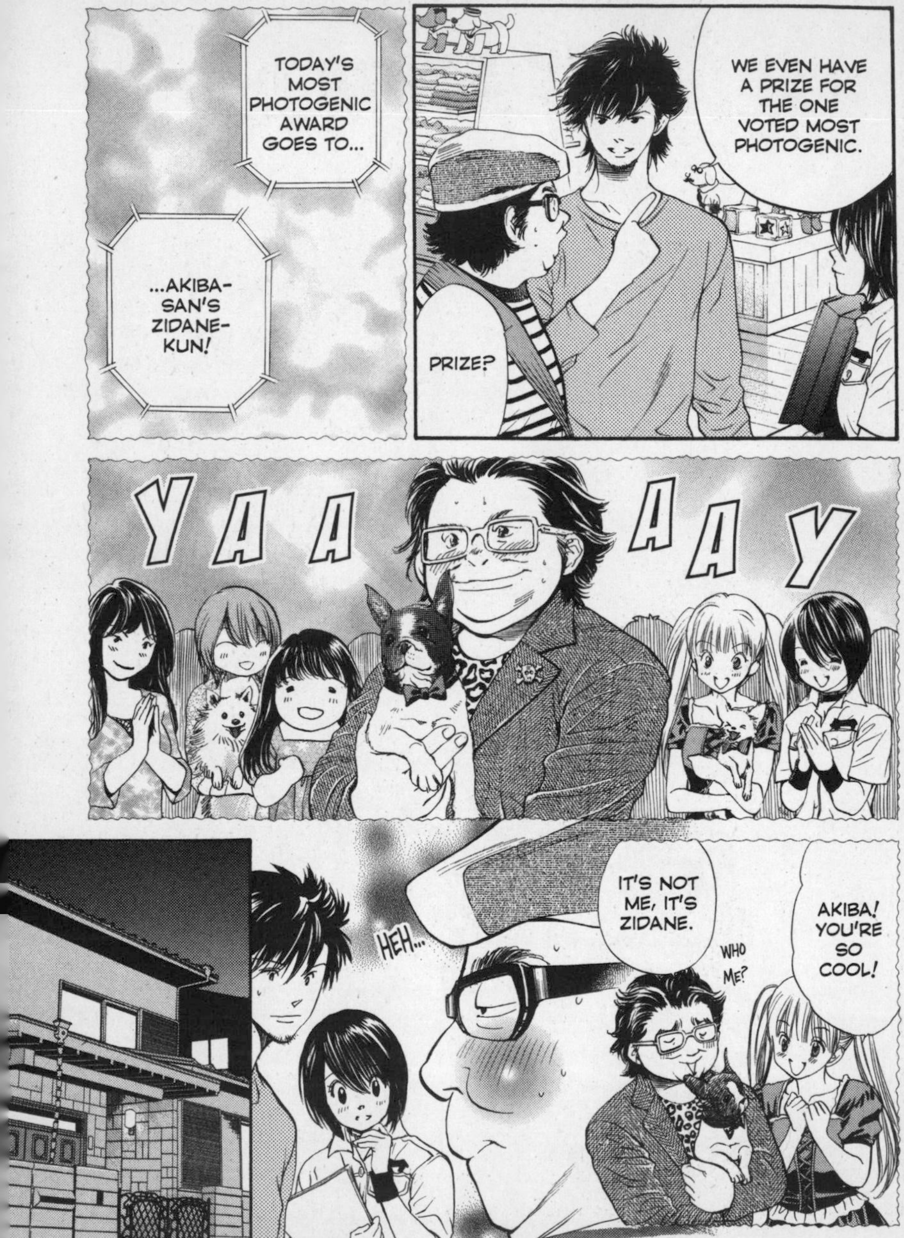
WE EVEN HAVE A PRIZE FOR THE ONE VOTED MOST PHOTOGENIC.
PRIZE?
TODAY'S MOST PHOTOGENIC AWARD GOES TO...
...AKIBA-SAN'S ZIDANE-KUN!
YAAAAAY
AKIBA! YOU'RE SO COOL!
WHO ME?
IT'S NOT ME, IT'S ZIDANE.
HEH...

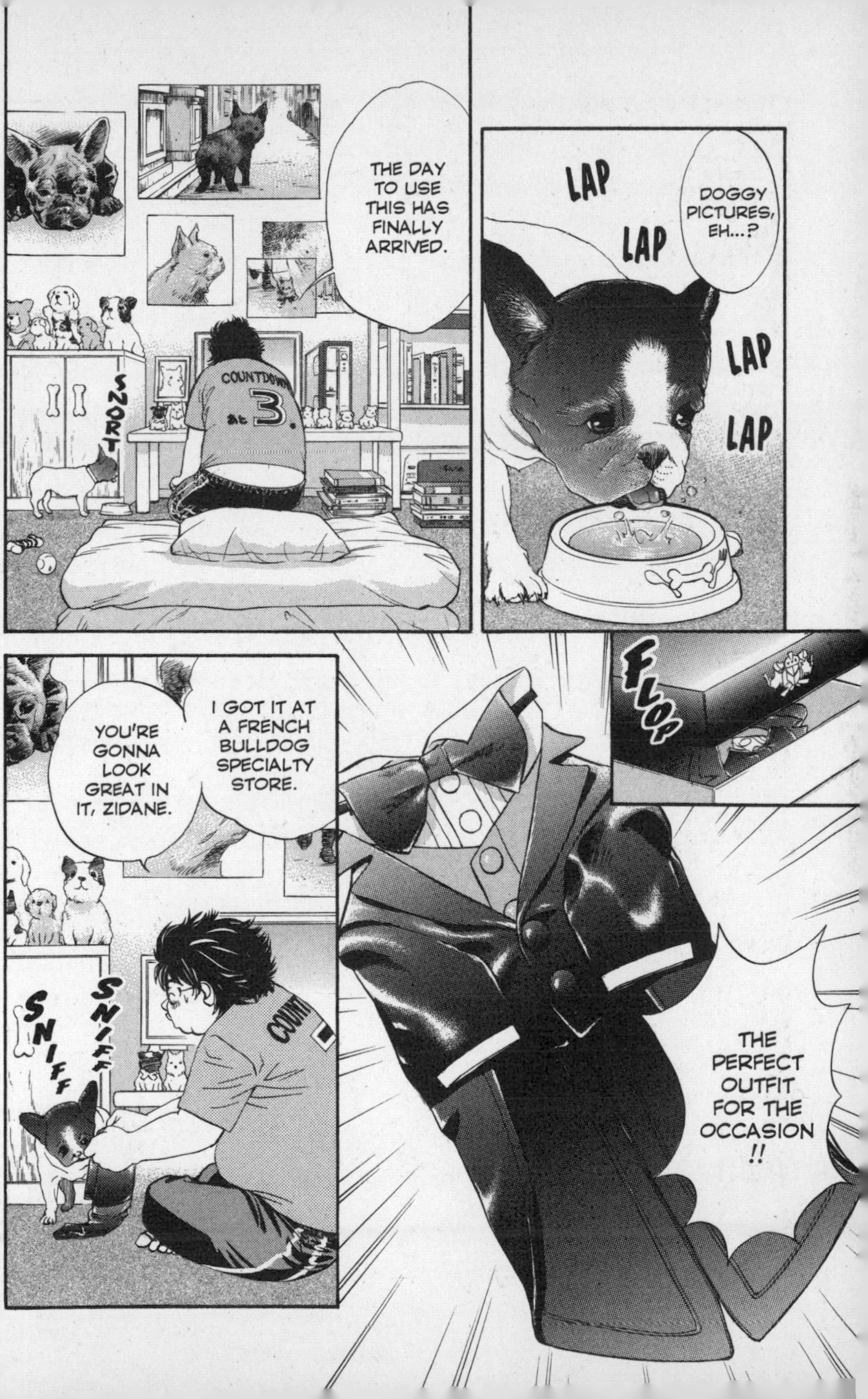
LAP
DOGGY PICTURES, EH...?
LAP
LAP
LAP
THE DAY TO USE THIS HAS FINALLY ARRIVED.
COUNTDOWN
SNORT
FLOP
THE PERFECT OUTFIT FOR THE OCCASION!!
I GOT IT AT A FRENCH BULLDOG SPECIALTY STORE.
YOU'RE GONNA LOOK GREAT IN IT, ZIDANE.
SNIFF
SNIFF

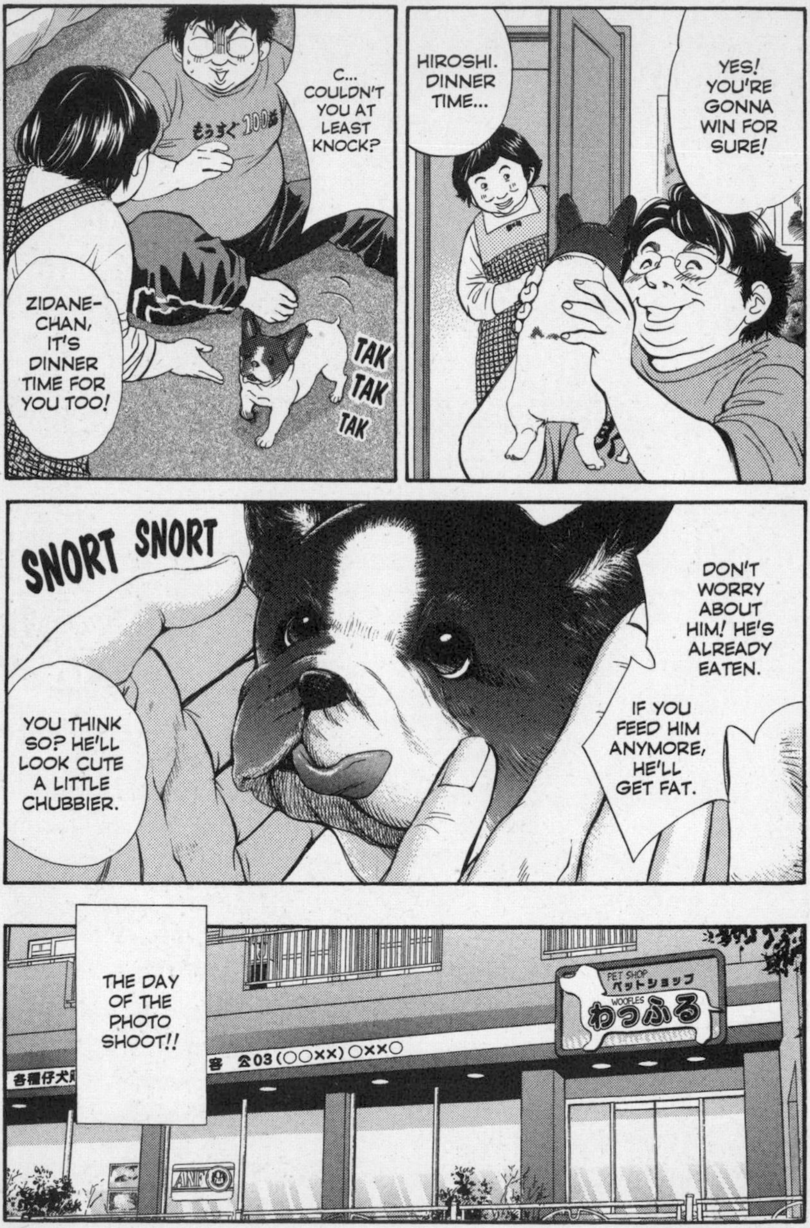
YES! YOU'RE GONNA WIN FOR SURE!
HIROSHI. DINNER TIME...
C... COULDN'T YOU AT LEAST KNOCK?
TAK TAK TAK
ZIDANE-CHAN, IT'S DINNER TIME FOR YOU TOO!
DON'T WORRY ABOUT HIM! HE'S ALREADY EATEN.
IF YOU FEED HIM ANYMORE, HE'LL GET FAT.
SNORT SNORT
YOU THINK SO? HE'LL LOOK CUTE A LITTLE CHUBBIER.
PET SHOP
ペットショップ
WOOFLES
わっふる
THE DAY OF THE PHOTO SHOOT!!

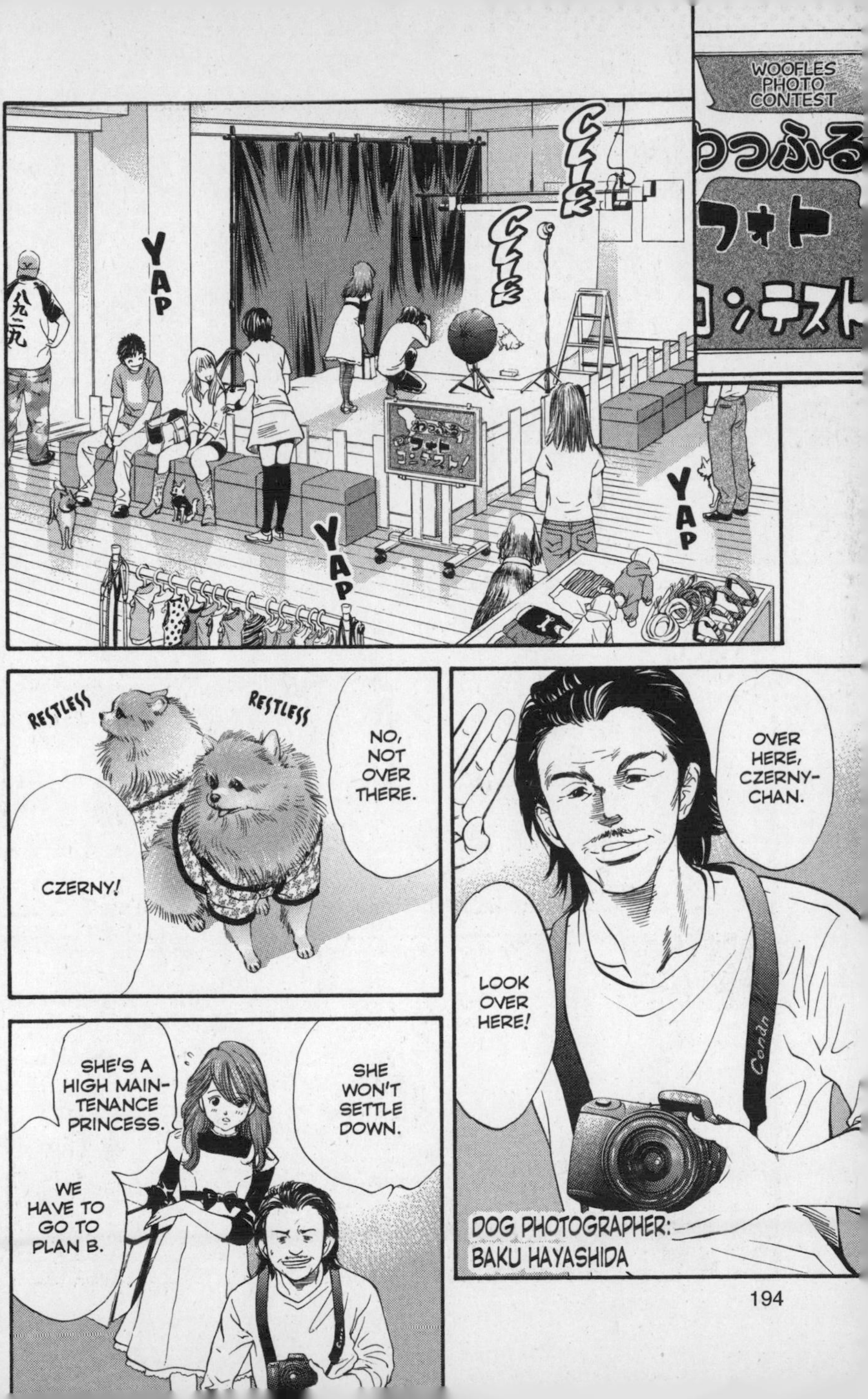
WOOFLES PHOTO CONTEST
わっふる フォト コンテスト
CLICK
CLICK
YAP
YAP
YAP
YAP
OVER HERE, CZERNY-CHAN.
LOOK OVER HERE!
DOG PHOTOGRAPHER: BAKU HAYASHIDA
RESTLESS
RESTLESS
NO, NOT OVER THERE.
CZERNY!
SHE WON'T SETTLE DOWN.
SHE'S A HIGH MAIN-TENANCE PRINCESS.
WE HAVE TO GO TO PLAN B.

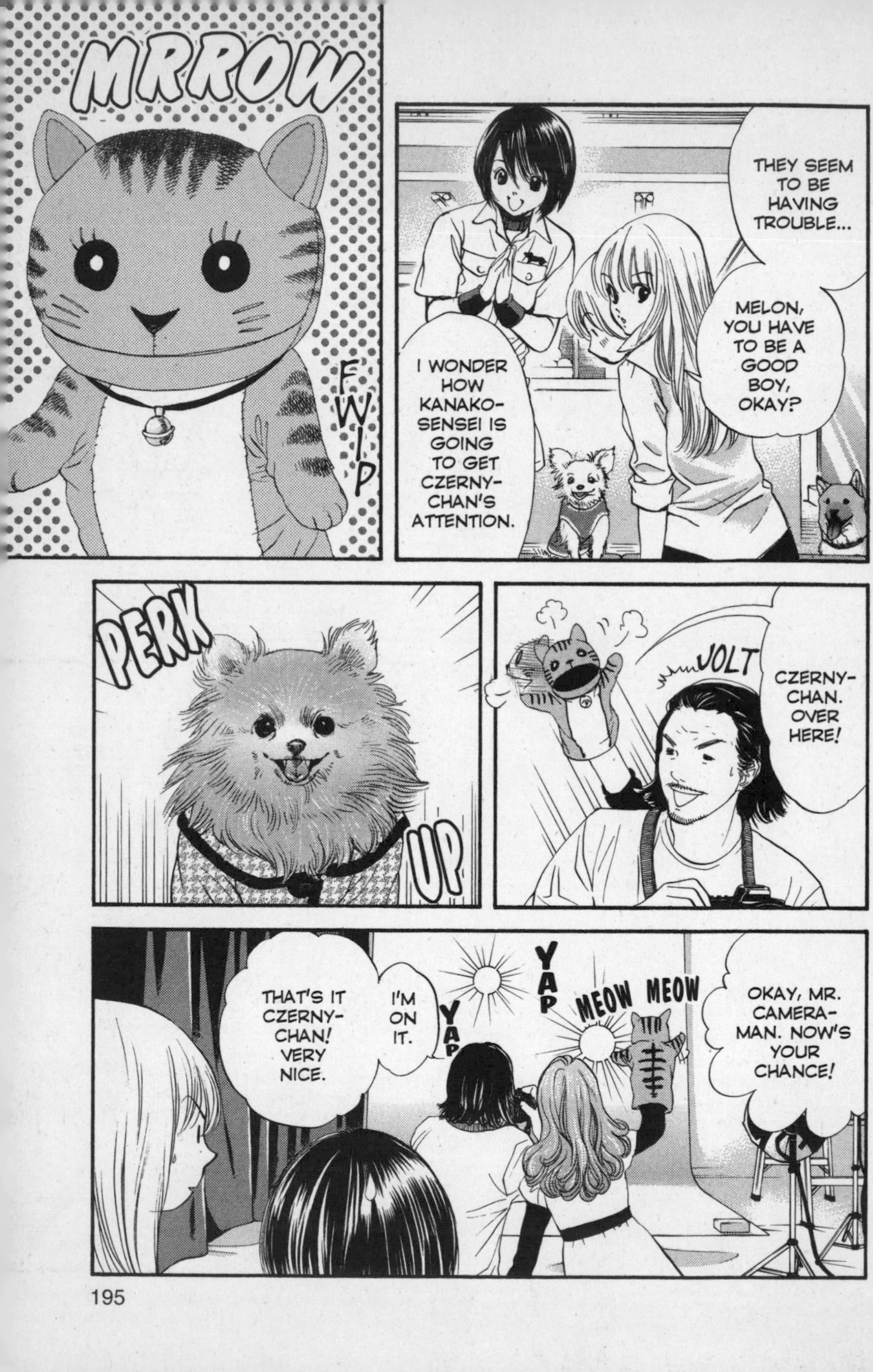
THEY SEEM TO BE HAVING TROUBLE...
MELON, YOU HAVE TO BE A GOOD BOY, OKAY?
I WONDER HOW KANAKO-SENSEI IS GOING TO GET CZERNY-CHAN'S ATTENTION.
MRROW
FWIP
JOLT
CZERNY-CHAN. OVER HERE!
PERK
UP
OKAY, MR. CAMERA-MAN. NOW'S YOUR CHANCE!
MEOW MEOW
YAP
YAP
I'M ON IT.
THAT'S IT CZERNY-CHAN! VERY NICE.

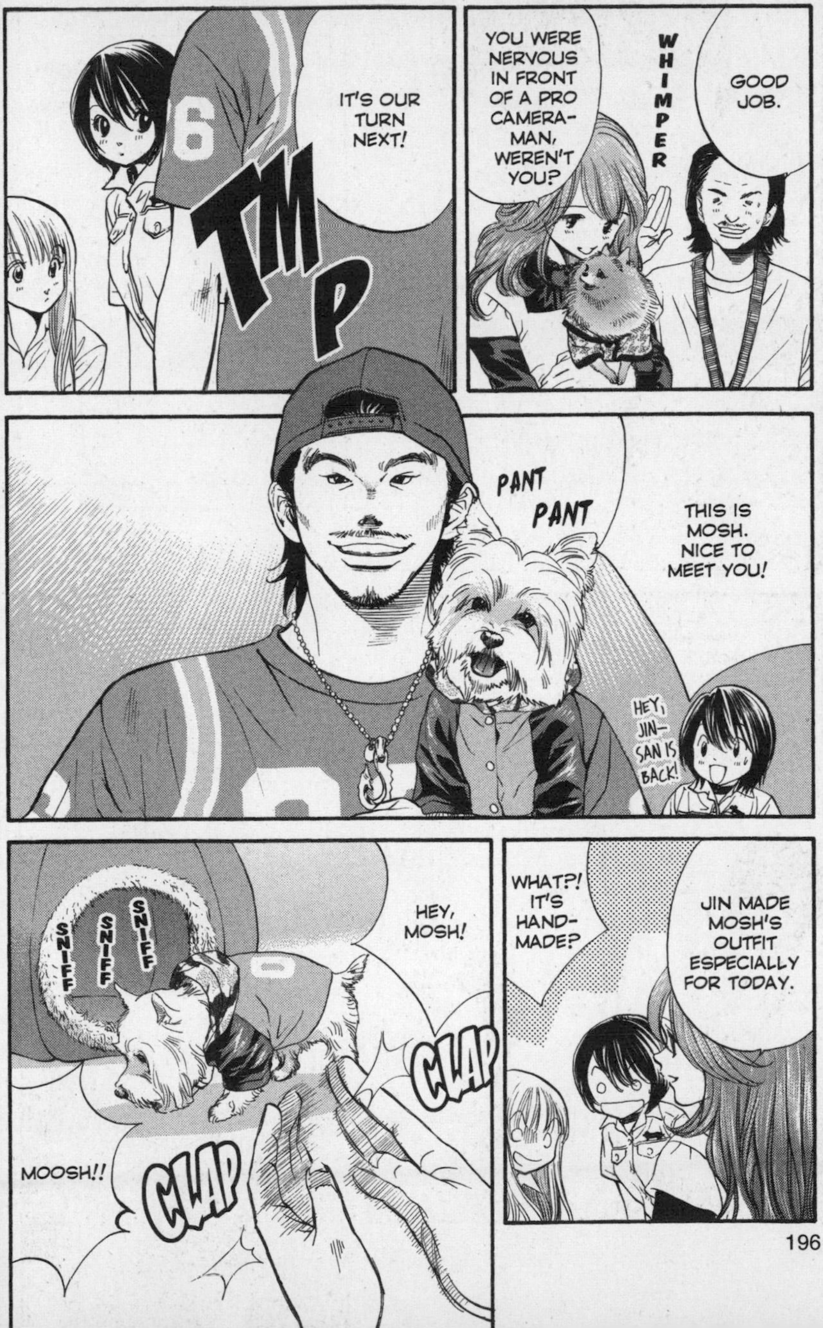
GOOD JOB.
WHIMPER
YOU WERE NERVOUS IN FRONT OF A PRO CAMERA-MAN, WEREN'T YOU?
IT'S OUR TURN NEXT!
TMP
THIS IS MOSH. NICE TO MEET YOU!
PANT PANT
HEY, JIN-SAN IS BACK!
JIN MADE MOSH'S OUTFIT ESPECIALLY FOR TODAY.
WHAT?! IT'S HAND-MADE?
HEY, MOSH!
SNIFF SNIFF SNIFF
CLAP
MOOSH!!
CLAP

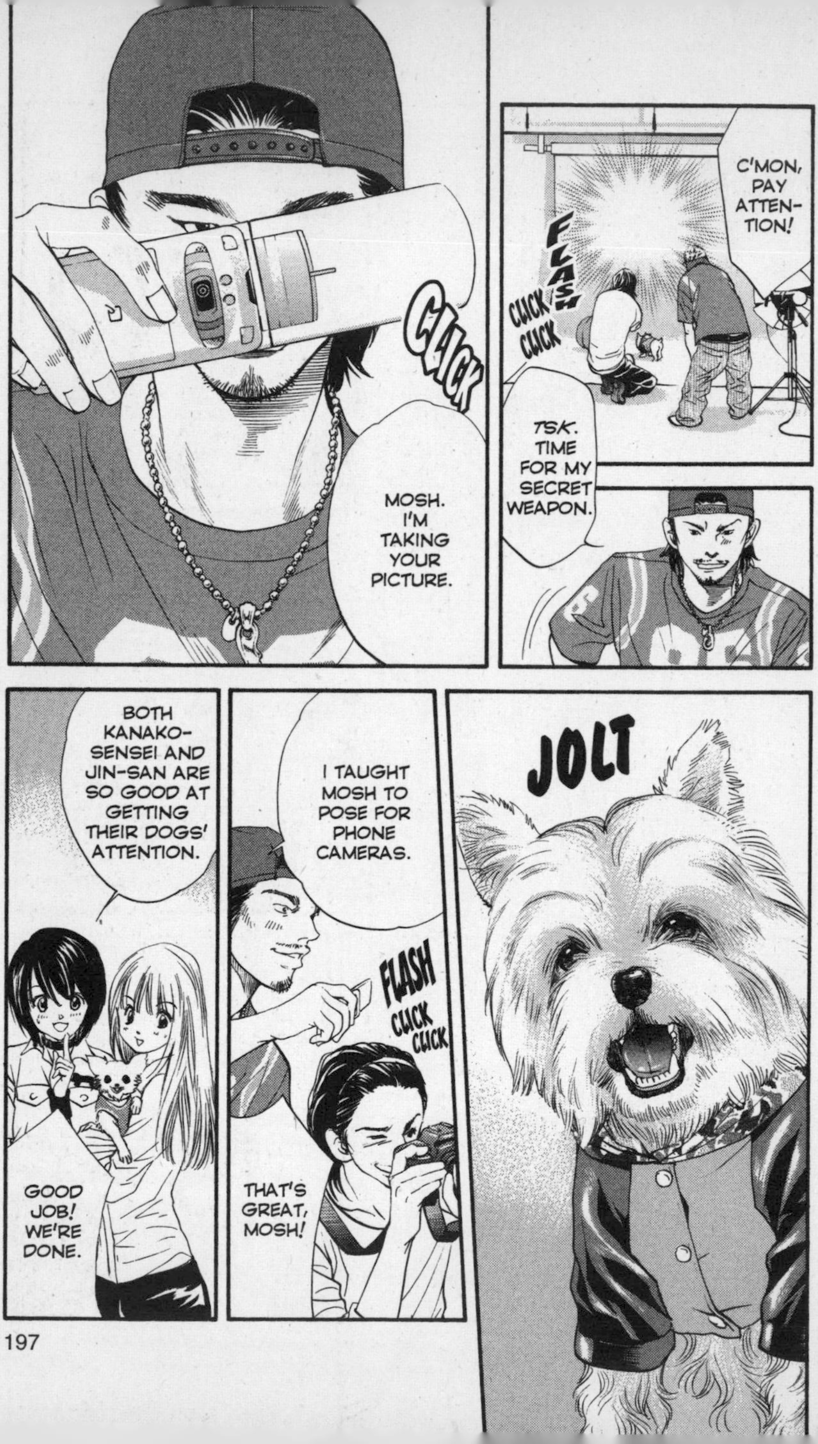
C'MON, PAY ATTEN- TION!
FLASH
CLICK CLICK
TSK. TIME FOR MY SECRET WEAPON.
CLACK
MOSH. I'M TAKING YOUR PICTURE.
JOLT
I TAUGHT MOSH TO POSE FOR PHONE CAMERAS.
FLASH
CLICK CLICK
THAT'S GREAT, MOSH!
BOTH KANAKO- SENSEI AND JIN-SAN ARE SO GOOD AT GETTING THEIR DOGS' ATTENTION.
GOOD JOB! WE'RE DONE.

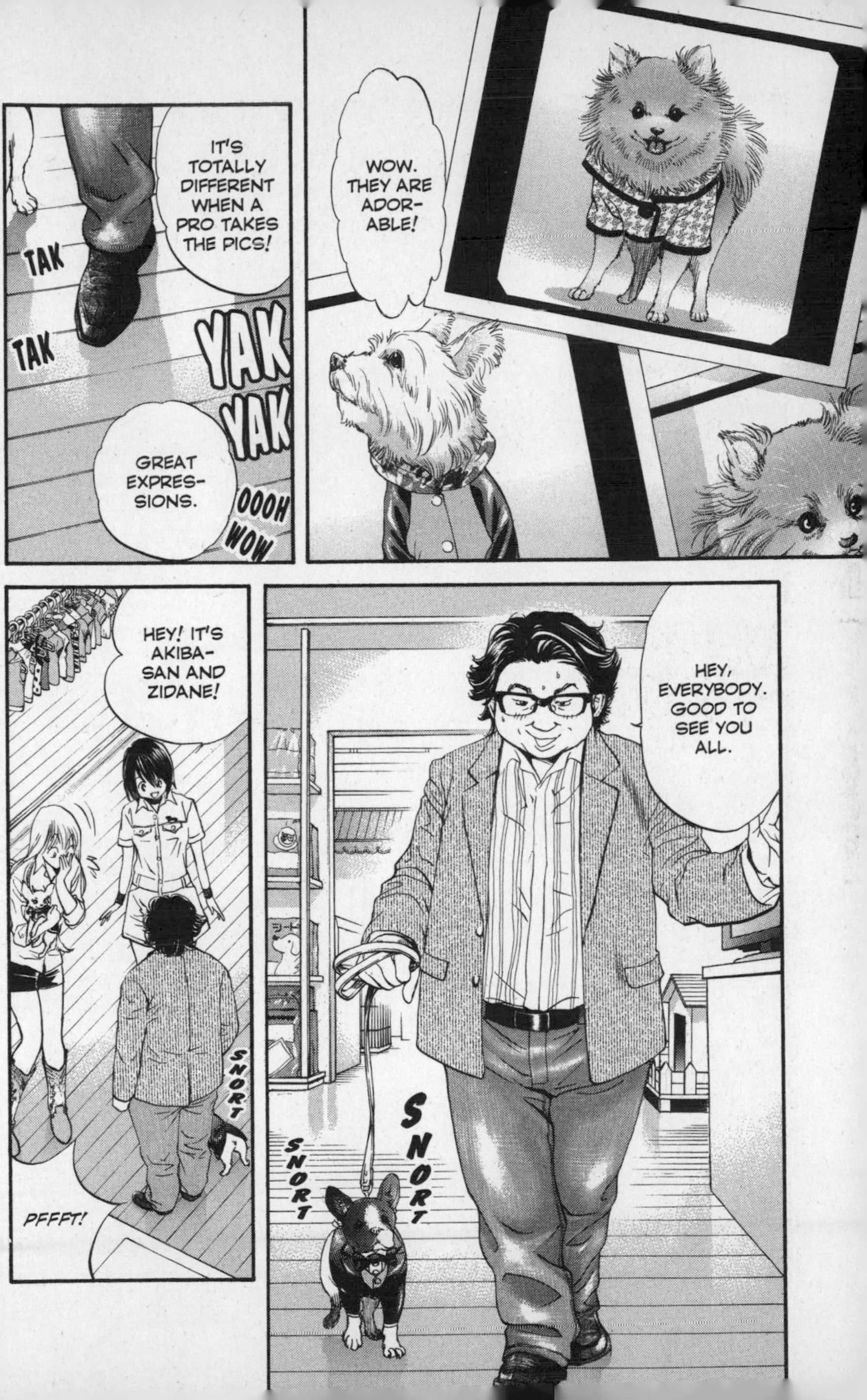
WOW. THEY ARE ADORABLE!
IT'S TOTALLY DIFFERENT WHEN A PRO TAKES THE PICS!
TAK
TAK
YAK YAK
GREAT EXPRESSIONS.
OOOH WOW
HEY, EVERYBODY. GOOD TO SEE YOU ALL.
SNORT
SNORT
HEY! IT'S AKIBA-SAN AND ZIDANE!
SNORT
PFFFT!

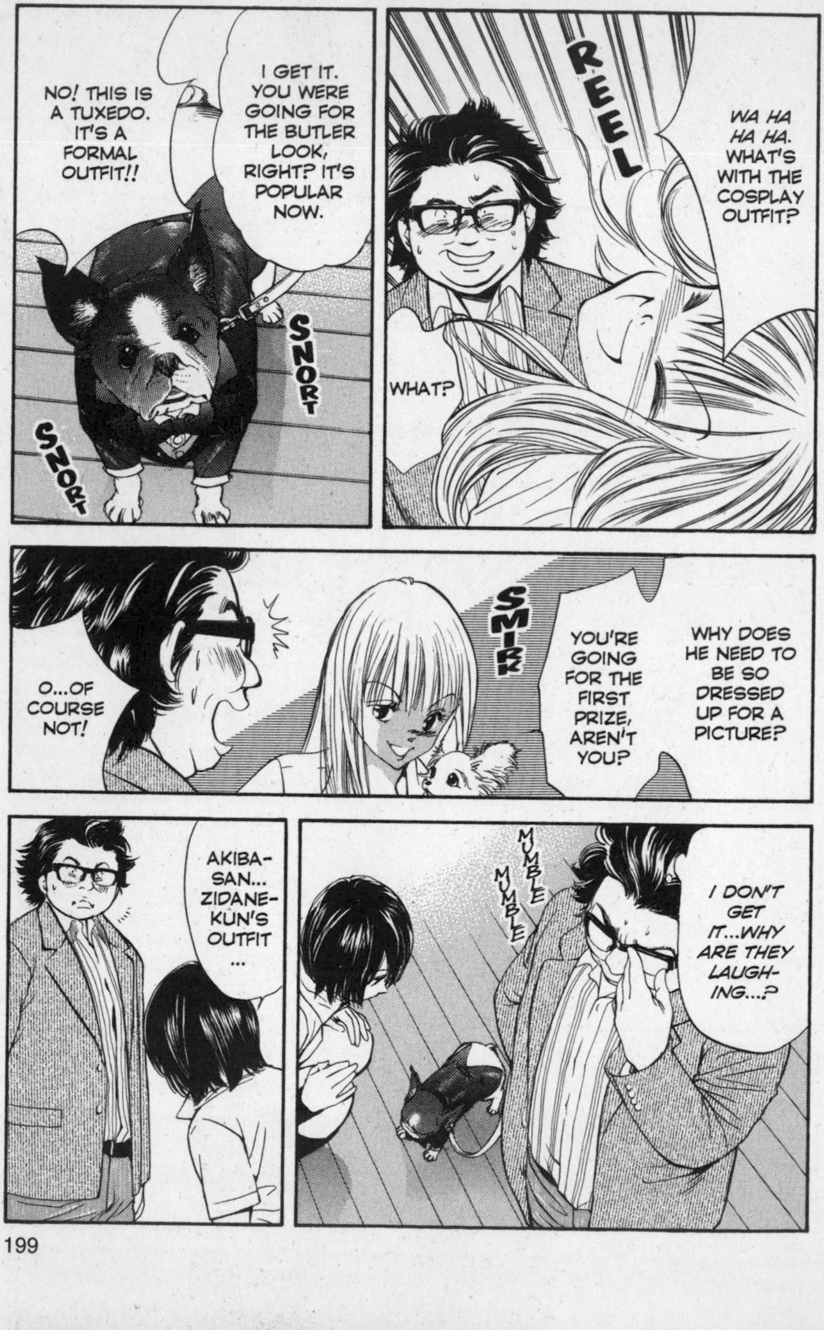
REEL
WA HA HA HA. WHAT'S WITH THE COSPLAY OUTFIT?
WHAT?
I GET IT. YOU WERE GOING FOR THE BUTLER LOOK, RIGHT? IT'S POPULAR NOW.
NO! THIS IS A TUXEDO. IT'S A FORMAL OUTFIT!!
SNORT
SNORT
WHY DOES HE NEED TO BE SO DRESSED UP FOR A PICTURE?
YOU'RE GOING FOR THE FIRST PRIZE, AREN'T YOU?
SMIRK
O...OF COURSE NOT!
I DON'T GET IT...WHY ARE THEY LAUGHING...?
MUMBLE
MUMBLE
AKIBA-SAN... ZIDANE-KUN'S OUTFIT ...

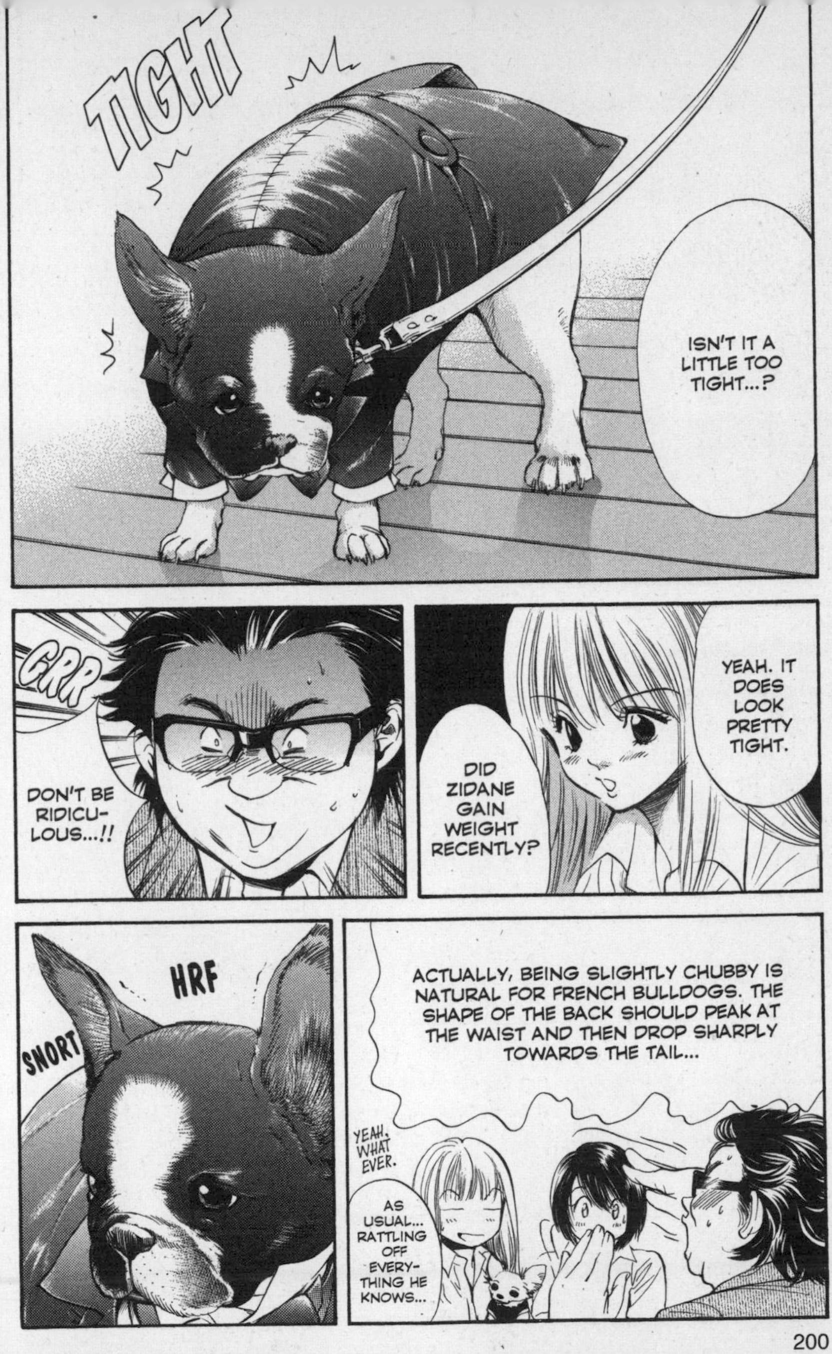
TIGHT
ISN'T IT A LITTLE TOO TIGHT...?
YEAH. IT DOES LOOK PRETTY TIGHT.
DID ZIDANE GAIN WEIGHT RECENTLY?
GRR
DON'T BE RIDICU-LOUS...!!
ACTUALLY, BEING SLIGHTLY CHUBBY IS NATURAL FOR FRENCH BULLDOGS. THE SHAPE OF THE BACK SHOULD PEAK AT THE WAIST AND THEN DROP SHARPLY TOWARDS THE TAIL...
YEAH, WHAT EVER.
AS USUAL... RATTLING OFF EVERY-THING HE KNOWS...
HRF
SNORT

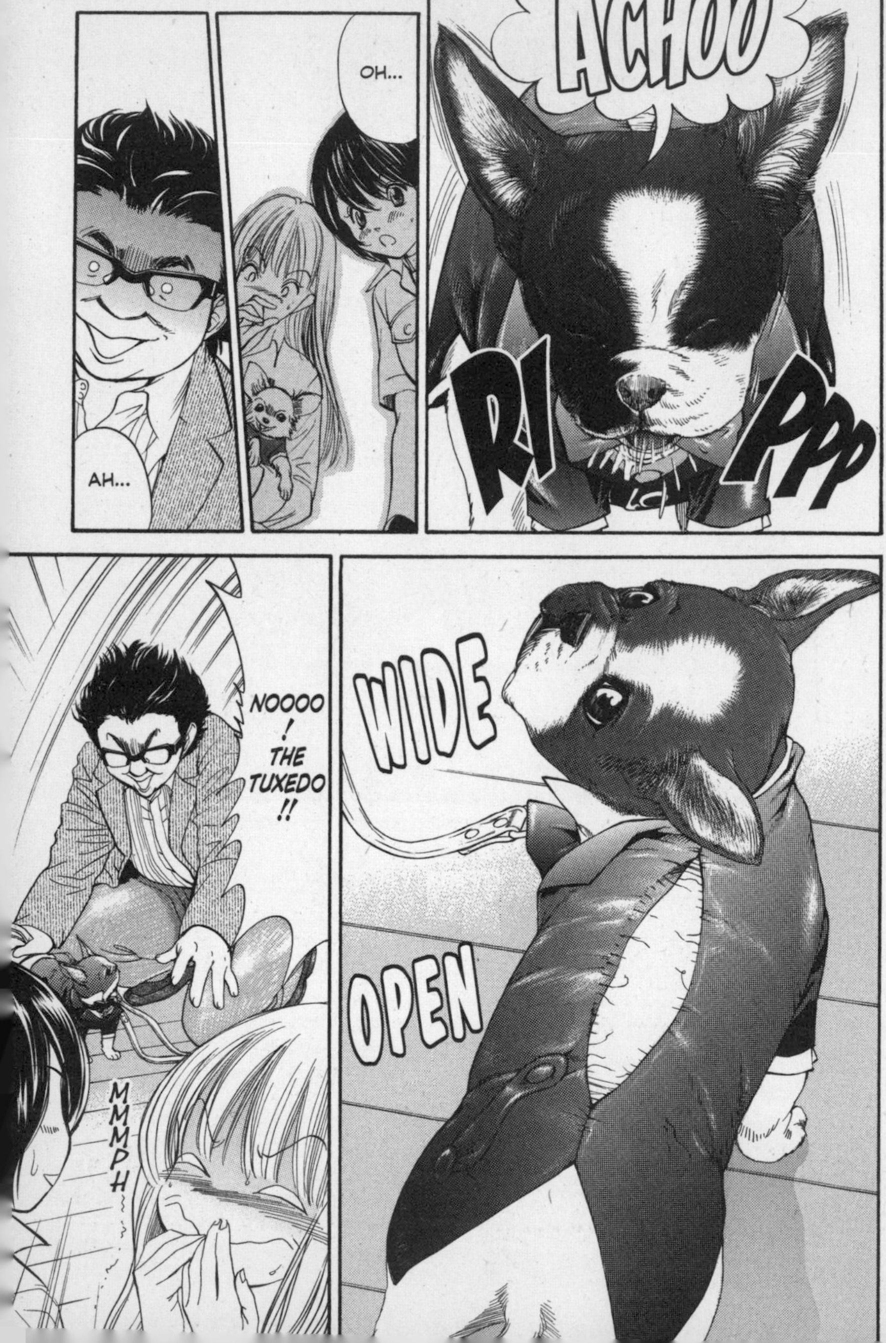

ACHOO
RIPPP
OH...
AH...
WIDE
OPEN
NOOOO! THE TUXEDO!!
MMMPH~

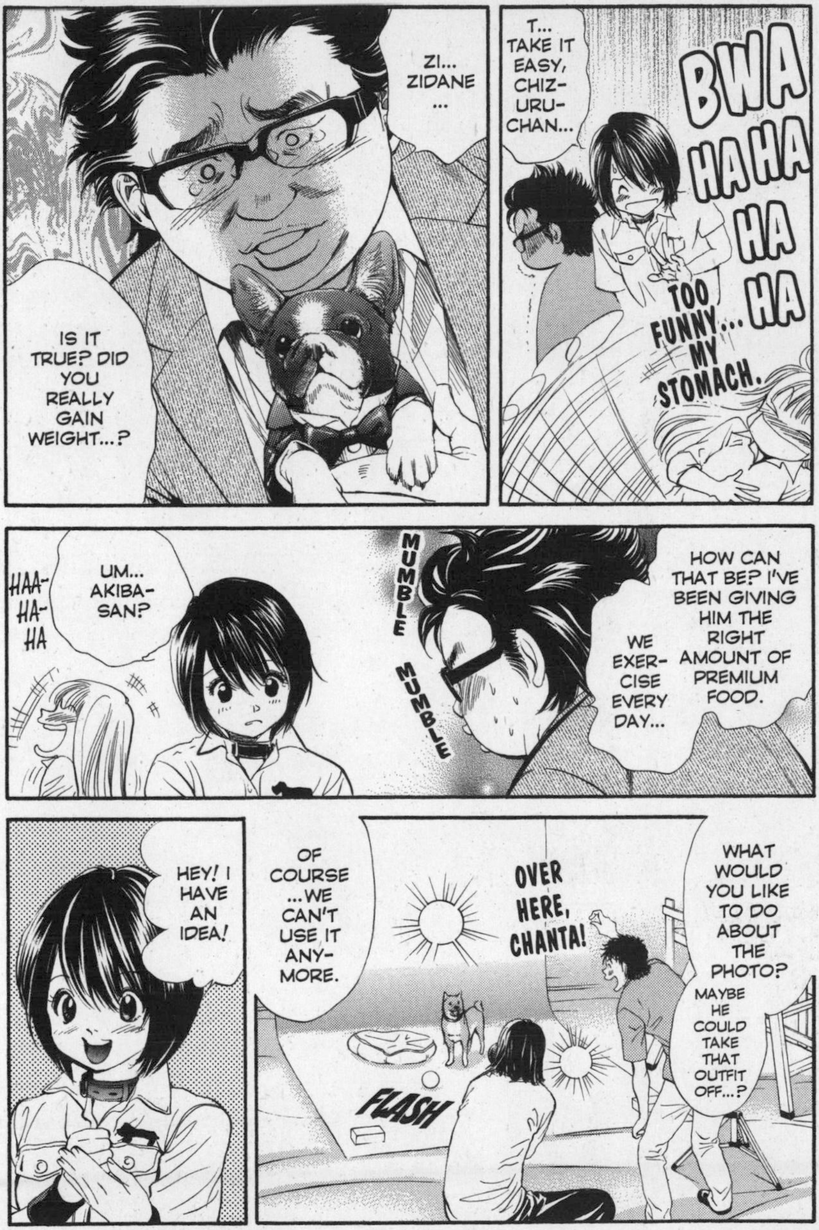
T... TAKE IT EASY, CHIZURU-CHAN...
BWA HA HA HA HA HA
TOO FUNNY... MY STOMACH.
ZI... ZIDANE ...
IS IT TRUE? DID YOU REALLY GAIN WEIGHT...?
HOW CAN THAT BE? I'VE BEEN GIVING HIM THE RIGHT AMOUNT OF PREMIUM FOOD.
WE EXERCISE EVERY DAY...
MUMBLE MUMBLE
UM... AKIBA-SAN?
HAA-HA-HA
WHAT WOULD YOU LIKE TO DO ABOUT THE PHOTO?
MAYBE HE COULD TAKE THAT OUTFIT OFF...?
OVER HERE, CHANTA!
OF COURSE ...WE CAN'T USE IT ANYMORE.
FLASH
HEY! I HAVE AN IDEA!

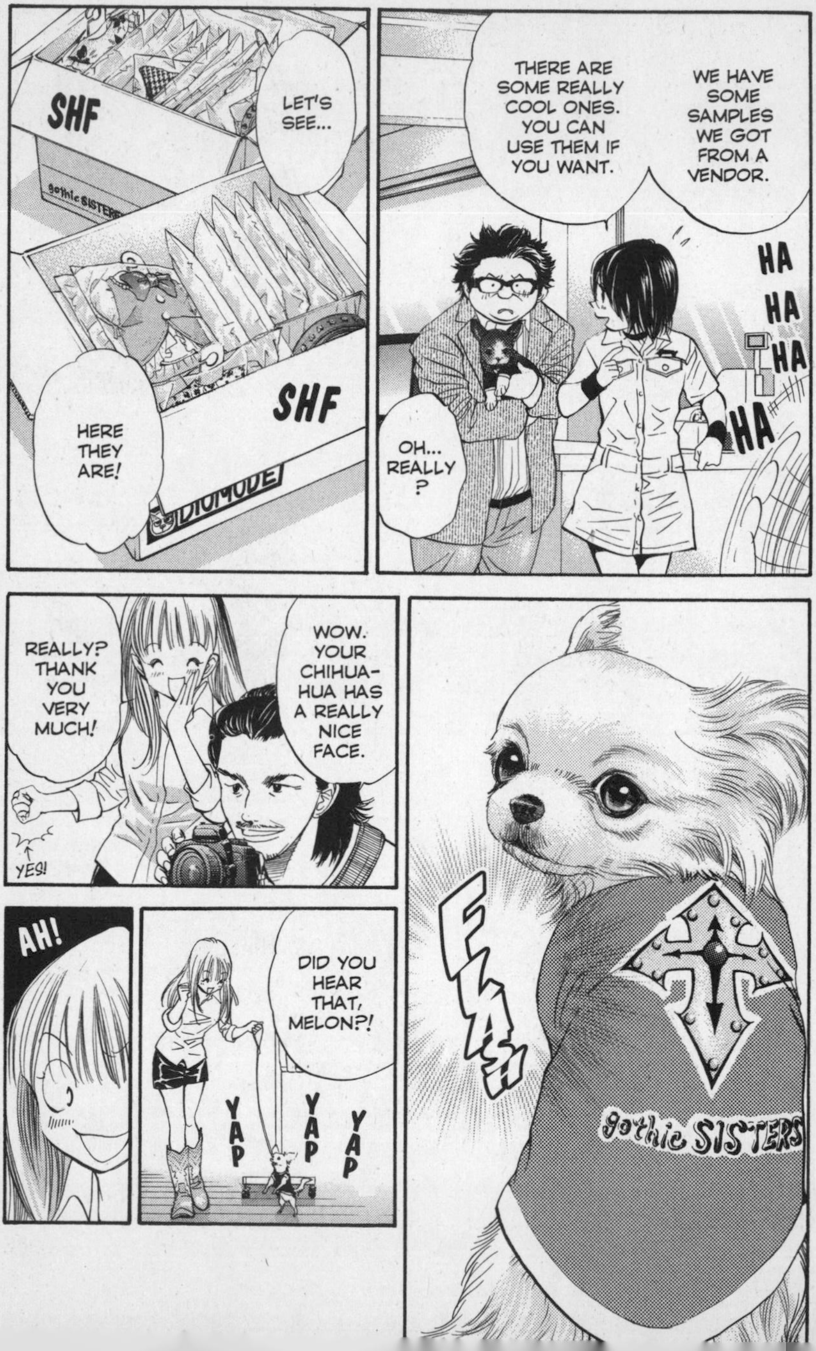
WE HAVE SOME SAMPLES WE GOT FROM A VENDOR.
THERE ARE SOME REALLY COOL ONES. YOU CAN USE THEM IF YOU WANT.
HA HA HA HA
OH... REALLY?
LET'S SEE...
SHF
SHF
DIOMODE
HERE THEY ARE!
FLASH
gothic SISTERS
WOW. YOUR CHIHUA-HUA HAS A REALLY NICE FACE.
REALLY? THANK YOU VERY MUCH!
YES!
DID YOU HEAR THAT, MELON?!
YAP YAP YAP
AH!

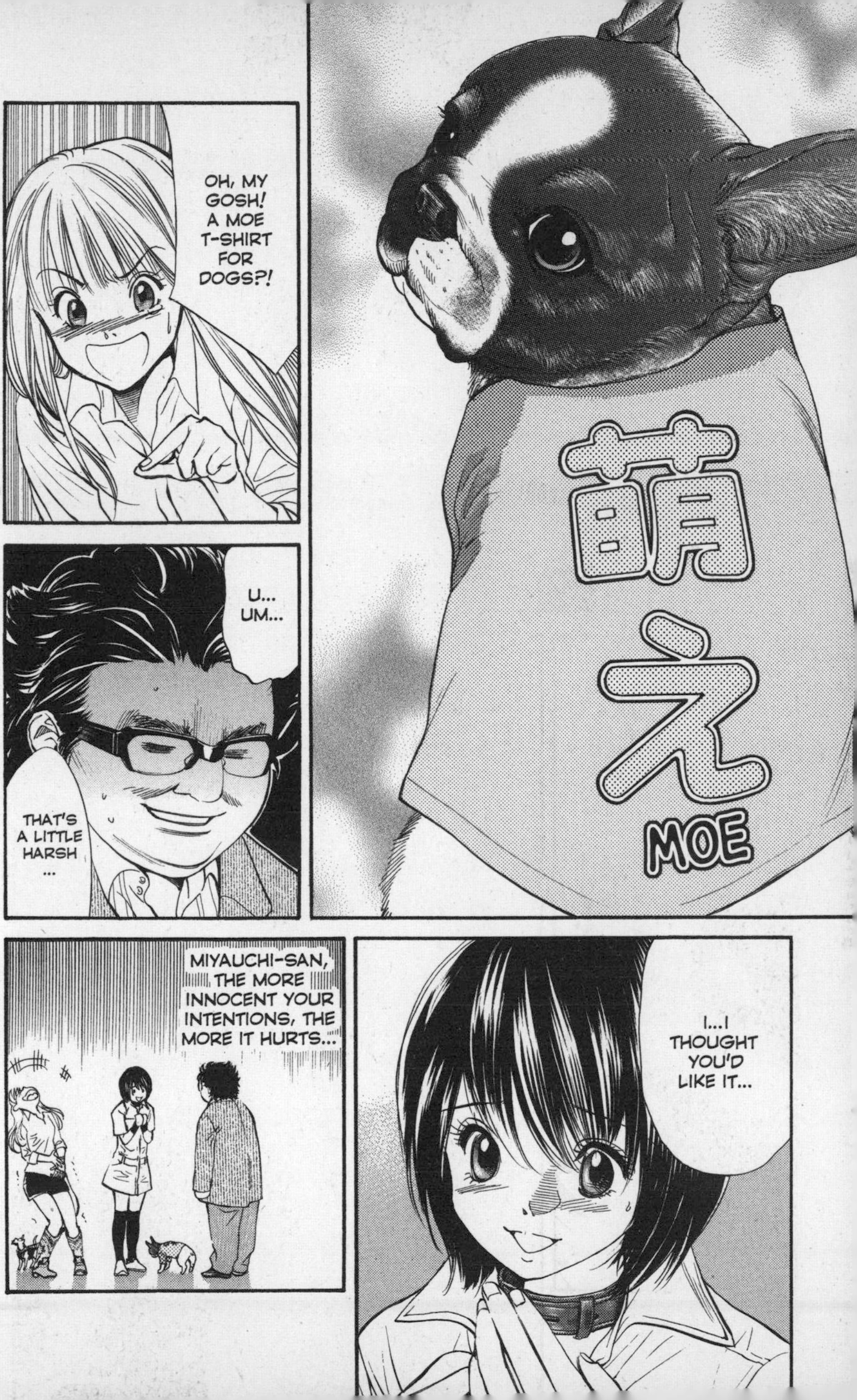
萌え
MOE
OH, MY GOSH! A MOE T-SHIRT FOR DOGS?!
U... UM...
THAT'S A LITTLE HARSH ...
I...I THOUGHT YOU'D LIKE IT...
MIYAUCHI-SAN, THE MORE INNOCENT YOUR INTENTIONS, THE MORE IT HURTS...

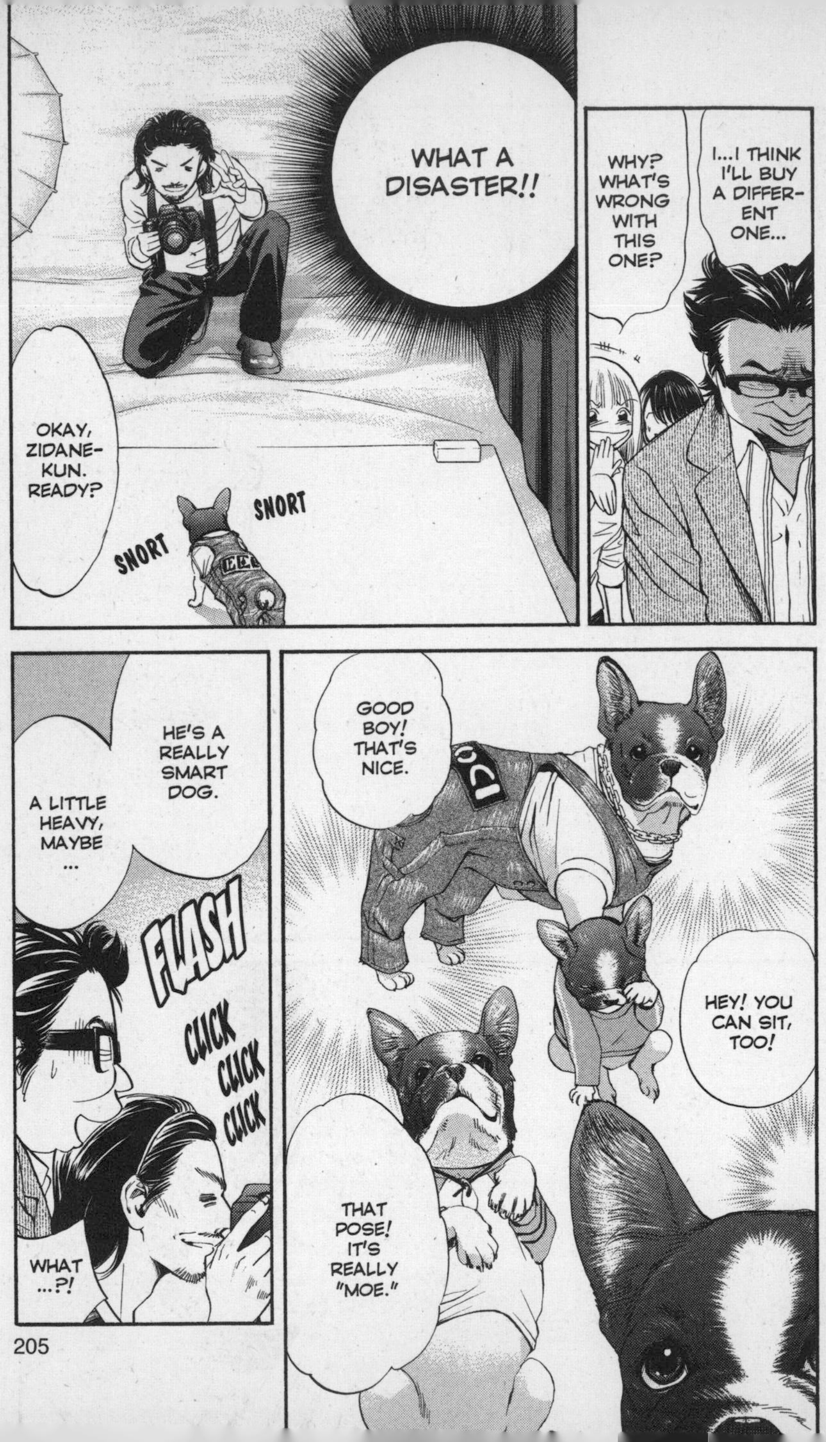
I...I THINK I'LL BUY A DIFFERENT ONE...
WHY? WHAT'S WRONG WITH THIS ONE?
WHAT A DISASTER!!
OKAY, ZIDANE-KUN. READY?
SNORT
SNORT
GOOD BOY! THAT'S NICE.
HEY! YOU CAN SIT, TOO!
THAT POSE! IT'S REALLY "MOE."
HE'S A REALLY SMART DOG.
A LITTLE HEAVY, MAYBE ...
FLASH
CLICK CLICK CLICK
WHAT ...?!

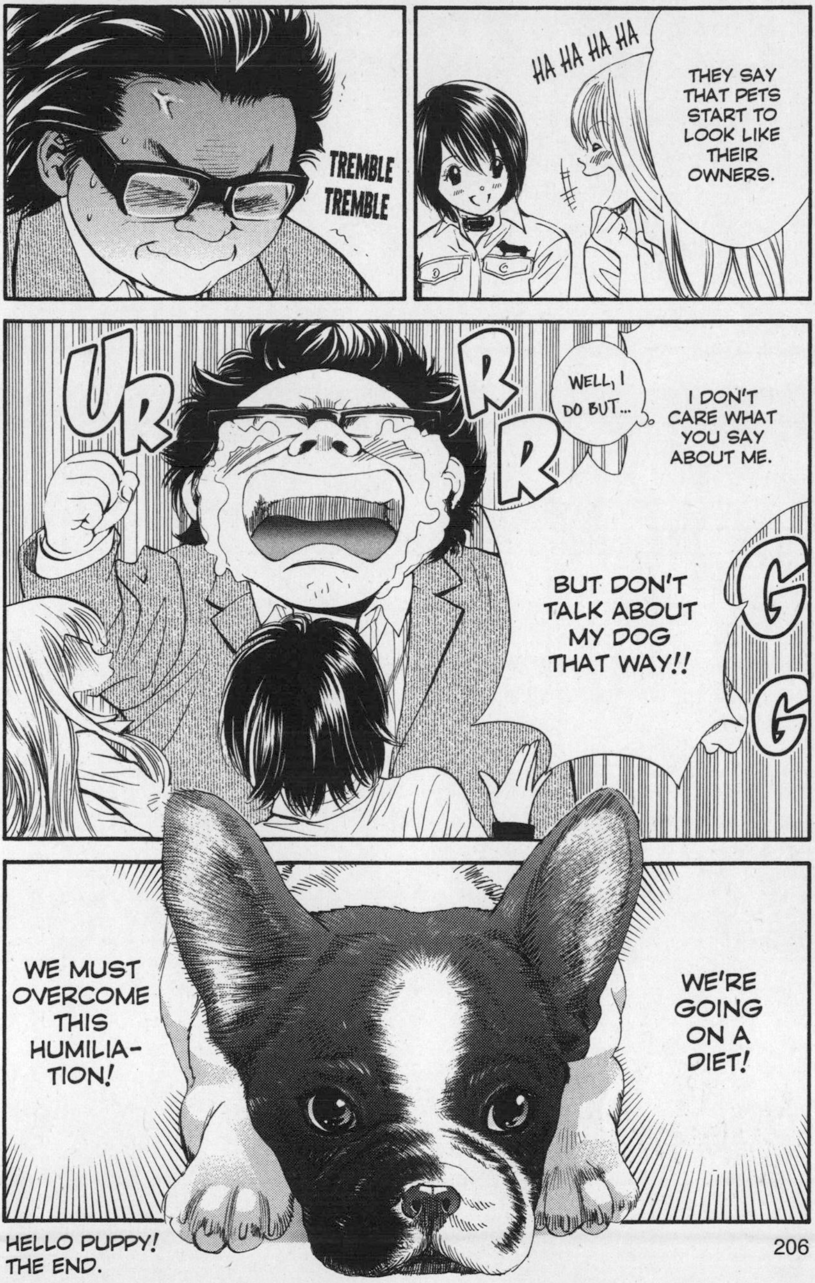
HA HA HA HA
THEY SAY THAT PETS START TO LOOK LIKE THEIR OWNERS.
TREMBLE TREMBLE
I DON'T CARE WHAT YOU SAY ABOUT ME.
WELL, I DO BUT...
BUT DON'T TALK ABOUT MY DOG THAT WAY!!
URRRGG
WE'RE GOING ON A DIET!
WE MUST OVERCOME THIS HUMILIA-TION!

HELLO PUPPY!
THE END.

INUBAKA

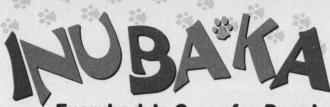

INUBAKA

Everybody's Crazy for Dogs!

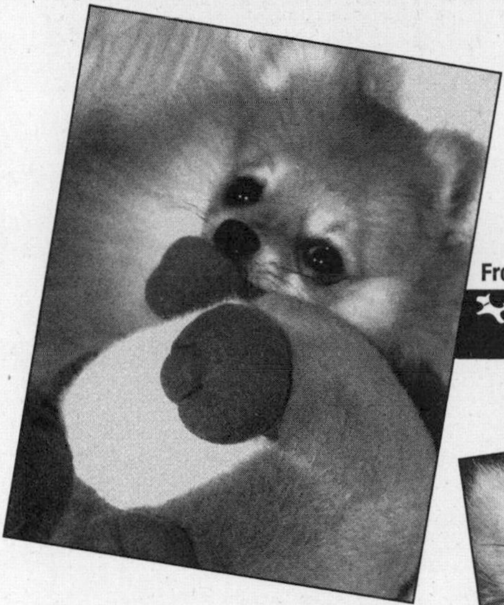

She never lets go of her favorite stuffed animal before bedtime. Even if it's hidden, she'll find it. Who can blame her? It ensures a good dream every night!

From Takagi-san in Saitama Prefecture

Marron-chan and Pudding-kun (Pomeranian)

Loves a good bath?! Pudding-kun loves taking a bath so much, he often wanders into the tub on his own. That must be where this photo is from! His innocent expression is precious!!

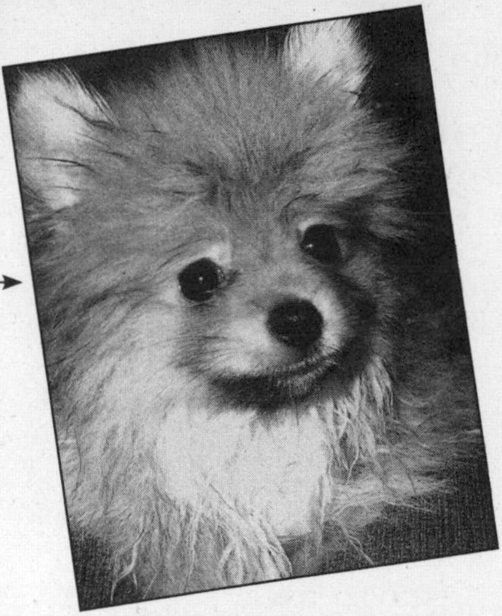

Yukiya Sakuragi

This is the kind of sweetness that hits you right in the heart. How can you not smile every day, surrounded by these cute faces?! To Marron-chan, the stuffed animal is an important friend. And Pudding-kun looks so refreshed after a bath! (lol)

From Okawara-san in Chiba Prefecture

Ron-kun (mutt)

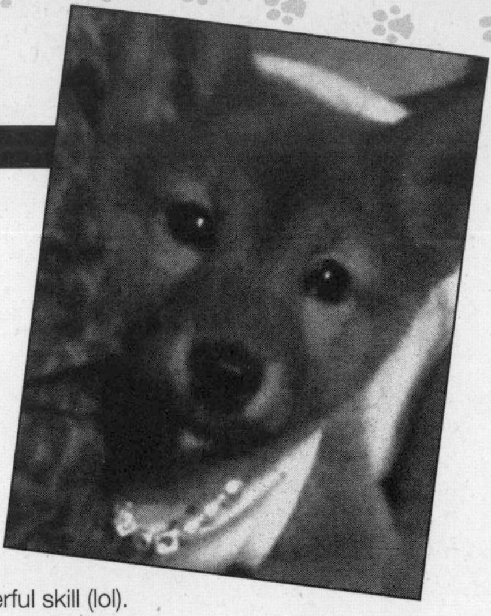

He can say "Hello." People say that it's just the owner's imagination, but as long as there is a connection between Ron-kun and his owner, that's all that matters. He just likes to communicate any way he can, right Ron-kun?

Yukiya Sakuragi

He can say a greeting! What a wonderful skill (lol).
They say dogs always know what people are talking about.
Keep on talking to him. Maybe he'll learn more words!

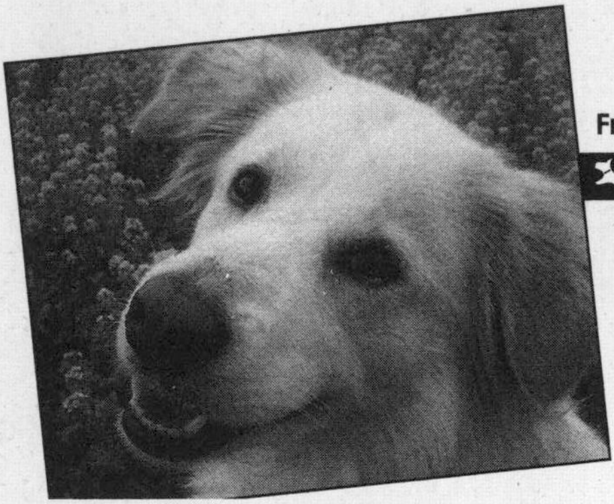

From "Miss Lassie" in Tokyo.

Islay-chan (mutt)

Islay-chan knows many tricks and loves nature. Her favorite thing to do is to take short trips with her owner in the car. Maybe this is a picture from one of those trips? What a great expression.

Yukiya Sakuragi

I hear Islay-chan used to be homeless, but when a dog is given lots of love, it shows in their expression, and Islay-chan is showing a lot of love here. Mixed breeds are wonderful dogs and are known for their various expressions, which are their greatest charm.

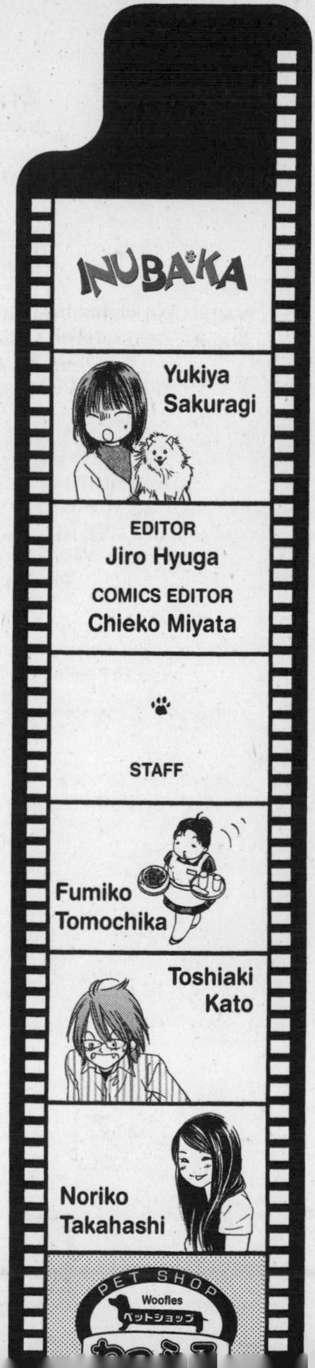
INUBAKA
Yukiya Sakuragi
EDITOR
Jiro Hyuga
COMICS EDITOR
Chieko Miyata
STAFF
Fumiko Tomochika
Toshiaki Kato
Noriko Takahashi
PET SHOP
Woofles
ペットショップ

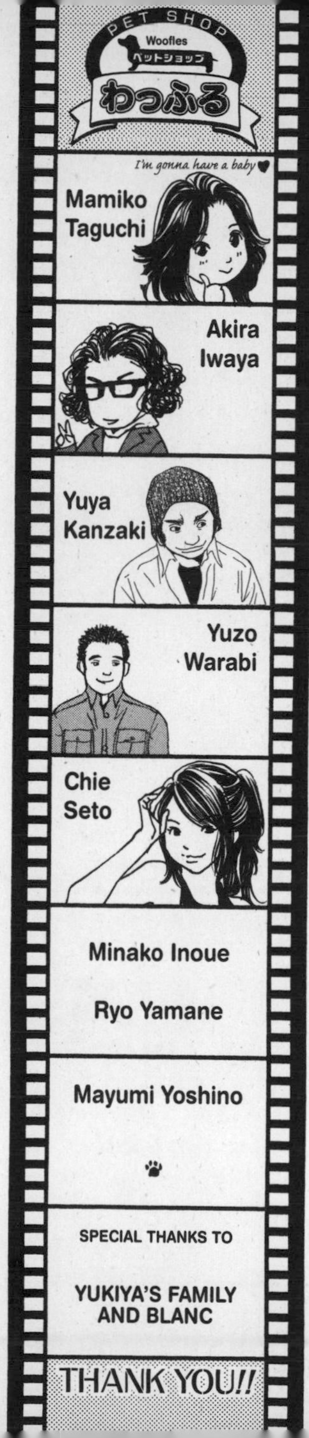
PET SHOP
Woofles
ペットショップ
わっふる
I'm gonna have a baby
Mamiko Taguchi
Akira Iwaya
Yuya Kanzaki
Yuzo Warabi
Chie Seto
Minako Inoue
Ryo Yamane
Mayumi Yoshino
SPECIAL THANKS TO
YUKIYA'S FAMILY AND BLANC
THANK YOU!!

Inubaka

Crazy for Dogs
Vol. #9
VIZ Media Edition

Story and Art by
Yukiya Sakuragi

Translation/Hidemi Hachitori, HC Language Solutions, Inc.
English Adaptation/Ian Reid, HC Language Solutions, Inc.
Touch-up Art & Lettering/Kelle Han
Cover and Interior Design/Hidemi Sahara
Editor/Ian Robertson

Editor in Chief, Books/Alvin Lu
Editor in Chief, Magazines/Marc Weidenbaum
VP of Publishing Licensing/Rika Inouye
VP of Sales/Gonzalo Ferreyra
Sr. VP of Marketing/Liza Coppola
Publisher/Hyoe Narita

Printed in the U.S.A.

Published by VIZ Media, LLC
P.O. Box 77010
San Francisco, CA 94107

10 9 8 7 6 5 4 3 2 1
First printing, June 2008 9.99

VIZ MEDIA

www.viz.com
store.viz.com

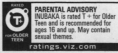

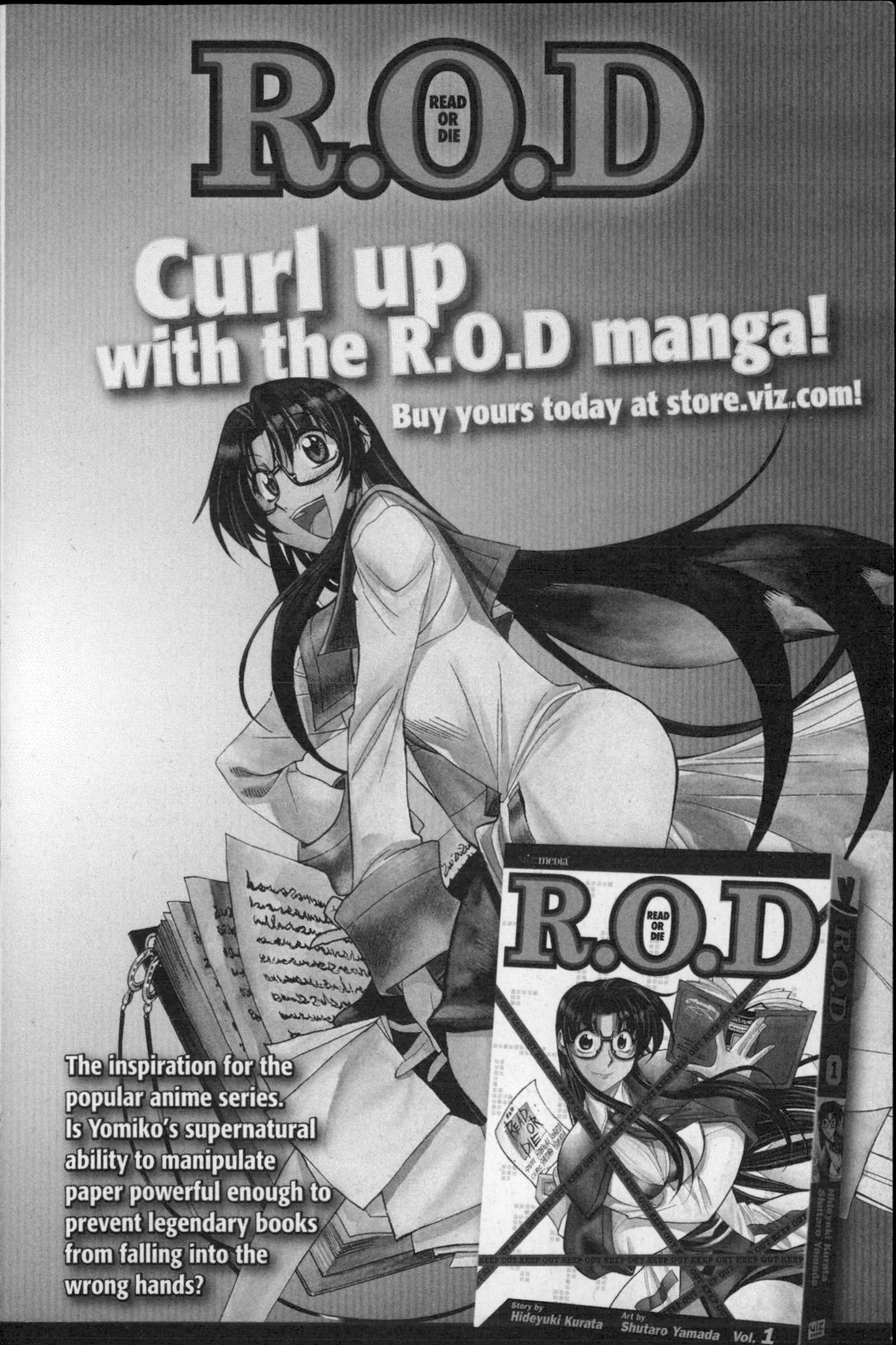
R.O.D
READ OR DIE
Curl up
with the R.O.D manga!
Buy yours today at store.viz.com!
The inspiration for the popular anime series. Is Yomiko's supernatural ability to manipulate paper powerful enough to prevent legendary books from falling into the wrong hands?
R.O.D
READ OR DIE
Story by
Hideyuki Kurata
Art by
Shutaro Yamada
Vol. 1

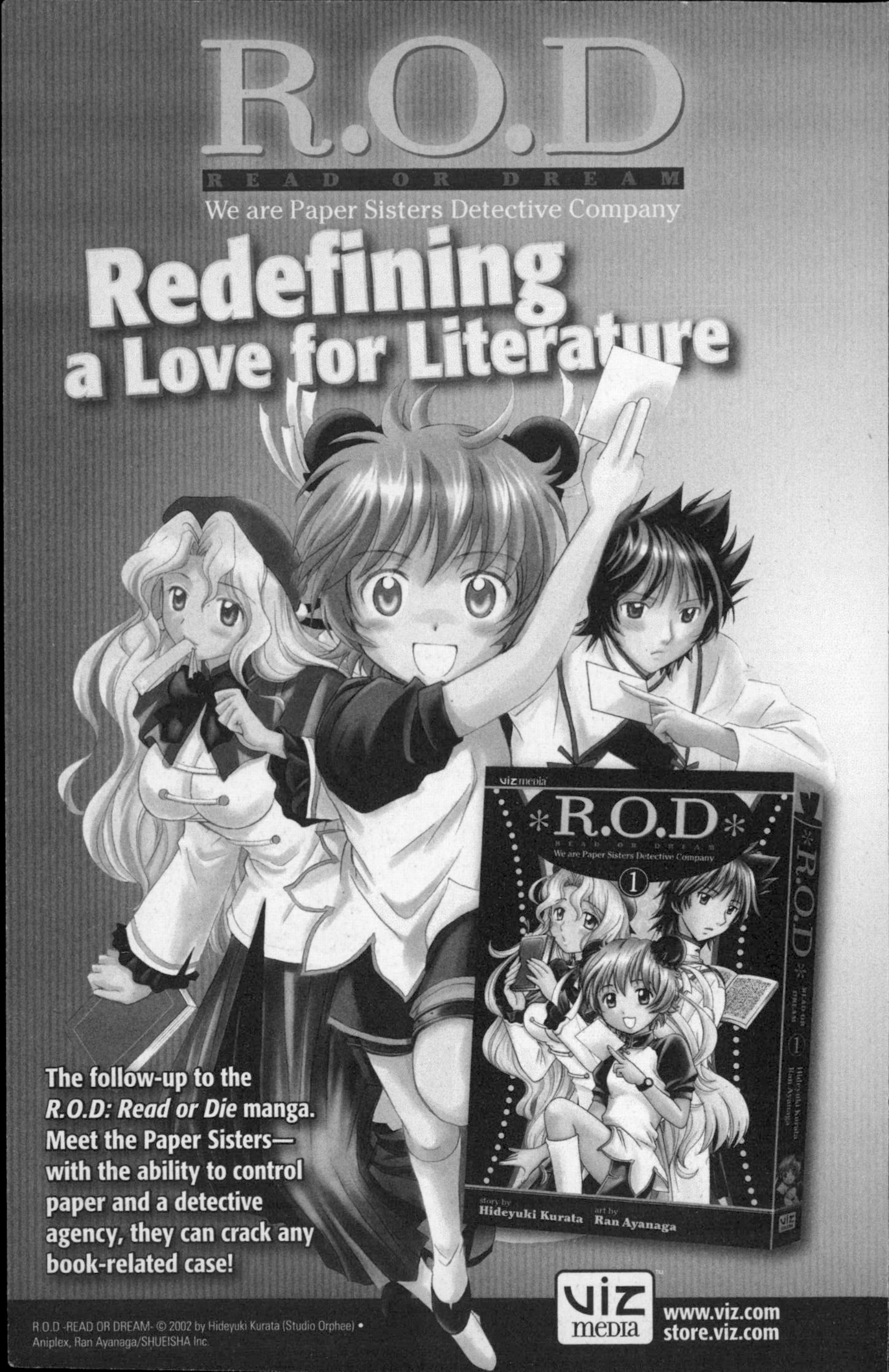
R.O.D
READ OR DREAM
We are Paper Sisters Detective Company
Redefining a Love for Literature
VIZ media
R.O.D
READ OR DREAM
We are Paper Sisters Detective Company
1
story by Hideyuki Kurata
art by Ran Ayanaga
The follow-up to the *R.O.D: Read or Die* manga. Meet the Paper Sisters—with the ability to control paper and a detective agency, they can crack any book-related case!
viz media
www.viz.com
store.viz.com
R.O.D -READ OR DREAM- © 2002 by Hideyuki Kurata (Studio Orphee) • Aniplex, Ran Ayanaga/SHUEISHA Inc.

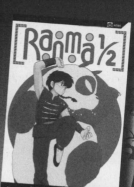
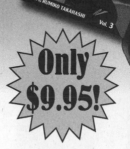